Shot and Shell

War in Earnest

Robert K. Lytle

Artisan Books LLC
1955 South Main Street, P.O. Box 23
Mountain Home, Idaho 83647

ISBN: 0615863027
ISBN-13: 978-0615863023

DEDICATION

For the great unwashed, and the great unwanted, who pressed to fight for their freedoms in our national cause. I ask the reader to remember that the Slaves and the Immigrants; both groups considered less than "Us" who paid their citizenship admission in blood. Ample volumes of blood, earning them a stake in this land. They did their part to determine the outcome, which resulted in a more comprehensive United States. We have to honor this to call ourselves "Americans."

CONTENTS

R E Lee

FOREWORD

The introduction of Robert E. Lee onto the national stage, in late 1862, as the Commander of the Army of Northern Virginia, turned the American Civil War into an absolute struggle to the finish. Lee, while of some renown, and emergent from a storied family, is unknown to the majority of his troops. Other officers who served alongside him are familiar based on shared experiences on the frontiers of Texas and the battlefields of Mexico. His aloof and serious nature provide little anecdotal legend of him, other than that of a penultimate professional soldier. Lee was a serious officer, given a Herculean task, with little hope of victory from the start. After a confusing assumption of command, following the wounding of Joseph Johnston in May of 1862, Lee gradually comes to know his army and the nature of his commanders. He learns how they have evolved upon coming into senior rank. The tragic result is a Southern Army that can and does win constantly, on the tactical level. The Army of Northern Virginia begins to operate in such an aggressive fashion, that they wrest the initiative from a Federal force twice their size. The Union Army, while vast in number and superbly equipped, lacks the leadership to wrest that initiative back despite continual experimentation with different commanders. General Lee imparts a will onto the Confederate Army, which becomes elementally irresistible. Fighting a war that he clearly knows cannot be won strategically, he dedicates his imagination and energy into constructing a force projecting the image of invincibility. Lee is forced into a gamble to persist in struggle in order to win a separate peace and international recognition from Europe. Recognition that could gain allies and support against the Goliath of the North. Each battle fought saps his army, poorly supplied, weak in depth, devoid of transport and lacking decent heavy weaponry. The only thing his Army is rich in, is spirit and force of will. It is this instrument that Lee wields in his desperate endeavor to buy time and impress the world. This pursuit is the only hope for the States in insurrection. What is to follow is the elemental change in the nature of the conflict. The killing is to intensify. The hearts of the combatants hardens and the human cost of each engagement increases, as Lee knows it must. In order to gain his ends he realizes that the war must be fought in deadly earnest. Late 1862 and early 1863 will be years of great struggle. The war will continue without meaningful pause even through the normally quiet winter months. It will continue at great cost to both sides and will ultimately exhaust the limited resources of the Confederacy.

CSS Planter

1
THE JUBILEE!

The May afternoon threatened thunderstorms. Large black clouds could be seen beyond the trees along the south bank of the Ashley River. Reid was stripped to the waist, his rough canvas pants secured to his form with a cast off fragment of hawser rope and he was barefoot as he swiftly moved about the deck of the steamship *Planter*. His task was to set blocks underneath great cast iron cannon which were being loaded onto the steamer from a large lifting gin, servicing the wharves near the Charleston Arsenal. Reid had been aboard, as a laborer, since March of that year. He recalled the confusion he had felt when E.J. Markley had loaded him and several of the other field hands, onto a buckboard wagon for the long trip to Charleston. E.J. had explained that they were to be rented out to the Government to help with the war. He had not understood that Mr. Markley would pocket a large chunk of the his laborer's pay, which. Reid would receive one silver dollar each month as his personal take of his wages. Twelve silver dollars would go into Mr. Markley's bank account in Charleston. Markley would also be relieved of the expense of feeding those slaves that he rented into wartime service.

Reid and Elzie had been the two field hands who wound up as laborers on the crew of the *Planter*. His only experience with boats had been plying the Santee in a flat-bottomed skiff to collect swamp bottom mud for enrichening the cotton fields. Now he was living aboard a great steam powered paddlewheel packet steamer that traveled all the waterways around Charleston. While the Captain and his white officers were stern and demanding, the work was nothing compared to the labor at Somerset Plantation. Most of the time, while cruising around the waterways, there was little to do.

Captain Relyea stood on the flying bridge, outside the small wheelhouse and watched as the brawny slaves unshackled the heavy 32-pounder gun resting on heavy pine blocks on the foredeck of the paddlewheel steamer. Relyea was to pick up two of the heavy guns which had been reconditioned and provided with stout iron reinforcing bands around the breeches at the Charleston Armory. Once he had his load on board, he would then steam back to the Southern Wharf and layover for the evening. He had planned an early morning run out to Fort Moultrie to deliver the guns. He would then proceed back to Charleston to pick up General Ripley, who was to visit Major Manigualt for an inspection of the batteries at James Island. His First Officer, Mister Parnell, had arranged for a fine supper at the Mills House that evening, so he was eager to complete the job of loading the guns.

As the dockworkers shifted the lifting arm back to the second gun to hitch up the lifting sling, Captain Relyea passed instructions to Mr. Smalls, "Robert, we shall return to the Southern Wharf tonight. Make damned sure you lay on a goodly supply of wood for tomorrow! We may steam most of the day, as we will be transporting the General again. And keep a sharp eye that the new slaves don't take a mind to wander off!"

Robert Smalls, a slave himself, had served Captain Relyea for a year and half as a wheelman. Had he been a white man they would have called him a "Pilot" but Smalls was content with his job and his wages. Smalls nodded as the Captain provided him with his instructions. When Captain Relyea had finished, Smalls expressed his concerns, "Captain, Sir, I'll be trustin' that you ain't gonna drive us close to them Yankeeman ships out yonder, they'll be shootin' at us!"

Relyea smiled and protectively responded, "No worries Robert, I aim to keep our ship safe tomorrow, so you can return home to your wife and children."

Smalls leaned against the great wooden wheel and thought on his wife and children. He had been saving his small earnings from his cut of wages, and his network of dealings in Charleston, to raise enough money to emancipate Hanna, and little Lydia, from the hotel proprietor where Hanna worked. The owner had raised the price from 700 dollars in 1861, to 800 dollars now, due to Lydia's birth. Smalls feared the price would continue to increase. He had carefully saved 600 dollars so far, but it had taken a painfully long time to earn and save that much. He was bound and determined that Lydia and her unborn sibling, would be free. He had become more and more doubtful of the promise made by Mr. Padgett, who owned the hotel and his wife, Hanna.

Captain Relyea and Parnell went down to the deck to supervise the securing of the gun, after the second iron tube had been carefully lowered onto the cypress decking of the steamer. They then had a lengthy discussion by the bow gun with the other white officer, Lieutenant Oakes. Oakes was an army engineer assigned to the *Planter* by General Ripley. Since the boat was attached to the Charleston District Engineer Department, they gained the Lieutenant, who also took command of the guns if they were needed for the defense of the boat. He had spent the past year training the slaves to load and man the fore and aft guns that made up her defensive battery.

Robert Smalls, watching the conference of the officers at the bow, gave the engine room telegraph a quick pull and returned it to the neutral position. The short signal brought Nathan from the boilers below up to the wheelhouse. Nathan was the boss of the engine room. He quickly mounted the steps to the small wheelhouse at the top of the steamer.

Nathan mockingly addressed Smalls, "You callin' Massa Smalls?"

Smalls grinned and replied, "You got dat right, Boy! We will meet tonight after the Captain and the other two leave the boat tonight. I want you to figure out a way to lose Elzie tonight. We can take Reid, but Elzie ain't got no sense at all. He is best to leave behind."

Nathan chuckled, and responded, "I wonder if you is gonna give this boy a dollar! We gonna have to gets some more wood loaded tonight, anyways. Fo' that fool, Elzie; I'm gonna give him something to do that will keep him gone all night."

Smalls nodded, and noting the Captain making his way back to the bridge, he nodded to Nathan to return back below decks.

After the cannon were stowed and secured, Captain Relyea instructed Robert Smalls to ease the *Planter* in full reverse away from the quay and into the Ashley River. Switching to all ahead full on his brass telegraph, Smalls steered the boat at the Captain's command around White Point Gardens to her berth at the Southern Wharf. Throughout the short journey the Captain maintained his customary place leaning on the rail with his hands spread wide on the rail, his large straw hat pulled low over his eyes. He preferred being on the outside where he could look ahead for shoals outside the enclosed bridge. Forward of the front swivel gun flew the tricolored flag of the Confederacy.

Pulling into the Southern Wharf, the *Planter* received a hearty welcome from flocks of gulls, which orbited screeching in hope of a meal. Robert watched as the half clad crewmen secured the hawsers to the cleats on the great wooden dock of the Wharf. They then checked and tightened the canvas covers protecting the large guns from the salt spray of the harbor. Captain Relyea provided Smalls with instructions to bank the fires, and keep light steam pressure, until their scheduled departure at 5 am the next morning.

An hour later, Captain Relyea, Lieutenant Parnell, and Lieutenant Oakes departed the boat wearing civilian frock coats and top hats. They were to have a "gentleman's evening on the town." Smalls watched them depart the vessel. He knew their real reason for the civilian dress. The guard mount, on the wharf section of town, was instructed to enforce the policy that naval officers remained on their ships, if needed. An entire crew of officers leaving at the same time was not allowed.

Smalls summoned Nate. When he arrived from below decks, he instructed him, "Go get our people! Tell them to lay low at the tobacco warehouse by the North Atlantic Wharf until we come. Get back here as soon as you can and get rid of Elzie!"

Nate quickly nodded and went below to get his shirt on. Once he returned on deck he secured his trusty wheelbarrow and an empty cask. When he moved about Charleston's streets, the wheelbarrow and cask was his prop to appear to be making a delivery. Slaves could not move about the city without a specific task to perform. If stopped, he would simply demonstrate that he was delivering an empty cask to the Hotel or any other destination he chose.

Back aboard the *Planter,* Robert Smalls assembled the remainder of the slaves who made up the crew, once Elzie had departed on his mission given to him by Nate. The sun had set behind the bustling city, and the lamps were slowly being lit along East Bay Street, beyond the Wharves. Smalls looked each of the remaining crewmen in the eyes, as they gathered in the small galley, below the wheelhouse. He addressed them, "We is all goin' to get our freedom tonight! If you be with me, you can stay. If you ain't, you will get off the boat, once we gets moving in the water. I ain't stoppin' for nothin' or nobody, once we start movin.' If them forts out yonder shoot at us, as we go by, I ain't stoppin'. If they sink us, I'm gonna die on this boat!"

The small cluster of men excitedly nodded their heads. Some chimed in during his speech with affirmative comments. Reid found himself filling with excitement. He wanted to see the North for himself and feel the freedom to go where he pleased. He had no idea how he would get there. The boats would be his best chance to get away. He worried that Elzie would report him as a runaway. The man was a fool and would gladly let Mr. Markley know he had willingly gone over to the Yankees. He hoped they would be successful or he would pay dearly for running.

Robert Smalls had taken an immediate liking to Reid. He could see the burning desire for freedom in his eyes, and while he never said much, he could clearly see he paid keen attention to everything around him. He had proved a quick study aboard the *Planter* and Smalls had directed him to assist Nate at the boiler, from time to time. He had learned most of the actions required when the engine room telegraph signaled them and Nate had also showed him what the valves should look like on the boiler to insure that the ship was not building up dangerous pressures. Smalls would need him to have these skills for his daring run, as Nate was needed to man the wheel in the morning.

The slaves spent a long and restless night preparing the boat. Robert Smalls peered from the wheelhouse from time to time, awaiting the return of Nate. He could see the sentries guarding the wharves by the illumination of the gaslights of East Bay Street. He would need Nate for the run.

After several hours and well past midnight, he saw Nate come around the corner wheeling his wooden barrow with its' ever present empty wooden cask. He became very nervous as the sentry guarding the Southern Wharf stepped out and challenged him. He watched as Nate pointed excitedly at the *Planter* and towards his cask on the wheelbarrow. The sentry finally waved him on his way. Smalls released a breath of relief as Nate rolled the barrow across the wooden gangplank.

Robert Smalls glanced at the ship's clock in the dimly lit wheelhouse, it was nearly 3 am. He quickly summoned Nate to the wheelhouse after he had stowed the fake load away, "Nate have the boys light up the boat like we is going to business! Move fast and have Reid watch the boilers."

Nate was shocked, "Where you wantin' me?"

Smalls quickly replied, "On this here wheel! You gonna drive this boat!"

Nate was even more surprised and asked, "What you gonna' do?"

Smalls gave a great grin and put the Captain's wide brimmed straw hat on his head, and replied, "I is the Captain!"

Both men laughed aloud. Since the Captain had left with his crew in civilian dress, Robert Smalls had found his uniform. With the ship brightly lit, he would pass for the Captain to distant observers. Smalls quickly donned, and buttoned up Captain Relyea's handsome naval jacket, and pulled the straw hat low over his eyes. He then directed the slaves below to untie the *Planter* from her cleats. Smalls showed Nate how to steer, after he showed him the method to signal to Reid below, on the telegraph, to set the engines to reverse. He then directed Nate to pull one long time and then one short time, on the steam whistle lanyard, which hung from the roof near the wheel. The long and short whistles were the codebook signal for official military boat traffic. Robert Smalls knew the code by heart.

After backing slowly out, Smalls instructed Nate in how to signal "All Ahead Half Speed" and Reid seeing the signal, made the necessary adjustment to the steam cylinders that pushed the long wooden shafts that turned the paddle wheel. The boat thrummed under the powerful vibration of her motor and the cascading noise of the turning wheels spinning in the water of the harbor, was like music to Robert Small's ears. Soon Lydia and her Mother would know freedom.

Smalls silently counted the wharves as he passed upstream on the Cooper River side of the city. The North Atlantic Wharf was ten docks down from the Southern Wharf. He remembered the Warehouse, that marked the destination, and as it hove into view, he instructed Nate to turn and signal on the telegraph handle for a full stop. Smalls intended to coast the *Planter* into the short wharf. The *Planter* smoothly coasted alongside the deserted wharf. The crewmembers quickly snagged the timber dock with boarding pikes, and pulled the steamer alongside the wharf. Smalls could see a sentry of the guard mount leaning against the building, which blocked the view of East Bay Street. He was continuing to stare in the direction of town, and did not notice the *Planter* as her crew lashed her alongside the dock.

Smalls then directed Nate to go over to the dark tobacco warehouse to bring over Hannah, and the children. Nate's wife was also there, waiting with her two children. Soon the 5 additional souls joined the 8 slaves on the steamer. The women gathered the sleepy children in the Saloon deck, and made them as comfortable as they could. They swiftly untied the *Planter* from the cleats, and began to slowly back out into the main channel of the Cooper River.

Soon they had the *Planter* running at her normal cruise speed of 8 knots as they passed Castle Pinckney Island, off to their starboard quarter. Smalls made sure the oil burning running lights were rigged to the stringent requirements of the forts, as they approached Sullivan's Island.

Smalls instructed Nate to guide the paddle wheel steamer close to the ramparts of Fort Moultrie, as the only channel clear of the exploding torpedoes in the harbor, were directly under the guns of the fort. Smalls showed the chart to Nate, as he nervously steered the boat away from where the locations of the exploding torpedos lay in the main channel. The engineers under General Ripley's guidance had emplaced them in a manner that denied the use of the middle section of the main shipping channel.

Across the channel on the ramparts of Fort Moultrie, a sentry called out the passing of a ship to the sergeant of the guard. The sergeant peered out into the misty harbor, and spying the ships lights, sternly directed, "Look sharp, the General usually travels on that one!"

The *Planter* smoothly slid past the silent guns of the massive fortress. The watching sentries could see the familiar figure of Captain Relyea in his large straw hat, keeping a close eye on the channel before him, outside the brightly lit wheel house. As the paddle wheeler hugged the shoreline, which led into Beach Channel, they naturally assumed the boat was headed to Fort Marshall on the far end of Sullivan's Island.

The Sergeant of the Guard instructed his runner, "Get over to the telegraph office and have them notify Fort Marshall that they have General Ripley's boat in-bound!"

Smalls leaned over, and shouted down to his crew to ready the linen sheet they had rigged for the flagstaff. He wanted to get clear of the guns before changing the Confederate Ensign to the white banner. The Yankee ships that lay in blockade, generally would fire first upon ships bearing down on them. He remembered watching a blockade-runner make an attempt that had to turn back, due to the volume of gunfire directed at it. He expected to be treated much the same. He quickly returned to the wheelhouse to study the charts. There was one more group of torpedoes laid across the channel that had a passage lane under the guns of Fort Marshall; he had one more hazard to pass. Smalls suspected that once he turned for the open ocean, the gunners at Fort Marshall would realize what they were doing. He decided to tell Nate to swing wide, like they would be making a turn towards the dock at Fort Marshall. He hoped that the maneuver would keep the gunners sleepy, by providing them with a normal looking approach. Down below in the sweltering engine room, Reid was stripped down to only his pants. Wiping sweat from his brow, he anxiously stared at the brass telegraph awaiting the next signal, while his helper, Johnny, constantly fed split wood into the open furnace that heated the boilers. Reid did not like the confines of the mechanical room with the hazardous collection of boilers and spinning and thrusting shafts. But, he was resigned to serving in the frightening machinery if it meant being free. He could sense that the ship was being sharply turned to the right, when the telegraph signaled all ahead full again. Johnny expertly added more split wood to the furnace to increase the steam. Reid paused a moment looking at the mysterious dial on the gauge near him, and then adjusted the lever that opened up full steam to the cylinders, driving the long shafts that turned the paddles on both sides of the steamer. The speed of the turning shafts increased noticeably, and the ship turned again sharply. He did not realize that they were narrowly missing several exploding mines placed in the channel. Hazards that were nearly impossible for Robert Smalls to detect, in the dark and misty waters of the harbor. He continually corrected Nate's course, as he peered nervously and carefully ahead.

Once they had crossed the bar, and proceeded towards the North Channel exit into the open sea, Smalls was relieved to not hear the guns on Fort Marshall fire. They had not been seen, or else the soldiers on the fort took them to be a blockade-runner. The thought of the blockade-runner caused him to remember the white flag. He leaned down, and shouted for the crewmembers below to pull down the Confederate colors and run up the white sheet in its stead.

Aboard the *USS Onward*, an older sailing clipper pressed into naval service last year, Lieutenant Nathaniel Chambers enjoyed an early morning pipe. They were the hunters where they sat, so the fears of being seen on the ocean were the problem for the blockade-runners, not the blockaders. The May morning air was freshening and he mused that it might signify rain in the morning. He had spent most of his watch pacing the deck along the silent rigging and weather deck guns. His watch, which had begun at midnight, consisted of two men above on the lookout posts in the masts and another six men on the weather deck. They watched both Port and Starboard, in order to detect inbound or outbound blockade runners.

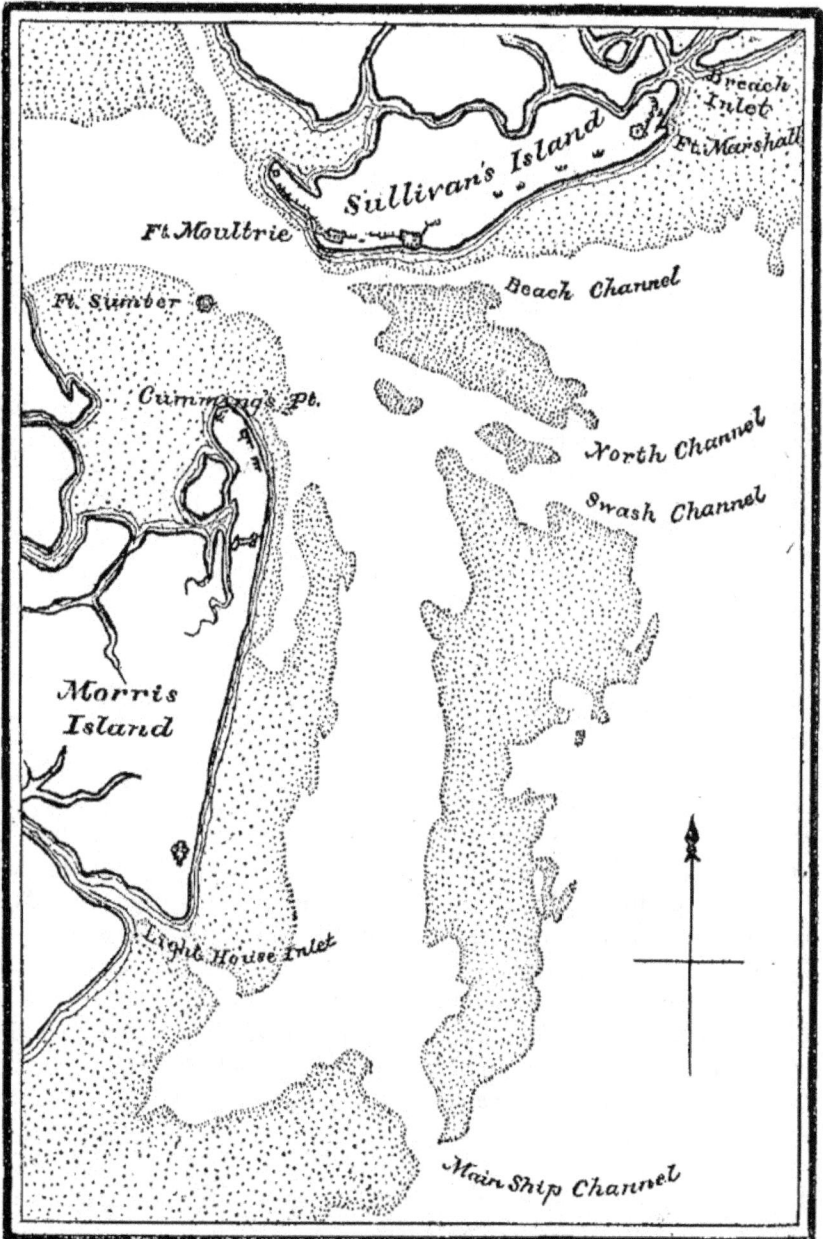

Entrances to Charleston Harbor.

He would be relieved at 6 am and was glad his watch was nearly done. Chambers turned his gaze from the open ocean back towards Sullivan's Island, beyond the bar towards the Swash and North Channels. It was then that he noted the running lights of the approaching paddlewheel steamer. It was bearing on a heading straight for the *Onward* and was running bold. It still bore its running lights, which was a rare sight for boats leaving Charleston Harbor.

Lieutenant Chambers nudged Mr. Holmes, the master of the watch who sat dozing beside him at the stern and ordered, "Beat to quarters, and direct the men of the starboard quarter to fire the recognition flares!"

On the deck of the darkened sailing ship, the crew of the weather deck guns removed protective muzzle covers, and the leather weather caps off the smooth iron guns, and began to swivel the heavy pieces towards the approaching steamer. They rapidly loaded the charges brought forward by the powder boys, and followed the charge with a saboted round shot. Once the crews had readied the guns the deck officer signified their readiness to engage the approaching ship. Coston flares hissed into the sky, and with loud pops, illuminated the approaching vessel.

Lieutenant Chambers shouted out, "Make ready to engage! Stern chaser will fire first!"

The crewmembers on the Stern Chaser heaved on the iron bars that provided leverage to swivel the heavy swivel gun truck, on the rails embedded in the deck, to improve the aim, now that the targeted vessel was illuminated by the bright flares. The assistant gunner's mate primed the iron gun and held the lanyard taunt, awaiting the order from his gunner.

Lieutenant Chambers raised his glass to look at the vessel. In the light of the third flare he could clearly see that the paddlewheel vessel had a forward gun, but he could see the form of a man standing oddly atop the carriage. As he began to focus on the vessel the Coston flares burnt out and fell back to the water in a trail of bright sparks.

Chambers quickly shouted out to the signalman, "Fire a Chromosemic signal rocket, and a Coston number zero!"

The signalman quickly rigged one of the paper rockets on the gunwale and expertly loaded the wooden handled Coston Launcher. He then lit the rocket with his slow match, and the firework leapt high in the air, functioning with a loud pop, high above the ship. The bright light of the rocket re-illuminated the *Planter*. Lieutenant Chambers aligned his glass on the approaching steamer as the red Coston flare was fired. To the rest of the fleet he had signaled the presence of a naval ramming ship. Chambers alerted the gunners to prepare to fire.

The strange ship bore closer. Lieutenant Chambers feared it was an attempt to ram the *Onward*. All the blockade men knew of the Trenholm and Frasier Company bounty that had been offered for the sinking of a Union blockade ship. He raised his glass again to study the ship. After a pause he shouted out to the gun crews, "I read the range at 800 yards! Stand ready to engage!" Lieutenant Chambers wanted to close the distance to 600 yards and hoped for a centerline shot in order to strike the vulnerable boiler of the paddle wheeler.

From the wheelhouse of the *Planter*, Robert Smalls began to feel very nervous. In the bright light of the flare he could clearly see that both of the big guns on the weather deck of the boat he was approaching, were pointed directly at him. He also could see no one waving or hailing him in any manner. Looking below he realized the white flag hung limply on the bow post, as there was very little breeze. He quickly yelled to Johnny, standing atop the bow gun, waving his arms at the boat, "Johnny! Make that flag move! Wave it!"

Smalls then realized that the ship ahead of him meant to shoot at him; he remembered Captain Relyea's talk of rams and of earlier attempts to attack the blockaders. To his horror he realized that the *Planter* looked like an attacker. He rushed to the wheelhouse door and shouted to Nate, "Move the telegraph to all stop! Do it quick!"

Reid was about to begin throwing in more split wood into the boiler furnace when the telegraph bell clanged. He saw the arrow move into the red painted part of the dial above his head that Nate had explained meant, "Stop." After a moment of thought, he stepped over to the boiler and pulled on the valve that vented off the steam pressure from the motor cylinders.

On board the *Onward*, the Master of the boat shouted to Lieutenant Chambers, "Sir, she is venting steam and it looks like they are displaying a white flag!"

Chambers had noted the venting of white steam in the bright illumination of the signal rocket and noticed that the crew appeared to be all contrabands. He shouted out to his crew, "Stand fast on the guns! Prepare

11

the gig and a boarding party!"

The sight of the crew of the warship lowering a whaleboat on the davits was what Robert Smalls wanted to see. He shouted out to Johnny on the bow to lower the anchor and have everyone assemble at the bow. Smalls then rushed down to the saloon deck to find Hanna and Lydia. They sat on the leather-upholstered bench along the paneled wall of the steamer, holding Lydia as she slept. When she saw Robert come in, she carefully laid the little girl's head onto the padded seat and rushed to embrace her husband. They had no time for greetings at the start of their voyage to freedom and Hanna had anxiously waited down below, knowing little of what was happening around her.

Robert smiled after hugging her tightly and said, "Wake Lydia, I want her to see the flag of freedom!"

Hannah gently shook Lydia awake, and as she rubbed her eyes with her tiny fists, Hanna exclaimed, "Rise up honey! You gots to see the Jubilee! Your Papa has set you free!"

They emerged under the light of the signal rockets, and clustered on the bow of the *Planter*, as the small boarding party under the command of an Ensign arrived alongside the boat. The oarsmen stowed their long oars upright, and hooked the gunwales of the *Planter* with boarding pikes. The Ensign and several musket-wielding Marines warily boarded the paddle wheel steamer.

Robert Smalls removed the large straw and announced to the Ensign, "Sir, I present to you the *Planter* and four fine guns! All of us ask you to give us our freedom in exchange!"

Ensign Robley D. Evans looked over the ramshackle collection of slaves and asked, "What have you done with the crew? Where are the officers of this vessel?"

Robert Smalls shook his head, "Sir, we is the crew! We only had three white officers and they went to town last night. I suppose they some kind of mad, right about now!"

Evans was astonished that the South was relying on slaves to crew vessels, and he asked Smalls, "What was your duty on this ship?"

Smalls explained his life aboard the *Planter* over the years; as he talked, the

Ensign glanced towards the marines as they searched the vessel. Reid, Johnny and Nathan simply stood and stared at the large Union warship. The morning sky was turning red as the sun began to rise. Ensign Evans asked where Smalls had operated the ship as a wheelman and realized as Smalls talked, that this man was a rare find. The Marine Sergeant returned and handed a chart and leather bound book to Ensign Evans.

The Sergeant reported, "Sir, the vessel is clear, there are no officers aboard, nor any white crewmen. The charts have every piling and torpedo charted for the entirety of Charleston Harbor as well as the rivers in and around James Island! The volume is the Confederate Commercial Code with their ciphers!"

Ensign Evans raised his eyebrows and asked Smalls, "How did you come by these documents!"

Robert Smalls grinned and replied, "This here boat is General Ripley's flagship for travelin' about Charleston Harbor. He is gonna be real mad when he figures out where we done went with her!"

Evans, realizing the import of this prize, quickly shouted out orders to the Marines to post a guard and he rushed back to the gig. He needed to get this information to the Captain.

Reid quizzically asked Smalls, "Mister Smalls, what is going on here? Are they gonna keep us as slaves?"

Smalls laughed, "Naw boy! They is digesting what they done found. I expect they will bring us alongside that ship over yonder. I hope they feed us some breakfast. We forgot to stock the galley yesterday. We ain't got nothin' but hard crackers!"

The Ensign and the launch returned after the sun had risen and he and several enlisted ratings, boarded the *Planter*. To the slaves delight they had also brought hot porridge and bacon in covered tins. Robert decided to skip breakfast and assisted the Ensign in explaining the operation of the ship. He paused to watch Hanna lovingly spoon small portions of the steaming porridge to Lydia, who was clearly hungry. It warmed his heart to know that they would be free. He had achieved what he realized was a lifelong goal. Now he would need a new goal. Perhaps a ship captain, he mused. Robert then noticed that the crewmen had brought over the Stars and Stripes, along with a proper naval ensign for the bow mast. As they raised the colors on the sternpost, Robert Smalls led Lydia by the hand over to the mast as the colors caught the rising wind with a crackling noise.

He picked her up so that she could touch the rustling fabric with her tiny fingers, "That flag means somethin' different now, Honey! It is now the promise of your freedom, child!"

Putting her down, he watched with amusement as she scampered across the deck planks towards her mother. He realized he would have to begin thinking about a new home for Hanna; he just had to determine what the Navy planned to do with them. A few minutes later Ensign Evans explained it to him. When Robert returned to the wheelhouse, Evans presented him with a small black badge embroidered with gold bullion thread. The symbol was a picture of a tiny ship's wheel.

Evans explained, "Mister Smalls, have your wife stitch this to your shirt. It is the appropriate rating for what you do. It is the badge of a pilot! Mind you in the United States Navy, that is the rating for an officer! Pray tell, can you navigate this vessel to Port Royal?"

Smalls eyed the small yet significant gift and nodded, "Yessir, of course it has been some time since I did it out of the main ship channel! Why is we going there?"

Evans smiled, "Why Mister Smalls you have an appointment with Admiral DuPont! He will more than likely insist on a personal audience with you! It seems that you have provided the United States Navy with a rather extravagant gift. It is what you know, Robert; that we greatly crave. We desperately need a man of these waters! A skilled pilot is what we lack!"

Robert Smalls shook his head in wonder. All this money and all these learned men, sent to fine schools and paid fine wages. Yet they needed a slave to show them how to sail to Beaufort. It made him laugh to himself. As they made the journey, Robert carefully explained every detail of the coast to Ensign Evans. Evans was astonished at the encyclopedic knowledge of the slave, who without charts had memorized every channel and shoal. Every hazard and signal of weather that could interrupt a voyage or lose a cargo. His sense of ship handling was also uncanny in practice, as he demonstrated an innate skill of employing the drift of current and thrust of the paddles, to maneuver without unnecessary commands to the motormen below. Ensign Evans found himself fascinated by Small's descriptive ramblings as they made the daylong trip to Port Royal. He resolved to advise the Admiral to keep this man close at hand.

⚓

Captain Relyea rushed down the stone walks along East Bay Street. He definitely felt ill, and according to his watch he only had half an hour to prepare prior to the arrival of General Ripley. He rushed past the early morning pedestrians and began to sweat in his rush. Thankfully, Lieutenant Parnell had departed ahead of him with assurances that he would get the crew ready. Relyea glanced at his watch again as he rushed the remaining blocks to the Southern Wharf, it was nearly 8 am. He regretted the previous evening. While entertaining, it was not worth how he felt now.

He finally reached the brick apothecary shop that marked the corner alley that led to the Southern Wharf. The sentry there stepped out and challenged him, "What is your business Sir?"

Relyea had been raising his hand to return a salute when he realized that wearing a civilian frock coat as he approached the wharf, made him appear just like everyone else in Charleston. His uniform was still aboard the *Planter*. He mumbled, "I am the captain of the vessel here! I am returning from leave!"

The sentry did not relent nor lower his bayoneted musket from port carry, "I will need to see your pass slip sir."

Relyea, feeling ill, became enraged, "Step aside boy! I am the captain of the *Planter!* I command you to let me pass! I am to meet General Ripley within the hour!"

The sentry gripped his musket tightly and began to sweat nervously before he could respond; the voice of Lieutenant Parnell rang out.

"Sir! The ship is not here!" he announced breathlessly. He had come running when he heard the commotion.

Parnell blurted out, "Sir a portion of the cargo to be loaded remains on the quay. She is not to be seen! General Ripley is to arrive in half an hour! What shall we say?"

Relyea stepped aside from the sentry and stared at the empty slip at the end of the alley and muttered, "Smalls!"

He then, overcome by the effects of too much wine from the previous night, doubled over and vomited on the brick cobblestones of the alley. Parnell hurried over to him to help him stand erect and asked, "What do we do? We must report this, Sir!"

Relyea flatly replied, "I am very ill, son. I am going to my home. I shall report the loss after you have checked the other wharves. Not a word until you have looked into this thoroughly!"

Lieutenant Parnell was astonished, "Sir, the General? What do we say to the General?"

Relyea, waved his hand behind him, "Make sure no one is here when he arrives! He will attribute it to a bureaucratic misunderstanding! Do what you can to find the *Planter!* Perhaps Smalls moved her thinking we were meeting at a different place." Captain Relyea knew that his boat would not be found. He knew he had made a fatal error. He only wanted escape. And escape he did. Lieutenant Parnell resolved to stay put. Someone would have to explain to the General.

⚓

The morning sun had melted away all threat of clouds and rain. The *Planter* made her bumpy way along in the choppy spring sea. Each time Lieutenant Evans had suggested a hazard on the charts, Robert Smalls had smiled and assured him that "he knew the way." Evans was taken by the older man's extensive knowledge of the Carolina Coast. Smalls had explained earlier that he had used this route many a year when they were hauling cotton up from the Sea Islands to the warehouses in Charleston. Smalls took time to explain the unique nature of the *Planter,* her wide breadth made her shallow draft, both lightly loaded, and heavily loaded. Such a design was essential to penetrate to wharfs up the Edisto to pick up bales from the Sea Islands.

On their port quarter, the *USS Unadilla* rode watchfully, under steam, as an escort for the prize on her way to Port Royal. *Unadilla* was basically coasting along at half her speed, to keep position on the slower paddle wheeler. It would take them the rest of the day to reach the great coaling base at Hilton Head.

Evans asked him how far he had sailed into the Inland Waterways about, and around Charleston. Smalls explained his trips around James Island, trips up the Stono, Ashley and the Edisto rivers. Evans was amazed and asked, "And you never ran aground?"

Smalls grinned and replied, "Sometimes if you missed the tide but there are many ways about them waters. They is always a way that I found."

Evans laughed and observed, "I think Admiral DuPont will want to make your acquaintance, Mr. Smalls."

Smalls nodded, and added a small warning, "Jus' one thing to remember Captain. Them Rebs, they knows the tight spots, as well as me. You'll always find them behind big guns, upriver. They knows all the tight spots!"

General Ripley's face turned a bright red when he arrived in his carriage and dismounted to the empty wharf. Lieutenant Parnell did his best to explain, but Ripley had stopped listening. The reports he would have to file filled his mind. The map of the harbor defenses and the nautical charts of the pilings and torpedo fields alone would endanger the general defense plan. The loss of the commercial code with ciphers would have national level implications.

Ripley turned to his adjutant, Captain Henson of the Engineering Corps, and ordered, "Place this man on close arrest! Find the Provost and have him collect up Relyea and the other Lieutenant and arrest the pair of them!"

He then eyed Parnell, "Lieutenant you know the regulations regarding crews of ships in this harbor! You are never to abandon your command to the care of slaves! You will be lucky if you do not hang!"

Two hours later, a provost detail of soldiers arrested Captain Relyea in his sleep shirt on the porch of his home on Rutledge Avenue. Lieutenant Oakes was found in a tavern, very drunk, on Meeting Street, and he too, was summarily arrested and spirited away to the Provost. Proceedings for a General Court Martial, under the authority of the Charleston District Commander, General Ripley, were swiftly drawn up. The Adjutant spent the remainder of the day compiling reports for submission to the Confederate States Government. The loss of the codebooks would be reported directly to Secretary Mallory. General Ripley hoped this event would not affect his current orders to report to Virginia, to assume a Brigade Command. He had intended the final trip about the harbor as a farewell tour of his command. It was a mission that would never occur.

His water taxi was now the newest Union vessel, which would be seen again and again, south of Charleston.

⚓

Robert Smalls was slightly nervous as he was ushered aboard the spotless and holystoned decks of the *USS Wabash*. He glanced about in wonder and marveled at the great iron stack. The high painted masts and the sleek iron guns fore and aft made for an impressive display. To him, it was a vast and well-maintained ship of a size that astonished him. Seamen were everywhere, and he imagined she must house hundreds of them. Well-trimmed and courteous officers showed him the way to the Admiral's Stateroom. A man everybody called "DuPont" awaited him and he did not know what to expect. His mind drifted back to yesterday, when they had arrived at the "Contraband Colony" which was a long row of barracks-like buildings set on a sandy flat near Fort Howell, on Hilton Head Island. The men from the North had built a massive wharf out of freshly milled wood that supported the arrival of hundreds of ships and assorted cargoes, which were piled in mountains near wooden buildings and warehouses. He was interested in seeing how much construction these business-like people had erected where he only remembered marshes and small shanties. They had kindly ushered the crew to some of the empty rooms in one of the long buildings. Their escorts were older white women who called themselves "Gideons." They talked of schooling and reading, and Robert knew he needed to find himself something on the water to do.

The next morning Lieutenant Evans had found him after breakfast, and summoned him to a visit with "DuPont." Robert gladly accompanied him to a launch by the wharf, manned by several brawny sailors. Smalls was greatly impressed by the collection of dark painted warships. He became fixated by the sight of the twin turreted Iron Clad *Weehawken,* and asked about her, to Lieutenant Evans, as they passed the vessel. Evans explained that she was to soon press an attack to Charleston, once additional ironclad warships were assembled.

As he entered the white painted stateroom, the escorting officers motioned to Smalls to take a seat in one of the nice wooden seats by a table with a white cloth and teacups on it. Smalls brushed his sleeves with his hands, fearful of marring the freshly laundered tablecloth. One of the officers offered him coffee, and Smalls gladly assented to having a cup. He nervously sipped a portion, and suddenly all the men stiffened.

"Good Morning Sir!" one of the men exclaimed, and Robert, taking his cue from his escort, rose from his chair and faced the Admiral as he entered. Robert was taken by the smallish grizzled man. His uniform was not as crisp nor clean as those of the younger men. The gilt had grown greenish from the exposure to the salt air. Like Captain Relyea, who had raised him, this man was clearly an officer of the sea. Smalls mused perhaps this was why his office remained aboard a boat.

"So you are Robert Smalls?" asked DuPont.

Smalls eagerly nodded.

"No small thing to filch a steamer out of Charleston Harbor under the guns of Sumter, and Fort Moultrie, whilst navigating a field of torpedoes to gain your freedom, son!" DuPont observed.

He looked him hard in the eye and asked, "I hear you were the pilot. Is this true?"

Robert Smalls nodded, and added, "I am called the "Wheel Man", Sir. You see, us slaves ain't near smart enough to be called 'Pilot' in South Carolina's navy."

DuPont grunted, "I would call you a Pilot, Mister Smalls! How long have you served in this capacity?"

Smalls quickly responded, "A year and a half, Sir! Before that I was just tending on the boat, helping them load and such. Captain Relyea moved me up, when the war came. They needed the extra white men for the navy."

DuPont reached behind him, and received a rolled chart from one of the officers. Rolling it out on the table before them, he asked, "Smalls do you know this harbor? Are these plots of torpedoes the truth?"

Robert Smalls nodded, and added, "Sir, that be the Lord's truth, hell I even helped lay some of them!"

DuPont was clearly intrigued and asked, "Did you observe the preparation of these devices?"

Robert quickly answered, "Yes Sir! They was real careful. They said they was the acid fuses, and we could not be rough with them."

DuPont knowingly nodded his head, and turned to another officer, who clearly was more important than the others, based on Small's observations of the stripes on his coat, and stated, "You see! That proves what we have heard. They have improved on the standard torpedoes in their possession. Gentlemen we can expect the worst when we attempt the harbor!"

Admiral DuPont looked at Robert, and said, "Son, I would like for you to serve as my personal pilot. Would you be interested in that?"

Robert Smalls nodded. The Admiral asked him a multitude of questions about his experiences on the waters of Charleston, and after he had explained in great detail of his life, DuPont turned to the man with the stripes on his sleeve, and directed, "Get him officially in my employ! Make him a contractor, I care not a damn! And get him a uniform of some sort! Contraband or no, I want this man!"

The officer nodded, and shouted instructions to one of the other officers who also nodded, and rushed out. Robert Smalls was impressed, and took another sip of coffee, which was now cold, but it was genuine coffee, nonetheless. He reveled in his newfound celebrity. Life was not bad, even if he was a slave. After a long afternoon of making his mark on various sheets of paper, and answering questions, Robert was hired on with the United States Navy as a skilled nautical pilot. Consequently, he received a promise of 14 dollars a month pay, with a 2-dollar advance, on signing. He was then shown to the quartermasters shack on the wharf, where he was issued a plain navy blue sack coat, and canvas trousers. He was also provided with new leather shoes. He was then sent on his way home, with the reminder to return to the wharf tomorrow at 8 am, to start his first day of duty. It took him a few moments to find his segment of rooms in the teeming barracks buildings. Women attended to chores and laundry outside, as swarms of shouting children ran about and played in the dirt commons, between the buildings. Finally Robert found the building he had been assigned to and saw Hannah sitting by an iron kettle over a fire in the yard. Spying Robert's approach she stood up and rushed to him with a hug.

Robert was taken aback for a moment, as she exclaimed, "Honey! They want to teach me and Lydia to read and write! Look at this!"

Hannah showed him the wooden hornbook and a McGuffin reader, "The Gideons say we don't need to be scared no more. It ain't against none of their rules for us to learn!"

Robert smiled, he knew the laws of the State were strict in regard to teaching slaves to read and write. Captain Relyea had ignored the rules and had taught Robert the rudiments of reading, just enough to function with charts and mechanical devices on the ship's engine. He envisioned Lydia would no longer be dependent on others. She would grow up free. They settled in for the evening in their new and cramped home, enjoying their first full day of freedom over a supper of sweet potatoes and salt pork.

After two weeks at Hilton Head Island, Reid was beginning to sour on the "Free" life. He had initially reveled in the thought of being a free man. He had willingly assented to attending the reading classes, put on by the Gideon ladies every evening in the meetinghouse. The structure served as both a schoolhouse during the weekdays, and a church on Sundays. He worked each day as a stevedore down at the docks; the army would pay each man 10 dollars a month to unload the never-ending parade of ships. They carried every manner of cargo.

In the evenings after a supper, he would struggle to stay awake and recite the alphabet and phonetic sounds to Mrs. Everette, who served as the night adult reading teacher. Initially the exercises made little to no sense to him. He considered quitting often. As there was little to do besides working and dreaming of a different place, he persisted. Reid quietly observed the activity around the harbor and learned of the origins of the many ships that came to deliver cargo.

By July he found that the pictures he saw on the many crates and boxes, were actually the letters that he had been memorizing. It dawned on him then, that they described what was within the thousands of boxes that he had been carrying, and stacking. As he labored and learned, Reid began to form an idea. He would learn to read. He would save the money he was earning, and he would travel to the place they called "Boston." It had become the first word he could read, as he saw it so much on the ships, the boxes, and the papers strewn about the docks that he used to start his evening and morning cook fires with at the contraband quarters. It was a word that also was often voiced in the conversations of the sailors, and soldiers that were constantly around him. Boston became in his mind, a magical place. A place where everything seemed to come from.

The Docks of Hilton Head Island

2

MARYLAND

Corporal Billy Cross sat cross-legged in the tall grass on the side of the Boonsboro Pike as his company foraged in the cornfield behind them for green ears of feed corn. The regiments in front of theirs had picked the field over pretty well, so they had been required to penetrate deep into the verdant green jungle of stalks in order to find anything to eat. Billy had found one ear halfway into the field. Since walking amongst the gnarly roots was difficult without shoes, he asked Gene to find him another. He had returned to their stacked arms and started a small fire to boil the last of their Yankee coffee they had scrounged in Manassas. They had eaten green corn for breakfast, dinner and supper since the 3rd when they had waded the Potomac to enter Maryland. He recalled there had been much ceremony by the crossing site. General Lee had arranged for a band to play as they had marched into the ford and entered the knee deep river.

It was that river which had softened the pegged brogans he had procured. The same shoes he had unflinchingly taken from a dead Union soldier in Manassas as they crossed the battlefield, following the retreat of General Pope's new army. The soles had peeled off the shoes after the first day of marching down the Boonsboro Pike. Gene explained that stitched shoes were far superior if you could find them. They had been finding that more and more of the Yankee soldiers had been equipped with the good ones. The men had called the desirable ones "McKays" as the soles were inscribed with that maker's mark on the instep of the sole. Thankfully, General Jenkins had paused for frequent stops in order to permit the stragglers to keep up with the remainder of the Brigade. Billy had found himself straggling as well from time to time as he found the going easier on the dirt roadsides rather than attempting to move barefoot down the graveled Boonsboro Pike. Many others were in the same boat as the improved Macadam surface destroyed the shoes of the marching soldiers.

Gene and George emerged from the stalks with haversacks full of stripped ears. Gene handed Billy two more. The men settled around the small fire and tossed a few of the ears on the coals to roast. Billy opted to eat one green. He had to force himself to continue to eat the tough feed corn. Sweet corn was preferred but it was rare to encounter a field that had not been picked clean of that variety.

Gene observed him and gently cautioned, "Gonna get the shits, boy! You should wait on the roasted ones!"

Billy looked at him with small bits of kernels clinging to his beard and responded, "Don't make no different one way or the other! We need to whup some more Yankees so we can get some salt pork!"

The noontime sun had made the crisp morning pleasantly warm and most of the men were in fine spirits, cheered by the lengthy Indian summer. Captain Kilpatrick strode down the line, and warned them that they had another 10 minutes until they resumed their march. Billy wearily finished a couple of more bites on the tough corn and put two more ears in his haversack for later. He then slung his ragged blanket over his shoulder and found his rifle in the stack and slung it. To the rest of his messmates he nodded for them to do likewise.

Gene took the remainder of the precious coffee and poured it into his half full canteen. "Next pot may be a might thin!" he quipped with a smile.

The men fell into the road. Those without shoes stood along the dusty sides of the road. Soon the Regiment began its march. Frederick, Maryland lay a scant three miles distant. The men had all had to listen to General Lee's general edict to the army yesterday, regarding their behavior in Maryland. The intent was to come as friends, rather than a conquering invader. That meant no foraging for meat or theft. No one explained why it was permitted to take corn off the stalk, but the men found it extremely hard to bypass pigs and chickens at the roadside farms they passed. They instead, satisfied themselves as well as they could with corn and apples, where they could find them. The campaigning of the summer had made them tough and lean, but the miles wore on and the hunger pangs became distracting. Most of them refused to grumble. All they needed was that one elusive clear victory and perhaps the war would end. Billy hoped that perhaps the move they were making would lead to that. In the interim he grimly continued forward, ignoring the pain of his feet.

THE
ANTIETAM
CAMPAIGN

As they marched towards Frederick, Billy noted that the occupants from the farms along the route, quietly and curiously watched. Old women on occasion would bring out baskets of food items to those fortunate enough to receive offerings. Yet there was none of the enthusiasm of liberation, evident from these Marylanders. None seemed anxious join the South, that they had been led to believe, from the Richmond newspapers and the suggestions of the officers. To Billy, the people seemed worried. They had not seen war, like most of Virginia. Looking west, Billy could see the beautiful misty forms of the Catoctin Mountain Range.

The land was hilly and fertile, and the weather was perfect for campaigning. The morning chills gave way to comfortable warmth during the day. Clouds in the distance to the north hinted at rain but the soldiers did not mind. They were acutely aware of how filthy they were. They had been constantly on the move since July, and had received little in terms of replacements for worn out uniforms. As they reached the outskirts of Frederick, Colonel Walker halted the column and instructed his officers have the men close ranks. Stern enjoinders were passed down the line for them to stick together and not to break ranks or wander off. This was the first major town in Maryland the invading army would pass through and General Lee wanted to insure the Marylanders witnessed the entry of a disciplined army of "friends."

Corporal Page checked the feet of the team horses in the first section, and shouted out to Joshua, "Sergeant Timmonds! Two loose shoes over here!"

Joshua nodded. He was still getting used to his Section Sergeant duties after having received promotion from Captain Haines, while they refitted at Aquia Landing in August. It had taken them a month to recover their caissons and refit the company after the disastrous debarkation from the peninsula. Sergeant O'Brien had contracted the fever and was invalided in Washington. They had been rushed north to aid General Pope at Manassas at the end of the month, but had arrived too late to do anything, but join in the retreat to Washington. Now Company M was racing to follow General Pleasanton again. It had been a week of near constant motion as the cavalry maneuvered to maintain contact with the flank of General Lee's fast moving invasion into Maryland.

Joshua dug into his saddlebag and extracted a small hammer and iron clinch tongs and tossed them to Page, "Here, just tighten them up, we can renail them tonight!"

Page caught the tools and proceeded to tighten the shoes on the team horses.

First Sergeant O'Keefe rode up alongside Joshua and paused to discuss what they could expect for the rest of the day. He had returned from eavesdropping on a session with Captain Haines and Colonel Hayes.

"We can expect to be moving all day! They are trying to keep up with General Stuart's flankers! The Rebs are hot footin' direct to Frederick. Regiment wants us to keep up at all costs in case the General has to block them from making a right turn towards Washington. So look lively! Captain wants us ready to move momentarily." O'Keefe gave Joshua a slight smile, adding, "Them stripes look good on you boy'o, take good care not to lose them!"

Joshua, returned the smile, and replied, "Thanks First Sergeant! No worries here. Remember you got nobody else but Micks to help ye!"

O'Keefe laughed and rode off to alert Newby's section. Soon the teams were checked and made ready. The sections pulled into staggered lines abreast in the fallow pasture; awaiting the move back into column and onto the road. The fine graveled roads of Maryland had polished the iron-rimmed wheels of the company to a bright gleam, which reflected the warm September sun. The refitting at Aquia landing had included new boots and uniforms. Noncommissioned Officers had been provided Colt revolvers, and the men had received a supply of Smith carbines, that many grumbled about, as they had to be slung on one's back, being the "artillery" variant. The men had wanted the cavalry version which was more comfortable to carry, but they were not "authorized," even for Horse Artillery.

Captain Haines was pleased at the sight of his company. They had taken on the air of professional veterans. Men who could be counted on to stand fast in any fight and defeat the Rebs wherever they met them. A rider approached and drew up alongside Captain Haines. After a short conference, Haines motioned with his arm and the company got underway again. The morning had warmed considerably and after a short time, the horses began to lather lightly where their harnesses rested on their short pelts. Joshua had hoped that their pause at Aquia landing would have resulted in mail, with news from home, but no mail had materialized. They had then been ordered north to Manassas. Following a short pause there, they were diverted. Company M had no part to play in General Pope's embarrassing defeat. The troops were cheerful now, since "Little Mac" was back in command and the army was on the move. The news of the Southern invasion had jolted everyone into speculation. It was clear to Joshua, as he listened to the news in O'Keefe's evening meetings, that this new turn would result in a huge battle. Perhaps this coming fight would be the last.

Lieutenant Pennington, newly assigned to the company, had been appointed to replace Lieutenant, now Captain, Haines. Joshua liked the young officer, who made it a point to share information when he got it. It was always on the men's minds, about where they were off to, and what they were going to do. Pennington soon rode up alongside Joshua to check on the progress of the section, as they moved swiftly down the graveled road.

Joshua saluted him as he approached, and asked, "Sir, do you know where we are going?"

Pennington, still looking straight ahead, returned his salute smartly and replied, "We are off to a town called 'Frederick.' General Pleasanton is pushing hard to reach its outskirts! We have word that Lee's main army is passing through there now. There is a chance we can cut them off and block any attempt towards Washington! Make sure you boys are ready for a fight! As you can tell, we are well in advance of our infantry at the moment."

Joshua saluted him again as he rode swiftly up the column to rejoin on Captain Haines. He then looked over to the team drivers and the caisson men behind him. They quickly nodded their heads. They had heard the news, despite the clopping of the hooves and the rattling of the gun carriage, limber and caisson.

The Palmetto Sharpshooters were not permitted to stop as they passed through Frederick. The men had found it strange that the citizens had not given them a rousing welcome. Most just stood, and stared dispassionately, as the men tramped through the rain puddled streets. The older women offered an occasional kindness and hungry marching men snatched up their offerings of apples or biscuits. Billy surmised that these were ladies who had sons of their own, fighting on one side or the other. He reckoned that a kindness offered to any soldier, might bring an act of Christian kindness to their own in some strange place, as they marched through. Some of the neat clapboard houses were decorated with the Stars and Stripes, bold and clear indications that the inhabitants were pro-Union and unwelcoming to Mr. Lee's army. Billy occasionally heard comments from the spectators about how dirty they looked. It caused him to be self-conscious of his tattered pants and bare feet. Had they looked closer, however; they would have noticed very clean muskets, full oiled cartridge boxes and burnished bayonets. They may have been bedraggled in their dress, but their effectiveness had given the Union Army pause at many a battlefield.

They marched another four miles out of Frederick, before setting up camp to cook their meager rations on a hillside bounded by a split rail fence. The majority of the top row of rails swiftly disappeared as the men spirited the rails away to make firewood. It was their way of getting around the strict orders not to destroy the fences. They merely made them, "less tall."

Gene and George hacked away at one of the rails with their bowie knives, until they got enough strips of the weathered wood to make a cook fire. Gene filled his tin cup with the thin coffee from his canteen, and George revealed a long saved gray lump of smelly cooked salt pork. Billy produced a small bag of cornmeal, and they commenced to start a fire. They had a frying pan, fashioned from one half of a Federal canteen, into which they placed the chunks of salt pork, after George had sliced it into small pieces. The fat meat began to fry, as the small smoky fire grew hotter. It had grown dark now, and all across the hillside small fires reflected the same tableau. Each mess, in their own manner, were cooking their supper of various scavenged, scrounged, and saved items. George had placed the cup by the side of the fire to warm the coffee, while Billy mixed some water with the corn meal to make a rough batter. When the salt pork pieces were browned, he poured the batter into the makeshift fry pan, and the men watched, as the cake fried in the grease. After several long minutes of waiting, and chatting, George lifted the pan by its makeshift wire handle off the fire, so it would cool. The corn cake steamed in the light of the fire. With his knife he carefully cut the cake into 4 equal pieces and passed a piece to each of the messmates. Gene then poured each a share of the thin coffee into their tin cups. The messmates ate the greasy bread, relishing the taste of meat after their days of green corn on the long march.

Across the hillside camp, men could be heard laughing and shouting to one another. The excitement of the campaign into Maryland was infectious. Billy and George began a discussion of the propriety of invading the North. George was against it, as he felt that the Southern armies were raised to defend the seceded states, and nothing more. Billy argued that, as the Union forces were doing to Virginia, the Carolinas and Louisiana, the South should do to the North. Gene only laughed and injected "Devil's Advocate" questions to keep the two going. When Sergeant Dennis stopped by to advise when they would move in the morning, Billy drew him into the discussion. Sergeant Dennis proved to be a pro-invasion man, but only for the sake of finding the Yankees, to fight them.

The weary men turned in for the night. As they wrapped their thin blankets about them, Gene paused to throw three shucked ears of green corn on the glowing embers of the cook fire, for breakfast.

Best's Grove had transformed from a pastoral peach orchard, into a busy military camp. Civilians from Frederick, and the surrounding countryside, were attracted to General Lee's transient headquarters in curious droves. Each strove to catch a glimpse at the famous Rebel Generals, who had so consistently frustrated the Federal Army. General Lee, General Longstreet and General Jackson had arrived at the camp by mid-morning. Lee and Longstreet had arrived in an ambulance, as both could not ride. Lee had his wrists wrapped due to an accident caused by Traveler breaking away from him while he was trying to mount. He had injured both wrists in the fall. Lee was pleased to see that Major Taylor and Colonel Chilton had already established his headquarters camp and the sight of white canvas and wood smoke was as comforting now, as arriving home. He mused that these field headquarters in their various locations, were his true home now.

Major Taylor, seeing the ambulance arrive, rushed out to greet Generals Lee and Longstreet, "Welcome to Best's Grove gentlemen! It is most effective secrecy to employ this here ambulance for your travels! Nobody would ever suspect your importance, traveling in such a conveyance!"

General Longstreet gave a disgusted grunt and General Lee said little. His humor was poor, due to his disappointment with the reception of his army at Frederick. His quartermaster had already submitted to him a report by courier, revealing the fact that Marylanders were refusing Confederate script or Confederate government promissory notes as payment for foodstuffs and supplies. The much promised enthusiasm had not been as forthcoming as Mr. Davis had imagined. Frederick had proven to be thoroughly pro-Union.

Accepting Major Taylor's extended hand on his elbow, General Lee quickly jumped to the ground. It was proving to be a fine Indian summer day. The leaves on the trees remained brilliantly green as if it was mid summer.

Lee thanked Major Taylor and directed, "Take me to see Colonel Chilton, we have orders to draft!"

General Longstreet deftly stepped out of the ambulance; he needed no assistance, as it had been a blistered foot that had interrupted his riding. He was resolved to regain his mount as soon as he could. He glanced down at the ridiculous carpet slipper on his foot. Seeing the crowd milling about the camp and embarrassed, he quickly followed General Lee. They had discussed a concept for dealing with the Yankee forces at Harper's Ferry. Since he did not like the direction General Lee was leaning towards, he was anxious to argue his point one more time. He also wanted to avoid being stopped with one foot in a slipper.

General Thomas J. Jackson and his staff also arrived mid-morning. He had abandoned the gift horse given to him by the citizens of Maryland at the Potomac crossing, and again rode on the sorry little pony that satisfied his need to move surely. Jackson occasionally rubbed his sore hands from the fall he had suffered from the gift horse. Major Dabney rode alongside him. Jackson was glad the Reverend had not found need to employ his customary umbrella for shade as he rode along. The catcalls from the troops were annoying and sometimes humorous. Jackson wanted to avoid the temptation of humor, particularly at the expense of his Chief of Staff, and spiritual advisor.

As they rode through the throngs of civilians wandering the camp, the cry went up, "There is Stonewall Jackson!"

The general stonily ignored another man who shouted out as he passed, "Where are you headed next, General?"

General Jackson turned to Major Dabney and commanded, "Major, insure that the Brigade Commanders post an alert Provost Guard! I will have no man slinking back into Frederick from this encampment. General Lee's orders are plain in that regard. I should suspect that there is many a man amongst our company that would seek strong drink there!"

Dabney seriously nodded, "Sir, I will happily see to it that they remain in place. I will instruct them to remain in camp and stay prepared to move at short notice. That should hold them still."

Jackson snapped in response, "Yes Major, please see to it! I shall not tolerate them engaging in speculation with these people. Such talk will surely get to the Yankees and they would be able to make useful associations from it. I refuse to be a party to them learning much of our intentions!"

As the two men dismounted by the tent camp established for them, a group of young ladies ambushed Jackson.

A very pretty girl with dark brown curls cooed, "General Jackson, are you intending on staying here for a spell? There is tell of a festival that the citizens of Frederick intend on holding, in your honor!"

The three other girls in her company giggled with lace-gloved hands covering their mouths. Jackson, stunned, realized that they were mere children, none more than sixteen years, at the most. He decided that since they were only children. Stern patience would be the Christian approach, "Ladies, as a married and chaste man, I do not partake in festivals. Mine is a mission that requires stern devotion and devout purpose. I suggest you repair to your homes and parents. There is no providence in association with soldiers on a battlefield!"

The pretty girl with brown curls, persisted, "Sir! We have read much of your exploits and admire your devotion to your cause. The stories of your fighting in the Shenandoah are on everyone's lips! Might we trouble you for a small token? It would be a keepsake to admire! Pray thee sir, a button perhaps?"

Despite Major Dabney's protests, Jackson assented. The girls were alarmingly quick and after a few moments he found himself short six buttons on his dirty gray coat. Dabney, having enough quickly shooed the girls away and rushed the general to his tent.

As the day wore into the evening, the generals did not mingle. Each was taken to examining the returns of their respective commands. Despite the proximity to one another, they focused inwardly, in order to prepare for a meeting that certainly would occur, as soon as Lee directed it. They had become accustomed to his taciturn ways and knew he was dedicated to thought and rest, when he could get it.

In the sparse light of a tin oil lamp, Robert E. Lee listened wearily as Colonel Chilton relayed the returns from the respective divisions of the Army of Northern Virginia. Lee was disturbed by the news that stragglers had increased in number, from what he had heard reported by previous movements. Chilton had relayed, that with what had been observed to date, he could only count on about 40,000 men being available if and when McClellan were to show his hand. Chilton droned on with spotty reports of contacts from General Stuart, revealing where Federal cavalry had been spotted south and east of Frederick. They had proven persistent and seemed to be wherever Stuart moved.

Chilton also relayed to General Lee, that many stragglers were, for all intents and purposes, invalided now. With the pressure of General Pleasanton's cavalry increasing, those stragglers were now prone to capture. General Lee could now see the hazard to the tail of his army, along the eastern side of the Catoctin Mountain Range. Looking at the map on the table before them, he studied his route. He mused, that perhaps, he would have to establish a collection point for those unable to join his main army, back at Winchester. He turned to Colonel Chilton and asked if he knew the strength of the isolated Yankee troops at Harper's Ferry. Chilton could only shrug and provide the common estimate of "no more than 10,000." Lee worried about that force. Were it to combine with the cavalry dogging him from the east, they could pose grave hazard to his lines of communication. He decided in that instant, that Harper's Ferry must be taken. He thought for a moment and realized he had exactly the general for such a mission, Thomas J. Jackson.

Colonel Chilton carefully recorded Lee's mutterings in a notebook with a well-used pencil, as the General ruminated over his marked up map of Maryland. He had off-handedly pointed to Philadelphia as his primary goal, but he gradually settled into thought of his immediate problems. Chilton had already jotted down the basic plan for Harper's Ferry. The stronghold would have to become theirs, in order to secure their lines of communication. If they were to venture deeper into the North those lines would have to be secure. Pausing, he noted that Winchester would become the collection point for the stragglers left behind by the progress of the army. A reserve would be formed by the reorganized remnants of the army. He shuddered to note that they had bled off nearly 8,000 men in the march so far. Chilton watched, as Lee traced his finger northwards to Hagerstown. Lee muttered aloud, "...should think Longstreet should move northward, in order to generate reports of our van..." Chilton rapidly recorded the inklings of that intent into his ledger as well. General Lee rubbed his chin, and traced his hand back westward on the map and left his fingertips resting on the Catoctin Range, and absently observed, "...then bring the army west of the range and guard the passes, to secure my eastern flank for the march north.." Robert E. Lee was acutely aware of Colonel Chilton's dutiful scribbling. It was their planning process, and Lee admired Chilton's ability to capture his nuance. His draft products were rarely deserving of edits.

The men were interrupted by a knock on the tent. It was Major Taylor with a tray of coffee and two plates of cornbread and bacon. Lee was surprised to note that it had grown dark outside. The time flew when he dedicated himself to planning.

Taylor cheerfully commanded, "Please gentlemen pause for something to eat! You must sustain your bodies as well as your minds!"

Chilton grunted sourly at the fine quality of the pork on his plate and asked, "Major, it appears that you have resorted to our commissary fund again?"

Taylor smiled and replied, "Sir, it only required a silver dollar! I can assure you we still retain nearly 20 dollars in silver coin and 30 dollars in greenbacks. I also procured several eggs for the morning!"

Chilton nodded, thinking on the bitter reality that only Union currency was good to the local citizens in the purchase of decent provisions. He wondered what the other 40,000 soldiers supped on at present.

General Lee absently munched on a piece of cornbread, as he intently studied the map some more. He then calmly directed, "Colonel, please draft up orders in regards what we have discussed here. I would like to discuss this with General Jackson, before noon tomorrow. I would also like to detach Major Taylor to be my representative in Winchester, until Harper's Ferry is reduced. Please see to it that you can provide a copy of this order to each of my Division Commanders, once I approve the final draft."

Colonel Chilton nodded as their eyes met. He softly admonished his commander, "Sir, I can attend to this. Please get your rest, Sir!"

Lee wearily nodded and left the tent, his wrists ached and he deeply desired sleep. As he exited the brightly lit tent, he paused for a moment for his eyes to adjust. In the moonlight he could see Traveler picketed nearby and the acreage of Best's Grove was lit with hundreds of smoldering cook fires. He felt comforted to be amidst his trusty army. While they looked ragged, he knew they would doggedly follow his every command. His heart filled with pride by their loyalty, despite the privations of his sudden campaign. He hoped the politicians of Richmond held them in similar regard.

Colonel Chilton summoned Major Taylor and ordered Captain Marshall to gather up the staff. They would draft an order and he needed Major Venable, the quartermaster and the commissary officer to be found. He also directed Taylor to build him a detail of couriers from each of the divisions. He would need men who could find their commands. Such couriers were only useful if the divisions were tasked to provide trusted officers to act in that capacity. Chilton knew instinctively that the carefully selected "pigeon" could always find it's "nest." Based on General Lee's seemingly reckless plan, he would need sure communications with the Divisions of the Army of Northern Virginia. Taylor smartly saluted, and went out into the dark night to find the commands to task them to provide couriers. Colonel Chilton remained amazed at the energy of the young Major. He never seemed to need sleep.

Colonel Chilton enlisted Captain Marshall to assist him with the creation of the draft order. After consultation in the Staff ledger, Captain Marshall informed the Colonel that the sequence number for this order would be number 191. Chilton remembered suddenly, that order 190 was the proclamation to the citizens of Maryland, from several days previous. As Chilton scratched out the draft from his penciled notes, he would pause to have Marshall clarify locations on the headquarters map and periodically confirm the proper units were identified. When the draft was finished, Chilton read the order aloud back to Marshall, who checked the map to insure the instructions would make sense to one who was unfamiliar with the plan. When confusion emerged, Chilton would scratch out words, and re-craft the sentence. Finally at 2 am he was satisfied with his product. Chilton looked at his gold watch and sighed, at that late hour he would pause to rest. He would consult with Lee first thing to obtain approval of the draft. In the interim he decided to attempt a nap. Blowing out the lantern, he directed Captain Marshall to meet him at the planning tent at 6 am on the morrow, and they would proceed to make copies of the final order, once General Lee had approved it.

Colonel Chilton felt as if he had just gone to bed, when Major Venable awoke him in his tent, "Begging your pardon Sir! General Lee would like you to join him in the Map Tent!"

Colonel Chilton sat up with a start and dug for his watch. He had lain on his cot in his pants, shirt and vest, having paused only to remove his coat and boots. The watch indicated 7 am and the sunlight shone past Venable, into the tent.

Chilton muttered, "Please be so kind as to inform the General that I am on my way!" He sluggishly pulled on his tall leather boots and stood to adjust his tie. He turned and found his coat. As he tugged it on, he grabbed his cap and exited into the bright sunlight. He quickly made his way around behind the tent to pee. He knew he would have little time for nature, once he was with the General. As he approached the tent and returned the salutes of the many orderlies holding horses by the entrance, Chilton could hear the low voice of General Longstreet. He also noted the ridiculously small Sorrel pony, a sure sign of General Jackson, wherever it was seen. General Lee was proofing his order with his two trusted advisors, it would seem.

General Longstreet continued without pause as Colonel Chilton quietly slipped into the tent, "General, what you propose goes contrary to all accepted maxims of War! Regardless of your imperative, you risk much to split your force in the very face of your foe!"

Lee waved his hand and calmly replied, "General, my foe is George McClellan and he will continue to be the utmost of caution. You witnessed first-hand, his alacrity before Richmond! I am comfortable that General Jackson can reduce Harper's Ferry with sufficient force provided. General Hill will have no problem holding the passes at South Mountain and we shall have ample time to continue to Pennsylvania."

Jackson absently mused to himself and chuckled, "It has been some time since I called on my friends from the Valley."

Chilton could clearly see one general was delighted and the other was dismayed. He took comfort in realizing that General Lee was not budging from the intent of the order he had drafted the night before. Lee stood and re-emphasized how formations would be detached and attached. Both men soberly nodded as they absorbed the instructions. Longstreet took on a very resigned visage, as he normally did once he arrived at the point where Lee no longer invited his counsel.

Lee closed the session, "Gentlemen, it is now time to prepare your forces for movement tomorrow. I shall have concise orders delivered to you by your couriers. It is essential that you safeguard these orders well! God speed to you and your men!"

As the generals departed, Colonel Chilton extracted the draft from the confidential ledger and offered it to General Lee, "Sir, here is the draft of the Special Order we created last evening. If you agree to it's content, we will prepare copies for distribution."

Lee nodded and after finding his reading spectacles in his vest pocket, he put them on, and read the penciled draft. He immediately put the draft down, secured a pencil and added a paragraph to the top. After he had finished, he then looked the rest of the document over. Here and there, he would pause and scratch out a word. Finally, with a nod of his head General Lee returned the draft to Chilton.

He removed his readers and instructed, "Colonel, the content of this order would prove calamitous to this army, were it to fall into the wrong hands! I will insist that you carefully control distribution solely to my Division Commanders. Please see to it that only trusted couriers deliver these, in the most expeditious means possible, today. I am anxious to move from this place by the morning!"

Colonel Chilton nodded and General Lee arose to clear the tent, to allow his tiny staff to commence their work of creating sufficient copies for the Army. Colonel Chilton quickly assembled the officers. He tasked Major Taylor to copy the draft down in the Confidential Book, as the master, while Major Venable, and Captain Marshall assembled clean paper and envelopes to transmit the orders. A half hour later, Taylor had finished the master. He passed the penciled draft to Venable, who placed the draft between himself and Marshall. The two men quickly began to copy the order in ink. Major Venable paused at the end of the first copy and asked, "Sir, who will sign?"

Colonel Chilton looked over from the map table, where he ate the remnants of the Generals breakfast tray and mumbled, with a mouthful, "My signature for General Lee. Oh, and we will need eight copies, one for each Major General. Label each as 1 of 8, 2 of 8, and so on!"

The Majors diligently applied themselves to making the copies. Captain Marshall blotted Colonel Chilton's signature and tucked each successive order into brown envelopes that he had written the name of each recipient in pencil. Major Taylor summoned an orderly to bring the respective courier officers over to the map tent and provided each with their envelope. He carefully instructed each man to return the empty envelope as proof of delivery. One by one, the couriers came and received their envelopes.

As the last courier departed, Colonel Chilton suddenly swore, "Damn! We have overlooked General Hill!"

Chilton quickly reopened the Confidential Book and took a clean sheet of paper out of the field writing table drawer. He hurriedly began to make a copy himself, using his pencil. He directed Major Venable to find another envelope. Soon he had the last order copy complete. He signed it and handed it to Venable.

Spying Major Taylor as he returned into the tent, Colonel Chilton directed, "Major please rush this order to Major General Daniel Harvey Hill!"

Taylor looked surprised and asked, "Sir, we provided a copy to General Jackson already. Does that not satisfy his notification?"

Chilton curtly replied, "No Major Taylor, it does not! General Hill is detached from Jackson's command to act as the rear guard. In that capacity, he receives the ninth copy."

The day had grown late. Walter Taylor grudgingly tucked the envelope into his coat pocket and mounted his horse. His mood grew increasingly fouler, as the very orders he was required to deliver, also required him to relocate back to Winchester. There, he would collect the stragglers and left behind units of the Army of Northern Virginia. The order required him to create a strategic reserve for General Lee. At the moment, he possessed no idea how he would achieve this task. He had yet to begin packing his meager belongings. He turned the black gelding towards Frederick, where he recalled from the map location, General Hill's encampment lay, just by Monocacy Station. As he passed the camps, he could see the men clustering around their leaders on both sides of the road. It was clear that the orders were going out. The Army of Northern Virginia prepared to move. Other couriers moved quickly up and down the road on horseback past him, as he rode. The vast enterprise of General Lee was awakening to their impending mission.

Passing the cluttered camps and scurrying couriers on the road, he suddenly recognized an approaching rider. He had met with Major Henry Douglas several days before, after Jackson's Division had come up. Taylor was surprised that Major Pendleton had taken furlough to visit sick family in Richmond and Douglas had been acting as the general's aide de camp in his stead. With a wave of his hand, Walter Taylor signaled a meeting with

Douglas. Douglas seemed bothered by the signal to stop.

Pulling up alongside Taylor, he sharply asked, "Major Taylor, how may I be of your service? Pardon my haste, but I am on a matter of grave importance to General Jackson!"

Taylor, in a foul mood himself, quickly replied, "Major Douglas, this order is for you to deliver to General Daniel Harvey Hill. General Lee has indicated it is of the utmost gravity that he receive it as soon as possible! I trust his Division still remains encamped with General Jackson?"

Henry Kyd Douglas took the envelope and opened it. He silently studied it for a moment, before retorting, "We have seen this order, Major Taylor. General Jackson is in possession of it now! Why one to Hill?"

Taylor impatiently turned his horse and called out as he rode away, "He is to be detached! See to it that he receives the order!"

Major Douglas quickly pocketed the envelope with the order, inside his frock coat. He decided that he would consult with General Jackson, before he delivered the order to General Hill. When he arrived back at the collection of tents, forming General Jackson's Headquarters, he was surprised to see parties of men collapsing the tentage.

Riding up to a corporal in charge of the detail, he asked, "Where is General Jackson?"

The Corporal, very preoccupied, responded, "Sir, He and Major Dabney left an hour ago. They were going to see General Hill, to give him his orders!"

Douglas decided, upon receiving this news, to go to his tent and gather up his things, and load his saddlebags. He did not want the detailed men tearing down the headquarters camp to filch his cigars. He still had to deliver coordinating information to the other regiments, which Major Dabney had given him earlier. He anticipated a long night. Arriving at his tent, he dismounted from his horse and packed the remaining cigars in his saddlebags. He then took four cigars and put three into his frock coat pocket. Having difficulty due to the order envelope already there, he took the envelope out and opened it. He carefully inserted the cigars, next to the redundant order. He quickly bit the rounded end of his fourth cigar and lit it with a Lucifer match, from the box on his writing desk. He took the time to pack some ham slices, wrapped in wax paper, that he had traded for earlier, in his larger saddle bag. After a thoughtful pause, he then took an extra box of pistol cartridges from his trunk, just in case. It was going to be a long night, as he had to locate all of General Jackson's Regimental Commanders and brief them on their place in the march tables, and their start times for the morning.

Just before the sun set that evening of the 9th of September, Major Douglas found Major Williams of Winder's brigade and advised him of his place on the march. He then found another officer, on the staff of Jubal Early's brigade and advised him of his times, not far from his first meeting. After a few questions, he was directed to take a side road through the woods near Monocacy Junction. He found the going difficult as the sun set behind the yellowing trees. Guiding onto a fire, he called out to the spectrally lit faces of the soldiers gathered around it for warmth and discovered he was near the Headquarters of Lawton's brigade and General Jackson's artillery. Douglas tied his horse loosely to a tree and dismounted. The animal eagerly began to nibble on the clover underfoot as Major Douglas wove his way among the campfires to a tent in the dark woods. There within, he found Major John Lowe. He pulled his march table from his coat pocket along with the envelope containing the cigars and the useless copy of the order for General Hill. For a moment, he considered burning the order, but thought better of it. Instead, he briefed Lowe on Brigadier General Lawton's place in the march. Lowe asked of the route, but Douglas could only shake his head. General Jackson was notoriously secretive of exactly how he got from one location to the next. He would usually intercept his forces at key intersections and direct them from there. Major Lowe sadly shook his head. The peculiarities of General Jackson were alternatingly humorous or infuriating, depending on your situation.

Henry Douglas took a few moments over Lowe's map, to find the three remaining brigades he had to brief. Fortunately, they were not too far distant from where he stood now. Offering his thanks, he stepped out into the dark night, to finish his rounds. It took him a few moments to find his way back to the pasture at the edge of the woods, as his eyes slowly adjusted to the darkness. Once he found his black gelding, he paused to relieve himself and tucked the envelope under his arm, as he peed. Noting the increasing chill of the evening, he buttoned up his frock coat and took the packet of orders, cigars and the march table and slid them into his breast pocket. In his haste, he did not notice that the envelope with the order and his cigars, missed the opening of the pocket. As he mounted his horse, the envelope slipped out and fell noiselessly into the deep clover. He rode off into the night to inform the other brigades. Later that night, when he decided to smoke another of his precious cigars, he realized that he had lost the envelope. At least he had the march table. That was the critical thing, now. General Jackson was a stickler for prompt departures and he was determined to insure his mission would be flawlessly accomplished.

Early the next morning in the hills and rolling pastures around Frederick, the great army of General Lee awoke to bugles and drumming. Bleary men finished cups of thin coffee and meager meals of corn and scavenged meat. The regiments began to file out onto the roads of Maryland, to commence movement in two separate directions. General Longstreet and his lightened Corps would continue north on the Hagerstown Road to Middletown and then on to Hagerstown. General Jackson would turn at Middletown towards Sharpsburg and recross the Potomac, to encircle Harpers Ferry from the south and west. General McLaws and General Anderson would follow to surround Harpers Ferry from the Maryland side of the Potomac. Colonel Dixon Miles and his tiny force defending the Federal Depot at Harpers Ferry, would have quite a job holding that ground from General Lee's approaching force.

The people of Frederick awoke to the sound of galloping horses and the tramping feet of Lee's Army leaving them on that chilly Wednesday morning. All around town vacant camps in trampled pastures were strewn with old newspapers and empty cans amongst smoldering campfires. The woods around the town reeked of excrement. The vast army of gray clad men was on the move in directions that caused the civilians, up early enough to observe the movement, to wonder where the Southern Army was headed to next. By mid-afternoon, all that remained were elements of General Daniel Harvey Hill's rear guard and small fast moving vedettes of General Stuart's jaunty cavalrymen. Farmers tending their crops and animals, early that misty morning southeast of Frederick, began to see small groups of cautiously moving cavalrymen, in sharp blue uniforms. They were maneuvering along the edge of the woods and in the pastures, as General Pleasanton probed for General Stuart's screen. An hour southeast of these small bands of cavalry, the long trains of the Horse Artillery Regiment began their early morning movement towards Frederick. The infantry regiments of General McClellan's vast army would spend that day in their camps, continuing to drill. He would not move further until he could determine the location of Lee's army.

Back in a clover pasture, a foraging Raccoon rummaged its way through the abandoned Confederate camp near Monocacy Junction. Near one

41

campfire, it found a partially eaten ear of green corn and ate a few bites. The smell of humans made the animal nervous. It paused only sparingly to investigate things. Twittering, it moved about and found a paper envelope, that had a strange odor within. The curious animal opened the envelope and sniffed the brown cylindrical objects inside. The pungent smell of the cigars repulsed the Raccoon. It dropped the envelope and its contents back into the dew wetted clover and continued to explore for more edible items.

Lottie was growing uneasy with the leering stares of the two soldiers in the hard wooden bench seats, one section behind her. Each time, the more persistent of the two caught her glance; he would flash a great gap toothed smile. Then he would spit tobacco juice on the floor. As she surreptitiously glanced about, she realized she was the youngest woman on the train. They still had an hour before they would reach the station in Raleigh. The slow moving train from Columbia was full of soldiers from a new South Carolina Regiment, on its way to Virginia. As the coach car gently swayed with the turns in the track, Lottie re-read the letter she had received in regards to her new position with the Confederate States Medical Commission. She was to be an accounting auditor for the Surgeon General's Office in Richmond. Her instructions indicated that she would be expected to report to the Surgeon General's office on the 15th of September at 1 pm. While she was excited about the prospect of doing something of significance for the National Government, she remained reflective about her father's concerns of a young woman traveling to such a large city alone. The behavior of the soldiers was proving to be reinforcement to his concerns. Her mother's voice also resounded in her mind, "Proper ladies never travel alone!"

The locomotive blew its whistle as it crossed the trestle bridge over the Neuse River. The outlying dwellings of Raleigh hove into view. The excitement of a new place, jolted Lottie from her reverie. Peering out the window of the car, she could see that the leaves were still mostly green but here and there the changing colors of fall were beginning to emerge. She paused to look back into her hand purse at her handwritten itinerary. She would have to board the Raleigh and Gaston Railroad over Weldon to Suffolk for the next leg of her journey.

This meant changing railroad lines and buying a new ticket from another rail company. While rail travel was indeed fast, the dizzying complexities of the new mode of transport created great anxiety for the traveler. Hopefully the wait for a connection would not be long. Soon the train slowed and Lottie could see the great brick roundhouse and terminal of the Raleigh and Gaston Railroad Station. She was impressed by the modern appearance of the station. It was nothing like the simple wood depots of Moncks Corner and Columbia. The train came to a jerky halt with loud squealing from the brakes and the passengers began to rise to debark. As Lottie stood and waited in the aisle behind an elderly woman and a small child. The two soldiers pushed up close behind her. She could smell them; they had not washed in quite some time. She could smell stale urine, tobacco and old sweat rising from their woolen uniforms. She was anxious to find a porter to assist her in transferring her portmanteau from the baggage car to her new connection, but the large number of passengers made the platform chaotic. The soldiers milled about and sergeants shouted for the various units to assemble out in the dirt yards across the tracks. As Lottie stood and anxiously scanned to locate a porter, she felt a strange pressure on her hoopskirt. Whirling around, she realized she was only inches from the leering soldier from the train. He smiled again with his hideous tobacco stained teeth and pressed towards her bottom with his free hand.

"Yer a fine filly I'd say! What would you say we gets us a room at a boarding house for the night?" The soldier was obviously quite drunk.

Without thinking, Lottie deftly pulled one of her hatpins from her traveling bonnet, and jammed it hard into his hand, as he continued to massage her rear. The man cursed loudly and dropped his rifle. His companion quickly moved to pick up the weapon. The wounded drunk grabbed Lottie roughly by the arm, shouting. As he brought his other hand up to strike her, a loud clicking noise injected itself into the scene. All Lottie could see, in the shock of the moment, was the finely blued and engraved barrel of a revolver. In the subconscious instant, she thought it quite pretty.

In a low and solemn voice, the bearer of the revolver stated, "Private, unhand the fine lady this instant! Make one more move and I will put a ball into your brain!"

Looking beyond the gun, Lottie beheld a smartly dressed man, nearly her age. She was immediately drawn to his gray green eyes and well trimmed goatee. From his uniform and accouterments, he was clearly an officer. He glanced at her for a moment and brusquely stated, "Excuse me for a moment, while I fix this situation!"

He then backed the two off the platform at gunpoint and had them stand to attention in the dirt lot across from the tracks. Lottie watched, as he carried on a one-way conversation, with his revolver pointed into the two men's chests for emphasis from time to time. After a few moments, he returned his pistol to its holster and the two soldiers hurried over to where the others were assembling. The young officer watched them depart for a moment and then returned quickly to where Lottie stood.

Removing his hat from his head, he apologetically said, "Please forgive us for your shabby treatment, Ma'am! These men are undisciplined militia that are entering Confederate government service from across the states! They are poorly disciplined!"

Lottie could only stammer, "I am deeply grateful for your service sir! I fear I am quite confused, this incident has not been helpful to me, you see I must get my connection to Richmond and I have no idea how to go about it!" She had begun to feel desperate, but found that she was mesmerized by his soft eyes.

The young officer replied, "Ma'am, you are fortunate to have found me! I too am bound for Richmond! I must apologize for my manners, as I was not availed the time to properly introduce myself!"

Extending his hand, he continued, "Madam, I am Captain Henri Philippe Tinchant of the Confederate States Army Medical Service."

Lottie happily smiled and took the proffered hand and replied, "Sir, this has proven to be a most serendipitous encounter! I, Sir, am Miss Charlotte Markley of Charleston, South Carolina. I happen to be traveling to Richmond, in order to start my employ with the Confederate States Medical Department!"

Captain Tinchant was amused at how her soft brown eyes danced back and forth as she looked at him. Her complexion reminded him of the French ladies of New Orleans, without the vocal inflections, so common to the Acadian areas of the region. He paused to look at his gold pocket watch, and commanded, "Miss Markley, if you would be so kind as to follow me, I will assist you in moving your baggage. We are in no hurry at the moment as we have nearly four hours until the next train to Richmond departs. I will suggest we secure your tickets, and then find a coffee house."

Lottie eagerly assented and followed Captain Tinchant, as he expertly summoned a porter and gave him instructions on the movement of her portmanteau. She was immensely glad that she did not have to handle the heavy case by herself. Tinchant then took her to the booking agent's window and she was surprised when he refused to take her money when he procured the ticket.

Handing her the ticket, Henri explained, "Miss Markley, I have procured your passage with a government voucher, as you indicated you were under our employ now. This is a seat in the very same second-class coach as mine. I will see to it that you get safely to your destination, as it seems you have experienced enough discomfort for one day."

Tinchant led Lottie to the café inside the rail station, but seeing it jammed with waiting passengers, he elected to take her to a restaurant he knew of, just outside the station. There, they whiled away the hours in conversation, over tea and imported shortbread cookies. Lottie found herself fascinated by Tinchant's tales of medical school in Boston, and how he had come into the service. She also discovered that he was quite familiar with her new employers. He promised her he would see to it that she was successful. He had commented, that while it was strange for women to begin working in offices normally occupied by men, he expressed understanding that a new age was arriving. The men would be needed, in full measure, for the fighting that lay ahead. To Lottie, the time seemed to fly by, and soon it was time to return to the station to board their train. As he held her hand to steady her when she climbed aboard the train, her thoughts flashed a memory of Joshua. Frowning, she remembered that she had seen no correspondence from him in over 5 months. She momentarily wondered if he was even still alive. Her mother's stern enjoinder about the "foolishness of a hopeless wait" came to mind. Smiling, Lottie resolved to see what this new encounter might lead to.

Colonel Henry Hunt and Lieutenant Colonel William Hayes rode north out of Alexandria, Virginia on a brisk September morning, on their way to Rockville for a meeting with General McClellan. Hunt's mind reeled with the tasks he needed to accomplish, in order to undo the damage wrought by the War Department and General Pope, to the structure of the Army of the Potomac. Now that McClellan was back in charge, there was a glimmer of hope in Hunt's mind. Perhaps they could bring order back to the chaos.

Hayes asked Hunt, as they rode north, "Sir, what news have you about General Porter?"

Hunt shook his head and shifted the reins to his left hand, as he rode, "That damned fool, Pope, has him under the supervision of a court of inquiry by the War Department! I think he is being arranged to serve as a "Scape-Goat" for Pope's very ample incompetence. What I cannot believe at the moment, is why Halleck is humoring that ass! The responsibility of a failed battle rests with the overall commander, not his subordinates!"

Hunt's mind returned to his more immediate problems. The reorganization at Aquia Landing had been interrupted by the news of Lee's invasion. This sudden movement by the Rebels, caused largely by Pope's disastrous defeat and the vacuum, it created, had resulted in a mad scramble to reassemble the Army. Refitting the artillery of the army and replacing lost leaders occupied all his energies at the moment. Fitz John Porter's problems were far too lofty for his immediate attention, despite his disgust for the whole situation.

Hunt turned and asked Hayes, "William, what is your estimate of our mobility? Do you have news in regards to horses?"

Lieutenant Colonel Hayes studiously replied, "Sir, my estimate is that we can move approximately 50 batteries, if we continue to cross level horses then perhaps up to 55. The last response we got from the War Department this morning was that no more animals were available!"

Hunt nodded, "Very well then, be prepared to provide as many details as possible when we see General McClellan. Also assemble ordnance teams to accompany the Inspector General of the Artillery Reserve, as we conduct the march north. I will have to finish the refitting and reorganization as we move! I am sure that will be a smooth enterprise! We have also taken all the available animals away from the siege trains, so no heavy guns will be available."

They arrived at Rockville, Maryland as the sun had begun to set in the western sky. General McClellan's field headquarters was a hive of activity. A sea of brightly lit tents marked where the returning commander had established his staff and supporting security escorts. The two paused to question a courier, on his way towards Frederick, where they could locate the General. The young sergeant hastily pointed behind him, and provided them directions, before rapidly galloping away.

Attentive orderlies relieved them of the care of their mounts and Colonel Hunt and Lieutenant Colonel Hayes entered into General McClellan's large white meeting tent. Inside General McClellan and General Heintzelman sat in a corner smoking cigars. Hunt noted General Marcy, in the far corner, busily writing an order. Their eyes met for a moment and Marcy gave Hunt a smile and a nod. Through the thin walls of the tent, Henry Hunt could hear the cacophony of an army on the move. Sharp bugle calls, the incessant hammering of a distant blacksmith and the clopping of numerous horse teams moving to and fro. Every soul was electrified by the Southern invasion and the return of McClellan to the army. Hunt mused that perhaps, McClellan's return was what they all needed. While some doubt remained in his mind after the campaign on the Peninsula. Those doubts were erased by the new energy that was apparent in the army everywhere he had traveled and observed.

General McClellan rose quickly when he spied Hunt, "Henry Hunt! Welcome, Welcome! We have been awaiting your arrival!"

Hunt, surprised, accepted the handshakes from General McClellan and General Heintzelman. McClellan offered him a cigar, which he gladly accepted and accepted a seat offered by General Heintzelman. Sitting in the tapestry upholstered folding chair, Hunt lit his cigar. Lieutenant Colonel Hayes also was provided a chair and a cigar. Hayes had been expected to be dismissed and he was surprised when General McClellan insisted that he remain.

George McClellan got right down to business, "Henry, how many guns will the army have available to it?"

Hunt took a puff from his cigar and motioned to Lieutenant Colonel Hayes. Hayes taking his cue, responded, "Sir, our best estimate currently is 55 batteries totaling 322 cannon."

McClellan nodded, "Colonel Hayes that is very good news. Very good news indeed! I have received reports of your difficulties with obtaining enough teams to move your pieces. I had expected far less, to be truthful. General Halleck can do little but grumble when the topic turns to Horses."

He then turned to Hunt and continued, "Henry, I have prepared orders making you the Chief of Artillery for the Army of the Potomac. John Barry has requested to be relieved to take a job with the War Department as the Army's Chief Inspector for artillery. Will you be willing to assume his responsibilities on such short notice?"

Henry Hunt was surprised and hoped Barry was not another victim of the latest War Department head-hunt. The news of Fitz John Porter's court martial flickered through his mind, as he replied, "Sir, I shall serve in whatever capacity you see fit, provided it is not at the expense of John Barry's good name! General Pope left him and most of the artillery structure behind in the last fight."

McClellan puffed his cigar a moment and thoughtfully responded, "Splendid make Hayes here your deputy, since he has already been functioning as such for the past month. You will need to know that I have passed your name up for nomination to promotion to Brigadier General of Volunteers to the War Department and I should hear back on that in a fortnight. Congratulations Henry, you have earned your star!"

Hunt nodded, he was stunned and could only quietly reply, "Thank you Sir, I shall try to live up to your trust."

McClellan swiftly rose, and motioned for Hunt to follow him to the map table, "Henry, we are tracking Lee's movements since he has crossed the Potomac. We are receiving reports that he is leaving Frederick now. I believe he is looking for a place to turn towards Washington. I intend to position our army close to him but retain our ability to move if he makes that turn. Our estimates have him at somewhere between 93,000 to 97,000 men. I will need you to finish your reorganization as you move to join the main army! Battle could commence anywhere along the Catoctin Mountain Range. I currently have General Pleasanton in contact with his flanking cavalry screen and the indications are there that he is still moving northeast. Bring my artillery reserve to Frederick as fast as you can!"

Hunt nodded and motioning to Hayes to stand, he replied, "Sir, I understand. Begging your pardon, sir, we must be on our way!"

The midmorning September sun warmed the day nicely. So warm in fact, that the hard marching soldiers of the 27th Indiana Volunteer Infantry were ready for some winter cold. The noise of scattered gunfire in Frederick as the cavalry skirmished with the departing Confederate cavalry had resulted in Colonel Colgrove ordering the approach march to proceed at the double quick. As they approached Frederick, civilians gathered on the sides of the road welcoming the sweating men. They then were denied entry into the town as their reward. They were to go into camp on orders from higher. There were shouts of dismay among the men, as word had it, that Frederick had a saloon at every street corner. Orders from on high had indicated an "undesirable" number of stragglers had been observed by the commanding general, therefore camps would be established north and south of town. Until the army could re-collect itself. Private Barton Mitchell listened dismayed to his First Sergeant as he briefed the panting men in formation alongside the road near a trampled pasture of clover. He had hoped for a little civilization after tramping through Maryland for the past week. The First Sergeant informed all the men that they would establish a bivouac where they stood. Directions went out for details to set up tents and dig privy trenches. Private Mitchell looked about him when the order to "Fall out and stack arms" had been given; it was clear that the Rebels had camped here, as well. Soon the privy trench detail was shouting out that the "nasty Rebs" had shit all about the woods, rendering the location with shade deliberately "untenable." The First Sergeant angrily instructed them to "shut up and start digging." After several hours work, a passible privy trench complete with a sitting log had been erected. The woods were surrendered to nature and the Captain directed a line of tents in the clover as an alternative to the unsanitary shady areas.

Private Barton Mitchell was delighted to have escaped election to any details. He gladly accepted orders from Sergeant Bloss, to have a sit and take it easy until camp was established. After securing his rifle in a stack with the rest of his squad, he found an untrammeled spot of deep clover and reclined with a groan. While they had only covered twelve or so miles that day, the double-quick order had left them winded. Mitchell quickly dug into his Meacham haversack and found a hardtack cracker to gnaw on while he rested. Sergeant Bloss joked with the men around him. He too, shared in their dismay at not getting to see the town of Frederick.

Private Mitchell pushed his forage cap onto the back of his head and craned his eyes about to take stock of his surroundings. The countryside was hilly and full of cornfields and nice woods. He mused it was a shame that the Rebels had camped here first. Much of the fencing was damaged and the place looked thoroughly trampled. Odds and ends of garbage lay about. As he continued to look, an odd package caught his eye immediately behind him. It looked all the world to him like 3 cigars wrapped in paper. Since he could rarely afford the sutler's tobacco, it was worth a look. He wearily got back up on his sore feet and walked over to the package.

Wary of the southerners' dirty ways, Barton elected to use his bayonet to examine what looked like a yellowish brown envelope. Surely enough, it contained three dark brown cigars that looked none the worse for wear after laying exposed to the weather in the deep clover. He exclaimed to no one in particular, "Well I'll be damned! Cigars!"

He quickly picked up the envelope, and returned to his spot. Sergeant Bloss asked, "Well Barton, what have you there?"

Private Mitchell plucked out one of the cigars and ran it under his nose, enjoying the smell of the fine tobacco. He asked, "Cigars Sergeant! Would you have a match?"

Bloss, being a hard dealer, agreed to share his matches for one of the cigars and despite the high cost in trade, Private Mitchell agreed. Bloss asked to see the envelope after Barton had bitten off the end of his cigar, and prepared to light it. He readily passed the package to his sergeant, with a stern reminder that the remaining cigar remained his, as he was the finder.

Sergeant Bloss agreed to honor the deal, and took the envelope and examined the inside. Noting a folded document, and thinking it a letter, he pulled it out, and began to read it. After a moment he exclaimed, "Well I will be damned!"

Clutching the envelope, he quickly rose to his feet. Private Mitchell shouted, "Hey, don't be runnin' off with my other cigar!"

Sergeant Bloss replied sternly, "Mitchell, follow me! We've got to find the Colonel!"

Several hours later, Colonel Samuel E. Pittman on the 12th Corps staff, after having ridden twenty miles at a gallop, breathlessly asked a courier for directions to General McClellan's headquarters. The courier agreed to escort him and soon they arrived before the sentries guarding a collection of several canvas tents in the Maryland woods.

Pittman stood quietly, as George McClellan quickly read the order. Behind him, General Marcy looked on. Colonel Pittman stated while he read, "Sir, I know Colonel Chilton personally and I can attest that this is indeed the writing of his hand!"

General McClellan exclaimed, "My God! If this order is indeed authentic and not some deception, Robert Lee would be last officer to do such a thing!"

He handed the order to General Marcy to read and asked him, "Tell me your thoughts on this. Do you consider it genuine?"

Marcy took the paper, and after taking a few moments to digest its contents, he replied, "Sir, I consider it genuine. This matches what is being reported and explains the lack of communications we have with Harpers Ferry. They have obviously cut the telegraph lines!"

Wanting to compare the order to a map, General McClellan rushed from his tent, towards his planning tent nearby with General Marcy in tow. With the order in his hand he intently studied the map of Maryland that was marked with pencil annotations of the latest locations of his Army. He reviewed the updated locations after the day's march and General Pleasanton's cavalry reports, noting Rebel sightings. As he studied the portent of the order generated by General Lee, McClellan discussed with General Marcy what routes would best support moving the army across the Catoctin Mountains. As the two men were in consultation, Brigadier John Gibbon, a fellow West Pointer and old army friend, entered the tent.

Gibbon announced, "General McClellan! I am pleased to report that most of the 1st Division has finally caught up with you!"

General McClellan looked up from his map study and smiled, "John! I have the most amazing news! We have intercepted one of Lee's orders!"

Gibbon laughed and asked, "I suppose this means we will be moving again?"

McClellan without pause waved the order in his hand and replied, "With this paper I can catch Robbie Lee in a trap of his own making! He has split his army!"

McClellan turned to General Marcy and directed that he cable news to Halleck in Washington of the find. McClellan also shared a discussion with Gibbon over the map about the best ways to move the army across the Catoctin range in order to assault Longstreet's portion of the Army. The rest of the afternoon was dedicated to drafting orders to the Army of the Potomac on movements in the morning necessary to bring the jaws of the trap to a close around the split elements of Lee's Army.

Joshua watched as his gun and caisson crew quickly hitched their teams in the dim light of dawn. Word had been spread that morning, that they would push hard for a place called South Mountain, to support General Reno's 9th Corps. They had chased the van of General Pleasanton's cavalry squadrons for the past week. They were taking part in a "cat and mouse" game of pursuit, with J.E.B. Stuart's cavalry from Frederick, across the Catoctin Mountains to the valley along the National Road. So far, there had not been an opportunity to employ the guns. The boys on the guns had begun to grouse about being "glorified teamsters," as they hauled the heavy guns across the Maryland foothills.

First Sergeant O'Keefe rode down the line of teams and spurred them to hurry, with the completion of making ready to move, "Move yer goddamned asses boys! We already got infantry on the road and we gots to get past them before they reach Middletown! The Captain wants to pick his own ground!"

Soon, the battery of three two-gun sections were pulling into column, onto the National Road. Ahead of them marched the long files of General Gibbon's troops. The width of the road did not permit passing and the pace of movement was painfully slow, for the majority of the morning. The columns of troops covered the roads for miles ahead of them and the bright morning sun illuminated the barrels of their muskets with a shimmering gleam that undulated through the Maryland countryside. The constant beat of drums governed the forward movement of the men as they hurried to intercept General Lee's army. By mid-morning, the spires of the churches in Middletown could be seen. The bells within them pealed, inviting the worshipful to services on the beautiful September Sunday morning. Soon the townspeople would be interrupted by thousands of trotting horses and tramping feet, as the Army of the Potomac followed the path of the Confederates from two days ago.

Nearing the outskirts of Middletown, a small delegation of horsemen waited by an intersection as they approached. As the company drew nearer, Joshua recognized the officer waiting as Lieutenant Colonel Hayes from the Horse Artillery Regiment. Captain Haines galloped past the marching infantry to consult with him.

Beyond the dust of thousands of tramping feet, Joshua saw Colonel Hayes wave his arm and shout, "Turn your battery off onto this road! It is a by-pass around Middletown."

Two members of the Pennsylvania cavalry squadron, from Haye's escort, escorted Company M as they raced south and west of Middletown, on the pike that Joshua saw signs indicating it as the "Old Sharpsburg Road." Passing the town, across fields of corn to their right, Joshua could catch glimpses of the marching troops in the main street of Middletown. Throngs of civilians lined both sides of the street, and they appeared jubilant to see federal troops. Ahead of him, Joshua could see several large foothills rising above the rolling farmland of the valley, several more cavalrymen could be seen descending a steep pasture to his right. They began to wave at them and Captain Haines indicated to the battery to depart the road, through a tumbledown gate off the right side of the dirt track that they were on.

The guns and caissons perceptibly slowed as the lathered team horses labored to pull their loads up the steep slope. Joshua noting Wilkins slapping the leads on the back of the off-leader, shouted out to him to stop it. "Let them adjust to the speed on their own! They know to follow the Captain!" he commanded. The teams surmounted the steep sloping pasture with heaving labored breathing and grunts as they struggled to pull the heavy loads up the hill. Joshua rode quickly ahead with the other section sergeants to get their positions from the Captain.

As he topped the hill, the entire panorama of the gaps in South Mountain came into view. Still slightly misty from the morning, the mountain was punctuated here and there with the early turning of color of the trees from the beginning fall. Off to the North, dust emerged from the crotch of Turner's Gap. With the naked eye, Joshua could see men in dusty brown uniforms spreading out along the crests of the hill on either side of the stark white gravel of the National Road. He quickly estimated the distance to the gap, at a mile and a half. All the activity he observed was within range. Looking left, Joshua could see blue-coated cavalry moving up the slopes to Fox's Gap. To him, it looked like the army had beaten the Rebels to the gap.

The guns came swiftly up once the horses crested the ridge. Quickly and expertly, the men of each piece dismounted and unhitched the guns from the limbers, rotating them to orient on the enemy in the distance. First Sergeant O'Keefe ordered the men to unhitch the limber teams from the limbers and lead them back over the hilltop. They could ill afford to lose the few horses they possessed. Soon all 6 bronze guns of Company M were in place and the men quickly unbuckled their implements. The carbines were rapidly shucked from their backs, as well and stacked back by the limber.

Captain Haines studied the line of Confederate troops through his field glasses and announced, "They are forming lines behind rocks along the eastern crest of the ridge! This will be a rough day for our boys coming up! Load shot and prepare to fire at 1600 yards!"

Joshua carefully turned his attention to his crew as Lieutenant Pennington repeated the Captain's command and range. With no fuse cutting required, Private Olson and Palmer quickly extracted and transferred the first fixed solid shot round forward to the gun. Palmer quickly passed the round over the axle to Mulcahy, who nimbly inserted it into the bronze muzzle of the gun. Private Lyttle quickly had the round home with his trademark long stroke of the rammer. Corporal Watkins obtained a sighting on the distant troops filing south of Turner's Gap and picked a rock outcropping that appeared to have swarms of butternut clad men taking positions along it. Joshua continued to watch quietly as Page pricked the charge through the vent. After which, Wilkins inserted a friction primer and attached his lanyard. Within moments, the three Lieutenants had announced their sections were ready. Down below, Joshua noticed long lines of troops in blue moving towards the foot of the mountain and off both sides of the National Road. Hookers 1st Corps would have the honors to assault the widest gap on South Mountain. Joshua could see little artillery down below. He imagined that they must be trapped in the slow moving columns, still coming up.

Captain Haines remembered his orders, which had been relayed to him by Lieutenant Colonel Hayes at Middletown, "Give them all the fires you can, as quick as you can! There is no plan for the Artillery Reserve for this battle! I will rush to you what I can find. Follow these men; they have picked you some dominant ground. Move quickly and commence firing as soon as you note targets!"

Satisfied that he had achieved the first part of the Colonel's intent, he decided to initiate the second part. He shouted, "By Battery....... fire!"

The guns spit out a great ragged salvo of shot as the six gunners turned and yanked their lanyards. As the carriages recoiled unevenly back, Joshua shouted out to Watkins, "Mark your shot!" He had noted a tendency of the new gunner to get focused on the next task, without following through.

Captain Haines studied closely as the arcing shot impacted all along the stone outcropping that sheltered the Rebel troops. The leftmost shot hit high on a rock, spraying dark gray rock fragments and dust over the sheltering men's heads and spooked a horseman who had paused on the National Road. The second and third shot impacted solidly on the great stones, and appeared to have shattered in a great cloud of dust. The remaining shots tore into the woods above the rock line, felling a tree, causing the men below to scatter. After a moment's pause, Captain Haines shouted out, "Load Shell, Cut Fuse at 5 seconds for 1600 yards!"

The Lieutenants again relayed the same orders to their sections. As the crews rolled the carriages back on line. Joshua noticed a horseman cresting the ridge. He noticed First Sergeant O'Keefe ride over to intercept the rider. Joshua realized it was Lieutenant Colonel Hayes. As the two sat on the ridge talking, with much pointing of hands and gestures, more teams appeared over the crest of the hill. Joshua could recognize the unmistakable silhouettes of 20 pounder Parrot Rifles as the limbered guns descended the reverse slope to their right. The crews quickly unhitched and manhandled the heavy iron guns in line with Company M.

First Sergeant O'Keefe rode back and gave a great wink to Joshua, as he sarcastically shouted out to the Captain, "Two batteries of guns to form the Artillery Reserve! It is to be Malvern fookin' Hill all overs again!"

The lack of planning was beginning to become apparent as Joshua looked down into the valley where vast lines of troops deployed into lines of battle to make the approach to the gap across the valley below them. On the ridge across from them, the scattered Confederate cannon wisely chose to engage the lines of troops forming below. The effects of their shot were horrifying to witness from his vantage point. He could plainly see in the clear morning, the effects of each explosion of case shot as the spray of lead balls beat down men in their dozens among the advancing ranks.

Joshua tore his eyes away from the struggle below in time to catch a mistake at the hands of Private Page. He shouted out, "Keep that thumb stall tight on the vent Private!"

Colonel Hayes had moved over to consult with Captain Haines and the Captain commanding the Parrot rifles, rode over. Joshua thought the man looked vaguely familiar. He then remembered from the training at Camp Barry. It was Captain Durell, with the battery of Germans from Pennsylvania. First Sergeant Mueller was over there, somewhere. The three officers consulted, as the clatter of musketry began to become apparent across the valley from them. The shouts of ready from the Lieutenants, jolted Joshua back to his duties.

Captain Haines shouted out, "Keep your fires on that pass, that's where everybody has to go to! By battery.... fire!"

The bronze Napoleons on the gun line again roared, filling the mid-day air with choking white smoke. Joshua noted that Watkins, a quick study, had danced aside to watch his shell as it left a smoky arcing path into the thick woods at the crest of South Mountain. It exploded in a distant white puff over the Confederates. Joshua realized at that moment, that while they were doing quick and professional work, it was too little, too late, to be of much consequence. Today would be an infantryman's battle.

General Joe Hooker sat astride his horse at the crossroad of the Sharpsburg Road, next to General George Meade and watched Mead's Division file past. Despite their early start, the day was growing late. The narrow roads had slowed the march to the point where Hooker had ordered the Divisional columns to break off of the road and march through the open adjacent fields. His Corps was to be General McClellan's primary object with the mission to force Turner's Gap and attack Lee's Army in detail starting at Boonsboro. Hooker dourly watched as Hatch's Division formed regimental lines at the foot of South Mountain. He looked north to see Ricketts' Division doing likewise on the right. Peering at South Mountain, and the approaches that lay before them, the woods looked deep and impenetrable. Here and there a large face of rocks could be seen protruding from the heavy trees. While the leaves were beginning to turn color all the leaves remained firmly on and dense. There was no way his supporting batteries could aid his men. They could see nothing to shoot at. Fortunately, he saw that unknown guns were engaging the Rebels in the pass from positions south of him. What bothered him the most at the moment, was the distant sound of artillery fire far away to the west. He reckoned it was the Rebels attacking Miles at Harpers Ferry. He hoped the man could hold on, until help arrived.

Hooker turned to Meade and commanded, "George, waste no time pushing up that ground! McClellan could not assure me, from what he had gleaned by the captured order, how long General Lee's army would require to assemble itself once more. Speed is of the essence on this day! I should like to own Turner's Gap, before the end of this day!"

George Meade quickly nodded, saluted his Corps Commander and dutifully moved back to where he could observe and control his command. He too, was impatient to strike while the opportunity presented itself.

General Lee walked out of General Longstreet's headquarters tent after a short discussion of his correspondence from the previous day. Longstreet had persisted in his doubts in regard to the danger that his commander had placed the army in, with the push to reduce Harpers Ferry. The splint on his left hand had made it tricky to manage Traveler's reins but he preferred the difficulty to riding about in that damned ambulance. He also preferred that the men of his army see him as he moved about. It clearly cheered them, as much as it cheered him. As he began to maneuver his hands on the pommel of his saddle to mount, a breathless courier from Stuart's Cavalry arrived. General Lee looked at the garishly dressed boy who carried no less than three pistols in his belt, and a cut down double-barreled shotgun. A long black peacock feather in a trail-worn hat was the finishing touch to the young cavalryman's attire.

"Sir! General Stuart sends his warmest regards! He wishes for you to review this dispatch of utmost importance! It's Yankees sir! The whole Yankee army is in the Middletown Valley! They are headed this way!"

Lee softly thanked the lad and asked him if he could wait to return a reply. The young man eagerly nodded. Lee opened the message and went back into the tent with the message in hand. He would need General Longstreet's help to handle this new development. Off in the distance a great rumbling, like thunder, emanated from the southwest. On such a clear day, it could only be Jackson's attack on Harper's Ferry.

Reaching into his coat for his readers, Lee found himself needing a chair as he finished the first sentence of the handwritten message. The looseness of Stuart's penciled script indicated that he had written it in haste.

General Longstreet, seeing Lee's composure shift as he sat down, asked, "Sir, what does it say?"

Lee looked up for a moment and read aloud a portion of the sentence, "I have received a report from a Frederick businessman that General McClellan has intercepted a copy of Special Order 191...."

After briefly pausing to read more, he continued, "Am seeing more than three Corps of infantry marching with purpose towards Compton's and Turner's Gaps. Estimate this is the van of McClellan's entire force. I will remain between Compton's Gap and Fox's Gap until further orders. Recommend reinforcing General Hill as soon as practicable."

General Lee looked up again to James Longstreet and quietly commanded, "General Longstreet, I will concede to your concerns now. I need you to reinforce General Hill, as soon as you can!"

James Longstreet solemnly nodded, but persisted in his argument, "Sir, I strongly recommend we move the remainder of our army to Sharpsburg! There is good defensible ground there, and it will shorten the distance that General Jackson will have to travel. Since McClellan intends to come to us now, let us prepare to greet him at ground of our choosing!"

Lee wearily nodded; the loss of the order was calamitous to his plan. He realized at that moment, that his freedom of movement had evaporated. His only hope of victory now required two things he could not control. Jackson's rapid success, and Hill's determined delay. He again looked to Longstreet and ordered, "General, send men that can stop him at South Mountain!"

The thick white dust caused Billy to tie his threadbare bandanna over his nose, as they hurriedly marched back through Boonsboro. They had just marched north through the same town on the 10th. Billy shook his head as he recalled Sergeant Dennis telling the men early that morning to get their gear on for a march in the wrong direction.

According to Captain Kilpatrick, who briefed the men as they assembled on the road at noon, "The entire Yankee army was hotfooting it to the passes at South Mountain behind us. We are to reinforce General Hill's rearguard."

As they marched back down the National Pike on that warm day, the men of the Palmetto Sharpshooters could hear the distant sound of cannon, and musketry emanating from the far side of South Mountain. As they passed through the town, the number of mule drawn wagons and artillery hitched to teams, impeded their march. The entire trains of the Army of Northern Virginia were ensconced in Boonsboro, under General Hill's protection. To make matters worse, the roads were clogged by the brigades ahead of them, dispatched by General Longstreet to reinforce the battle.

As they waited at one intersection, where a quartermaster officer engaged in a hot argument with one of Brigadier General Jenkins's staff officers, over who had the right of way, Gene, leaning on the muzzle of his rifle, asked Billy, "Now don'cha wish you was one of them fine officers in charge of this mess?"

Billy smiled, spit some dust out of his mouth and shook his head, "I'll leave all that to them gentlemen. Soldierin' is my lot, and I'm thinkin' about quitin' it before too long."

As the Regiment paused, a quick-fingered South Carolinian spotted a box of Yankee crackers in the back of one of the stalled quartermaster wagons. The soldiers quickly snatched the treasured army bread up, broke open the box and distributed the crackers, in a mad tumble, amongst each other in the column. It beat raw corn and gave them something to do, while they waited.

General Daniel Harvey Hill raised his field glasses to his eyes from his perch atop a hastily erected wooden signal tower by a small dwelling that everyone had taken to calling, "Mountain House." Were it not for the war, he would have enjoyed a day's ride about this valley. As the leaves had begun to change, it offered an abundance of wild beauty. At the moment, however, he beheld another wonder that also possessed a terrible beauty.

Lowering his glasses he turned to his Aide De Camp, Major Ratchford and observed, "Major, despite having faced them much in the past, I must say this is truly the first time I have beheld General McClellan's army in nearly its entirety!"

Below them in the Middletown Valley, the Divisions of three separate Union Corps were beginning to transition from columns of march into lines of battle. They could clearly hear the bugles signaling the maneuver, while commands and the drums indicating the pace. Regimental Colors of all hues were visible as the regiments formed below. The burnished barrels of the soldier's muskets glinted in the sunlight, that caused the huge mass to take on a glittering sheen.

Hill turned and asked Ratchford, "What number of troops would you estimate that you see?"

Ratchford glumly answered, "Sir, I would guess more than 50,000! Sir, I am sure you are aware you have at best 9,000 men to stop that?"

General Hill avoided a direct answer, "It is like something out of the Bible Major. A "terrible army with banners," or at least that is what I recall the passage was."

Far across the valley, Yankee artillery began to fire upon his soldiers, as they filed into the woods on either side of the National Pike. Hill was surprised at the initial accuracy of the first volley, that killed several men amongst the rocks and felling trees to his right. He tucked his field glasses back into their case and suggested that they descend the tower to conduct a reconnaissance of Fox's Gap and find General Garland.

As General Hill retrieved his horse and mounted, another salvo of Union shell sailed over their heads, exploding in loud booms to his left and right and in and amongst the trees before him. His horse reared slightly and he soothed the anxious animal. With a wave of his hand to Major Ratchford, they rode down a rough trail on top of the mountain ridge that led to Fox's Gap. As they neared the pike that went through the gap, they could hear shouts and commands in the woods to the east and below them. A quiet figure on horseback hoarsely whispered, "Ya'll best come back my way! Them's Yankees down there!"

General Hill and his aide rode towards the figure, who turned out to be one of General Stuart's mounted scouts, the man seeing that he was addressing General Hill, lifted his hat and continued, "Beggin' yer pardon Sir! Them Yankees just came up. It is just skirmishers now. We heared that we would get some infantry up here soon. I would imagine that sooner than soon, would be better about now!"

General Hill nodded and quickly turned his horse to ride towards the pike using the western side of the ridge. To his great relief, he saw Brigadier General Garland astride a lathered bay ahead of a column of dusty men. They had obviously executed the climb at a double quick as the men were clearly out of breath.

Hill returned Garland's salute and said, "Samuel! Thank God you have made it! You must deploy your men north and south of this pike as quick as you can! There are Federals on the other side of the ridge already! Have your men sweep through the woods and drive them back!"

The young General nodded quietly and General Hill continued, "If you have artillery, see if you can counter those Yankee guns across the valley! Their fires are focused on Turner's Gap, just north of here. From this vantage you will be closer to them! Hold this ground firmly! You are the only thing between them, and our quartermaster trains. Can you do this?"

Garland gave him a great wicked smile and exclaimed, "Sir, it would be my pleasure!"

Garland then whirled his horse around, pointed to his right with his sword, and shouted for the leading companies of his small brigade to the north of the pike. The men decamped the road with a shout and began to file through the woods with fixed bayonets. As the trailing men of the lead companies cleared the road, Garland gave a great whistle with his fingers to his mouth to attract the attention of Captain Bondurant and his four guns who were in the middle of the brigade column.

As the Captain rode up adjacent to Garland, the General commanded, "Captain, set the guns off to the south just east of the ridge, there are Federal cannon across the way! I will need you to silence them if you can with your rifles."

Bondurant nodded, he had wanted a chance to avenge his losses at Gaine's Mills. Behind him were two brand new Whitworth rifled guns that were just the solution for the problem he had been provided. After saluting, he ordered his battery up and pushed down the pike to find a good spot.

General Hill and Major Ratchford paused long enough to watch the rest of Garland's trail companies enter the woods to the south of the pike. He was relieved that his reinforcements had arrived in the very nick of time. As they rode back up the ridge towards Turner's Gap, they could hear the high pitched yelps and whooping hollering of the North Carolina Regiments below them and the firing of their muskets as they drove back the Union skirmishers from the deep wooded eastern ridge. General Hill paused to listen halfway up the ridge. In the distance, he could hear the ominous thundering of artillery to the west. Instinctively he knew it was Jackson. Hopefully the man would overwhelm the Federals there. He had too many exposed flanks and too few men to cover them all. Around them, the crescendo of musketry filled the woods as the lead Regiments of General Hooker's Corps reached General Evans' men at the foot of the mountain. Hill spurred his horse and moved to Turner's Gap with a purpose. His next task was to find Longstreet's reinforcements and place them.

After General Hill found his way back to Turner's Gap, he directed Major Ratchford to get a situational dispatch back to General Lee's Headquarters. He paused, to look at his watch, it was nearly 2 pm in the afternoon, and the National Road behind him to the west was distressingly empty. Nothing was to be seen of Longstreet's help. Turning to look east again, he could see General McClellan's vast army uncoiling towards him, like a giant blue snake.

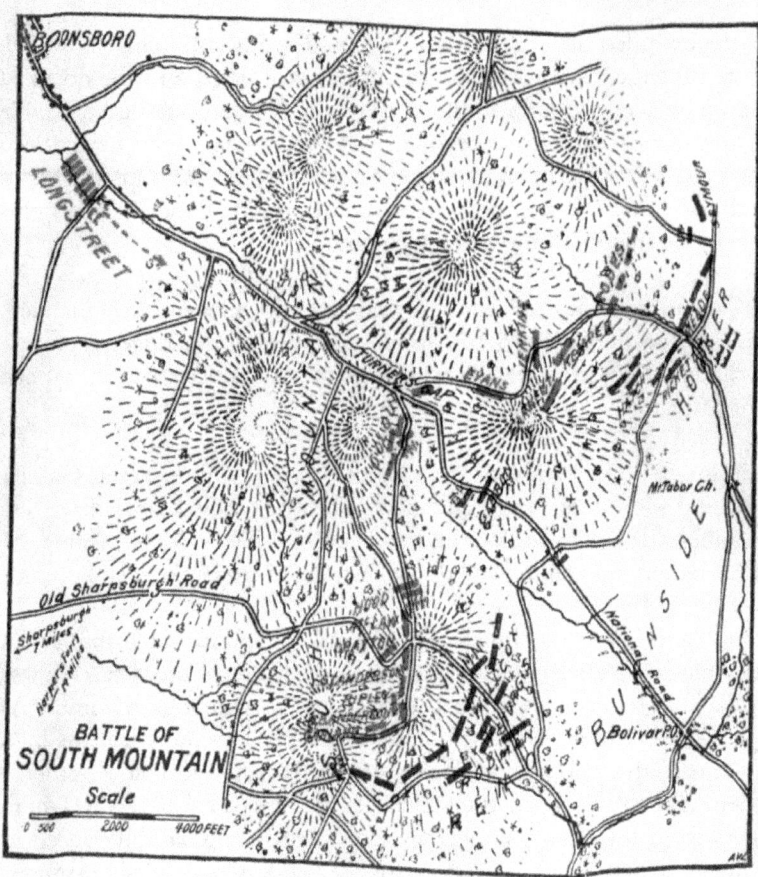

South Mountain 14 Sept 1862

First Sergeant O'Keefe rode over to Joshua as the crews loaded to fire their 6th salvo at the pass. The crews were in their paces now, and the drill exhibited was flawless. Joshua felt grateful that they were not attracting the attention of the rebel artillery. He did not envy the infantry below as he watched the clouds of smoke emerging from the deep woods at the base of South Mountain.

O'Keefe leaned over on his horse, and posed a riddle to Joshua, "OK, boy'o, when your section fires this next round, I want you to be watching your two gents on the lanyards and tell me the problem that you see."

Joshua was puzzled, but waited and watched as he was instructed. As the Captain gave the order to fire, he noticed that Wilkins on the first gun, and Private Terry on Newby's gun both were holding the lanyard down nearly at their knees as they turned and yanked them to fire the friction primers.

O'Keefe, watching just as intently, observed, "When your number four starts going lower and lower on his lanyard, it's a clear sign the primers is slippin'. When we be done today, I will have Mills order up some ordnance men. We got worn out vents!"

Joshua nodded. He recalled the last gauging they had done was back in July. They had fired close to a thousand rounds since then. Joshua silently watched, as six more shells burst in the woods at the crest of Turner's Gap.

Joshua watched and listened as Lieutenant Pennington shouted out orders for the next load and the range, echoing Captain Haines. His section quickly and efficiently repositioned the guns as the smoke rose lazily into the sky from the last engagement. Turning to his right, he watched in fascination as the Pennsylvanians handled their rifles. Their rounds were not fixed like Company M's, instead; they were pulling powder charges from tin cans sealed with thin lead foil. The men would first insert a black molded charge, followed by a streamlined shell and then ram the combination home. O'Keefe informed him that they were employing Schenkl shells with Hazard's Patent powder charges, which were compressed cylinders of powder, coated with lacquer, to make them somewhat waterproof. He also explained that the shells themselves required no fuse cutting, as they had an impact fuse. "Bormann fuses don't work so good in rifles," O'Keefe observed, between puffs on his pipe.

Durrell's Battery was attempting to disable the signal tower that rose above Turner's Gap. With little else to shoot at, they sought to isolate the Rebels from outside communication. The battery of Parrot guns fired by file, each attempting to hit the tower. The Parrots, each in turn, recoiled with a great crack, and long tongues of flame as they fired. Joshua noticed that the time of flight of the streamlined rounds was very fast. By the 3rd shot, a round impacted on one of the support legs of the tower, exploding in a white and orange explosion punctuated by large dark chunks of wood from the shattered logs. Men could be seen falling from the collapsing platform at the top.

Captain Bondurant saw the smoke as the battery across the valley fired by file at Turner's Gap. From the sound, he knew they were Parrot rifles in a typical Union configuration of six guns. He raised his field glasses to locate them and called out to his section leader the general location, once he noted the distinctive silhouette of the Parrot rifles. As he scanned, he realized that 12 guns were there; six bronze Napoleons and six Parrot Rifles. He would fire upon the Parrots first and then turn his attention to the Napoleons. Inwardly, he wished he were equipped as well as the Yankees across the way. He had two very good guns, with his new Armstrong Whitworths and two antique 1841 12-pound Flank Howitzers that could not even range to the far batteries. As his crews adjusted their aim and swung open the screw breeches of his two rifles to load them, he voiced to himself one word, "audacity." He then shouted to his section leader, "Load solid bolt, 2000 yards!"

The rebel gunners carefully inserted the fixed solid bolts with their odd hexagonally shaped copper powder cases into the breech. The number three, and number four, then turned the large iron toggles to screw the breech closed. A friction primer was then inserted into the center of the breech and the lanyard was fixed. The gunner carefully inserted his brass sight into the socket drilled into the reinforce, and carefully elevated the barrel until he was satisfied with the azimuth and elevation of the rifle.

Bondurant then asked his gunners, "Ya'll both on them Parrots?" The two gunners nodded. Captain Bondurant nodded and raised his field glasses back to the location of the Yankee battery. The Jefferson Davis Artillery was fixing to deal some harsh cards to the Yankees. He shouted out, without lowering his field glasses, "By Section….. Fire!"

The two Armstrong Whitworths barked with a load crack and recoiled violently backwards. The guns spit tongues of flame out of their long barrels as the hexagonal bolts screamed across the valley. The gun crews quickly rolled the heavy carriages back into position, and the crew at the breech expertly screwed them open again. Extracting the smoking copper cases, they then dipped rags into buckets of water to clean the screw surfaces and interior of the breech, before reloading. The gun was notoriously prone to sticking, if not frequently cleaned. Captain Bondurant watched carefully as the rounds streaked towards their distant targets.

First Sergeant O'Keefe and Joshua continued to sit side by side on their mounts as the crews rolled the carriages back up on the gun line and began to go through the reloading drill. Suddenly in the distance, they noted cannon firing across the valley, from the lower gap nearly straight across, from where they sat. Two high pitched, shuttling howls passed in front of the battery as the crews reloaded, and tore into the two leftmost guns of Captain Durrell's Parrot rifles. Joshua watched, stunned as the rounds impacted diagonally on the left hand cheek pieces of the guns. With a great ripping noise, the oaken carriages shattered in a great cloud of splinters, segments of iron strap, and bolts that burst away from the impact hurtling straight through the bodies of the crewmen closest to the impacts. The heavy iron tubes, first bounded up and then crashed down onto what remained of the ruined carriages. The spent solid bolts sailed off in altered directions with an unearthly howl. The number four crewman, of the first gun in the line sat upright, hatless, staring dumbly into space. His left arm was missing at the shoulder and a large chunk of oak protruded from his chest. From what Joshua could see, parts of the body of number one, lay beneath the gun tube, which nearly touched the ground. The German crews shouted and rushed to ready their pieces.

O'Keefe shouted, "Long range rifles! Likely a Whitworth, Captain!"

Captain Haines had come to the same conclusion, at the instant of the impact, and shouted out, "Counterbattery Fires! Load solid shot, 2000 yards, action left! Set your elevation at 5 degrees! At my command!"

The gunners feverishly insured the guns were loaded and adjusted their trails to the left where the smoke continued to rise from the wood. Captain Haines knew that the Rebel gunners were doing the same as he. Speed would be essential. He trotted the line, and corrected the aim of two of the guns. He worried that their own troops were climbing the same ridge, he was going to engage. Glancing to his right, he noted that Durrell was also orienting his remaining four guns in the same direction.

Haines then shouted, "By Battery!...... Fire!"

Company M's guns roared as one, obscuring their vision forward, as the great cloud of smoke rushed down the hillside. O'Keefe slapped Joshua on the arm, "Get the Limber teams for all the guns forward, now! Get the Limbers hitched to teams, as fast as ye can! Trust me this won't go well for us if we stay here!"

Captain Bondurant ducked his head, as six solid shot ripped through the trees several feet over his head. One shot tore straight through a thick oak trunk in an instant and exited in a spray of stark white splinters. He had noted that the Napoleons had fired in response, but the rifles remained his primary focus. His men were nearly complete with the reloading of the next two rounds. He had elected to load point impact shell for his next shots. Bondurant had carefully watched the limber men, to insure they had removed the packing properly from the finely manufactured Armstrong fuses and had tightly screwed them into the longer Whitworth shells.

After the crews had loaded the two rifles and firmly screwed the breeches shut with the iron toggles, the crews stood back. Bondurant waited patiently, as the gunners sighted in on the next two guns of the Yankee battery.

When they indicated that they were ready, he lifted his field glasses up to his eyes and shouted, "Fire!"

His two guns cracked again, sending their deadly loads towards the Union battery, which returned fire at nearly the same instant. Bondurant was pleased to see only four discharges. He lowered his field glasses, to shout out the command to limber the guns, when the bursts of the incoming 3.67 Schenkl shells, caused his horse to rear. The Yankee commander on the far side had done precisely what he would have done. As the rounds burst among the trees around his battery, he saw both men and horses fall. The woods were full of smoke, and falling leaves.

He shouted hoarsely, "Limber the guns!" It was time to move. He paused to look across the way. The sight of a limber exploding, was all he could make out through the thick white smoke that hung in the afternoon heat.

As his men hurriedly brought the teams and limbers forward to hitch up the guns, he suddenly heard the increasing volume of musketry fire, erupting all around him. The Union regiments had run into reinforcing Confederate troops, who were pouring out through the woods.

Colonel Roberts, of the 1st Pennsylvania Reserve Volunteer Infantry, pushed his men through the thick trees, and tangled Mountain Laurel. The undergrowth was thick as the darkest jungle he could imagine. He shouted to his Adjutant to ride the line to insure the companies of the Regiment were maintaining their dress and alignment with the colors. He secretly hoped, in this green, and dark mess, that they would find an exposed flank. He had abandoned his horse after the first hundred yards of travel, as movement by foot was easier than fighting an excited mount. South of him, he could hear heavy musketry emerging from the more open areas by the National Road. General Seymore had instructed them several hours ago, to find that exposed flank, and roll the Rebels up, for destruction by General Gibbon's, and General Hatch's Regiments. He pulled himself up the steep slope through narrow game paths in the laurel and turned from time to time to insure the bugler, and colors were following him.

As he pushed with his men through the thick growth, he suddenly heard cries above him in distinctly rustic accents, "Hyar they come boys!"

A sudden crackling roar of musketry filled his ears. The noise was deafeningly loud and hurt his ears. He could feel the heat around him from the blasts of hundreds of rifles above him. It was at this moment that he realized he had almost walked into a steep face of rock to his front. 30 feet above them, were the men of the 3rd Alabama Infantry. They were lying atop the massive rocks in order to fire down upon the Union troops as they struggled through the tangle. Colonel Roberts shouted out to his men, to rally on the colors. As he looked around, he saw many blue clad forms lying very still on the ground. Just as several men gathered near him, another volley of muskets erupted above their heads. The hail of minie balls tore through the leaves of the trees and laurel bushes around them. Colonel Roberts could hear the cries of the wounded all around him. Turning back, he grabbed his bugler by the arm and commanded, "Sound retreat! Then I want you to run down the hill a hundred yards and sound the rally!"

The shocked young bugler nervously nodded and made his call. After crashing back down through the brush himself, Colonel Roberts then moved to his bugler as he made the rally call. There he found his Sergeant Major, who informed him, "Sir the 5th Company has found a path off to the right where those great rocks have a gap in them! There are Rebs there too, but at least we can get at them!"

Colonel Cullom Battle of the 3rd Alabama carefully trod along the jumbled rock, atop the rock face commanding the foot of the mountain, where he had arrayed his Regiment. A brief encounter with Yankee infantry had ended too soon for him to establish how big the attack had been. He was comfortable that no one could get through the point where his men had driven back the first attack. He worried greatly about his left flank. In reality, he had not expected the Yankees to attempt an attack through the awful tangle below him, yet they had appeared. He recalled earlier, how his Aide de Camp, Major Warren, had complained bitterly as the sounds of battle raged south of them. Warren had wryly observed, "Old General Hill has done gone and put us too far outta the way sir! We ain't gonna see no game out in these parts!"

Colonel Battle reckoned that the probe they had observed was a Yankee attempt to find General Hill's exposed flank. Sensing imminent danger, Battle strode off to his left to find Major Hobson, who commanded the 5th Alabama, on his left flank. Where their two regiments met, lay a trail that they had used to find water earlier that morning. As he passed by his waiting men, who nervously fingered their loaded rifles, while peering over the rocks, many stated as he passed down the line, "Sir, we can hear them down there!" To each group in passing, he ordered, "Don't shoot at nothin' you can't see in your sights! Wait for good targets!"

After pushing through the thick brush and carefully stepping over the tumbledown stones coated with thick mats of dead leaves, he found the wiry bearded Major Hobson looking down the same path with the commander of the company assigned the defense of that segment of the 5th Regiment's line. Hobson looked over and seeing Colonel Battle, asked, "Sir was that your boys doin' the shootin?"

Battle nodded and replied, "That's why I am huntin' you Major Hobson! From the noise they are making down there, it is my guess they have seen this here gap."

Hobson introduced Captain Snyder, from Montgomery, who was assigned the flank between the regiments. Snyder held a ball in his hand. He offered it to Battle to observe, saying, "We gots a surprise for them Yankees when they come this way!" He grinned broadly and continued, "These here are 6 pounder shells with 5 second paper fuses in them. Once they show, we are gonna drop these on them!"

Colonel Battle and Major Hobson agreed to place a company each, on either side of the steep path. Hobson insisted that they allow them to get halfway up before they opened fire. Colonel Battle agreed, and moved back over, to reposition his 1st Company to cover the draw, closer to the flank of the 5th. As he went back towards the center of his line, he shouted out to his regiment in his best parade ground voice, "Get ready for them boys!.... Fix Bayonets!"

Colonel Roberts realized that he was drenched in sweat, as he located his bugler. He paused to reach awkwardly behind his map case and found his canteen. He uncorked it and gulped down a couple of swallows of tinny tasting water. His Sergeant Major and Adjutant found him and after they arrived, he pointed back towards the gap between the rocks and ordered, "Major Emerson, put a company back from each side! One on the left of the gap, another on the right! Leave a hole in the middle. I want a gap wide enough to pass the other companies through, a hole big enough for a company moving by platoon lines of battle! I want the two forward companies on either side of that gap to place volleys on the rim of those rocks above! Put some skirmishers forward that can correct the aim of those companies. We must keep their heads down! Do you understand?"

Both men nodded in understanding, as he continued, "Let me know when you have those two companies up. I will lead the men making the assault through the middle!"

He walked back down the hill until he found the Captain of the first company of the regiment and instructed him to form his men into a column of platoons on line. He then found the third company and instructed their commander to follow the first. He turned to his bugler and color sergeant, and ordered them to follow him like children. The two anxious men nodded.

As Colonel Roberts waited for the Sergeant Major to report, he could hear the distant rattle of musketry to the south. The sounds led him to believe that no one had gotten any higher up the mountain than he was at the moment. He dug his watch out of his vest pocket, and looked at the time. It was nearly 4pm. They had been up, and moving since 5 am. It would start to get dark in another 3 hours. They would have to hurry. In the distance above him, he could hear Rebels shouting down to them, "Come on up, Billy Yank! Bring us some new shoes, boys!"

Sergeant Major Lyman soon returned. He nodded to the Colonel and removed his hat to wipe his sweaty hair on the sleeve of his frock coat, "Sir, they are in place! Should we fire now?"

Colonel Roberts solemnly nodded and then turned to the bugler, as he unsheathed his sword, "Corporal, sound the advance!"

When the Bugler sounded the advance, the 1st Pennsylvania rushed up the tangled approach with a shout, as the flanking companies delivered a great volley at the rim of the rocks. As the smoke from the volley dissipated through the tangled laurel thicket, Colonel Roberts led the lead company up the steep and narrow path. The rocks narrowed to the point where no more than 4 men could move up the path abreast. The ground was slick with fallen leaves lying over wet earth and the men slipped and stumbled as they ran. The steep incline slowed their progress and many rapidly became winded, as they advanced. A second volley was fired from below and Colonel Roberts thought he could see where the path opened up to the rim of the rocks just ahead.

As they neared the top, a loud shout from above was heard, "Give em hell boys!"

As the companies below reloaded, Sergeant Major Lyman looked up. He first saw the colors then he made out the form of the Colonel with his sword drawn, leading the first company up the narrow path between the great boulders. Suddenly, he saw large masses of butternut clad men rise on both sides of the draw, with long bayoneted rifles. Some of the men threw what he took to be stones, down on the advancing troops. One in particular caught his eye, as it appeared to be spewing smoke. He turned to his men as they struggled to quickly ram their charges home and cried, "Ready... Aim..... Fire!"

Private John Warner of the 1st Pennsylvania Volunteer Infantry winced as a hard object hit him painfully on his shoulder. He then immediately felt a sharp burning sensation on his neck. He dropped his right hand from the wrist of his Springfield musket, to rub the burning area of his neck and he looked down. At his feet lay an iron ball; at one end it emitting a flame burning like a dull red flare. He stared fixated at the strange object for an instant. Suddenly all he saw was a bright flash. The 6-pound shell exploded, shredding his sack coat and sharp shards of iron ripped into his crotch. The last thing he heard in this existence, was a thick-throated southern accented voice cry out, "Fire!"

The loud explosion behind him, stunned Colonel Roberts for a moment then in his peripheral vision, it seemed like a vast number of men were pointing long sticks at him. All he could see was smoke and tongues of orange flame. He felt a sensation of something hot and fast passing through his shoulder and he suddenly felt violated in his chest, with a shocking sensation of something passing violently, malevolently through him. He fell to his knees weak, his sword dropped from his hand and something draped over his head. With his last strength, he turned his head, and saw alternating bands of white and red. The fading light of the sun gently illuminated the colors. Fine stitching connected the bands, he muttered, "The colors," before everything went black.

Seeing the Colonel, and the colors fall, Sergeant Major Lyman screamed, "Fire!"

His men, finished with their loading, fired a volley that caught many of the Alabamians at the moment that they had discharged their muskets into the draw. Lyman had the satisfaction of seeing many of them fall from the rocks, into the draw below. Men in blue and butternut now mingled in the rocky path. Some moaned and cried out. Others simply lay still and quiet.

Captain Kirkpatrick called out to the marching troops to halt, as they neared the top of the narrow mountain road. He echoed the commands that came down the line. The sounds of battle came up to them, from the far side of the pass.

Gene asked aloud, "Where we at, Ya'll?" A voice off to the side of the column replied, "Maryland!" The men chuckled and shouted back curses. Sergeant Dennis informed him that they called the spot "Turner's Gap."
The men waited and wiped their sweaty brows, running their dirty hands through long hair that was the natural result of months afield. The army had paused little, since the early summer. Billy thought about where he had been as the musketry far below them continued in a near constant roar. The Seven days fight, Manassas one more time, Chantilly and now South Mountain. This fight sounded big, but nobody seemed in too great a hurry to get deeper into it. Another man from behind them called out, "Where are we going Captain? We goin' in?"

Captain Kilpatrick called back, "Don't worry me right now!"

Soon Colonel Walker called up the commanders and gave them their orders. They were to spread out north and south of the narrow lane where they stood. They were in support of Colquitt's and Garnett's brigades. "Stand ready, if they come running back up this here road! If that happens we will be next!" Captain Kilpatrick walked the line as the men spread into their assigned positions. Billy, Gene and George began to gather old logs to augment the scattered rocks that marked where they would make a stand. An occasional Yankee shell would tear through the heavy timber at the pass and explode deep in the woods behind them. Heavy smoke smelling of sulfur and burning wood wafted through the woods. Down below, the sound of musket fire would intensify and then die down. It seemed to come slowly closer, to where they waited, but the wood was too thick and deep to see much. Billy began to notice that the shadows had lengthened. The day was growing late.

Another quarter mile down the road from the Palmetto Sharpshooter's lines, General Daniel Harvey Hill sat on a large rock with his horse tied off to a small tree behind him. Couriers were coming to him with reports. The newest one was a grimy and dusty Lieutenant who reared up his lathered horse, and saluted, "Sir, General Colquitt begs to report that he has been able to hold his line. The Yankees are coming against us strongly but their losses are great, and he is in no danger of losing his position! He asks if he has supports if they attack again!"

General Hill nodded and simply replied, "He has. Thank the men from Georgia for their gallantry!" Hill raised his field glasses towards the open pastures beyond the burning barn where General Garnett had rushed his brigade of Virginians in to plug the gap between Colquitt's and Evan's Brigades. The lines continued to hold and as he watched, great clouds of white smoke emerged from the dark lines of men arrayed in regimental lines, along the fenced edges of the tall cornfields below. Lowering his field glasses, he remarked to Major Ratchford, "It would seem that our 9,000 have stopped an enormous legion, Major. It is a simple miracle."

Soon another courier came up the road from the west. He bore orders from General Lee. Ratchford took the message from the rider, and asked, "Does the General require an immediate reply?" The young corporal shook his head, and once Major Ratchford nodded, he turned, and rode back down towards Boonsboro. Ratchford handed the folded message to General Hill, who paused, then opened the folded message and read it silently. After a few moments he folded the note and tucked it into his frockcoat pocket, "Major begin to prepare orders. We are to leave this ground at midnight. General Lee wishes us to move the trains and the artillery reserve to Sharpsburg tonight."

3
ANTIETAM CREEK

David Miller rose early to hitch his wagon to his two mules. He would have to ride over to the Meeting House as his wife had forgotten her prayer book in the pew of the simple structure, where they had attended services yesterday. It was a warm morning and the Indian summer promised to last a while into September. He was in a hurry, needing to go into town to pick up some nails and flour from the general store. He paused to listen after attaching the mules to the singletree of his wagon. The worrisome thundering of the war had quieted from yesterday off to the south and east. He hoped that the fight was going to move somewhere else. Turning his wagon south on the Hagerstown Pike, he could see off down the road towards the Meeting House and town, large groups of men in light brown and tan looking clothes gathered in the open pasture below his cornfield. Miller became agitated; he realized that the war had not left. It now resided on his land. He deliberately moved his mule drawn wagon at a walk as he passed his corn. Soon it would be drying and he would harvest the dried kernels for feed and meal. It reminded him to check the condition of his Sheller when he returned home in the afternoon.

Ascending the low rise that the Meeting House was built on, he could see men on horseback under a tree by the simple white structure. Three men appeared to be studying the ground to the east. They wore finer gray uniforms with all manner of trim on the sleeves. Miller imagined that they were in charge and he made up his mind to talk to them after he had secured his wife's prayer book. The three men on horseback gave him only a passing glance when he pulled up to the structure. He tried to contain his agitation as he entered the structure. Moving inside he found her book on the ladies side of the meeting house and returned with it to his wagon.

General Daniel Harvey Hill listened intently to Colonel Rooney Lee's descriptions, detailing of how the land flowed up from Antietam Creek to where they sat. General Hood had accompanied General Hill, his Cavalry's attachment would remain in effect, until General Longstreet's Headquarters established itself, forward of Sharpsburg. For now, General Hill would position Hood's Division, just across the road from where they sat. Colonel Lee explained to General Hill that reports were coming in, suggesting that McClellan's main body, was now passing through the passes of South Mountain, and would likely arrive in Porterstown, along the east side of Antietam Creek, by tonight. Hill nodded and observed, "I suspect we should busy ourselves in placing troops and artillery then. I will establish my headquarters back towards town shortly, once my men come up. I would appreciate another meeting, Colonel Lee, so we might study this all on a map." Lee nodded, and good humoredly patted his already ample belly and replied, "Yes Sir, after supper would be a good idea." Hill smirked and gave him a nod. General Hood extended his hand to Lee and offered congratulations, "Colonel, before you depart, I have just heard rumor that you are to be promoted! Congratulations!" Lee thanked him and with a tip of his hat, he turned his horse and departed on one of the many dirt trails that led to the northwest.

As the two generals continued to sit and discuss the ground, they scarcely noticed the gray-headed farmer who approached them from the white building until one of the staff orderlies intercepted him. General Hill noted that the man was clearly agitated and told the orderly to leave him be.

David Miller removed his hat and asked, "Would you be the man in charge of these men?"

General Hill nodded, and replied, "Yes sir, at least the ones in this vicinity. How may I be of assistance to you?"

Miller continued, "Mister, I am David Miller, a simple farmer. That is my place up the road. I sincerely hope you are not planning on fighting this unholy war on this property! This is the property of the German Baptist Brethren. This is our church that your actions are defiling!"

75

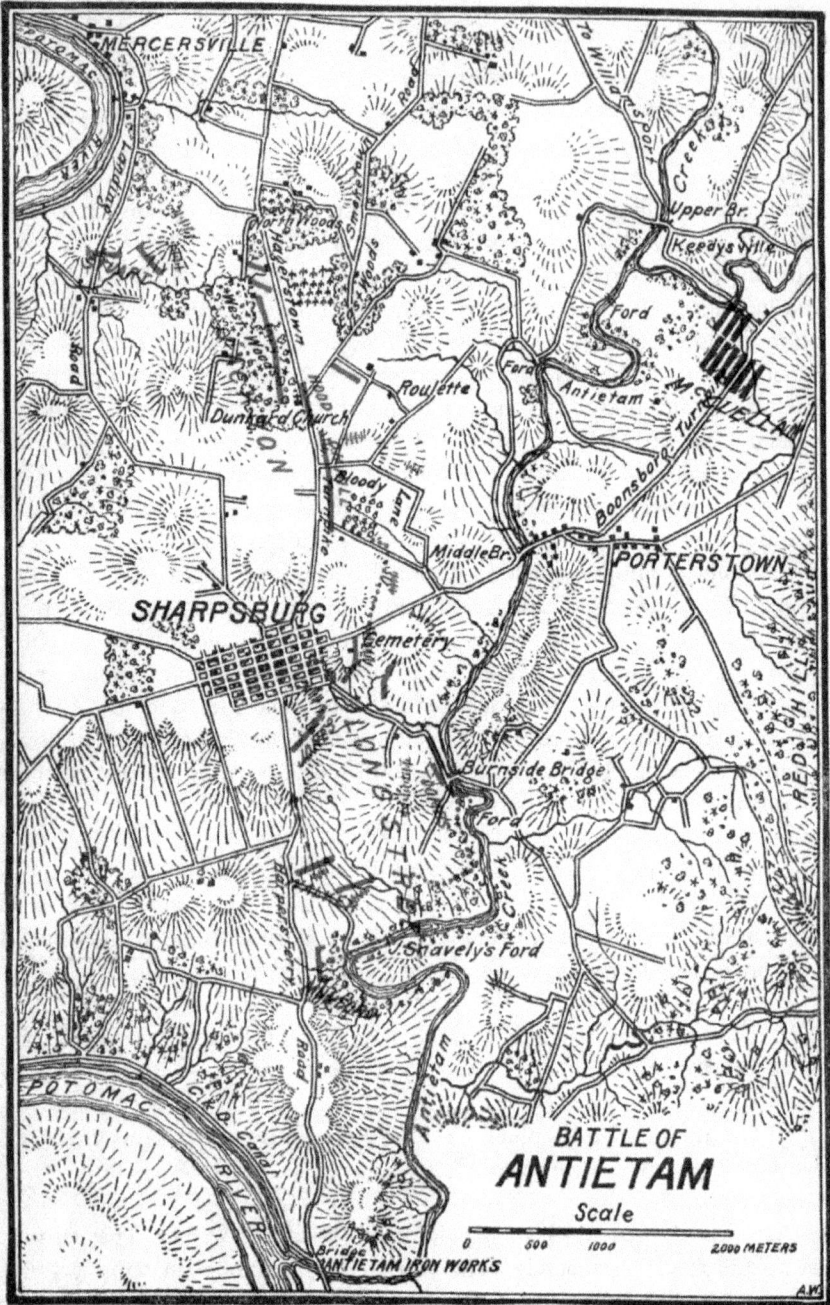

BATTLE OF
ANTIETAM
Scale

0   500   1000   2000 METERS

FROM HISTORY OF THE CIVIL WAR, BY COMTE DE PARIS.

General Hood leaned towards Hill and quietly stated, "Lee said the locals called this the "Dunker Church" earlier. Even though it don't look like a church to me."

Miller, hearing the comment, grew angry but suppressed his temper and retorted, "Gentlemen, those who adhere not to our beliefs, call us "Dunkers." That I will not dispute. My family and the Mumma Family, down the road, are founding members of this congregation. We reject this war, which is a sin that you will answer for. I must insist that this Meeting House not be a battlefield! This is God's house!"

General Hill removed his hat and ran his hand back over his head and replied, while holding his hat in his hand, "Sir, while I respect your beliefs and your property, military imperatives require us to be here."

Before Miller could reply, he continued, "Mr. Miller if the sky to the east darkened with a great storm, could you stop it from coming here and blowing houses and trees down?"

Miller shook his head and was interrupted again, as he tried to speak, by General Hill, "East of here is the Union Army! They are marching here as quickly as their feet can carry them! That is a host of 100,000 men who mean to make war against us here, here in this place! If it is God's will that your Church is unmolested, then so be it. As for myself, I intend to use this ground to preserve this army! Sir, my advice to you would be to leave this place with your family."

General Hill then directed his orderlies to escort Miller away. David Miller, now knowing the worst, quickly remounted his wagon and rode with some speed towards town. Halfway there, he encountered Samuel and Elizabeth Mumma coming his way. Miller pulled his wagon alongside Mumma's, and Samuel exclaimed, "David, you must turn and gather your family! This entire area is to be a battleground! I have held a meeting with the brethren this morning. We are going to shelter at the Manor Congregation in Hagerstown."

Miller nodded and sadly replied, "Yes brother, I have also just learned. They have already placed cannons around the Meeting House. I fear the worst!"

Mumma nodded and slapped the reins of his team to begin moving again. He was anxious to find his son, who had departed before dawn with his other horses. He had heard that the armies had a tendency to take horses for their own purposes. Miller watched him pull away and sadly turned his own wagon around at the Porterstown Road intersection, to go back. As he turned around, he could see large groups of men dressed in the peculiar light brown and gray uniforms of the Southern army, lounging along the sunken banks of the Porterstown road. It appeared as if they intended to use it as a position to fight from.

Joshua studied the ground as they pulled their guns up the grade through Turner's Gap. Blue and butternut clad bodies lay strewn about in grotesque positions on the torn pastures and trampled cornfields along the pike. Details of men from the attacking regiments had already begun to lay the blue clad corpses into ragged lines for burial. He noticed that none of the bodies had shoes on anymore. The Rebels had obviously been busy in salvaging those badly needed commodities during the night. First Sergeant O'Keefe had informed the Sergeants that morning, that they would push through the pass to a town called Boonsboro and then the company would wait there for Lieutenant Colonel Hayes. They were to be returned to the Horse Artillery Regiment for the move forward. General Pleasanton's scouts had reported the Rebels were fortifying Sharpsburg. Their backs were to the Potomac, and it appeared to him to be building into a large fight. Joshua hoped that they would be able to reload the limbers at Boonsboro, as his limber chests were nearly empty from the firing yesterday.

Passing the burning barn that marked the narrowing of the pike as it wound through the dense woods, he could see the shattered signal post and fallen trees, displaying the terrible work they had wrought, yesterday. The trees were torn and splintered from the solid shot and exploding shell that they had concentrated on the area. Most of the dead wore the ragged butternut uniforms of the Rebels. These bodies too were shoeless. The dirty feet of the corpses spoke volumes. These men possessed no shoes to steal. As the column halted behind some wagons in the pass, he looked down at several bodies by a shattered split rail fence, running along another trampled field of corn. The dead men had long hair and sallow faces, marked almost universally with long beards. They had a wolf-like and wild appearance. This army had clearly waged ceaseless campaigning since the early summer.

Lieutenant Pennington arrived alongside Joshua as he waited and asked, "You don't recognize any of them do you? I hear there were many South

Carolina regiments defending this ground."

Joshua shook his head and spit, "Sir, I try not to recognize any of them. I know my brother is a cavalryman for them, but I have no idea where. I suppose we follow different fates, him and me. None of this is our making. This war overran me!"

Pennington quietly nodded, "If it is of comfort to you Sergeant, there are many southern men of some renown who serve the Union. And to the contrary, there are some northern men who serve the rebellion. Fate has been odd in this regard. For myself, I am grateful that you made the choice that you did!"

Joshua looked the young officer in the eyes for a moment. It was rare to receive praise from officers. He quietly replied, "Thank you sir for the kind words. This army has been my home for eight years now. I am content with my lot."

Pennington clearly wanted to talk and he continued, "Timmonds, the word is, this coming fight could decide the war in the east. Colonel Hayes shared his concerns with us last night. It seems that General Lee and his army have split their forces. General McClellan is rushing us to Sharpsburg because an officer in Lee's army lost a copy of an order indicating a very unwise decision by General Lee. That is the reason for our hurry. We stand a very good chance of defeating a divided army with it's back to the Potomac River. This development is providential, I feel. Please relay this to the men of your section. I think we are poised on the brink of a historical event."

Joshua, uncomfortable with the philosophical aspect of the conversation, raised the practical considerations of a Sergeant. He imagined this was the reply O'Keefe would give, "Sir, I think that history will be disappointing if we don't get some ordnance men on these guns! My vents are worn and we noted some difficulty yesterday. If we can get them redrilled before the next fight it would make a difference!"

Pennington smiled and promised he would emphasize that fact to Captain Haines. The artillery always demanded attention to the technical realities of the guns. He was glad to serve in a unit where the Sergeants kept a close eye on the details.

By late afternoon, they had pulled the guns through Boonsboro, the town was full of signs of the Confederate occupation. The pastures and crops around the town were trampled from encampments hastily abandoned. All the roads were rutted and covered with animal dung from the pause there by Lee's supply trains and artillery park. General Pleasanton had directed the horse artillery to rest there until morning to reload limbers and attend to the guns. They would push to Porterstown at dawn. Pleasanton did not tarry at Boonsboro, instead, he pressed forward towards Sharpsburg with his cavalry to scout out the terrain and find the screen of Stuart's Rebel cavalry. The general had come to prefer the quiet work in half-light that his troopers excelled at. He left one troop of regulars from the 5th Cavalry behind to act as security for his horse artillery. The troopers left behind wasted no time and cantered through the hamlet to look things over. After Joshua got his section parked, he had the men unhitch the teams and attend to the horses. First Sergeant O'Keefe convened a quick Sergeant's meeting to share the news he had received from the Captain.

"Stay by yer guns until the Ordnance men come up. Mills has found them and is bringin' them up directly! Make them gauge your vents, I have done seen at least 4 that are worn! Each section Sergeant also needs to make a personal inventory of your limber and caisson chests. Captain says we are riding into a big fight soon. Ammunition is still stretched out far behind us due to this country, so be mindful that you have good stocks! Tighten all your carriage and cheek piece bolts and grease yer hubs!" O'Keefe looked for a moment as the road was filled with marching infantry moving towards Sharpsburg. The dust from their marching drifted slowly past him, as he continued, "Cook rations tonight for 3 days march, we will move out tomorrow before dawn!"

Newby looked up, after he finished packing a pipe with tobacco and asked, "How is the fight going for us, First Sergeant? Have you heard any news?"

O'Keefe spit and narrowed his eyes to reply, "It don't look good! The Rebs have General Myles and Harpers Ferry surrounded. The Captain heard that Lee has an army of over 100,000 men, just west of us. We are going to attempt to hit a portion of that Army hard tomorrow as they are split up. If we are lucky, we'll do that! If we ain't, then you best be fookin' ready to fire fast and true! Fook that up Newby and you may get yer chance to use them silly little carbines!"

As they were breaking up the meeting to return to their sections, Sergeant Mills arrived with an Ordnance wagon in tow. The artificers soon arrived at Joshua's guns and began to look at the vents. The grizzled old sergeant in a tattered frock coat, bearing Quartermaster Sergeant stripes, gave his vents a quick glance and growled to his young assistant, "Get the brace and bit and tap! No need for gauging – these two are unserviceable!"

Joshua watched as the Sergeant patiently drilled an oversize hole with the hand drill. He was slightly alarmed at the size of the hole that was defiling his gun. The artificer noting his alarm, winked after he finished the hole and said, "No worries sonny! Soon she'll be as good as new!"

His young assistant then produced a steel tap screw from his wooden toolbox. The bearded artificer began to slowly cut new threads into the enlarged vent hole. He would periodically back the tap out to clear the bronze filings from the sharp steel teeth of the tool. After fifteen minutes of cutting threads, he directed his assistant to fetch him an "insert."

Joshua watched fascinated as the man took a threaded bronze plug from the younger soldier, and after a quick measurement of the tapped hole, he made a pencil mark on the plug and inserted it into the threaded hole in the gun. He then obtained a mechanics adjustable wrench and fitted it to the squared off top of the threaded plug. He then quickly, yet carefully, screwed the plug in, until he could see his pencil mark, flush with the top surface of the gun's barrel. Looking at Joshua, he directed, "Have yer crew run a rammer down the bore to make sure she ain't catchin' on nothin." Once they had complied and were satisfied that all was flush inside the bore, the artificer obtained a fine-toothed saw and patiently sawed off the plug flush with the top of the barrel. Once the excess was cut away, Joshua noticed that a perfect diameter vent hole, had been partially drilled through the plug. The artificer then packed up his tools and instructed Joshua to have his crew use a hoof rasp to smooth up the edges to match the contour of the barrel. He moved over to Newby's gun to repeat the procedure. Joshua took a friction primer from Watkins's pouch and checked the fit. He smiled as the primer seated perfectly, with hardly any side-to-side play. They were back in business. Joshua then walked over to check on the progress of the limber, and caisson crews as they broke open ammunition, from an adjacent blacktopped ammunition wagon.

Henry Hunt hurried his mount past the endless lines of marching regiments on the Boonsboro Pike. He ashamedly caught himself trying to look at his shoulder boards, from time to time. He had been promoted to Brigadier General the day before and he was having a hard time believing it. It was only a brevet rank of volunteers, but to wear a star was not something he had ever envisioned happening to him. A courier had found him while he had been inspecting ammunition trains, with news that he was to join General McClellan on a hilltop above Porterstown for a reconnaissance of the Rebel defenses of Sharpsburg. General Hunt noted that a majority of the army had arrived and were establishing camps along the east bank of the brown waters of Antietam creek. He noticed through the trees how the ground rose to a ridge lined with trees that masked the town of Sharpsburg. Only the tops of the church steeples beyond were visible. General Lee had occupied good ground. He sensed as he rode, that many of the men encamped along that river would be having a difficult time, when that time came, to take that ground from General Lee's army. As he rode into the hamlet, and scattered farmhouses, and barns that marked Porterstown, a Sergeant waiting on horseback by the side of the road, saluted him, and directed him to a farm trail that coiled up, and around a hill overlooking the town. Hunt quickly trotted his mount to the top. Arriving there, he could see that his friends from the 15th Engineers had already arrived. They were mounting stakes into the top of the hill and affixing powerful telescopes, atop the stakes, to observe the Rebel positions. Looking about, he could see another detail erecting a log tower to support signalers, and beyond that were orderlies holding a knot of horses. As he approached the orderlies, he saw a familiar face, Brigadier General Humphries. The Army Engineer greeted him, "Henry! Let me be the first to congratulate you on your promotion!"

Hunt took his warmly outstretched hand, after he had dismounted, remarking jokingly, "These days anyone can become a General! I just hope they decide to keep me!" He paused to pull at his collar. The late afternoon was unseasonably hot, and heavy clouds were gathering from the north.

Humphries motioned with his hand, "Come, come, General McClellan is anxious to see you!"

Approaching the group of Generals, looking out to the west towards Sharpsburg, Hunt recognized Fitz John Porter and Alfred Pleasanton. General McClellan was in a high state of excitement as he observed, "There before you, is a portion of General Lee's army! In a way I am grateful that Halleck did not take my advice in evacuating Harper's Ferry! General Miles has drawn part of his great strength away from this ground."

McClellan turned, and noted Hunt's presence, "Henry! You are arrived in the nick of time! We need to ride the ridge below us. I have a spot for your artillery reserve! I should like to hear your thoughts on the ground."

Hunt quietly replied, "Sir, I am at your disposal." He paused to look at his friend Porter. He seemed to have aged and had lost the inspired visage he normally displayed. The court martial charges from General Pope and the army bureaucracy had obviously killed something inside him. Pleasanton nodded when he caught his eye and remarked, "I last saw Hayes in Boonsboro"

Hunt nodded as he pulled his gloves back on, and prepared himself to accompany General McClellan. He curtly replied, "Sir, I ask you to keep the Horse Artillery as close as possible to the center of the line. This ground will break up our effects. I may need every gun before we are done here."

Pleasanton laughed and nodded, "Damned things slow my boys down anyway, Henry! I shall not ride off far with them; that, I can assure you!"

Hunt quickly mounted his horse and followed General McClellan and his aide de camp as they galloped back down the hill, in the lengthening shadows of the late afternoon. The general waited on Hunt at the bottom of the hill. Henry Hunt, a gunner all his life, was not nearly a horseman of General McClellan's caliber. They rode briskly up another hill on the south side of Porterstown and upon reaching the top, Hunt could see he was on a long ridge running parallel to Antietam Creek. McClellan shouted as they cantered along the ridge, "Henry this is my center! I want your rifled guns to control this ridge. As you can see you dominate the Rebel positions on those far heights. From the study of my maps I think you can range most of their positions on the far ridges!"

As they rode further along the ridge a Rebel gun on those far ridges near Sharpsburg fired. McClellan brought his mount to a sudden stop and the shrieking projectile kicked up a spray of dirt 50 yards in front of them. He turned to Hunt as he spurred his horse towards the shelter of the eastern lee of the ridge, "They have the range as well! Can you get guns up here by daylight tomorrow?" Hunt nodded, he wearily realized that his reserve was badly scattered and he replied, "Yes sir. I would like to study your map this evening to see your other plans, if possible."

McClellan readily agreed and they rode back down the ridge to Porterstown. There they crossed the road again and rode to a farmer's barn that was surrounded by brightly lit tents. Hunt noted that the general had selected his headquarters to be sited at the base of the tall hill, that he had climbed earlier.

Inside a brightly lit tent a map maintained by the inimitable General Marcy lay spread out, on a pine topped table. Hunt sensed, as General McClellan described the ground, that he was acting as a sounding board for the General's ideas. He formed the impression that he was likely not alone in this feeling.

General Marcy directed an orderly to bring coffee and Henry Hunt listened as McClellan laid out his concept, "General Hunt, I am proposing to hit General Lee hard on his left flank here, north of Sharpsburg. I should think that Joe Hooker, Sumner and the recently arrived corps of General Mansfield would be the sort of men to aggressively attack him on this flank. As you can see, there is good ground to maneuver towards that flank. I will position my reserve, General Porter, in the center with General Pleasanton's cavalry in support. The Artillery Reserve will control the center with their fires, with Sykes's regulars supporting your guns! General Burnside will on my command attack the right flank at the most opportune time. I should be able to trap this portion of Lee's army in its entirety at this pocket around Sharpsburg, before he can pull his other forces back from Harper's Ferry!"

He looked up at Hunt from his map and asked, "What do you think, Henry?"

Hunt motioned to the left, "Sir, from what I could see of the ground to the north here, it is controlled in places and broken up in other places by hillocks and ridges. I think you will have to reinforce those Corps with additional artillery, to establish dominance there. I suspect Lee has carefully placed his guns to control the approaches. While the ground appears to offer approaches it will be tough work for the infantry without artillery support." Hunt did not like his own suggestion, as it took away his ability to mass his guns, but Lee was the only one at this juncture with that option. He had gotten to the best ground, first.

McClellan nodded as an orderly brought them hot cups of coffee. Henry Hunt took a sip, as McClellan stated, "Have your rifles on the ridge first thing tomorrow. Move your ordnance rifles and Napoleons to Hooker's and Sumner's Corps. I should think the Napoleons would be best there."

Looking at his watch for a moment, Henry Hunt excused himself, he had to find his staff and get orders out to the batteries. There would be much movement and planning required through the night. Exiting the planning tent he noticed that it was gently drizzling rain. The night was unusually warm. He found his horse and began the dark ride back to Boonsboro to find Lieutenant Colonel Hayes and Major Arndt.

Sergeant Lloyd Chriscoe of the 28th North Carolina laughed as he watched his men clamoring to pick up their salt pork and hard tack cracker rations from the captured Yankee supplies at the Harpers Ferry Arsenal. They had marched in behind General Branch, after General Hill had officiated the parole of the 11,000 Union troops, many of whom watched sullenly as the Regiment had marched in. The capture of stocks proved to be a tremendous boon to the weary men. They quickly found replacement shoes, and many, Sergeant Chriscoe included; found new frock coats to replace their tattered and lice infested uniforms. When asked by Private Coates, about the unfortunate choice of color, Sergeant Chriscoe had smiled and replied, "We'll just have to stick close to General A.P. Hill! Them Yanks will see that red shirt of his and know who we are, despite all this Yankee blue!"

General Jackson had given strict orders that his divisions were to have rations for three days drawn and cooked, as he planned to march towards Sharpsburg, beginning at mid-afternoon. Many of the famished troops could not help but eat portions of those rations as they cooked them. The captured Union pork was irresistible after weeks of living on raw corn and apples from the fields.

As the men sat around their cook fires, cheered by their re-equipments, they watched as Colonel Lane held a short conference with the Company Commanders under the overhanging roof of one of the ruined Arsenal warehouses. From what Chriscoe could overhear, they would sit tight for a fortnight, until General Hill had evacuated all the paroled Yankees, and gathered up their rifles, and artillery. This news pleased him, and his men immensely, as they had plans to sleep in that nearby warehouse, if fate allowed them a night to tarry. Captain Sykes returned and briefed his Lieutenants, who in turn instructed groups of men to form details to load rifles into wagons that would be moved to Winchester in the morning. When the details were finished, General Hill's men rested in the strangely empty arsenal. A gentle rain began to fall near sundown and the North Carolinians rested under the shellfire perforated tin roofs. Their full bellies made them quiet. The quiet pattering of the rain on the leaky tin roofs lulled them to sleep in minutes.

Lottie awoke early and rummaged through her portmanteau for the appropriate clothes for her meeting that afternoon. She settled on her dark blue visiting dress as the most businesslike for such a meeting. She decided to wear a white chemisette underneath with plain sleeves buttoned on, so she would not be bare armed. She really had no idea what would be best for government business. Looking in her mirror on the chest of drawers in her small boarding house room, she examined her hair. She decided to keep the bun, despite the unruly auburn locks that framed her face. Her hair was what it was, she decided and left it alone. She then finished her dressing. Standing and studying herself, she decided to pin on her mother's blue velvet secession cockade, adorned with one of Tom's Arsenal cadet buttons. Looking again, she decided that she was presentable. Peering out the window at the bright September day, she decided to wear her lightest bonnet and gloves. She glanced at her small locket watch, Captain Tinchant would be by shortly. She was anxious to see him again. He was proving to be most pleasant company and his assistance had enabled her to quickly become settled in the busy Richmond society.

As she descended the stairs into the foyer of the boarding house, she saw that Henri was waiting on her. He looked striking in his buff lapels and gray frockcoat. His uniform bore the gold trim of the cavalry, as Confederate regulations directed cavalry accouterments for the Medical Service. As he saw her descend, he gave a mock bow and said, "My, Miss Markley you are quite striking this morning!"

Lottie laughed, "I feel quite road weary this morning, Captain! I hope the Purveyor is not shocked by my ragged appearance!"

Tinchant smiled. She was clearly a striking young woman. He felt fortunate to have met her on that train. Her company would make his time in Richmond abundantly more interesting than some of his other postings. He took her hand, as she reached the final step, and liked its soft feel. As she gathered herself, and put on her gloves, Tinchant announced, "Charlotte, I would like to take you to a charming Inn near here for a light lunch before your appointment. I can prepare you, while we eat, for your meeting with Colonel Johns. I have had a close association with him for the past year."

Lottie smiled, and agreed. She had been too nervous for breakfast, and now she was very hungry. She realized that she had no idea where to eat, except for what Mrs. Newland served at the boarding house. After a short walk they entered a small café and Inn on a street corner, near the Medical Department offices. Henri commented, as he picked up a copy of the Richmond Dispatch from the reception table of the restaurant, "Charlotte, we often have dine here when we are in town on business. I think you will enjoy it!"

Over a nice plate of a rather fine Smithfield Ham and red potatoes, they whiled away an hour in conversation about the office politics of the Medical Department. Lottie learned that she would be doing a great deal of travel, as the job entailed inventory of medical supplies in field hospitals. As an auditor, she would be required to conduct inventories of those supplies that were controlled formulary items. Henri explained, as she ate, that many of the items were in high demand by the remainder of the population, as shortages existed due to the war. Taking another bite of ham, he observed, "The opiates are quite popular items that are pilfered for resale. It is becoming a problem lately."

He paused, and glanced at his paper and exclaimed, "Well now, it would seem that General Jackson has captured Harpers Ferry! That should prove a boon for us. Quite a lot of medical supplies were stored there!"

Lottie was unaware of the invasion of Maryland and was surprised to hear the news. Captain Tinchant explained the latest developments to her. He advised her to take up the habit of familiarizing herself with the news as she would likely be required to venture near the front, from time to time, depending on the location of the hospitals.

After lunch, they walked together to the Medical Department offices. Henri took her to the second floor, where Colonel Edward Johns maintained his offices and introduced her to the young clerk that functioned as his receptionist.

The young corporal directed her to take a seat and after a 15-minute wait, two men exited the door. The corporal rose and indicated to the older bald man, "Sir, Miss Markley is here."

Colonel Johns smiled and walked over to Lottie, as she stood and offered his hand, "Miss Markley welcome! Please accompany me to my office, we have much to discuss!"

She settled into a chair in Colonel Johns' cluttered office. He held up her letter of introduction and asked, "Tell me of your accounting education, Miss Markley."

Lottie matter of factly replied, "Sir, I was educated at the Ecole de Bousinnaire in Charleston, in the Italian Method of double entry book keeping. I also kept the books for the school, following my graduation, for 6 months. I am experienced in maintaining a fairly involved ledger, as the concern where I was employed supported over 60 students. The payments were not regular."

Johns nodded and stated, "This job entails traveling in environs not particularly civilized, nor safe. Often times near fields of battle. The hospitals you will visit are grotesque places. I trust you understand my reservations, despite the shortage of skilled male practitioners, in regards to employing ladies in this capacity. Do you feel you can satisfy the requirements of a job requiring audits of the formularies of such hospitals?"

Lottie quickly replied, "Sir, I was raised the only girl among three brothers on a working plantation. I have gutted deer and pigs with my momma and I have ridden with my brothers on foxhunts! I could keep up with them and jump. I dare say, I rode better than they!"

Johns laughed and replied, "Well, young lady, we will equip you with a horse then. I would suggest we get you a pistol as well." He leaned forward and added, "In all seriousness, Miss Markley, you will find this a very demanding job. Your returns from the audits will constantly adjust where we prioritize shipments of supplies, which are scarce, to say the least. We are employing audits to force medical staffs to safeguard supplies from theft, primarily in order to relieve strain on our supply system. You will be required to be persistent in your examinations! There is much profit available to those who would illicitly sell opiates. I hope you understand there is an element of danger involved as well, particularly if you uncover wrongdoing underway. We will arrange your visits to be always with a military escort."

After a few more minutes of talking, Colonel Johns led Lottie to show her where the master ledger was maintained. She would share an office with three other auditors, who also would travel to a network of locations all over Virginia. As she looked at the map of hospital locations on the wall, she realized she would have the chance to see more than she had ever envisioned. Colonel Johns directed her to spend the remainder of the day studying the master ledger in order for her to understand the formulary of the Purveyor's Office.

Travel of the nature mentioned by Colonel Johns made her think, while she examined the entries in the ledger. She resolved to shop for riding clothes and boots that would be more suitable for her new duties. She also pondered if she should try to obtain a horse.

Brigadier General Henry Hunt paused with Colonel Hayes atop the ridge south of Porterstown, as Captain Weed brought his battery of 20 pounder Parrot rifles up to the crest. They could see little, as the early dawn mist obscured their view of Sharpsburg. Weed saluted Hunt astride his horse and remarked, "Sir, Good morning! I trust the Rebels across the way are in range?" Hunt nodded and replied, "Set up as fast as you can! This ridge orients directly at Rebel batteries that I noted yesterday with General McClellan. Stay on your toes; I expect them to fire upon you when this mist burns off. You are to be the northernmost battery here, expect five more batteries to come in to your left!"

Colonel Hayes pointed out to them the next battery as the lathered teams of horses struggled to pull another six guns up the steep ridge. The early morning sun cast a reddish glow on the horizon as it rose in the east. Hunt continued down the ridge to greet the next commander. Riding down further, he found Lieutenant William Van Reed with his battery of 3-inch Ordnance rifles. Reed, seeing General Hunt, also saluted, and announced, "Sir, General Sykes sent us up! He says we can't do shit down below, so he sent us up. I hope that is acceptable Sir!" General Hunt smiled and replied, "Good to see the 5th Artillery Lieutenant! Keep your eyes to the west and northwest! Expect to receive fire when this fog clears! Respond sparingly, and only if you have good targets. Remember ammunition is expensive!"

Hunt, and Hayes continued to ride the ridge, taking the time to talk to each of the commanders coming up. Colonel Hayes had done an admirable job of rounding up the scattered elements of the Artillery Reserve in Boonsboro and getting them moving towards General McClellan's rapidly accumulating forces. Last up the ridge were Captain Durrell's Pennsylvanians. They only had four Parrot rifles, after having lost two at South Mountain. Hayes, and Hunt spent a few moments with Durrell, and assured him that they would prioritize replacement guns and crews as soon as they could. Hunt directed Durrell to orient his pieces to the southwest to cover a bridge that afforded a southern approach to Sharpsburg.

As the two officers rode back north along the ridge, they moved at a deliberate pace as the crews unlimbered the guns and drive the limber teams back across the spine of the ridge to mask the horses from Rebel fire. The crews scrambled to unshackle their implements to prepare the guns to engage. The mood on the ridge top was urgent, as word had spread that Lee was desperate and was assembling his army with his back to the Potomac. The men had been instructed that the Rebels may soon launch an attack on the assembling Union forces. Satisfied with the placement of the batteries on the ridge, Hunt suggested that they find the Horse Artillery Regiment to consult with General Pleasanton. He wanted to have those guns in the fight, regardless of the Cavalry's mission. Colonel Hayes explained that he had dispatched them to position with the Cavalry Division that lay east of Antietam Creek, just south of Keedysville. They swiftly rode back down the ridge and onto the Boonsboro Pike. The road was full of General Sumner's Divisions who were completing their early morning march to positions overlooking a ford north and west of the Pike. After a half hours ride past the marching columns of dusty troops, they found Pleasanton's cavalry in an orchard hollow alongside the Little Antietam Creek, that branched off of the main stream. Long lines of horses were picketed among the trees, and the cavalrymen were in small clusters making coffee in the morning mist. As Hunt arrived, a small mounted detachment was crossing the ford below them. Occasional shots could be heard in the mist on the west side of the creek as the cavalry patrols discovered Confederate pickets on the hills dominating the west bank of the creek.

General Hunt guided on the Divisional colors and soon found General Pleasanton, enjoying a cigar and a tin cup of coffee, while he pored over a map on a table in front of his tent. Seeing Hunt and Hayes riding up he stood and warmly greeted them, "Good morning! Gentlemen please pause for some coffee, I am sure you have arrived to take away my Horse Artillery Regiment!"

Hunt shook Pleasanton's hand and assured him, "No sir, I shall only ask you to push them forward soon!" He accepted a proffered cup from an orderly and looked to the map in front of Pleasanton. He explained, "Since General McClellan wants to push hard on Lee's left, this high ground across the way will enable enfilading fire onto the enemy when General Hooker makes his assault on the army's right. Can you secure this ground for the Horse Artillery to fire from?"

Alfred Pleasanton nodded, "Henry, that is the reason I am pushing patrols across now. There are Rebel pickets along the creek but I have found no infantry yet. They appear to be further back towards the ridge here, before Sharpsburg." He paused, puffed his cigar and continued, "I am still awaiting the arrival of the horse artillery batteries, they are currently stuck behind Sumner's columns. I expect them to arrive this afternoon."

Hunt nodded and replied, "Very well, with troops still arriving and due to the thickness of this fog, I doubt General McClellan will do much today. I understand that he has a meeting tonight. I would presume that we will attack tomorrow. Don't have them cross too soon. They will need to have support when they do cross."

Hunt then decided to ride back to the observation point established by General McClellan, above Porterstown. He would like to see what would occur as the rising sun burned off the mist of the creek. Colonel Hayes asked to be allowed to continue northward, he wished to find General Hooker and determine the condition of his 6 batteries before he moved.

As General Hunt rode south again towards Porterstown, he began to hear the distant rumble of the Rebel guns. The mist was clearing and he imagined that his line of guns on the ridge before Porter's Corps were now in plain view.

General Lee read the script of the message in his hand carefully. He was pleased that General Jackson was hurrying his troops to Sharpsburg. Cavalry reports were also coming in that large numbers of Union troops were coming down the Boonsboro Pike and the message he held indicated that Union cannon had been spotted on a ridge over Porterstown, across the Antietam. While disappointed that his invasion plans were now untenable, Lee resolved to show George McClellan a fight. He was satisfied with the choice of ground, but he knew he needed his far-flung Divisions back within his control as soon as possible. Finishing his reading, he saw Colonel Chilton quietly come in to announce a visitor. "General Pendleton has arrived Sir."

Lee removed his reading glasses and warmly welcomed him, "Good morning Reverend. I hope you are faring well this day!"

Pendleton nodded, he greatly respected Lee, they had shared much over the years. Lee was even a vestryman of his parish in more peaceful times. The Older white haired General politely listened as General Lee got down to more pointed business, "General, I shall need you to bring all my guns up, and to be sure, spare none for a reserve. Please see to it that the rifled pieces are situated thus, to strip away the Union guns that may interrupt troops moving from the center to either my left, or right. Until my whole army is once more come together, I must be able to maneuver the forces I have, from flank to flank, as necessary."

General Pendleton nodded, and replied, "I understand General Lee. We have nearly all the guns up, now, save those guarding the Potomac crossings. It is a shame hearing the report of 70 additional guns being captured by General Jackson at Harpers Ferry. If we had sufficient horses, they could be added to your force. Unfortunately very few animals were taken there."

Lee nodded, "Have Colonel Alexander move them to Winchester by whatever means exist. General, please also inform the Battery commanders to conserve their ammunition. They must have plenty when McClellan shows us his infantry!"

Lee bid General Pendleton a good day, and his Chief of Artillery departed. When Colonel Chilton returned, Lee asked if there was word of General Jackson arriving yet. Chilton slowly shook his head. He assured General Lee that he would notify him the instant Jackson arrived. In the distance he could hear guns beginning to fire. From the noise, he knew it was his artillery. The fog of the morning was burning off.

To the dismay of Joshua and his section, they hardly paused when they arrived at General Pleasanton's bivouac site at noon. Instead a patrol of cavalrymen intercepted Captain Haines and directed him to follow them. Mindless of the slow pace of the guns and caissons, the horsemen led them across a bumpy field and began a galloping ascent of another steep hillock on the eastern side of a tree lined copper colored creek. Beyond the hill they were climbing was a taller hill rimmed with trees. Joshua could see the red and white flags of a signaling detachment atop that hill performing the odd movements of the communication corps system. He wondered, as he leaned forward on his straining mount, if it was something he could learn. It would be a nice life sitting still and waving flags.

O'Keefe, sensing the grumbling of the crewmen, denied a pause for rest, moved among them as they unlimbered on the bald crest of the smaller hill shouting, "Be quick boys, be quick! Thank yer lucky fookin' stars you ain't campin' in the shit of 3,000 cavalrymen and their mounts! Step lively now!" He looked off to the west. The spot was good, as they could see above the trees and the lower hills across the wide creek below. Squinting through the thinning mist he could make out a bright white structure across the valley, situated in a shady grove of trees. He rode the line and directed the gunners to center their aim points on the building. In the near distance they could hear the occasional booms of distant cannon. Looking to the southwest he could see white smoke slowly rising from the ridge far distant from where he sat. Behind that smoke he could see the steeples of Sharpsburg.

The crews had their pieces quickly set. The drivers trotted the teams and their limbers towards the reverse slope of the hillock behind them. Lieutenant Pennington told the men to use hobbles on the leaders. Since the distance was greater than the standard fifteen yards, he wanted extra men to haul charges forward. They would risk no holders for the horses. Horses were too critical to hazard loss at the moment. Captain Haines walked the gun line while the men unhitched implements, set out their water buckets and arrayed their tools. He paused by first section and raised his field glasses to the west and asked Joshua, "Timmonds, what say you the range is to that white school house yonder?"

Joshua put his pendulum hausse back into its carrier and held his hand over his eyes, squinting, "Sir, I would say 2000 yards at the most! If you like, we could figure it exact!"

Haines shook his head replying without lowering his glass, "Nope, never known you to be far off, Sergeant. Just keep a sharp eye on that place. Call out any movement you see over there."

As First Sergeant O'Keefe rode behind the gun line one last time, Corporal Newby shouted out, "Hey First Sergeant, what you want us to load?"

O'Keefe turned his mount and shouted back, "Nuthin' Corporal, we is waiting orders! Make us a cup of coffee!"

Smiling, Corporal Newby directed his number five to bring up the pot and some kindling. The sun was warming the September afternoon, over on the ridge beyond, little could be seen in the still and humid valley. Both armies paused for a few hours. The occasional shot boomed out, but neither side did more than eat and rest. In the northwestern sky, clouds were forming. They would likely bring more evening rain.

Corporal Billy Cross sat contentedly on a smooth limestone rock on a rocky face of the hill, which housed the cemetery of the good folk of Sharpsburg. Having arrived there yesterday, and with little to do, save rest and eat rations taken from dead Yankees at South Mountain, the men of the Palmetto Sharpshooters were in high spirits. He studied his new shoes. He had taken them from dead Union infantryman early in the evening after the fight had died down. The man even had a spare pair of socks in a knapsack on his back which had "2nd WIS VOLS" stenciled in white paint on the slick black leather. He had also found two thick chunks of salt pork and a half-dozen hardtack crackers in the dead man's tarred canvas haversack. After securing the shoes and socks, he elected to take the haversack in its entirety. The shoes were mostly new, very stiff and of the right kind, "MacKays."

Gene lay on the grass beside him with a ridiculously tall beaver hat from Hagerstown covering his eyes. He tipped up the hat, and asked, "You heared any news from the Captain or Sergeant Dennis? When are them Yankees coming?"

Billy looked over towards the battery of iron guns on the edge of the cemetery above them. He knew they were from Virginia, having engaged some of the gunners in conversation yesterday evening. They now were somewhat alert, with the noise of firing north of them, they all were peering east. Billy lazily replied, "Looking at the boys up there on them guns, I'd say they are here now."

Another louder boom reverberated through the humid afternoon. This one was closer. Billy plucked a long stem of a weed and picked at his teeth. He looked east and below their position. Where he sat, he could see a fine stone bridge crossing the slow moving creek at the bottom of the hill. He had never seen such a fine bridge in Old Berkeley County. "Folks up here got lots of money," He muttered to himself.

The heat of the day lulled them into drowsiness, and they lay dozing for another hour until they began to hear music and drumming faintly behind them.

George Simon came breathlessly running over the lip of the hill. He shouted out, "They are a comin'! It's Old Jack and his boys from Harpers Ferry! They done took the whole thing from the Yankees and they are comin' up! Get up boys, you gotta see it! They are bringing cattle with them! We got meat boys!"

Suddenly, the Virginians on the Parrot rifles above them began to shout commands and revert to their crew drill. The two iron pieces closest to Billy's messmates, erupted in a loud roar. The heavy smoke hung in the humid and breezeless Indian summer air. In the distance, Billy could hear the sighing sound of the 10-pound shells as they sailed across the valley.

General Lee had reclined for a short nap on his iron folding bed when the sound of the Headquarters Band playing "Dixie," and the shouts of men, caused him to wearily sit up. The afternoon had grown insufferably warm and caused the weariness of the summer to return.

An urgent knocking on his tent pole, marked the arrival of a breathless Major Venable, "Sir! General Jackson has arrived!"

Lee's mood immediately improved and his weariness was swept away, "Major, if you would be so kind, it would please me to see him. Please locate him and direct him to this place, as soon as you can."

As the Army of Northern Virginia wildly greeted the arrival of General Jackson's advance guard the artillerymen on the ridge east of Sharpsburg began to fire in earnest at a tempting target. Off in the distance, a group of horsemen bearing colors, rode the ridge above Antietam Creek. The Gun Captains shouted commands and the gunners adjusted their pieces with care. Shot after shot was fired by the long-range guns. Large sprays of dirt were kicked up near the horsemen. The determined group of riders pressed on, seemingly ignoring the hazard they had placed themselves in. After an initial series of firing, the Union guns on the far side emitted silent puffs of white smoke from their muzzles. Traveling in, with the booms of the discharges from the far side, the screaming shells impacted around the

Confederate positions with loud cracks as they plunged into the hard limestone studded ground. Several guns were hit and dismounted, killing, and maiming crews and horses. Spent shot tore furrows in the deep pasture grass, before plunging into Sharpsburg below, scattering marching soldiers and curious civilians watching the arrival of Jackson's troops in the street. The cannoneers on both sides settled into a deliberate grudge match and spent the afternoon trading shot for shot, heedless of the affects of their battle on onlookers beyond.

As General Thomas Jackson's dusty and weary men trooped down the emptying streets, companies of men were often forced to rush for cover, as ricocheting shot and shell fragments plunged through the clapboard and brick buildings in the town. General Jackson was greeted by Major Venable, halfway through the hazardous streets, and received his invitation to meet with General Lee. He beat the dust off of his threadbare and dusty coat and accepted the invitation. He turned to Major Dabney, and directed, "Move them north out of this town and have them find shelter in the trees behind the ridge! I shall return to you there."

Fifteen minutes later, Jackson and Venable arrived at General Lee's Headquarters camp on a hill west of Sharpsburg. He saw Lee sitting hatless under a canvas awning, awaiting his arrival. The artillery contest continued unabated behind them. Jackson dismounted, his back sore from the long night and morning of riding, and strode over to greet General Lee. Jackson removed his hat and took a seat in a folding chair, at Lee's invitation, under the white canvas awning. "General, I appreciate your rapid arrival here. Please tell me of your operations in Harpers Ferry!"

Jackson thoughtfully replied, "It all started and ended rather quickly, General. Positions and careful placement of guns on those heights was all that was required. I regret to report that my boys may have mortally wounded Dixon Miles. It was God's will I trust."

Lee gravely nodded; he remembered the old soldier, having met him many times. He reflected on the nature of a war where friends and associates battled one another. Stories he had heard from his father had taught him that the revolution had been the same. The two men quietly talked until Lee was satisfied that he knew what he had gained. The delay of Ambrose Hill's Division concerned him somewhat, but Jackson assured his commander that Hill would arrive in time. He always did.

Jackson asked Lee where he wished to locate his men. Lee simply told him to center on a white church on the Hagerstown Road, behind Daniel

Harvey Hill's men. Jackson rose after accepting General Lee's thanks for a job well done, and responded, "It was really light work General, Miles had no chance. No chance at all. The ground for him was poor. I should rather assault such a place 40 times over, than be compelled to defend it once."

Lee rose to see him off. He was concerned about the continuing firing of his guns. He resolved to get a message to General Pendleton to have them reduce their firing. He would need that ammunition later.

Down below the meeting place the citizens began to depart the town, first in small groups. Then in larger groups, as the unstoppable torrent of artillery shells continued their paths of destruction through their homes. By the early evening, Sharpsburg was nearly deserted, save the long lines of Jackson's troops, wearily marching north.

Major General McClellan returned to his headquarters beside Mr. Prye's barn at 4pm. Handing Dan Webster's reins off to his orderly, he quickly summoned General Marcy for a review of the orders to be dispatched to his Corps commanders. His exhilarating ride of the lines had inspired him to make a slight change. He would order Joe Hooker to move today, instead of tomorrow before dawn. He explained to Marcy that it would enable Hooker's Corps to clear the ground for Mansfield's approach. They would move swiftly to block any further northward movement of General Lee's left. After the short consultation, General Marcy assembled his staff to draft up written orders for distribution. McClellan resolved to give each of his commanders orders that would provide them clear actions to take to realize his grand plan. He saw little need to pull them away from their commands to provide them the overall concept. He would manage that as best he could. With six complete Corps merging on the Confederate defenses, it escaped him how he would find time to meet them all.

One of the hard-pressed couriers finally found General Joe Hooker's Corps headquarters, as they were marching through the northern fords of the Antietam that afternoon. Hooker had already decided to cross, to feel out the Confederate left flank. Hooker had chafed all day for his chance to maneuver on Lee's Army, and he had decided to form up his corps and move at 2 pm on the 16th without orders. He had directed General Meade to assemble his Pennsylvania Reserves as the van of the Corps. The men gamely collapsed their camps on that hot afternoon, adorned themselves with knapsacks and rifles, and moved towards the fords. The 1st Pennsylvania Rifles, recently renamed the 13th Pennsylvania Reserves Volunteer Infantry, to the chagrin of the men, acted as the advance guard of Meade's Division in the approach march. Colonel McNeil led his men who wore distinctive deer tails attached to their forage caps, the mark of backwoods riflemen. After crossing the Antietam Creek near Keedysville they moved west on the Williamsport Road at the head of Hooker's Corps. After they had crossed the creek, Colonel McNeil dispatched the Cameron Rifles, under Captain Gifford, to press ahead of the Regiment to act as skirmishers behind the Cavalry. As they ascended a hill that led up from the creek bed, they could see a wooded area to their left that came all the way up to a split rail fence marking the left side of the Williamsport Road. Colonel McNeil was uneasy as he rode with his staff in between the skirmishers and the rest of his regiment, marching in column behind him. Somewhere to his left would lay the Rebel left flank. So far the wooded lane was quiet. They were somewhere ahead of him, but he knew not where. Off in the distance, the sound of cannon fire, emerged in short spurts of activity, followed by periods of quiet. The day had grown quite hot. He noted that the marching men were frequently pulling their canteens up to their mouths to drink. Tempted, he reached for his own canteen then stopping as he decided to conserve his water. As he peered ahead at the distant cavalry, he noticed that they halted ahead where the road passed between the wood to the left and a hillock to the right. The Cavalry had seen or heard something. A horseman ahead turned his mount and returned at a gallop towards the marching men. Suddenly off to his left Colonel McNeil heard the stuttering roar of musket fire as Rebel skirmishers emerged from the woods on his left. He wheeled his own mount and rushed back to his color bearer at the head of the marching column behind him. He shouted to the Corporal, "Stand fast here, Son! Mark the center of the line!"

As his adjutant and bugler came up from riding along the right flank of the columns, McNeil spread his arms wide along the road and shouted at the top of his voice, "Prolongue to the left! Center on the colors!" His skirmishers had already posted themselves along the fence line and were trading fire with the Rebel skirmishers, only a few yards distant. The smoke hung lazily in the humid air.

The 13th Pennsylvania, on hearing their orders, pushed companies forward past the colors at the double quick to get their men centered on the colors. The skirmishers stubbornly exchanged fire with the Rebels in the woods. Once they had formed, the companies faced to the left and formed a line of battle. The cry "Load" was echoed along the line. McNeil was fixated as a great group of brown and gray clad men emerged from the woods 30 yards distant on his left in line of battle. The Rebels presented their muskets and released a massive volley at the line of blue clad Pennsylvanians before they could finished loading. McNeil grew angry as numbers of his men fell. He instantly shouted, "Fire!" The blue ranks presented their rifles, the barrels sparking in the bright sun, and fired in response with a thunderous stuttering roar. Dozens of men in the Rebel ranks fell. The smoke from the volleys hung heavily in the air. McNeil then shouted out to his regiment, "Advance!" His men pushed towards the rail fence and began to pull the wooden fence down in order to move towards the woods. To his satisfaction, the Colonel noted that the Rebel troops had withdrawn back into the dark forest. The skirmishers disappeared into the dark woods in pursuit. McNeil could hear the firing continue amid the thick trees and brush. After his men had torn great gaps in the split rail fence, the companies crossed and reassembled their lines, moving in line of battle into the dark trees, dressing their alignment on the colors. Looking behind him, McNeil could see many of his men lying on the dusty road. Some were moving and others were crying out in agony. Another sharp volley tore his attention back toward his new front. Turning his horse, he rode through one of the gaps in the split rail fence into the woods behind his line of men.

As his eyes adjusted to the dark of the shade, the firing of the Rebels could be seen as orange smoky flashes in the darkness. The woods were heavy with acrid smoke that smelled of rotten eggs. The well-trained and drilled men of the 13th needed no orders. They attended to the task at hand continuously trading volleys with the slowly retreating Rebels. No one noticed Colonel McNeil fall from his horse as a minie ball slammed into his temple, killing him instantly.

Behind them, General Meade pushed his division westward on the now cleared road. Behind him, General Hooker urged his Corps forward. He paused to dispatch a rider to find Captain Naylor, who was forward with his cavalry screen. The orders were simple, "Ride to the Potomac. Report back when you find it. Confirm we are on the Rebels' flank."

By 6 pm, as the sun settled low on the western horizon the dispatch riders returned. Lee's flank to the north was closed. The skirmish in the north woods slowed as darkness fell. The weary soldiers of the 1st Army Corps settled down for a cold supper without fires.

BATTLE OF
ANTIETAM
Scale

General John Bell Hood sat and listened while his staff reviewed the reports with him late in the afternoon. Colonel Liddell, and his 11th Mississippi had been directed earlier in the day to push north into the woods beyond the cornfield, adjacent to the white church on the Hagerstown Pike, to counter a large force of Yankees crossing the Antietam. Now he learned that Liddell had been killed. His concern grew as more and more reports indicated that his men were short rations and had been issued little to eat in nearly 3 days. With reports of a large force to his north, he resolved to secure proper rations, a place to rest, and to feed his division. They would be of little use to General Lee without sustenance. Hood directed Major Blanton to locate some of the beeves brought in by Jackson, and attempt to draw several. He had to secure decent rations for his played out men.

The General next made his way to General Lee's headquarters, seeking permission to pull his men off the line, to allow them to cook that evening and get some rest. General Lee directed him to secure this permission from General Jackson, as he now was his direct commander. Swearing under his breath, Hood quickly strode back to his horse to make the ride back out of town and back up the Hagerstown Pike to Jackson's headquarters, behind the Dunker Church. After some searching, he finally found General Jackson asleep under a tree. The sun had passed below the trees, and it was growing rapidly dark. He awoke his commander and asked his question again. Jackson groggily directed, "General Hood you may do as you ask but you must be prepared to move quickly come dawn. I expect them to come at us then!"

Hood replied, "General, I can do that in an instant! I would like to bring them back across the pike into the woods yonder, behind the Church."

Jackson slowly nodded and then tipped his ragged cap back over his eyes. General Hood's command wasted no time in moving into the woods. Major Blanton had secured four cows from the captured Harper's Ferry herd and they were led deep into the woods for slaughter. The experienced Texans had them quickly gutted, skinned, and began to slice cuts for issue to the hungry men who clamored and lined up at the butchering station with pans and cups to receive their ration of raw beef. Some got kidney, liver and tongue cuts, resulting in deal making and trading among the waiting soldiers. Soon the woods behind the German Baptist Brethren Meeting House were lit by hundreds of small fires as the soldiers set to cooking their rations. Each mess also received a small handful of Yankee coffee beans. The noises of makeshift pulverization of the precious beans, could be heard throughout the woods. From the clacking sounds emerging from the dark woods, General Hood surmised that most of his men were employing the plentiful limestone rocks to grind their beans. The men were cheered by the food, and soon the sounds of fiddles and harmonicas filled the warm night air. As Hood looked east towards the direction of his enemy, the woods were strangely dark.

The night air was warm as the Texans settled in to sleep. Many had gone to bed soon after eating, as the good food lulled them into drowsiness. In the distance, beyond the cornfield, occasional shots rang out in the distance as the pickets nervously fired at sounds in the North wood. A light rain began to fall that persisted until the early morning.

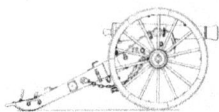

Captain William Poague gladly accepted a tin cup of scalding hot, sugared tea from his First Sergeant. He stood by his horse on the crest of the hill that dominated Mr. Nichodemus's farmhouse below. The old Dutchman had been somewhat bitter about them casting aside his gates and fences to get the guns up across his pasture. As the sky began to glow off to the east with the rising sun, he had decided to double check the orientation of the two 10 pound Parrot rifles, brought up by Captain Barnwell last night from the Artillery Reserve. Poague was happy to have four guns now, as he had been required to detach his 6-pounders two days ago to secure the ford by Shepherdsville. General Stuart had visited the two batteries last evening to emphasize the dangers posed by a large number of Yankees to the North of them. He had explained that they had moved in late yesterday evening. Poague had napped only fitfully that evening and had readied his crews by 5 am, just in case.

As the guns had come up in the darkness last night, Captain Poague directed the gunner near the first piece he approached to send his Number 5 forward with a shell from the limber chest for inspection. It would not be the first time he had found mismatched ammunition and guns. The man brought forward the fixed 16-pound shell and charge bag. Poague inspected it. He smiled as he recognized a Yankee Read shell. This was probably a gift from General Pope, back at Manassas. Nodding his head, he directed the gunner to go ahead and load the guns with percussion-fused shell. The opening shots would clearly be at maximum range, once the Yankees decided to come. Pogue then went over to his two 12 pounders which made up the rest of his battery. He informed those gunners to employ solid shot for now, as he knew they did not have fuses that would reach the extreme distances that the Parrots could, for his opening shots. He looked down below to the east; light smoke from the cook fires of Jubal Early's boys drifted up from the woods below as the soldiers began to cook their breakfast rations. He felt naked on his hilltop. His guns were nearly a quarter mile forward of any supports. Handing the empty teacup back to his First Sergeant, he flatly observed, "Keep the teams ready in the event that we need to leave this place!"

The hot tea soon inspired him to pee, so he ducked back beside his horse and relieved himself. He realized from the mugginess of the morning that it would be a hot day. There was hardly any breeze yet, and the rain from the late evening shrouded the valley of the Antietam to the east, in a low hanging mist. The sound of cracking gunfire back to the north impelled him to quickly button his fly on his trousers and dig for his field glasses from the leather case on his hip. Retrieving the binoculars he faced north ,and looked up the Hagerstown Pike. The road was full of distant marching columns. The troop's blue uniforms looked almost black in the morning half-light. Slightly to the right of the Pike, he could see the firing coming from the edge of the woods that General Stuart had called the "north woods." He could not see lines of infantry there yet, and the action appeared to be from skirmishers firing into the woods from an open pasture north of the cornfield. Scanning back to the columns moving down the road, he cried out, "Yankees on the Pike! 2000 yards, prepare to fire!" His crews scurried to their places as the gunners adjusted their aim, resighting the already loaded and primed guns.

His two section lieutenants shouted, "Ready!" as their gunners retrieved their sights, and stepped clear of the carriages. Poague lowered his field glasses, and shouted, "Fire by file 1st Section, 2nd Section!"

First one, then the second Napoleon guns roared with bright orange flame and clouds of smoke followed by the sharper and longer tongues of flame from the two rifles in the second section. The obscuration from the smoke was difficult to see through in the early dawn light. Poague trotted off to the right of the guns to attempt to see his result. Training his glasses on the column on the pike, he saw, after several seconds, a burst of white smoke on the pike in the middle of a dark mass of marching men. He then saw a second impact again in the midst of the column, further back. The shells of the rifled pieces had arrived first. He then saw troops running off to the left and right of the road further up the column as the bounding solid shot from his two smooth bores ripped through the marching men. He shouted aloud again, "Load Solid Shot and exploding shell!" The crews rolled their pieces back into line and began the reloading process.

General Hooker sat astride his mount at the intersection of the Smoketown Road and the Hagerstown Pike. He had started his morning with the skirmishers of Lieutenant Colonel Anderson's Pennsylvanians as they approached the woods on the left of the pike. As they entered the woods, he could see bright tongues of orange flame from the Rebel's muskets erupt in the deep shade of the trees. He turned his mount, and followed by his headquarters guard he galloped back up the pike past Doubleday's divisional columns. He found General Meade there and quickly consulted with him on his progress. Meade indicated that the woods before them on the east side of the road was full of Rebels, and he was compelled to fight through them with his brigades. Just as the skirmishers fire had slackened, two shells screamed in from the south and exploded in the columns of General Doubleday's advancing divisions. The fire was accurate, and damaging, as he saw scores of men fall. Hooker turned to Captain Reno, and shouted, "Find Monroe! Get his guns up to fire on those heights!"

Reno quickly saluted and galloped back down the pike to the north. Hooker looked back to George Meade and stated, "This is the day we will repair this Republic, General Meade. Make sure your men push and push hard! This is a clear flank and Lee is weak! There may never be another moment like this one!"

Joseph Hooker then spurred his mount back down the road filled with his approaching Divisions. To each commander he encountered, he directed each to form lines of battle and to clear the road. The fight had begun. As he watched his men march and form up on the clover pastures approaching the woods, he hoped that Mansfield was making good time coming up to support his left. He realized with certain clarity. This was a moment of opportunity if he could achieve momentum with his attack. More shells streaked in from the heights beyond the woods to the south. With each blast from the guns, the sound reverberated in the dense humid air. Peering forward, he could see the Rebel guns spewing clouds of dense white smoke on a high cleared pasture, above the white building by the pike, which marked his initial objective. He turned and trotted his horse back north on the pike to find his artillery.

Private Michael Haws lay by the edge of the plowed field, adjacent to the woods, where he had lain all night with his musket propped up on a mound of earth, pointed into the deep woods. Himself, and the rest of the boys from Company E, of the 31st Georgia Infantry, had spent the night shouting taunts to the Yankee skirmishers in the wood and firing ineffective shots into the darkness to "keep them on their toes." The rest of the brigade was behind them in the dense and deep cornfield, marked by a split rail fence, back across the plowed field. If the Yankees came through the woods, they would have to hot foot it back across the deep furrows and clamber back over the fence to re-join their brigade. Looking over his shoulder, he did not relish putting his back to the bluebellys to make that trip. In the distance, cannon had begun to fire. The suns' rays began to illuminate the morning and he could hear rustling and clinking emerging from the woods. Captain Tanner shouted out to his men, "Boys get up! Get ready, they's a comin'!" In the woods, Haws could hear the Yankee officers shouting to their men to dress their lines. Peering along the long burnished barrel, Private Haws could make out dark moving forms amongst the tree trunks. He gripped his musket as he stood and took aim while leaning against a pine tree. Captain Tanner then shouted out to his thin line of skirmishers, "Let em' have it boys!"

Private Haws pulled the stiff trigger on the musket and the dark woods disappeared behind a white cloud of smoke as the weapon rocked back into his shoulder. Instinctively, he brought the musket back down and retrieved a buck and ball cartridge from his cartridge box. As he bit open the cartridge, he could hear men crying out from the woods. After he had rammed the load down the barrel with his ramrod. Captain Tanner shouted out, "Fall back on me boys! Get ready to fire on them again!"

As the men of Company E backed away from the edge of the wood across the plowed field, the Union skirmishers in the woods fired back. Haws could see the orange flashes of their rifles in the dark woods. He ducked his head as an angry whizzing object passed his ear. Moving back, he stopped in loose alignment with the rest of his company, spread across the furrowed field, in a thinly spread line. He then secured a percussion cap from the pouch on his belt and cocked the hammer on his musket, replacing the old cap with a fresh one. Captain Tanner waited until the first group of men, also loosely arrayed in a long line, emerged from the wood. Tanner then ordered, "Make Ready!..... Aim!" After a short pause, as Haws noticed the men in blue were loading their weapons, Tanner shouted out, "Fire!" Again they fired, filling the still air with white smoke that hung like a fog in the early morning air. Haws could clearly see that he had hit the man opposite him.

The men in blue, Haws noted, as he stumbled back again over the furrows, had what looked like fur on their hats. They presented their shiny rifles and returned fire with a loud crackling volley. This time their aim was better, once they had clear targets, and several of the men from Company E fell onto the tumbled and churned ground. Haws attempted to extract a cartridge from his box and dropped it. Looking up after retrieving the paper cartridge, he could see that his entire brigade, behind them, had come up to the fence at the edge of the cornfield in a great gray line. Soldiers against the fence were waving for them to come back. General Lawton was shouting, as he stood by the colors, "Fall back to your lines boys!"

Private Haws needed no further encouragement as he heard the clatter of the Yankee's muskets and the whizzing of minie balls zipping past him as he sprinted the rest of the way across the broken earth to the split rail fence. He quickly clambered over the fence and found a place amongst men of other companies, whom he did not know, and finished loading his musket. His new associates taunted him as he arrived, "Why didn't ya kill more of them?"

Haws looked up from his loading to see the Union regiments emerge from the woods and form battle lines to their front. The uniformity of their equipment, and the order in which they assembled was impressive. The sight reminded him of his grandfather's tales of the Revolution. Another Union Regiment with colors emerged from the right side of the woods and formed another line of battle, further down towards the Smoketown Road. Haws heard a loud roar of cannon fire from behind them, some distance away from the south. He then heard the Captain in the rear of the line nearest him cry out, "Ready!" He also heard the command echo all up and down the line of men on the fence. As he dutifully followed suit, a loud shuttling noise shrieked over their heads and with sharp cracks and white smoke, a salvo of shells exploded in front of the blue troops to his front. He thought he heard the order to "Aim" so he picked out a blue form in the distance. He could see the men in blue falling, as the command, "Fire!" was shouted down the line. The Georgia brigade released a great killing volley into the Union line of battle in the plowed field. The blue line after taking the brunt of the volley and losing dozens of men, took aim and returned a volley. As Private Haws feverishly reloaded, several men near him grunted and moaned as they fell. He was aware in his peripheral vision that a minie ball had blown a chunk out of the tall split rail fence near him.

Again the order was shouted, "Ready! Aim!" and he once again elevated his musket. The men in blue were now advancing with fixed bayonets across the plowed field. As he aimed his musket again, he noticed a great spray of dirt erupt in front of the blue ranks, and watched, amazed, as an iron sphere ripped a man in half within the Yankee ranks. The command to "Fire!" was heard again and the brigade fired another massive volley. The smoke hung thick in front of the rail fence as more hurtling artillery shells swept in from behind them, this time exploding in loud cracks that in turn kicked up clods of dirt around the Union battle line. Many more men in blue were falling. After he had loaded another charge of buck and ball, the orders were called out to leave skirmishers on the fence. The rest were ordered to fall back into the corn. The Yankees in front of them were withdrawing back into the north wood.

A Captain he did not know, pushed him and the other men back into the corn, holding his sword at the level in front of him. He simply ordered, "Push back! Push back, we are gonna form a line in the corn." He backed them off about 30 yards into the tall and dense stalks and formed them on a line. The men around him were excited and were exclaiming how they "whupped the bluebellies" as they feverishly reloaded their muskets. The sound of cannon fire continued and the urgent rustling of shells could be heard, over their heads, as an unknown battery behind them poured shells into the woods beyond. The air was thick with smoke and the noise of exploding shells. Throughout the cornfield, multiple officers commanded, "Fix Bayonets!" The Captain, whom the men called "Taggart" walked the line and explained the concept, "We are gonna let the next line get to the fence and we will meet them there with the bayonet first! Then we will give them a volley!" He then ordered them to stand in ranks and ordered them to place their arms at right shoulder shift, to insure no one got impaled by his neighbor's bayonet in the movement forward again, when it came. They stood and idly conversed amongst each other while they waited. No one was paying attention to the fact that their bayoneted muskets protruded beyond the top of the tall corn stalks, catching the rays of the rising sun.

Major General Joseph Hooker paused by the edge of the woods, where a large plowed field opened up beyond the trees and descended down towards a large field of corn. He pulled his pocket watch from his vest and studied the time. It was nearly 6am, and he was still short of his objective,

Robert Lytle

the white schoolhouse, further down the pike. He listened, as he put the watch away, and he was pleased to hear artillery firing behind him. He glanced up in time to see shells striking in the vicinity of the Rebel battery on the high hill west of the Pike. Captain Monroe had obviously gotten his message. He then looked east; he had expected Meade's troops to be closing in on the cornfield by now, but all he could see were blue clad bodies lying out in the plowed field before it.

As he sat, absorbing the battlefield, a courier arrived from General Meade. The young Captain saluted and reported, "Sir, General Meade begs to report that he has encountered a large rebel force before the cornfield, and the attack of his Division was repulsed by heavy rifle and artillery fire. He is going to attempt another attack with Magilton's Brigade and supports from Ricketts' Division!"

Hooker raised his hand to pause the report, saying only, "Wait a moment, son!" He dug his set of field glasses from his pommel bag and peered towards the cornfield. Something had caught his eye. A cloud's shadow blocking the early morning sun, passed, and the bright rays again played on the silent stalks of tall corn. The light glittered and gleamed off of thousands of bayonets in the midst of the lush green stalks. He turned and summoned another rider of his headquarters guard. Find Reno or Monroe! I want artillery up here now! Also get word to General Hunt through the signalers! I want to place artillery fires on that cornfield. Lots of artillery fires! Go now!"

He lowered his field glasses and ordered General Meade's courier, "Tell General Mead to wait on his next attack. I will bring fire on that field of corn first! Then I will order when he tries it again. You go tell him and then get right back! Do you understand, Captain?"

The young man saluted with a smile, "Yes Sir, I got it! I shall return in an instant!" He then turned his mount and galloped furiously back down the Smoketown Road to the east.

Captain Steven Weed of Battery I, 5th United States Artillery, had expected the attack at dawn to be a little more stimulating than it was proving to be at the moment. He had set his men to swabbing the bores of his rifles from

108

the duel of yesterday, and the men groused that there seemed to be no interest on the enemy's part to continue the contest, as the sun rose.

Weed watched the men, as they finished cleaning the bores of his rifles. His gunners were watching off to the north where all the firing seemed to be coming from. Everyone knew that it was Hooker's attack. The artillery firing and musketry would reach a crescendo, then taper off momentarily, then inevitably, it would rise again. Weed idly looked at the tall hill to the north on his side of the Antietam and noticed the signalmen waving their red and white flags wildly. After a few moments, he saw a horseman come riding at a gallop down the winding road from the top of the hill. The horseman crossed through the empty streets of Porterstown and began to ascend the hill towards him. It was Lieutenant Colonel Hayes. He pulled up alongside Weed, and breathlessly ordered, "Captain Weed, ready your guns for some long range work!" Hays dismounted and pointed northwest towards a distant and small white building, "Captain Weed, train your glass on that small white building by the pike, yonder. Do you see it?" Weed put his own field glasses to his eyes and found the structure, replying, "Yes, I can see it."

Hayes then said, "Now scan to the right. The ground dips down a ways and then you will see a broad field of corn. Can you see that?" Weed studied for a moment, and responded, "Sir, I see two fields, one near a road and another far off by some woods." Hayes quickly replied, "It is the far one!" Weed then replied, "Sir that is nearly 2500 yards off, just guessing of course!"

Hayes instructed, "Captain Weed, General Hooker is requesting firing from every gun available into that field of corn. He is asking for 10 rounds per gun from your battery. Give him something good! It is full of Rebel infantry, and they have pushed his attack back. Can you shoot case shot that far?"

Stephen Weed's mind raced, images of his firing tables danced in his head. He turned and shouted towards his nearest limber crew, "Nance, what is the time of flight for 2500 yards?"

The Private hearing his name, nodded and quickly lifted the copper covered lid of the limber chest, and studied the table on the underside for a moment before shouting back, "six and a half seconds sir!" Weed's thoughts were on calculations, time fuses did not work well with rifles. The Bormanns were notorious for not lighting properly, paper ones would be better. He shouted out to his First Sergeant, "Sergeant Tice! Do we have paper fuse wells and fuses?" First Sergeant Tice, without hesitating replied, "Yes sir, in the battery wagon!"

Weed shouted back, "Get them! I will need sixty of the 10 second fuses!" He then turned to Lieutenant Colonel Hayes, "I'll give it a try sir! I am not very sure we will get this to work, but it is better than scratchin' our asses on this hill doing nothing!" Weed then turned to his crews and shouted, "We got infantry at 2500 yards! Case Shot! Employ paper time fuses cut for six seconds!"

The crews scrambled to prepare rounds as the First Sergeant distributed the rarely used fuses and fuse wells to the limber crews behind the gun line. Two crews were short the saws used to cut the fuses, and the limber crews tossed them the tools after they had cut their own fuses.

Weed hoped that the cutting process would enhance the performance of the time fuses. The brass obturating cups on the Parrot case shot and shell did not allow charge gasses to pass around the shell. The fuse would not ignite until the projectile exited the barrel. He hoped that by cutting the 10-second fuses off, thus removing the lacquered surface of the prepackaged paper fuses, he would obtain greater reliability.

As the crews finished their loading, the section lieutenants shouted out "Ready!" in a sequence that was slower than usual. Weed then trotted to each gunner and confirmed the lay. They did not have a clear understanding of their target. After he had finished, he returned back to Lieutenant Colonel Hayes'. He had now gotten back onto his mount. Weed looked up at him and asked, "10 rounds per gun?" Hayes nodded.

Weed nodded and then shouted, "By Battery! Fire!"

The six 20 pound Parrot rifles fired in near perfect synchronization, each spitting a long tongue of orange flame and white smoke into the early morning air. The heavy guns and carriages violently rolled back on the top of the ridge. Weed raised his field glasses and mentally counted off six seconds, as the long Read case-shot projectiles screamed across the Antietam Creek valley towards the distant cornfield beyond. One round appeared to burst well short of the field, but the remaining five appeared to be right in the middle of the distant corn. He lowered his glasses and watched his crews preparing the second volley.

Captain Gibbs and First Sergeant Mace rode at the head of Company L of the Ohio Light Artillery behind General Gibbon's infantry brigade. They were unfamiliar with the leadership of the brigade as they had been detailed away from the artillery reserve to General Hooker's Corps two days ago. Since then, they had dutifully followed Gibbon and his troops across the Antietam and wherever they had camped. As they approached, the increasing noise of battle could be heard, further south on the Hagerstown Pike. A rider galloped up to Captain Gibbs and anxiously asked, "Sir, do you have an assignment?" Gibbs turned to Mace with a shrug, and then turned back to the anxious Sergeant, "No Sergeant, but I suspect I am about to get one!"

The Sergeant replied, "Sir, Captain Monroe needs you to report to the front of the column! You shall be placed by the Corps Commander!" He then turned his mount and rode back to the south shouting to the infantry on the road ahead of them as he passed, "Guns up! Clear the road! Guns up!"

Sergeant Mace turned and rode towards his sections shouting, "Stay on the Captain, and the colors! Move fast lads, we have a dance card!" The drivers on the leaders slapped their reins on the necks of the horses and the battery picked up speed, rumbling, and shaking the limbers and carriages of the guns. They raced down the Hagerstown Pike, towards a patch of woods to the front of them, shrouded in white smoke of artillery and musketry. As they approached the edge of the woods, an officer on horseback waved for Captain Gibbs in a motion that clearly indicated for the racing company to follow him. As they rode between the woods, First Sergeant Mace became aware of heavy firing in the trees to his right as they passed. His instincts immediately told him they were too far forward. He muttered to himself as he rode, "We are about to get buggered here!" Their guide, a Captain who introduced himself as "Monroe," pointed out a clear spot, just short of a plowed field near two stacks of wheat straw. Mace looked beyond the plowed field and could see bodies of men in blue in the middle of the furrowed earth. Beyond that, he could see a wide cornfield that extended the width of the field and ended quite near their designated position. A tidy farmhouse with a horse barn, marked their right flank. Mace wondered if they were the first to have reached this farmyard, as he could see no bodies near where they had stopped. He ceased his pondering, nevertheless, and resumed his First Sergeant's role, shouting, "Move it boys! Quit yer gawkin' and unlimber the guns!"

The teams swiftly pulled forward and the crews disconnected the pin tails of the limber chests from the lunettes of the Napoleons. After they had rolled the guns to face about, Captain Gibbs cried out, "Load spherical case! Cut your fuses to two seconds! Report ready by section!" Mace carefully watched his men as they executed their gun drill. He noted one man in second section bringing up his fixed round in his hands instead of using his pouch. He made a mental note to fix that, later. He glanced off to his left and could see in the distance another battery being pulled up across the wide plowed field from the Smoketown Road. He understood, at that instant, that their target was troops in the corn. Looking toward the vast green field before them, he realized just how close the corn was to them. He shouted out quickly for emphasis, "Look lively boys! Remember your drill!" He decided to ride over to Captain Gibbs as the men completed their loading drills.

Arriving beside the Captain, who was intently staring at the vast field of corn, Mace asked, "Beggin' your pardon Sir, but will we have supporting infantry here?" Gibbs, preoccupied, replied, "They are supposed to be in the woods to our left. Captain Monroe did not mention what was to the left. The cornfield has at least a brigade of Rebs in it." Mace quickly responded, "I suggest canister next, Sir!" Gibbs gave him a worried look, and retorted, "Start preparing double shotted canister, First Sergeant! I like this posting far less than you!"

With admirable rapidity the Section Lieutenants shouted out, "Ready!"

Captain Gibbs tersely shouted, "By File! Fire!"

In the tall corn, Captain Taggert had just finished with a visit from General Lawton who led his white horse by the reins on foot in the dense corn. Men were stepping out of line and grabbing ears off the stalks for later. The sounds of firing were increasing in the distance, but the corn they stood in seemed to be a peaceful refuge. The shade afforded to the men by the tall stalks took the edge off the growing heat of the morning. The men in the company Private Haws found himself stuck with, continued with their cheerful banter. One had extracted his ramrod and twirled it about, occasionally employing it to emphasize a point in a discussion, or tipping up the brim of a cap of one of his company mates. Hawes noticed that the General had moved his horse off to his left, and paused again, holding it's reins, as he chatted and encouraged his men further down the line from where he stood. He wished he could leave the spot where he was and get back to his friends, but the thickness of the corn and the scattered way they had come back, discouraged that.

Six sharp cracks erupted very near where he stood. They were ear splittingly loud, like a close strike of lightning, followed by an evil and rapid ripping noise. The broad white flank of General Lawton's horse erupted in a spray of hot red blood, splintered organs and meat, as a spherical case shot tore through the animal with a loud hollow sounding thump. A large gory chunk of horsemeat slammed into Haws chest and knocked him backwards onto the ground. He lay dazed as six corresponding bangs erupted behind him, deeper in the corn. He could hear the shrieks and cries of men as more of the horrible blasts erupted all around him. Large objects were tearing through the stalks of corn with rattling shredding noises as the projectiles tore into the flesh of men, cobs of ripening corn, and the tough green stalks of the corn plants. Haws could see yellow kernels of corn mixed with red blood, falling like rain, and spraying through the air, along with fragments of green fronds. He rolled over onto his stomach and pushed away the still hot chunk of horsemeat from his chest. He could see nothing but the legs and boots of the men who had stood around him. He smelled the intense coppery odor of blood and entrails mixed with the smell of fresh corn. He began to crawl towards the fence, low on his belly. He had secured a musket, having lost his own, and drug it with him as six more loud claps sounded out spraying more smaller objects that ripped through the stalks with urgent intensity. As he crawled, he could hear blast, after blast behind him and high overhead. Following those noises, he heard hard thumps as other projectiles impacted the dark ground all around him. He realized they were being fired upon by artillery from all sides. After what seemed like an eternity, he reached the brushy edge of the cornfield. He noticed several frightened men had possessed the same idea. Another spaced series of claps, like the strikes of lightening, slammed into his ears. Too late, he brought his hands up to plug his ears. He sensed that objects were passing mere feet above his back as he tried to make himself as low to the ground as he could lie. For the next 20 minutes he lay and endured a perfect Hell, colored green and deafeningly loud.

The firing stopped, and Haws looked up through the tangled weeds at the edge of the field. The edge of the wood filled with lines of troops in blue that advanced across the plowed furrows to the beat of drums. Thousands of men approached with glittering bayonets. Rising to a crouch he signaled to the other men, "We best get back!" He half ran, and half scrambled. Much of the corn had been knocked down where he had sheltered. Finding

General Lawton's dead horse, he noticed the General laying by the animal. He was clearly dead. A few yards behind him he found the colors of his regiment. He pried the staff from the stiff hands of the dead color bearer and ran back to the west through the remaining high corn. As he scrambled over the fence at the far side of the cornfield, Haws could see troops forming lines in front of him, in a field of wheat stubble, approaching closer, he could recognize the colors of the rest of his Brigade. The men waved to him to hurry. As he rejoined the survivors several officers he did not know, clapped him on the back and congratulated him on saving the colors of the 31st Georgia. Private Hawes had, by virtue of surviving, become the regiment's new color bearer.

Major General George McClellan folded the dispatch after reading it and returned it to Lieutenant Colonel Colburn. Colburn had just received the message from his signalers atop their rough timber tower on the crest of the prominence above Mr. Prye's farm. McClellan turned to General Porter and the Prince De Joinville, who were spending the morning with him, and calmly remarked, "Joseph Hooker has been wounded and is being carried from the field! It is a report from Marcy."

General Porter looked shocked, and replied, "Damn! I recommend you name Meade to take charge, Sir! He should be next in seniority! Hopefully it is not mortal." McClellan gravely nodded, and he turned to Captain Custer and motioned him over. When the long-haired cavalry officer trotted over, McClellan ordered, "George! Send word to General Sumner to commit his corps to the right! Also get word to Brigadier General Marcy to inform George Meade that he is now the commander of the 1st Corps!" Captain Custer smartly saluted and trotted to his horse. Prince De Joinville, seeing the General's growing urgency, offered helpfully, "Sir, I shall ask your signalers to attempt to obtain an update on General Mansfield's Corps!" McClellan gratefully nodded; he had expected Hooker's dawn attack to have progressed further. From what he could observe from the prominence, stubborn resistance lingered north of the white schoolhouse on the ridge in the distance. Clouds of white smoke rose from the woods and the fields in a semi-circle around the small distinctive structure.

McClellan had earnestly hoped that he could have caused Lee's flank to collapse. He extracted his watch and looked at the time, 7 am. The guns below him to the left fired another long-range salvo into the fray that was developing on the far right of his lines. He wondered what number of troops Lee held available across the valley around Sharpsburg. George McClellan slowly began to realize that Lee must have rejoined his divided forces. He resolved to keep Porter and Franklin's corps close by. He might require a large reserve.

Joshua bit the end off of a cheap sutler's cigar, it was his last one, and lit it with a Lucifer match that he struck by dragging the tip on the rim of the wheel of the number one gun. The crewmen had been standing in their positions for two idle hours watching the growing battle off to the northwest. They had no orders, but they could see large groups of troops massing beside General Pleasanton's cavalry below. Captain Haines explained to them that they were Sumner's Corps. Haines had opined that they were coming up late from his limited understanding of what was supposed to be happening in the grand plan of the battle.

Joshua found it interesting, as he puffed on his cigar, he could make out the paths of long-range fires crossing his front, from the slight trails of smoke that emerged from the burning fuses of the shells in flight. Someone with rifled guns was shelling a cornfield far off in the distance. He wondered how they could tell friend from foe at such distances. He idly watched as another series of the rounds exploded in mute white puffs above the field.

The booms of the explosions could be heard after a short delay. He did not envy whoever was underneath those shells.

After a few more puffs, he realized that the firing far off to his left had ceased. He noticed movement far off to the right. Long lines of men in dark uniforms had emerged from the woods to the far north. More lines of men were moving towards the white building at the center. Captain Haines saw the movement as well and shouted out, "Look to the right! That has to be General Hooker's men!" From the great distance the lines disappeared from view as they entered the cornfield. Only the bright flags of the regimental colors could be seen as the lines of battle made their way through the corn. Joshua noticed that columns of more men were coming down a pike that separated the cornfield from the woods. They too, quickly transitioned into lines of battle and made their way through the large cornfield. Cannon that had been firing on the flanks had ceased as their line of sight was masked by the advancing ranks of blue clad men.

O'Keefe paused on his rounds by Joshua and observed, "Many an orphan and widow is about to be made down there! Keep on yer toes, boys! That vast movement yonder will likely bring something for us to shoot at from across the way!"

Down in a hollow, west of the cornfield, they could see remnants of Rebel regiments forming a line to counter the approaching blue clad ranks. The leading lines of battle had emerged from the far side of the corn. The outnumbered Rebel troops fired a volley into the approaching blue ranks and the long advancing lines halted, delivering a heavy volley in response. Joshua expected the outnumbered Rebels to disperse and retreat back up toward the woods and the white structure, but they stood their ground, responding with another volley. He looked above them and could see more troops in blue approaching down the Hagerstown Pike. They had nearly come adjacent to the white building, when a massive eruption of white smoke emerged from the wood to their west. The impact of the flanking volley seemed to cause a shudder in the ranks of the distant troops. They quickly faced the threat and formed a line of battle, but were too late to deliver a volley in response before receiving another great killing fusillade of musket fire. Joshua watched as the advance column disintegrated into individual fleeing men. He then saw further south, on the Hagerstown pike below the white building, teams of horses emerging from the woods to the west. The Rebel artillery was unmasking.

Joshua turned to shout, but First Sergeant O'Keefe, seeing the same development, cried out, "Stand to! To your places!"

Captain Haines turned and trained his field glasses towards the axis marked by O'Keefe's outstretched arm. After a seconds study, he shouted, "Load solid shot, 1900 yards! Just south of the white barn!"

Joshua shouted out to his men words of encouragement as he watched them load the guns. He knew the Rebel guns, that were quickly forming a line of batteries, were far beyond their range for any munition, except solid shot. At best, they could strip horses away and disable their mobility. He glanced down below and saw men of General Sumner's lead divisions, marching up the hills that led towards the fight developing in the west. Long columns of men behind them waded across the knee-deep ford in the creek.

Lieutenant Pennington shouted out, "Ready!" when his two guns had completed their loading. He was soon followed by Lieutenants Platt and Woodruff, as their men had prepared their guns. Joshua walked well to the left; he noted a slight breeze blowing to the north. At these ranges, every eye would be necessary to assist Captain Haines in marking his effects. The Captain gave the command, "By file! Fire!"

Joshua watched as the first bronze gun, trunnion number 003, his old gun, as it fired. As the great orange flame spewed from its four inch bore, he noted the characteristic dip of the muzzle as the great mass of the breech slammed onto the elevating screw and bounced up, then down, emitting a bell-like tone. The heavy olive drab carriage violently rolled back, halting 10 feet back from its original position. Corporal Page's crew quickly laid hands on the great wooden wheels and the handspike, rolling it back forward. He turned his gaze swiftly out and looked towards the Rebel batteries that had begun to fire at the approaching lines of Union troops advancing across the broad pastures and wheat fields, beyond the corn. He saw a puff of dust short of the Rebel guns, marking the first skip of the iron sphere, as the other guns in his battery fired in sequence. In the distance he saw a disturbance in a limber team by the nearest Rebel gun, and then he saw several horses down on the ground. Page had wisely aimed for the biggest target he could find, which was the Rebel commander's horses. Joshua then could make out more puffs shy of the Rebel guns, marking the skips of successive rounds. Hopefully, they would compel the enemy commander to leave his ground. It was the only way they could make a difference.

General Jackson rode into General Hood's camp as his men were cooking their breakfasts. The crackling of musketry to the north, and now to the east, had the men on edge. They knew the call would be coming soon. General Hood had just received report that General Lawton, whom he had sent forward last night, was down and presumed dead. He had already issued the order to his men to be ready to move, soon. He absently dug into his vest pocket, when he saw General Jackson approaching his camp with his entourage. Glancing at his watch he noted the time, 7 am. Unfortunately, his men would likely have to wait until later to eat.

Jackson casually returned John Bell Hood's salute and stated, "General, I have need of your division. You are to counterattack with all you have to drive the Federals from the field! You will receive supports on your right by General McLaws and the forces of General Hill. Push them back to that wood to the north. I will hold this ground with General Early refusing the left! See to it, General!"

Hood nodded, and shouted for his adjutant. The young Captain, after receiving his orders, found a young drummer nearest to him and commanded him to begin playing the long roll. He then rode through the woods and ordered every other drummer he could find to do the same.

Sergeant Charles Ake and his messmates were attempting to soften the chunks of tough meat they had cooked the night prior, over their breakfast fire. The men were somber as they heard the sounds of battle increasing in the woods north of them. They all knew their turn would soon come. When he heard the long roll, Sergeant Ake announced in a weary voice, "Shit! Grab your rifles, boys! We got work to attend to!" As if to punctuate the urgency of the moment a stray Union shell tore through the treetops overhead, bursting deep in the woods behind the Dunker Church. Ake heard other men cursing and shouting in the distance. Once they had shouldered their bedrolls and had fallen into line with the rest of the 1st Texas, Ake walked along his line and let them pluck the still hot chunks of beef from the makeshift frying pan. Private Simmons had to bounce his particular hot piece of beef from hand to hand until it cooled. He then offered his remaining piece of meat to another Private from another mess, who looked particularly hungry, saying, "Here boy, it ain't much, but it should hold you till we get back!"

Colonel Work trooped the line on his buckskin gelding, shouting, "First

Texas! It is my honor to serve with you! Let's show them how Texians fight! Fix Bayonets!"

All along the lines of General Hood's division, the clatter of men fixing bayonets onto the muzzles of their muskets could be heard. The officers then ordered the lines in the shade of the wood to move towards the Hagerstown Pike. The early morning sun had brightened the green pastures beyond the trees. As the men advanced, they could see and smell the acrid white smoke drifting by in the open. The regimental lines were then halted at the edge of the woods under the shade of the last trees. The officers shouted, "Wait on them to come up to the pike! Load!" Again the clatter and clanking of thousands of ramrods shoving home cartridges echoed up and down the lines.

After several minutes of anxious waiting, Sergeant Ake saw a Union line of battle come into view. To his amazement, they were marching perpendicular to their lines. The soldiers in blue were marching past the line of woods, completely unaware of their presence. He was impressed by their flawless step, and alignment. Behind the well ordered ranks, drummers beat common time, governing their rate of approach, while the officers in advance of the double ranks of troops pointed their swords towards the Dunker Church and several batteries of the Reverend Pendleton's guns that were shelling other approaching Union Regiments.

Nearly all of them heard Colonel Work cry out, "Ready!........ Aim!" before the Captains of the Regiment echoed the command. The cocking of thousands of hammers made a low and ominous chatter, like a legion of crickets, as the soldiers brought their muskets up. As each man selected a point of aim on the marching target, Ake commented, "This is fixin' to be a bushwackin'"

The cry went up from the officers, "Fire!" The woods edge was blanketed in dense white powder smoke as their initial volley erupted in a loud crackling roar. The enfilading volley shredded the closest of the marching troops, a single round in many cases, hitting more than one man. Blue clad bodies marked the clover pasture as the confused soldiers ran in multiple directions. Their sergeants and officers vainly attempted to rally them. The men of the 1st Texas instinctively began to reload, without waiting on the orders. Colonel Work, sensing their actions, paused a moment before ordering, "Charge Bayonets!" Each man in the regiment then brought his rifle up before him with the bayonet pointing slightly up and out. Work, satisfied that they were ready, shouted out "Advance!" The drummers beat the time as the brigades emerged from the shady woods towards their opponents. After they had crossed the pike, Ake could see the next regiment in the Union line of advance was turning and forming a line of battle to meet the advance of Hood's Division as they emerged from the woods. The Union commander, unnerved by the development on his flank, gave the order to aim and fire at nearly 150 yards distant from the approaching Texas brigades. The incoming volley hit low, but dropped men, nonetheless, with wounds to the legs. Colonel Work coolly advanced his regiment until they were quite close to the feverishly reloading Union regiment and ordered his men to fire their next volley. The impact of the volley cut great gaps in the Union ranks, but the men gamely closed ranks and returned the fire. Sergeant Ake saw one of his messmates fall, clutching his face. There was no time to stop and help, as the command to advance was shouted by the officers again, after they had reloaded. Work closed his command to 50 yards, before he halted and ordered the next volley. At that distance, the men could clearly see the eagles on the Union soldiers cartridge box straps. The Yankee soldiers had just returned their ramrods to their channels and were capping their rifles when the order "Fire" was heard. The volley broke the resolve of the Union soldiers, and they broke and ran.

Sergeant Ake became preoccupied with keeping his men in dress as they stepped out through the downhill open pasture. He could see as he glanced forward that they were approaching a large cornfield that spanned their entire front. As they neared the edge of the cornfield, another Union regiment stepped out of the tall stalks facing them. Colonel Work turned, and shouted out, "Charge men! Bayonets!" He then spurred his horse with his sword pointed forward. The men forgot the choking smoke and their thirst after battling two regiments in the open pasture, and ran yelling and screaming with their bayonets thrust forward. Sergeant Ake had practiced his bayonet thrusts plenty, and had taught his men the same, yet he had never actually had to employ that weapon until this instant. As he closed in on a short man in blue, a corporal he noticed, he brought his musket up to shoulder height, as practiced in "epi melee," and shoved his musket forward. He had instinctively turned the musket sideways as he plunged down pointing the tip at the left side of the man's chest to avoid the leather shoulder strap of his cartridge box. He saw the shock in the Corporal's eyes as the sharp steel penetrated his chest. The man dropped his rifle and fell backwards. Ake, expertly turned his rifle and yanked the point back out. Seeing another man, who was rapidly backing away into the corn, he brought his rifle up, and after cocking the hammer, fired. Through the smoke, he saw the man drop to his knees and fall face forward. The next several seconds were a blur. Another man in blue attempted to lunge his bayonet at him. Ake brought his rifle up with both hands and parried the stroke as another Texan impaled his assailant in the stomach. Soon they had pressed into the corn chasing men ahead of them that could be heard, rather than seen, running before them. Ake could hear the shouts of their officers, "Keep in line! Keep your dress!" None of them were listening. Up ahead, he heard a voice shouting, "Present! Fire!," and a loud roar of musket fire was heard. A wave of minie balls swept in with a crackling and snapping noise as they clipped through corn stalks. Ake could see men on either side of him fall as the balls smacked loudly into them. He saw Captain White for a brief instant, running diagonally in front of him, with his sword drawn, but soon lost sight of him. He was aware of his charges following him, but there was little time to pause. They needed to rally as confusion reigned in the tall stalks. He could not catch sight of the colors.

Ake, and several of the men from his company, warily followed their leveled bayonets through the tall corn toward where he had last seen Captain White. Screams of men mingled with rifle shots and the occasional whizzing shells, overhead filled the stifling smoky air. Over the din, he heard voices calling out to his left amidst the deep and shredded corn, "First Texas! Rally on me boys!" He pushed through the stalks following his bayonet until he spied several men in butternut, milling around Captain White. White, hatless, pointed his sword towards the open field that was barely visible through the thick stalks, and commanded, "Quick! Form a line on me! Load your muskets! We got a line of Yankees forming in the field out there by a battery!" The men scrambled to form a line. Ake noticed that many were missing, but he could hear more men coming up behind them. The men in the ragged ranks feverishly scrambled to load their muskets.

Brigadier General John Gibbon rode to the farmhouse off to the right of the Hagerstown Pike as his brigade deployed from line of march. He found Colonel Bragg and directed him to push off the road to the left and establish a line between the battery by the haystacks, over to where another regiment was aligning, halfway down a plowed field. Looking over the confused field, he guessed the troops he saw forming there were Meade's Division. Things looked bad, as troops were exiting the cornfield in an obvious rout. He pointed out a reddish colored flag in the middle of the corn to Colonel Bragg, and commanded, "The Rebs are gonna come out of that corn soon! This will be a close thing! Stand fast here and support this battery to your right. When the Rebs show at the edge of the field, facing you, stop them! Coordinate with the battery commander and anchor your line on his position!"

Gibbon paused by the battery, which sat silent, and found the commander, Captain Gibbs. Gibbs saluted and said, " I appreciate the supports, Sir! The General put us way too close to the action, and it has been a near thing here for the past half hour! We had to cease our fires when those Pennsylvania boys rushed into the corn. Before that, we put six salvos of canister into that field. I've got it loaded now, double-shotted!"

Gibbon nodded; sometimes he wished he had stayed in place as an artilleryman himself. The rank offered to regulars to command volunteer troops had tempted him away. He asked, "What battery is this Captain?"

Gibbs smiled and replied, "Battery L, Ohio Light, sir!"

Gibbon replied, "General Doubleday sends his regards, Captain! Can you anchor my brigade? What is your ammunition supply?"

Gibbs replied, "Sir, if your boys will stand, then I will likewise! I still got lots of shell and case shot, but I will be out of canister after three more engagements, unless you brought up wagons, sir!"

Gibbon shook his head, "Captain all I have with me is my brigade, they took my artillery for the fight on the right of us. I will send a runner to see if I can locate resupply. For now, stand fast where you are!"

As the troops of the 6th Wisconsin Volunteer Infantry Regiment established their line adjacent to the battery, First Sergeant Mace met with the Sergeant Major of the regiment where the right flank of the troops met his number one section. Mace advised the Sergeant Major, "Keep a sharp eye out when the last bunch of infantry retreat out of that corn! I am noticing fewer and fewer coming out! My fear is the rest of our lads in there are wounded or dead. I would propose to you, Sergeant Major, that the next visitors to that fence forward would be our Rebel friends!"

The two Sergeants shook hands and returned to overseeing their commands. Mace was concerned by his count of canister. The corn lay only 80 yards away. He believed he had seen the last of the fleeing Pennsylvanians, and smoke from the battle raging off to his right eerily drifted through the quiet corn. He did not have a good feeling about his position, and shouted out to his Captain, "Sir, I recommend to you to have them prime the pieces and stand ready!" Captain Gibbs nodded and gave the command. Quartermaster Sergeant Boldman trotted over to Mace to report, "Caissons got 6 rounds each for each of our guns, First Sergeant! That makes three shots only, if we keep double-shotting!" Mace grimly nodded, and replied, "Double shot it is, lad! Tell the caisson and limber crews to remove the shipping plugs from the spherical case, double quick!"

Sergeant Boldman made a worried face and trotted off. Mace decided to watch the men close once they had exhausted canister. If the Rebs made a hard push out of the cornfield, they would be in for some dangerous work.

Captain White commanded in a sharp whisper, "Alright boys move it up! Don't show yourselves until we get to where the corn is down. When we shoot, put your first volley on them guns off to the left!"

Sergeant Ake repeated the instruction, in case the remaining men of his mess had not heard it. He focused on keeping them dressed, and on line, as they carefully trod forward through the tangled corn stalks. Looking forward, he could see where the field was shorn by the fire and the number of motionless bodies they had to step around, increased. He decided to stop looking down as each glance at the still forms revealed a new horror. The leaves brushing his face felt wet as if they were covered with dew. Wiping his hand on his face and looking at it, he realized it was blood. They stopped short of the exposed edge of the field where only four rows of tattered corn protected them from observation. Ake could see new rows of Union troops forming lines across the full frontage of the plowed field, separating the cornfield, from the wood beyond. Soon the deep voice of Colonel Work could be heard as he walked the line, "Steady boys! When I order ya'll to advance, come out of the corn quick! I don't need to give you the order to make ready and we won't show the colors till we get clear of the corn. Ya'll fire, when I call for it!"

Sergeant Ake had the men around him check to insure they had capped their muskets; there would be no time once they had exposed themselves. As they waited, the battle off to their left had apparently increased in intensity, as the firing of cannon and muskets filled the air with a violent clatter. Ake wiped his face on his sleeve. He realized that his clothes were soaked with sweat and the sweat from his brow burned his eyes.

Colonel Work again came down the line exhorting in a hoarse voice, "Push them as hard as you can boys. We'll have the 5th Texas following us!"

First Sergeant Mace carefully watched the pair of soldiers by the breeches of his six guns as they ran the priming wires down the vents to puncture the charge bags and insert the brass friction primers into the vents of the large bronze guns. The number four crewmen on each gun had each attached their lanyard cords to the loops on the friction primers, when movement in the corn caught his eye. A loud cry of "Advance!" emerged from the segment of the field closest to him, and a cluster of men began to emerge, barely 80 yards distant from the men and guns of Battery L. Mace, to his horror, noted that they had emerged from an angle on the right of field; all of his guns were oriented towards the center of the field. His command beat the Captain's, "Action right on the oblique!"

The crews rushed to their carriages and laid hold of the handspikes to swivel the guns, the Rebels emerging from the corn delivered a loud sputtering volley. A hail of minie balls instantly impacted on and around the men of Battery L. First Sergeant Mace felt an angry tug on his frock coat, as a minie ball grazed the upper sleeve. All the men of gun number one fell, and three of the crewmen of number two gun were also down. The noises coming from the horses and the shouts of the limber crews, told him that horses were down as well. Captain Gibbs scrambled to his feet after he extracted himself from his wounded horse. He screamed in a desperate tone, "By Battery, Fire!" Three of the six Napoleon guns of the battery fired in a great roar. First Sergeant Mace ran forward and locating the lanyard cord for gun number one, turned and yanked the lanyard firing off the fourth shot. Lieutenant Anderson, wounded in the arm by the volley, seized the lanyard of 3rd Section's first gun, with his wounded hand while holding the bleeding arm with the other and awkwardly fired the fifth gun. When Mace cried out for the limber men to come up to replace the fallen crews, he was dismayed to see only three men come forward for the decimated 1st Section. He heard Captain Gibbs call out, "Load Canister!" And seeing no one else, he made his way to the limber and grabbed two and cut away the charge bag on one with the limber chest knife to prepare a double shot. The infantry regiment to his left responded with a heavy volley that struck many of the now exposed Confederate soldiers. Yet, more and more gray clad men were appearing from the corn now, as the follow on regiments pushed their way out of the thick stalks.

As First Sergeant Mace trotted back to the number one gun, he was surprised to see the Sergeant Major of the 6th Wisconsin again; he had brought a dozen men with him. Seeing the First Sergeant he shouted, "First Sergeant! I have volunteers to man your guns! If you can show them how, they can help!"

Mace placed the fixed shot into a man's hands and instructed him how to place it in the bore. Another volley of minie balls ripped through the air and into the dirt around the battery, and one of his new volunteers fell, struck in the head. The men, while confused by their new roles, did as instructed, and the battery got another salvo of canister into the corn as the Regiment beside them unleashed another thunderous volley. The Rebel troops were advancing now in lines out of the corn into the plowed field. From Mace's perspective, it appeared that it was more than three regiments with their red battle flags hanging still in the humid mid-morning air. As they fired their last battery salvo, the cry went up from the limber teams, "We're outta canister!" First Sergeant Mace looked towards Captain Gibbs, and catching his glance, the Captain simply nodded. Mace cried out, "Load Rotten Shot!" Turning to his infantrymen manning the guns he directed, "Once you got this load down, get way back from the front of the gun! Do you understand?" He then ran to his volunteer limber crew and pointed them out, "Get the red painted ones! Bring them to the gun as they are!"

The advancing Rebels brought their rifles up as the crews of Battery L completed their loading. As First Sergeant Mace glanced down the line, he was astonished to see General Gibbon, himself, elevating one of the guns on foot, and shouting instructions on Point Blank to one of the infantrymen. Captain Gibbs' cry, "By Battery, Fire!" was heard above the din of musketry all around them. The six guns roared as one, followed instantly by six loud claps as the spherical case shot rounds exploded at the muzzles. Two of the volunteer crewmen, who had lingered too near the muzzles when the pieces fired, fell wounded by the fragments of the exploding rounds. Suddenly, another great volley of musketry emerged from the eastern side of the cornfield. General Sumner's Corps was attacking from the east. As the firing increased, the Rebel troops retreated back through the shredded corn, leaving men in piles in the plowed field and hanging on the fence of the cornfield.

General Lee sat under his awning by his map table reading returns from Daniel Harvey Hill when a new courier arrived and handed a folded message to Major Venable. Venable opened the message and scanned it before announcing to the General, "Sir, General Jackson reports that he has stopped a Union attack in the west wood and that General Hood pushed all the way back to the north wood but is now under heavy pressure from the north and east. General Jackson thinks we are receiving another Corps attack towards the center! Lee silently nodded and asked, "What news have you from General Longstreet?" Venable shook his head and replied, "No news sir, and we have no additional news of General A.P. Hill either."

Lee rose from his chair and looked at the map on the wooden table under his awning. He silently ran his hand over the positions of his army from north to south in a thoughtful fashion. After a few moments thought, he commanded Major Venable, "Major, if you would be so kind, advise General Jackson to prepare to commit General McLaws to support General Daniel Harvey Hill. I imagine he will be next to be tested by this attack." Lee found the action on only one side of his defense to be strangely comforting. It seemed to him, that General McClellan was taking a very simplistic approach to this fight. It was clear to him that his opponent was paying all his attention to an attempt to roll a flank without considering supporting attacks. Other returns were causing him concern, as the powerful Union artillery was costing him guns, horses, and trained men. He grimly accepted that such was the cost of great battles. Perhaps, he reasoned, if he could hold the Federals at bay here, the world would notice.

Joshua saw the blue clad troops forming on the ridge across the creek from them, as he heard First Sergeant O'Keefe shout, "Limber the guns boys! We are masked!"

Joshua directed his men to remove the hobbles from the caisson leaders as the cannoneers stowed and latched down their implements. Once the last items were secured, the limber teams drove the horses out in front of the guns, as the crews reversed them by pulling on the wheels and the handspikes, and lifted the lunettes up to hitch them to the pin tails of the limbers. Company M had all their guns hitched in a little less than four minutes, and at Captain Haine's signal, they followed him and the color bearer back down the steep pasture, towards the ford below. As they reached the ford, O'Keefe shouted out, "Drive through the ford slow! It won't hurt the wheels to get a good soakin'!" The drivers fought the team

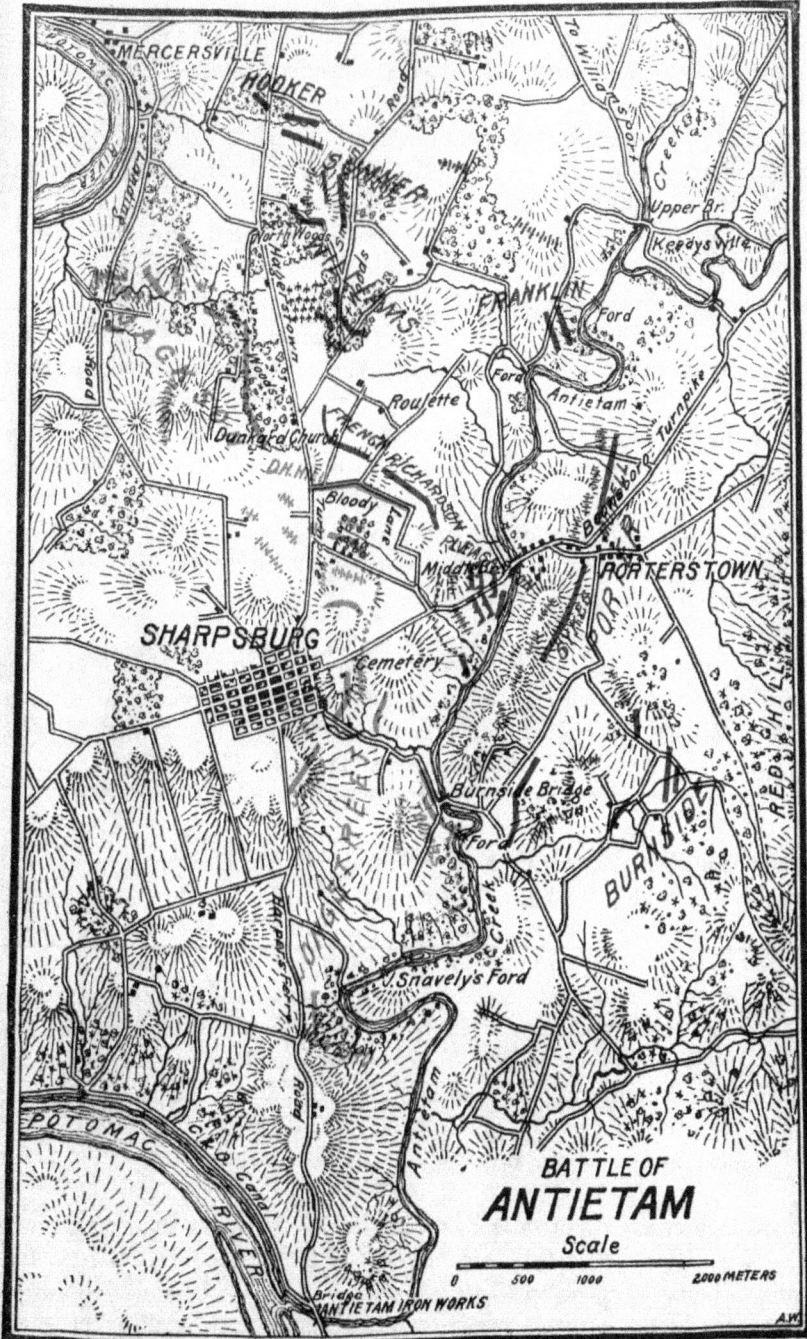

BATTLE OF
ANTIETAM
Scale

horses as they tried to pause to drink and the company gradually made their way across the waist deep ford. As they ascended the steep hill on the far side of the Antietam, they found all the prominent knolls on the far side occupied by the staging regiments of General Sumner's Corps. Beyond the masses of troops, Joshua could see the steeples of Sharpsburg behind the ridges that masked the town. The firing off to the north had settled to a low rumble. Captain Haines, after a short consultation with O'Keefe, shouted out for the battery to follow him as he led them on a wide swing over the rolling hills to the left. They heard the shriek of shells over their heads as the rifles on the ridge, east of the Antietam, fired at Rebel guns that were unlimbering on the ridge to face the new threat emerging near the center. On his wide swing left, Captain Haines, noted a low hilltop back closer to the creek. While it would increase the range, it would allow them to see the upcoming approach. Arriving at the low hill the men scrambled to unlimber the guns, and establish a battery. After the guns were emplaced, Joshua gazed over the panorama of the battlefield. It appeared to him that Sumner's troops were swinging back southward and advancing almost perpendicular to the ridge.

As they watched from their new position, great columns of Union Troops began to form lines south of the white building, and proceeded to advance towards Rebel troops positioned in a sunken road that appeared to cross the Antietam towards Porterstown. Joshua looked behind him, and he could see General Pleasanton's cavalry crossing the ford below them.

Captain Haines evaluated his new position. He was concerned as he was located south and east of the Union lines of battle forming to attack the Rebels, who had formed long lines of battle north and west from his point of observation. The geometry of his location, in aspect to theirs, meant that any overshots or duds could potentially land amidst the approaching Union ranks. He would have to leave the troops in the sunken road to the infantry. He would be forced to focus on the Rebel artillery and any reinforcing troops that approached from the southwest. As he analyzed the Rebel's position through his field glasses, First Sergeant O'Keefe shouted out, "Rebel guns are comin' up! Make ready on the guns!"

Captain Haines swung his glasses to the left, looking first at the troops in the sunken road then past the orchard behind them. On a bald pasture hill, south of the orchard, he spied Rebels guns coming up behind their teams, as they conducted a nicely executed occupation of their firing position. Haines estimated them to lay around 900 yards distant. The distant Rebel gun crews quickly, and expertly, unlimbered their pieces, preparing to fire.

Haines, lowered his field glasses, and commanded, "Load Spherical Case Shot, 900 yards! Cut fuses for four and one half seconds!" He listened as his section officers repeated the commands. Haines returned his attention to the Rebel battery to his front; they had begun to fire upon the advancing Union ranks as they approached the sunken road.

Joshua watched his section. The limber crew threw open the lid on their chest and extracted the red painted case shot, busily screwing in the Bormann fuses. Private Olson then took his "T" handled auger and bored a hole in the soft tin at the appropriate mark then handed the readied round to Private Palmer, who advanced the charge to the gun. He then studied Corporal Page as he adjusted the lay of the gun while adjusting his pendulum hausse to the range. As the battery completed their loading, and the Lieutenants cried out, "ready", another volley of shells from the batteries behind them on the distant ridge soared over their heads. Following Captain Haines order to fire, the guns roared. As they fired the shells from the rifled guns began to strike around the hapless Rebel guns. In the distance, a limber and team could be seen running south across the pasture, fleeing from the terror of the bursting shells. As the smoke and dust from the impacts drifted slowly away in the late morning breeze, the six hurtling case shot from Company M burst in a neat cluster of airbursts, just shy of the line of guns. Joshua wished he possessed field glasses as he tried to analyze the impact they were having. Captain Haines ordered a repeat of the last engagement, and the crews quickly prepared their guns. Off towards the target, Joshua could see the Union ranks had begun to trade volleys with the Rebels at the sunken road. At least they had stopped the firing of one battery that faced them.

Corporal Alan O'Rourke cursed as his slick soled Jefferson boots slipped in the muddy road leading up from the ford across Antietam Creek. Nathan Bannion, his trusty messmate taunted him, as he broke step ahead of him on the difficult climb out of the creek bottom, "There ya go! Ya just had to be fookin' up General Richardson's glorious advance! You've obviously been drinkin' lad!"

O'Rourke adjusted his grip on the heavy 1842 musket on his shoulder and laughed as he climbed the slope, "Ya shouldna' worry so much about me as you should for the Colonel!"

The troops in the ranks had become greatly amused by the antics of

Colonel Meagher. Some had seen him fall off his horse after they had crossed the creek. He had clearly been enjoying some grain for breakfast. Private Oates, marching adjacent to O'Rourke, volunteered additional information, "I heard Quartermaster Sergeant O'Brien say he keeps a wee flask of the stuff in his coat pocket! He says if ya watch closely, you'll see him takin' a nip from time to time." The men all laughed as they made the painful advance up the hill. They could hear the noise of a great battle being waged ahead and were wishing to be anywhere, but here, at the moment. As they topped the hill and got on easier ground, O'Rourke thought of home and wondered whether he would be better off there. The streets of New York and his life as a dockworker and hustler, brought only bitter memories to mind. Aside from battles, the Army life was a vast improvement of his standard of living. Even the common soldier got his whiskey ration, and it cost one nothing.

Oates continued on his observations on Colonel Meagher as they marched in a column of fours down a cart rutted farm path, "They was sayin' it took two Lieutenants and a Captain to get him back on his horse!" The column halted for a spell, and the Officers and Sergeants shouted out commands to dress the lines and close up the column. The rattle of musketry increased in intensity up ahead. Deep reverberating booms of cannon caused the air to vibrate from time to time. O'Rourke remembered Malvern Hill and felt a deep sinking feeling in his gut. He mused to himself, "I'll be seein' the elephant again." Soon the drummers and fifers had been prepared and the 69th New York, the elemental regiment of "The Irish Brigade," would arrive to the battle in style. Once the musicians began playing, the march resumed. Rumor had it that Colonel Meagher needed the music to keep him at the front of the column. O'Rourke continued the discussion, "The Colonel can drink as much as he pleases so long as he stays up with us whens we gets in the range o' the buck and ball!" The men deliberately clung to their secondary standard, 1842 muskets, the lesser weapons, seen as the only armament fit for arming dangerous Irishmen with, had become a badge of honor in the Irish Brigade.

O'Rourke only liked the heavy thing because it was quicker to load. He could never recall where having a rifle made any difference. The fights had all been close things, and he believed that they were surviving because they fired faster, with four rounds per shot, to boot.

After marching another half mile, the column of fours echoed cries of "Halt" as the Officers repeated the order down the line of march. The next order was "Left Face!" that was repeated down the line. Facing left, O' Rourke could see nothing but tall corn. As they stood waiting, a long

Confederate shell burst 50 yards in front of them with a loud clap. Oates exclaimed aloud, "Jesus, Mary and Joseph! That was close!" Private O'Malley behind him joked, "Shit, Boy'O! I'm sad to tell ye that nobody has spare underpants to help ye!" The men in earshot snickered. O'Rourke commented sourly, "Just wait till they shoot some canister at ya before ya go shittin' yourself!"

First Sergeant Ainsworth, who happened to be walking the line and hearing the chatter, called out, "Shut yer fookin' yaps! No talkin' in ranks!" Once he had passed, O'Malley remarked, "That ones a Tammany man for sure! I heard he's a regular at the Colonel's Fenian meetings!" The mention of the Fenian meetings caused Corporal O'Rourke to spit in disgust. Oates, behind him, noted his disgust and asked, "What's wrong Alan?" O'Rourke growled, "It's all lies, boy! They just tolerate it to keep us fightin'!" Oates asked him, "You mean they won't send us home?" The innocence of the boy often bothered Corporal O'Rourke, and frustrated, he tried to school him with a dose of reality, "This fookin' land can't even keep itself together, much less free the fookin' 'ould country,' can't ya see that! Don' be believing all the shit ya hear!" The order "Stand at ease!" was repeated down the line of march. O'Rourke sensed that they were waiting for orders to advance. Ahead of them, beyond the corn, the sounds of the battle ahead intensified and the volleys of musketry were rising to a constant roar.

After a half hour of waiting, as the sounds of battle continued ahead, Captain Sands walked the line with First Sergeant Ainsworth. He halted at the center of his company and announced, "Take off yer hats boys, the Father is coming to give us absolution." Private O'Malley could not resist it and uttered in a low voice, "Now ain't that fookin' special!" The comment earned him a hard stare from First Sergeant Ainsworth, who seemed to be able to hear everything. Corporal O'Rourke remembered that this was his third absolution he had received on a battlefield. First it was Gaines Mills, then Malvern Hill, and now here. He imagined that the fight was going to be stiff, ahead. Soon a balding man in a black frock coat, adorned with an emerald green vestment, emerged before the Regiment. Lieutenant Colonel Nugent was with him.

The Padre called out in a reedy voice, "Kneel, if you please, Lads!" The brigade priest performed the rite in Latin, and the kneeling men, duly genuflected, as was right for all Irish Catholics, regardless what each individually felt. After all, they all had mothers somewheres. Lieutenant Colonel Nugent walked the priest over to the next regiment, and soon appeared again before the men.

As the men were standing back up and returning their hats to their heads, he said, "Boys! It is my honor to stand with you on this day! We are about to attack. I promise you that if you cannot see me at your front, then you can feel free to leave this field! The Rebels have a strong position before us! Steel yourselves for a hard fight today! If we can win today, it might be the last time we have to fight!" O'Rourke and all the boys in his mess, cheered him, along with the rest of the Regiment. They did this, because of his great decency. He had never failed them.

The orders came, shouted down the line in quick succession, "Form into line of battle!" The men wheeled, as duly drilled, into a line of battle, two men deep, as the officer and sergeants took their places behind them. For a moment they stood in ranks that way until the order was shouted down the line, "Advance!" The young drummers began to sound "Common Time" and the men stepped off and waded through the tall cornfields. The heavy crops, made dress and interval difficult and it took much shouting by the officers to keep their lines even as they crossed the field. After exiting the far side, they encountered a field of stubble that inclined before them towards a ridge. Atop the ridge, another regiment of troops was paused to dress alignment, prior to entering into the fray. O'Rourke could see Rebel shells bursting in the air above the distant unseen fight. The claps of the airbursts were lost in the general din of the battle.

O'Malley was now his neighbor in the line of battle, and as they paused, to again dress the line, he made a screwy face at O'Rourke and remarked, "We must be crazy as shit-house rats to have signed on to this line o' work!" Colonel Nugent shouted out to the Regiment, "Affix Bayonets!" To a man, they promptly withdrew the wicked steel blades and attached them by their sockets onto their muskets with a great clattering noise. One clumsy soul down the line dropped his bayonet into the dirt, which elicited howls of abuse from the Sergeants and his mates on the line. Private O'Malley leaned out to look as the man quickly retrieved the bayonet, "Yep, knew it was Mulligan! The only thing he won't fumble is his wee pecker!" The men chuckled, despite their growing anxiety of the prospect before them of "going in."

Corporal O'Rourke looked up and noted that the regiment on the ridge ahead of them had now stepped off towards the roaring battle beyond the ridge. He watched until the bobbing bayonets of their shouldered rifles, disappeared from view. The drummers began to beat time again on their instruments and the regiment advanced again, keeping their dress on the remainder of the brigade that extended off to their right and left. As they advanced up the slope of the ridge, Colonel Meagher rode the lines with emerald green colors and his entourage following. Meagher had his sword drawn, and he shouted out as he rode the line, "Sons of Erin! Rise up to your colors and follow me!" He then rode further down the brigade line, shouting out again to the next regiment. Bannion remarked, as they ascended the hill, "He's lookin' a tad loose in that saddle, boys!" The fifers had now been ordered to play as they neared the crest of the ridge. O'Rourke had yet to see the Rebels that they were approaching, but he noticed scattered men coming back over the crest of the ridge in disarray, to his left. He also saw bloody walking wounded coming back, being helped along by their comrades.

As they crested the low ridge, the tableau of the massive battle emerged before them. Corporal O'Rourke beheld a broad sloping flat of wheat stubble that held a sunken road lined by a broken down split rail fence. Behind the road lay a corn stubble field. Long lines of Rebel troops were both within the sunken road, employing the feature as works, with a line of rebel regiments behind them in ranks amongst the stubble of the cornfield. Blue clad bodies lay in scores amid the wheat stubble, and the regiment that preceded them was in the process of disintegrating, as only small groups of shouting and determined soldiers were firing at the massed Rebel troops. The rest were turning to run and helping wounded men escape the carnage. The officers below were shouting for the men to rally, but the heavy bursts of musketry melted the regiment down like wax.

Cresting the ridge behind the emerald green colors, O'Rourke heard the command come down, repeated by their officers, "Load!" As he extracted a cartridge from his box and bit off the end, Corporal O'Rourke was jostled by the men beside him as they feverishly attended to the same task. He whipped out his tulip headed ramrod and easily shoved the opened charge down the smooth barrel of his musket. Swiftly returning the rammer to its channel, he brought the musket up and capped it. The officers sounded the command; "Advance!" and the ranks of the Irish Brigade advanced another 20 paces before meeting a concentrated volley from the Rebel ranks behind the sunken road. The hail of minie balls slammed into the Irish Brigade's ranks, felling men along the line. The impacts of the balls made sickening thuds and thumps on the bodies of the struck. Colonel Meagher's horse fell, and the men nearest him rushed to pull him from underneath the animal. The sergeant bearing the colors, fell face forward, killed instantly by a head shot, and he lay cloaked in the colors, soaking them with his blood. One of the fifers took a hit into his chest, emitting a loud off-key tone and he fell backwards, still clutching the instrument.

The surviving soldiers presented their muskets, before the officers could order the movement and released a great smoky volley, in return. O'Rourke say many gray clad men fall across the way, as the compound loads of the smoothbores ripped into their massed ranks. The cry of "Load!" was heard by men, who already were ramming charges down their slick bores. O'Rourke could hear O'Malley shouting out, over the clamor, "Keep standin' there! You gray back bastards!" Again they presented, as swiftly as they could and delivered a ragged, and unordered volley into the Rebels, still struggling to reload their fouled rifles. Colonel Nugent, practical enough to know that orders were useless to men with their blood up, simply walked the line behind his men, shouting, "Pour it into them boys!"

Colonel John Gordon, commanding the 6th Alabama, strode the clay-surfaced road as his men reloaded to fire into a newly emerging Yankee Regiment. He limped, having taken a painful graze on his leg only moments before after his men had poured a killing volley into an advancing blue clad Regiment. He could see his men employing the bodies of the dead to improve their breastworks, formed by the waist high banks of the sunken road. He remained determined to stop them at this road. He had promised his commander, General Rhodes, that he would rather die than give an inch of ground. Seeing an emerald green color coming over the ridge, he knew instinctively that the Yankees were sending the Irish against him. Based on what he knew of the Yankees, they were sending men they cared little for, just to wear them down. He grew concerned as he watched men pick up rocks to hammer ramrods down dry, and severely fouled barrels. The Yankees just kept coming. There seemed to be an endless supply of hirelings approaching this critical ground. The men in blue came forward, in well-ordered ranks, and as his men struggled to load, his supports behind him, thankfully, responded with a great volley. To his satisfaction, he saw many of the men in blue fall. The volley had dropped the colors, as well as an officer on horseback, on the ridge. Like the others had before them, the Yankee Regiments gamely responded with a great volley in return. As the smoke billowed from their muskets, he felt a sharp and new pain in his already wounded leg. The Irish were firing buck and ball! He glanced at the small hole in his pants leg as the butternut fabric turned dark with blood. He swore and hobbled down the line on his rounds as the men moved their fallen comrades out of their way. The smoke was choking in the humid morning air. He shouted out as he walked his lines, "Keep your fire swift, boys! Pour it into them!" He had long since abandoned commanding volleys, as it wasted time. They knew what to do. He instinctively hunched down as another unwelcome Union artillery salvo unleashed bursting case shot into the supports behind him with loud cracks. Turning, he could see more precious men falling in the wheat stubble behind him from the wicked shrapnel within the bursting shells. Another series of bursting shot erupted over his head, he felt a burning pain in his shoulder as one of the multiple projectiles, within, penetrated his back with an impact that knocked the breath out of him.

Colonel Gordon could feel the hands of his men on him as they attempted to revive him. One of them had placed a rag under his shirt to stem the blood coming from the fresh wound to his shoulder. He brushed them away, and rose, enraged. He stood and dusted off his uniform, despite his dizziness, and drew his Tranter revolver from it's patent leather holster and quickly unleashed six shots as fast as he could at the blue ranks on the ridge. He heard a man behind him, exclaim, "Gawd damn! The Colonel still has fight in him! Pour it on, boys!"

Gordon felt woozy and uncertain on his feet, but he doggedly hobbled along his lines, shouting out words of encouragement to his embattled men. The pain in his shoulder would not go away. He sensed something was broken within, and he favored his right arm when he pointed out things to his men. As he worked his way along the line, he noted a distressing number of dead and wounded accumulating in the sunken road. There were just too many men in the Yankee ranks approaching. He paused to reload his revolver; he found it painstakingly difficult due to the soreness in his shoulder. As the sharp roar of the firing rung in his ears, he finally completed his task. Standing again, he returned the pistol to his holster, and he turned to look at the Yankee Regiment approaching him. He saw them, in the distance, as they raised their muskets again and a great cloud of white smoke emerged from their ranks. He then sensed a great shock, followed by blackness, as one of the heavy caliber balls tore through his cheek and impacted his skull. He would be found a day later, still alive, under piles of dead men, by a burial detail.

The soldiers of the 69th New York continued to fire as fast as they could. The heavy volume of fire had slowed the Rebel response down the hill. Corporal O'Rourke, reaching for the next cartridge, found that both of his top tin compartments were empty in his cartridge box. Cursing he pulled the tin insert out to obtain the cartridges in the bottom compartments. In his haste, he dumped the last rounds into the pouch and discarded the tin insert. He could not recall ever firing as much as they were at this moment. Soon cries emerged from the ranks, "I'm out!" and "We need more rounds!" The regiment was exhausting their ammunition. Colonel Nugent, now acting Brigade Commander, found the Brigade Bugler and ordered the young soldier to sound recall. Nugent then sent a runner to find Major Duryea, the Brigade Quartermaster, to direct him to find resupply of ammunition.

The men of the Irish Brigade backed off the line and gave the battle over to the Ohio Regiments behind them. As Corporal O'Rourke glanced over the ground where they had stood and fought, he saw that the ground was covered with the bodies of the dead and wounded. As he glanced to his left and right, he realized that Nathan was no longer with them. He swore aloud as they backed away through the dense smoke of the battle. After the ranks had passed through the Ohio Brigade, Colonel Nugent ordered the men to route step, and they descended the opposite slope of the low ridge to a vale to rest and resupply. They could hear the Ohioans unleash a great volley of rifle musket fire into the Rebels on the far side.

On the far left of General Richardson's advancing Division, Colonel Francis Barlow had been charged to lead the 61st and 64th New York Volunteers to secure the left flank of the division. Both Regiments had been severely reduced in strength by the fighting during 2nd Manassas and had yet to receive additional recruits from the New York State depots. He paused his command of barely 350 men in the sheltered lee of the far left side of the ridge, and then proceeded on foot to the crest to look things over. His adjutant, Captain Thompkins, trotted along beside him. The Colonel mounted the crest of the ridge with his trademark cavalry saber in his right hand. He was prone to slapping the butts of straggling men with it; he used it now to point out the Confederate defensive line to Captain Thompkins.

Off to the far right, Barlow noted the next assault that pushed through the retreating Irish Brigade. The battle lines were being halted by the stubborn Rebel infantry in the long fence lined sunken road. As his eyes followed the trace of the road, he noticed their exposed right flank. At that moment, he realized his good fortune. When he and his men had swung wide to General Richardson's left flank, they now were poised perpendicular to the Rebel lines in the road. He estimated that he was 300 yards distant from the Confederate flank. Barlow gave an urgent command to Captain Thompkins, "Captain! Have the men load their rifles, and bring them up at the double quick. Center the colors on me!"

Moments later, to the sound of drumming, the Regiments came up; the men were out of breath from climbing the ridge at the double. Barlow quickly formed his line and commanded the small group of men, "Fire into the road, boys! You can aim high or you can aim low, but keep your fire into that road!" Barlow then quickly pushed his way through the center of his ranks to get out of the way. He then shouted out, "Make ready! Aim!.......Fire!" The men brought up their long barreled Springfield rifle muskets and poured a punishing volley into the Rebel troops sheltering in the sunken road. Barlow pushed forward in order to see. In the road the shocked Rebel troops fell by the dozens, he could see many pointing towards his small force and shouting orders. Barlow shouted out, "Fire at will, boys!" The soldiers quickly settled into loading and firing as accurately as they could. Barlow could see men leaving the road and fleeing south.

Captain Haines shouted out, "Cease firing!" The limber crewmen advancing the next charges stopped short of the carriages and looked towards him, expectantly. Lowering his field glasses, he looked towards them and commanded, "Return the rounds to the limber chests!" He then returned his field glasses to observe. The lines of attack had spread until the last regiment had been able to flank the Rebels in the sunken road. He could no longer fire as the attacking regiments that quickly advanced and filled the sunken road were pursuing the retreating Rebels. Reaching the fence of the road facing south, some started firing at the backs of the retreating Rebels. Other regiments continued to move in lines of battle towards the orchard, south of the road. First Sergeant O'Keefe rode his horse down the gun line, and shouted out to the crews, "Swab yer bores, goddammit! You ain't paid to watch other men fight! See to your guns!"
The crews quickly snatched their implements up and ran wet sponges down the hot barrels. The bronze guns were black at their muzzles from the powder fouling of the heavy firing. Joshua watched the crews of his section as they swabbed. The boys were in high spirits, their hands and faces were blackened by the sooty powder residue as well. Seeing the Rebels retreating from the road was encouraging. Joshua scanned the front, directly across from where the guns pointed now, towards the far north, where the battle had begun. Smoke rose from the entire front as both sides continued to fire all along the lines. The movement to their front seemed to be the only hot action going on at the moment. The lines south of Sharpsburg remained strangely quiet. Looking back over towards the center of the

battery, Joshua noticed that First Sergeant O'Keefe was in conversation with Captain Haines. O'Keefe nodded his head several times as the Captain talked. He then turned his horse and shouted, "Limber up!"

Brigadier General Jacob Cox stood on the high prominence that overlooked Rohrback's Bridge that connected Sharpsburg to the Porterstown Pike. Cox had spent several uneasy days as the acting IX Corps commander, since the death of Major General Reno three days ago. He had assumed that Major General Ambrose Burnside, with whom he had spent the past two days, would have assumed the Corps command, following General McClellan's decision to abandon the concept of Wing Commanders, each, who controlled two Corps. Burnside had been in a foul mood at what he termed, "the betrayal of a good friend," after McClellan had made the decision, and he had obstinately refused to resume command of the Corps that once was his. In this awkward arrangement, and in constant contact and consultation with a sulking Major General, Cox wanted nothing more than to return to the command of his beloved Division of fellow Ohioans that were waiting in the woods behind them. Their original orders from Major General McClellan had been to open the battle with a diversionary attack on the narrow and tiny bridge down below. McClellan had placed a caveat on that order, with the phrase, "when ordered." The troops had been rousted from a cold night and morning with no fires to cook rations or make coffee. Then they had sat, and sat, while a major battle erupted to the north of them. They had watched, as many columns of Rebel troops had exited Sharpsburg and moved north to reinforce the raging battle beyond them, yet no order came. Burnside, in his present mood, was proving to be devoid of initiative and refused to even send a message asking for those orders. The situation reminded Cox of his Ohio senate days and the political games played by his opponents on the floor of that august assembly. They stood on the hill and watched the smoke of the great battle, until 9am that morning. Their troops in the wood below waited and wondered why they were rousted from their beds so early, to do nothing.

The only action they had observed so far, had been a desultory artillery duel between Lieutenant Benjamin's 20-pound Parrots on the ridge adjacent to them and Rebel batteries on the far ridge that overlooked the bridge. A short sharp exchange of shells at sunrise had quickly compelled the Rebels to move their guns. The men below had loudly cheered when Benjamin's guns had exploded a caisson in a spectacular explosion on the crest of the Rebel held ridge.

At 9:30 am, Colonel Sackett, from General McClellan's headquarters, arrived with orders that he handed to General Burnside. Cox thought it odd for the Inspector General of the Army of the Potomac to be in service as a courier. General Burnside coolly accepted the folded dispatch and handed it to Cox without reading it, saying only, "This communiqué is obviously for the Commander of the Ninth Corps, Colonel! I am not sure why you hand it to me!" Sackett looked amused, but said nothing. Cox opened the note and read the order as Sackett, intoned, "Sir, that was drafted by General McClellan at 9am. He insists that you now force the bridge, and cross the Antietam with your Corps. The General is concerned that we must press the enemy now on all fronts!"

Cox looked at Major General Burnside, and Burnside replied, "General Cox give orders to General Rodman to take the ford to the south and pass word to General Crook to assault the bridge! We shall follow our plan of last night."

Cox waved his gloved hand to his Adjutant to come over, and when the man arrived, he instructed him to transmit the order to commence the attack. A few minutes after the Adjutant had departed, he could hear the drummers sounding the long roll.

General Robert Toombs walked the heavily wooded ridge with his manservant Ben, who led his horse by its bridle. Toombs needed a battle to make his name. He had enough of dealing with West Pointers and all their foolishness. Today did not look like it would be the day for him to get his name in the Georgia newspapers. Aside from the artillery fight in the morning, it appeared that General Longstreet, and his friend Robert Lee, had relegated him to a dullard's job. His men had spent their morning hunkered down along the stone fence, near the crest of the high wooded ridge that overlooked the Rohrback's Bridge. Not one blue belly had shown his face all day, and he wondered what was happening amidst all the noise off to the north. Ben helpfully asked, "Gen'ral Toombs, sir? I can water this horse for you, if'n you wish." Toombs, preoccupied with his thoughts, absently replied, "No, Ben. Make him wait. Too much waterin' will make him want it all the time." Toombs raised his field glasses, and studied the hill where he knew Yankee guns waited. He had ordered his twelve supporting guns to mask, as he knew the Federal's had better guns than his. Fighting them too early would result in the loss of the only thing that he had to support barely 600 muskets in stopping an attempt on the narrow bridge below him.

The long roll of drums, beyond the far ridge to the east, alerted his attention across the creek. He motioned to his Aide de Camp, who followed Ben and the horse a few paces distant. When the young Major approached, he commanded him, "Tell the boys to pay attention! The Yankees are up to something over yonder."

As he watched, his Adjutant spread the word down the lines, Toombs imagined himself returning to Georgia with a hero's laurels. It would be useful for reelection to the State Senate, maybe even the Governor's office.

He heard a man shout out to his right, "Here they come!"

The Yankee guns on the high ridge across the way began to fire again, and an instant later, their first shells began to burst on the ridge top above them with ear shattering cracks. He cried out in the midst the din of the exploding shells, "Make ready boys!"

Soon the orderly blue clad soldiers emerged over the ridge, across the creek, behind which they had sheltered all morning. Toombs waited until they began to approach in lines of battle, halfway down the open field that led towards the road, running parallel to the creek. He counted the colors as they approached. After a quick analysis, he realized he had seen twelve flags. That made for six Regiments. He motioned to his Aide de Camp again. When the young Major appeared, he directed, "Major Spence, go tell the battery commanders to fire their pieces only after my first volley! Insure they understand that they must displace frequently, so the Yankees don't get their range!"

Spence quickly nodded and trotted back to his horse. He sprang into his saddle and galloped back up the tall ridge to find the gunners.

Toombs patiently watched as the Union troops approached his bridge in neat ranks, arrayed as if on parade. When they had closed to within 100 yards, easy range for his Enfield rifle equipped men, he shouted out, "Fire upon them, men!" The waiting men did not pause for him to complete the order. A great roar of muskets drowned out the final syllables of his command. Scores of the men in blue fell in the sunlit field. The survivors closed ranks and returned fire at the smoke of the Rebel's muskets. The volley was largely ineffective, falling well short of the stone fence. Toombs listened as his subordinate commanders shouted out, "Reload!" Their echoing commands were drowned out by the roar of the twelve 6 pounders above him as they spewed loads of case shot on the approaching blue ranks. Amid the white puffs of the air busting rounds, Toombs could see more blue clad bodies falling in the stubble. The massed fires of his second volley caused the ranks to break apart, and the Yankees ran back to the safety of the far ridge. The Federal batteries, far off to the east, returned fire again at the smoke of his guns. He could hear their shells bursting on the ridge above him and he hoped his gunners had moved in time.

General Toombs watched as the stubble field emptied of approaching troops and he again summoned Major Spence. When he arrived, he instructed him to send a runner to General Longstreet to inform him that the Yankees were attempting to take the bridge. Major Spence saluted and made his way back to where the staff had their horses and couriers.

A new crackling of musketry to the south of him, caused General Toombs to look to his south. The Yankees were obviously attempting the ford, downstream as well. He had few men there and he hoped that they could hold that ground, as he had nothing to spare.

Brigadier General Cox watched dismayed, as the second and third attempts to approach the bridge failed under the heavy fire of the Rebel defenders. The stubble field below them was dotted with bodies. The narrow road on the bridge was covered with bodies as well. Smoke from the last volleys of the Rebels shrouded the woods across the way with a lazily rising haze. Reports coming in from General Potter indicated that the ford to the south was impassible, due to the steep banks of the creek. Headquarters was impatient as well and Major General Burnside had received another visit from Colonel Sackett, of General McClellan's staff. As he watched the men run back across the stubble field to the safety of the ridge, the two officers near him were in a heated discussion. After a few more minutes of often loud discussion, Burnside returned to Cox. He flatly instructed, "Go down to General Sturgis. Have him commit the remainder of his Division to try again. Tell him to do it smart! They cannot pause in the field on our side, nor can they use the road! The must attack it on the main, and damned quick!" Brigadier General Cox nodded, and motioning to his orderly, he retrieved his horse and rode down behind the ridge.

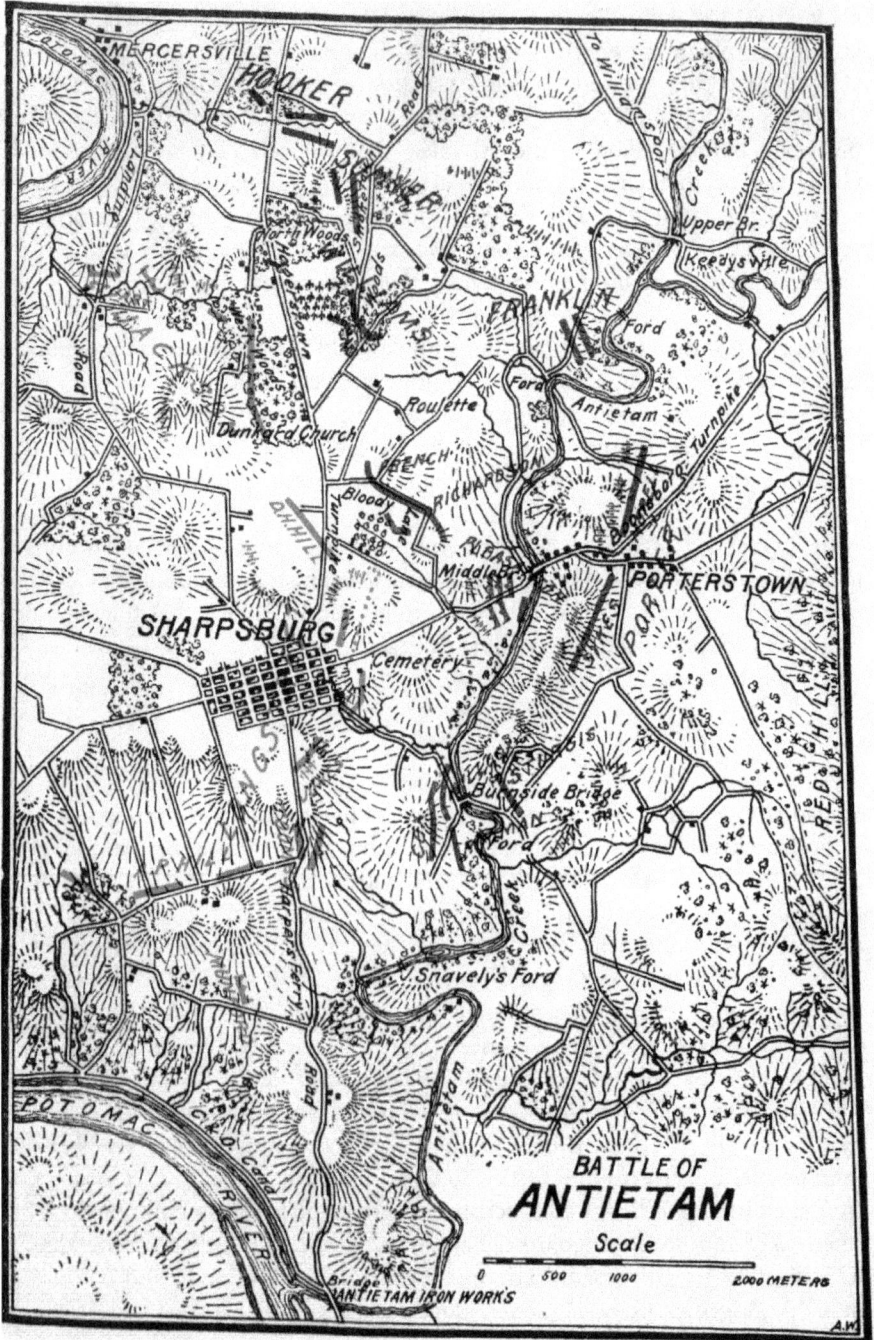

BATTLE OF
ANTIETAM
Scale

0   500   1000   2,000 METERS

In the camp of the 51st Pennsylvania Reserves, Corporal Lewis Patterson attended to his team of mules. They had been forced to stand all day hitched to the Quartermaster Sergeant's wagon. Patterson was the driver for the team and he was solicitous to the finicky animals. He was increasingly frustrated with the Infantrymen's constant requests to provide them with their whiskey ration. The Brigade Commander had suspended issuance of the coveted fluid since three days ago. There had been a spate of fights that had angered the Colonel. This resulted in stern enjoinders from the Quartermaster to suspend the ration. Quartermaster Sergeant Wilcox was a burley man, and fearsome to the men, so they had taken to approaching Patterson, instead. He had grown tired of their begging. He paused from his curry combing when he saw Colonel Ferrero ride into the camp and engage Colonel Hartranft in an urgent discussion. After several minutes of conversation, Hartranft shouted out to his Sergeant Major, "Get the boys up! Have them gather around!"

Colonel Ferrero also found Colonel Potter of the 51st New York Volunteer Infantry next to them in the woods, and had them gather as well.

When the men had assembled in a large semi-circle around Colonel Ferrero, he addressed them in his heavily Italian accented voice, "Men, You are requested directly by General Burnside, himself, to make this next attack to gain the bridge down there! We will attack the bridge with two Regiments side by side, and you will not stop until you have crossed it! I have recommended, that my two 51st Regiments take the lead of this attack as you have proven you like to fight!"

The men looked back at him with stony stares. Most thought the former dance instructor to be a posturing fop, and resented his recent suspension of their whiskey ration after South Mountain.

Ferrero, after an uncomfortable pause, asked, "Will you take the bridge for us?"

Corporal Patterson, sensing an opportunity to make his life easier, shouted out his own question from the rear of the gathering, "Will you give us back our whiskey ration?"

Other men voiced the same frustration in loud voices from separate locations in the crowd, "It ain't right! Give it back! Men are dying over yonder!"

Ferrero looked stunned, and for a moment, found himself speechless.

Then he gathered himself after noting a nod from Colonel Hartranft and shouted, "Yes! If you two regiments take that bridge, you shall have all you can drink, by God! Even if I have to buy it with my own pay!" He paused and looked angrily at the men, before continuing, "But, only if, you take the bridge!"

Colonel Ferrero took his two Regimental commanders off to the side as the Sergeant Majors shouted for the men to form two columns of fours behind the sheltered crest of the ridge. Each Regiment stood in line of columns, side by side, awaiting the order to advance. Corporal Patterson trotted back to his wagon, picked up his cartridge box and musket and ran to join the men in ranks. He could hear Quartermaster Sergeant Wilcox shouting out behind him, "You're gone crazy! Get back here!" He glibly smiled and ignored the commands. His company mates, pleased by his act slapped him on the back and welcomed him into the ranks.

Colonel Hartranft commanded his column, "Load your muskets and fix bayonets!" The men quickly attended to their tasks. Above them, two batteries of artillery began to fire heavily into the Rebel positions across the creek. Hartranft, then commanded, "Advance boys! At the Double Quick!" Corporal Patterson and all the men around him gave a great throaty cry. They ran over the ridge, stumbling, and catching one another as they crested the ridge and entered the deadly stubble field. Patterson found himself occasionally tripping over the bodies of fallen men as he approached the bridge. He could only catch glimpses of the triple arched stone structure as he ran between the backs of the men in front of him. He could hear the shells shuttling overhead, as he ran. This noise was followed rapidly by shattering cracks as they impacted into the woods across the creek and exploded. Glancing to his right, he saw that the lead company had diverted and had begun to fire volleys from behind a low stonewall by the bridge. The Captain, in front of his company, ran straight for the bridge. When they were 50 yards from the stone escarpments of the bridge, the defending Rebel troops fired a great volley, accompanied by shots from cannon, on the commanding heights over it. The minie balls from the Rebel volley tore into the advancing column as they closed on the bridge. Patterson felt one buzz closely by his head as he ran. The man, before him, fell heavily and Patterson tripped and fell headlong onto the man's back. He looked down and saw a gaping hole in the back of his comrade's head, a stark white flap of bone from his skull lay open like a hatch where the projectile had exited. Shocked, he picked himself up and rushed to rejoin the thinning column, still approaching the bridge. As they came up onto the span, Corporal Patterson tripped, and fell again. The road surface across the small span, was covered with the bodies of the dead and wounded of the Connecticut Regiment that had made an earlier attempt. As he put his hands down to break his fall, he felt the still warm blood on the road underneath his palms. After rising to his knees, another volley erupted from the Rebel troops barely 50 yards away. Another soldier to his left, was struck and dropped his rifle, heavily on Patterson's arms as he struggled to rise. Shaking free, he could see his Captain laying still a few feet before him. He rose and followed the survivors across. He ran as fast as he could, and joined thirty other men sheltering behind a low stone wall on the left side of the road that led up to Sharpsburg. Afforded cover, they began to fire as fast as they could reload, into the deep woods up the hill. More, and more men got across and joined them.

Soon the Rebel fire, in response to their volleys, slowed. Corporal Patterson heard someone shout out, "They're skedaddling! Pour it into them boys!" He continued to load, and fire, until he realized he had no more cartridges in his pouch. He looked towards the bridge, thinking he could salvage more from the dead, when he saw the following Regiments crossing in ordered and undisturbed ranks. The "two 51st Regiments" had earned their whiskey ration back.

The men in the following Regiments swiftly marched up the hill towards Sharpsburg. After they had advanced for 10 more minutes, the sounds of heavy volleys erupted before them. They had hit General Toombs' second line of defense.

The couriers arrived one after the other, in an urgent sequence. All bore messages for General Lee and each communicated desperation. Colonel Chilton intercepted each and he acted as the screen for his commander, who quietly sat under the awning. He was listening to the sounds of the battle, while ruminating over his map.

Chilton read them, as they were delivered. One told the tale of men without ammunition who watched an entire Union Division forming to their front. Another indicated that General Hood had apparently lost most of his Division in his counter attack towards the north wood. Another indicated the death of General Lawton. Yet another described the retreat of Rhodes from the sunken road under heavy Union pressure. The latest described the loss of the Rorhrbach Bridge to the south. Chilton digested the collective content, then went to visit his commander.

Chilton cautiously approached General Lee as he sat hatless in the shade. The day's heat had slowed him down. When Lee looked up, and saw his Chief of Staff, he asked, "So how goes this battle, Colonel Chilton? The firing seems to have subsided to my north, yet I hear much more to the south!"

Colonel Chilton calmly answered, "Sir, we have several units short of ammunition with Federals continuing to approach. General Hill has been pushed from the Porterstown Road and the Federals have also taken the Rorhrbach Bridge and are on the move towards General Longstreet's right. That, Sir, is the sound of battle, you hear to the south. Sir, were it my duty to describe this situation, the word I would employ would be, "Dire.""

Lee rose and placed his hat on his head, and asked, "What news of A. P. Hill, Colonel?" Chilton silently shook his head. General Lee softly directed, "Colonel Chilton, be so kind as to summon my orderly. Have him bring Traveler to me. I think I should go to General Longstreet now. Please see to it that General Jackson understands the necessity of holding my left!"

Chilton watched as the General painfully, and slowly mounted Traveler, his injured hands slowing his every move. Since he could not properly rein the animal with the splints on, an orderly rode alongside him to control his horse. Once the General had departed for his ride through Sharpsburg, Chilton found Captain Marshall, and directed, "Send a rider down the Shepardstown Road! We must have an update of General Hill's Light Division! Everything now depends on his arrival!"

Sergeant Lloyd Chriscoe shouted out to his weary men, "Ain't far now boys! Heard a rumor that it might lay off of the next bend of the road!" His shouts of encouragement resulted in only curses and spitting from the weary men of Yadkin County. They made for an odd sight, dusty blue Yankee sack coats with muddy wet trousers from crossing the boggy ford at Shepherdstown. Many of them had their precious Yankee shoes off, dangling by their laces over their shoulders, to preserve the leather from wet ruination. Chriscoe was keenly aware of how his feet hurt; the Captain had pushed them hard since early morning. The only guidance he had given, after complaints were heard at the brief noontime halt, was, "We got 17 miles to make today! No stragglin' and there is likely to be a fight at the end of this march!" The sounds of the battle increased in intensity off to the north. It was an unsettling noise that had become apparent when they had crossed the ford. All day General Hill had ridden along the column in his red shirt, their clearest indication that a fight lay ahead. He would shout out the need for urgency, and then repeat his urging to the next Regiment in the line. They passed men straggling off the side of the road, in numbers that increased after they had crossed the Potomac. When Chriscoe looked at them limping along, most would reply, "Tell the boys, up ahead that I'ma still comin'!" Chriscoe good-naturedly advised them, "You best keep movin' son! They's likely to shoot you if you ain't moving in the proper direction!"

Ascending the hill that led to the town of Sharpsburg, he could see broad fields of still green corn. Chriscoe admired the straightness of the rows, and the dark richness of the soil. This was obviously good land. Much better for farming than fighting on. Neat farmhouses and well built barns stood at various points off in the distance. After another mile of walking, the column inexplicably stopped. The men around him asked, "Why are we stopping, Sergeant?" Chriscoe irritably looked at them, asking, "Ain't you just walked all day with me right beside you? Did any of ya'll see the General come by to give me the news? Why are we stopping?" He thrust his rifle to the man next to him, "Here hold this!" Chriscoe left the column, and climbed a tall split rail fence to look further ahead. After peering for a moment he gingerly climbed down, to avoid splinters in his bare feet, and replied, "It looks like a rider has stopped the General. I reckon we are gettin' orders!"

Captain Sykes briskly walked down the line with his sword in its sheath, carried resting on his shoulder, he shouted out, "Get yer shoes on men. We got work ahead of us!" The men of the 28th North Carolina, unslung their Yankee boots, and quickly put them back on. Up ahead the drummers began to beat the rate of march; the weary men stepped off and again made their way north on the road.

On the road ahead of them, General Ambrose Powell Hill galloped with the messenger sent by Colonel Chilton to find and report his arrival to General Lee.

Private Elmer Peck, and the rest of the men of Company C of the 16th Connecticut Volunteer Infantry marched up the steep sloping western bank of the Antietam Creek watershed. He recalled the early attempt to take the bridge behind them, that morning. For all the men the 17th of September would be a day that none would forget. It had been the first time they had been under heavy and determined resistance. Word had flowed through the ranks that the Colonel had been grievously wounded in the assault on the bridge. Major Ward had taken command of the Regiment when they had rallied at the morning camp that they had been forced to abandon earlier in the day. Heavy Rebel artillery fire had disrupted their breakfast at sunrise and many had little chance to eat. The men had been forced to scavenge rations remaining amongst the ruins of their camp. Before long, word that the follow on Regiments had taken the bridge. They had fallen in and received orders to make a general advance back across the bridge to assault the retreating Rebels into Sharpsburg. Upon crossing the ridge, leading down towards the bridge, they were forced to wait an hour for the columns ahead of them to cross the bridge. It seemed that General Burnside was pushing most of his corps across the narrow structure.

As they ascended the steep road, the men were quieter than usual, shocked by the ample evidence of the realities of battle. Bodies lay in ragged lines in front of the porch of a shot up farmhouse, many missing heads or limbs. The company had already lost twenty of their comrades and many did not relish facing what lay ahead.

On the road ahead of them, Colonel Harland looked back at his depleted brigade as they struggled to maintain their pace up the steep road. Looking back towards Sharpsburg, he noticed the gaudily dressed New York Zouaves deploying into line of battle off of the right side of the road. General Rodman, commanding his division, had directed him to form his brigade to the left of the Zouaves and press towards the southern side of the town. He could see the steeples of several churches in Sharpsburg but only the tops above the rolling hills and ridges that surrounded it. The fields were mixed between dense cornfields and recently harvested wheat. Various fences and low stone walls divided each farmers property. He realized that keeping in line with the units at his flank would be a challenge, particularly in an approach uphill against the defending Rebels. Urgently he signaled his adjutant to come up. When the officer arrived beside him, he ordered, "Major, detail the regiments to assign more guides! Inform them to deploy off the road to the left, on me!" Once his adjutant had departed, he galloped up to the point in the road where the Zouaves had deployed.

Soon the column of panting men came up and he directed first the 4th Rhode Island, followed by the 16th Connecticut, and finally the 8th Connecticut to depart the road and form a line of battle off to the left. Glancing over to his right, he could see that the advancing Zouaves had found a small detachment of Rebel skirmishers behind a stone fence. They began to trade musket fire as they continued to advance. Harlan turned his horse and centered himself on the 8th Connecticut, so he could keep the Zouaves in sight. Raising his sword, he commanded in his loudest voice, "2nd Brigade! Charge Bayonets!.... Advance!" Behind him a drummer began the beat the time and the lines began to move to the west with their rifles carried bobbing at charge bayonet.

Private Peck, near the right of the line of the 16th Connecticut, brought his bayonetted musket up at the command of Major Ward and attempted to keep pace with his company as they advanced through a dense field of corn. The firing of muskets had begun to increase far off to his right, but he could see little beyond the dense stalks of corn he was pushing through.

General Lee had arrived near Longstreet's lines along the Hagerstown Pike, when he spied a large approaching mass of troops far in the distance. Lee turned to his entourage and summoned up Major Ransom, General Pendleton's liaison, to his headquarters. Turning to Ransom, Lee asked,

"Major Ransom, can you see the colors of those approaching troops?" Ransom, who did not like the European field glasses, raised his trusty naval telescope. The troops were quite distant on the Harpers Ferry road, to his estimation. He carefully adjusted the telescope. They wore what appeared to be dark clothing. The still, and hot afternoon air ruffled the flags they carried, very little. After another glance, he muttered, "Sir, they look like Federals!' Hopefully, he continued to stare, and suddenly a flag dipped further down the column, and he could clearly see the new model color that had the diagonal cross of Saint Andrew adorned with white stars. Ransom lowered his scope and cried out, "No Sir, those are General Hill's men!"

Lee released a deeply held breath; the day may be saved after all. All up and down his lines the rattle of musketry and the booms of cannons troubled the humid afternoon air. In the near distance, he saw a group of riders approach him. They had seen his headquarters flag, carried by another orderly, several horses back. The rider in the lead wore a red shirt. Lee instinctively knew. Ambrose Powell Hill had arrived, to quote General Jackson, "At the right time."

General Lee gingerly dismounted and walked on foot towards the riders as they reined their horses to a stop. General Hill, swiftly dismounted as it would be unseemly to remain mounted before his Army commander, and to his great surprise, Lee warmly placed both hands on his shoulders. General Hill stammered, "Sir, We made the march as quick as we could! My apologies if we were delayed!"

Lee stepped back, his eyes wet and red about the edges, and said softly, "No, General, you have arrived at the right time. Your arrival is indeed very appropriate!"

He then regained his normal commanding visage, that Hill knew and expected, as he received his orders, "General Hill, our situation is dire! Form your men south of Sharpsburg along the Harpers Ferry Road and drive them from the southeastern approaches of Sharpsburg. Drive them back to the creek!" Hill nodded his head and rushed back to his horse. Wheeling the animal when he was back in the saddle, he rendered a quick salute and galloped back to the south to his men.

General Hill easily covered the distance to his approaching columns as they closed on favorable ground. It would be a downhill assault all the way. Batteries near the cemetery had begun to fire on vast ranks of Federal Infantry that were arrayed in long lines spanning the stubble fields and large green expanses of corn, as they approached. He swiftly commanded his lead column, Maxcy Gregg's South Carolinians, "General! Turn your men now, and attack! You shall form my left! Do not pause for the others!" Gregg nodded, and shouted out commands. Hill then rode further down his lines and pointed with his sword to his next commander, General Branch, "General, form your men and push through that field of corn, yonder! Push them to the creek! General Lawrence O'Brien Branch acknowledged his directions with a salute from his own drawn sword. Branch then turned and shouted out orders to his adjutant who galloped off to form the left wing's line of advance. General Hill continued to pass orders to each Regiment he passed, until he pushed the final two back south to cover his right flank. He then returned to his center to watch.

Sergeant Chriscoe forgot about the pain in his feet as he heard General Branch shouting, "Turn right and attack boys! Form your line of battle as you find them! Push them down the hill!" The men of his Regiment turned off the road still in their march column. They ran at the double quick until they were on line with a rapidly firing battery by the cemetery on their left. There, the officers had the companies wheel into line of battle. As he checked the alignment of his squad, Chriscoe glanced to his front. Long lines of men in blue were approaching them in well ordered ranks. In front of them a Regiment was slightly ahead of the others. They were strikingly dressed, wearing red baggy pants. The men around him commented on their appearance. Chriscoe remarked, "They call them "Zoo ayes" or somethin' like that. It's some French thing. Mighty fancy!" Captain Sykes ordered them to fix their bayonets, and to load their Enfields. Soon, Colonel Lane rode the Regimental Line and shouted out to the loading men, "Boys! We are fixin' to advance! Keep your alignment on the colors! Guide on the Yankee Zouaves yonder! They should be easy enough to see!" Lane then positioned his horse on the center of the Regiment and signaled for his drummers to begin the pace. The 28th North Carolina advanced with their rifle muskets pointed forward. Most of the advancing men had unbuttoned their captured sack coats, due to the heat. They had no awareness of their appearance from a distance. As the lines of General Branch's Brigade had finally formed across the front, the great mass of approaching men resembled their opponents, save their colors, and their odd collection of hats. Grimly determined, the North Carolinians closed the distance between themselves and their foe. Sergeant Chriscoe called out to his squad, "Steady boys, make ready to give them hell!"

As the ranks of the 16th Connecticut exited the tall cornfield, they found themselves in a wide plowed field, across from which stood another wide field of green corn. Private Peck looked off to his right and realized he could no longer see the men of the 8th Connecticut. He felt very uneasy by the sight. Something had gone wrong. He tried to gain the attention of Sergeant Holmes further down the line, but his effort was interrupted by several loud bangs over his head. The Rebel guns on the ridge above them had begun to fire exploding shell into their ranks. After rising from his instinctive crouch, Peck could see that men had fallen to the ground and were being left behind by the advance. He could hear shouts from their officers through the thickening white smoke, "Close ranks! Close up!"

Peck struggled to maintain his pace as the men on his left and right jostled him as they clumsily closed ranks. Raising his head, he could see Rebel troops ahead running towards them off of a road. They were forming ranks in their path in the distance. Another volley of rustling shells passed over their heads and burst with loud claps behind them. He could hear men screaming in the distance as the hot iron found flesh. Despite the dense heat that had his woolen uniform soaked in sweat, he found he had begun to tremble uncontrollably. The only way to fight the trembling was to continue to walk forward. Soon they entered another large field of tall corn. Peck immediately felt better not being able to see.

A quarter mile away General Rodman turned on his nervous horse and surveyed his division's progress. To his alarm, he noted that Harland's Brigade was developing a wide split in his lines. While the 8th was keeping up with the 9th New York Zouaves, he saw that the 16th Connecticut and the 4th Rhode Island were moving on a diverging axis towards the southwest. The misalignment was creating a tempting opening to the Rebels forming for battle up the slope before him. Spurring his horse to a gallop, Rodman rode to Colonel Harlan to his right. Reining in his horse when he arrived by Harlan, General Rodman shouted, "Colonel Harlan! Your brigade has separated! Continue to guide this regiment on the 9th New York! I shall push your center and left back to you! Stand fast as their guide!" Harlan nodded, surprised at how far in the wrong direction his center and left had drifted in the deep corn. General Rodman then spurred his horse to a gallop and rode out across the plowed ground towards the wayward regiments. The air filled with the clatter and smoke of musket volleys as the Zouaves found the Rebel main line.

Corporal Billy Cross and Gene Gerrard spread more of the fodder on the hayloft floor of the tall barn they had established themselves in. They had been there since noon, patiently engaging in long range shooting of targets of opportunity in the approaching Federal ranks. Once the Yankees had taken the bridge down below their original position, First Sergeant Otis had instructed them to occupy the barn with the Whitworth rifle as part of the skirmish line duties assigned to the Palmetto Sharpshooters. Another group, from his company, was along a stone fence just outside the door of the barn. Billy settled back down on the cushion of fodder and found it more comfortable to lie on than the hard wooden floor. It was now nearly 3 pm, and the number of Yankee troops had reached alarming proportions. Gene had calmly observed, as he peered through his telescope, "I suspect we will have to get, shortly!" Billy nodded, as he stood to swab his bore before reloading. So far, he had taken 10 shots with seven hits. He still had 10 cartridges remaining. Finished with his wiping, he carefully opened another of the long hexagonal tubes and poured the powder down the bore. He then inserted the long hexagonal Whitworth bullet into the muzzle and carefully rammed the round home with his ramrod. After he had returned the rod to its channel, he capped the rifle, and settled back down into the hay, adjusting his shooting position. They had been careful to establish themselves in the middle of the hayloft to avoid allowing the long plume of muzzle smoke from exiting the structure. Many field glass assisted eyes, on the other side, looked for that tell tale sign. Any sighting of such smoke would invite the attention of the Yankee cannon.

After scanning the approaching Union regiments, Gene called out, "Billy, look out to the right! Gotta messenger on a horse, in a big hurry!"

Billy lifted his head away from his scope, to better see the action to the right, and asked, "How far off?" Gene quickly replied, "I'd say near abouts 800 yards, or so."

After a short scan, Billy saw the horseman breaking away from one of the blue clad regiments. The man was riding towards two others, that were heading in a slightly different direction. He could clearly see the wide separation developing in the nearly solid lines of blue clad men. He quietly said, "I see him! Ain't easy, hittin' a running target!" Gene replied, "Shoot the horse, then." Billy settled in and adjusted the rifle with his knees, until he found the horseman in the Davidson scope. He muttered, "Even the horse won't be easy, boy!" He reached without looking and cocked the hammer. He took in a breath and held it. He then followed the rider momentarily and then held the cross hair in the scope off further to the right, to give the round lead. Gently squeezing the trigger, he surprised himself with the discharge of the rifle. The rifle violently recoiled and filled the loft with dense smoke. Gene had risen, as he had become accustomed to, and stood by the opening of the loft with his telescope propped on the sill to avoid the obscuring smoke. After a pause, he called out, "Hey! You got the horse for sure, they both went down pretty hard!"

Suddenly the men below shouted and began to fire their muskets in a loud clatter. The Sergeant below, shouted up to the loft, "Time to skedaddle boys! We got lots of Yankees a' comin'" A perfect hail of minie balls suddenly passed through the rough sawn timbers of the structure, filling the air inside the barn with flying splinters as Billy and Gene scrambled to get to the ground floor. At least a regiment was firing volleys at the structure.

None of the Officers of the 16th Connecticut saw General Rodman fall. They had already blindly entered the tall corn. The heavy hexagonal bullet had passed through his thigh and into his horse. Both died together in the dusty plowed field.

Ahead in the corn, Major Ward peered through the stalks, towards his front, as his men struggled to stay aligned. They were approaching another cleared field beyond and through the stalks he thought he could make out masses of men in blue in the open field. He turned and grabbed Captain Elliot, who was the acting Adjutant, and directed, "Go forward with the Colors and ascertain the Regiment ahead, perhaps we can align on them!"
Captain Elliot quickly nodded and rushed over to the color guard and drummers to direct them to follow him. With the men in tow, he trotted forward through the thick stalks of corn. As he came closer he could begin to make out the dark mass of men before him. He turned to insure his color guard was keeping up, as he neared the edge of the field. Emerging into the brightly sunlit field of stubble, Captain Elliot realized that the mass of men before them were not another friendly Regiment. It was a long line of men wearing bits and pieces of both Rebel and Union uniforms.

As he turned to return to warn Major Ward, he heard an Officer within the Rebel ranks cry out, "Ready!"

Sergeant Chriscoe and his squad were amazed to see a small cluster of men emerge, barely 50 yards away, bearing large and lovely blue State color along with the Federal Flag. General Branch had shouted out as he rode the lines, "Ready your arms men! Give them hell!"

Chriscoe and the rest of his men hastily shouldered their rifles when Colonel Lane had echoed the command, and they waited until he shouted out, moments later, "Fire!" All the regiments of Branch's Brigade unleashed an earsplittingly loud stuttering volley into the green corn field. As the great cloud of smoke obscured the view forward, Chriscoe could hear screams and cries from the stricken men in the corn, as they feverishly bit off the ends of cartridges to reload. The officers had called out down the line, "Load!" With great clanking and thrusting of arms, the brigade recharged their rifles and brought them up in near unison to cap them as the Colonel cried out again, "Make ready! Aim...!" Thousands of Enfield Muskets were brought to shoulders again and erupted again as the repeated calls of "Fire!" were heard. The drumming then began as they reloaded. They were hardly given enough time to complete their task before the Officers directed, "Advance!" The Regiments began their measured advance into the tall corn. As they entered the cornfield, a weak volley coming in response, blew wafts of smoke through the stalks. Only a few of the North Carolinians fell. Chriscoe could hear the Yankee Sergeants in the smoky green jungle of stalks, as they shouted for men to close the ranks and align themselves.

After they had gone 20 yards into the corn, the order was shouted, "Charge Bayonets!" Chriscoe and the men around him gave a great shout as they brought their rifles up, pointing before them as drilled. They soon encountered the first of many fallen men, laying in rows, as they had stood in the tall stalks. Some still moaned and held their hands up as the grim North Carolinians ignored their pleas and pressed on through the corn.

Private Peck became aware of a commotion of shouting, forward of him and off to left, before a great eruption of musket fire sent a deadly hail of lead splattering through the tall green stalks. The men to either side of him went down heavily, and he felt something hot and wet spray onto his face. Looking down, he saw the man to his left with a gaping hole in the side of his head. Peck wiped his face and realized he was covered in blood. Desperately looking around, he could only see few men who were still standing. A wide-eyed Lieutenant behind him, shouted, "Close ranks men!" Peck rushed over fallen bodies and nervously got next to a man he did not know and blindly followed the shouted commands. As they fumbled with their muskets, another great volley erupted before them, and a second shattering wave of minie balls tore through the corn. Peck heard loud and violent pops as the balls struck home. Trembling, he raised his musket on the command "Ready!...Aim!" and pulled the stiff trigger on the command, "Fire!" Their fire in response did not sound like much, maybe a hundred muskets at best.

The trembling had returned, deep in his gut, as he shakily struggled to reload his musket. He felt something deep emerging within him. The feeling rose, irresistibly, seizing his ability to think, totally possessing him. Ignoring the commands being shouted, and dropping the opened cartridge to the ground, he turned, and ran. Despite tripping and falling in the tangled roots of the corn, he kept scrambling to escape. To his surprise, despite the great heat and choking smoke, filling his heaving lungs, he felt he could run all the way back to Hartford. Descending the slope that lead to the bloody bridge below, he began to slow as he noticed he was not alone. Many others were doing the same. As he approached the road that led back across the bridge, an officer on horseback shouted out to him and several others descending the hill, "Rally on me boys! Stand your ground here with me!"

An old grizzled Sergeant walked along the growing group of panting men. Seeing Peck heaving to catch his breath, he offered him a canteen, and said, "Here boy take a drink." As Peck took the canteen, and hastily swallowed, the sergeant soothingly said, "No worries son, after a few more fights, you'll learn how to calm the rabbit in ya." The Sergeant moved on to the other men, checking each before ordering to the bunch, "You all just sit tight and rest. We will figure out your regiments in a little while!" More and more dejected men were coming back down the road. While columns of new men pushed up the hill. The clamor of firing back up the hill, continued without pause.

A dusty courier galloped up the prominence where General Lee stood with General Longstreet studying the smoke arising from the battle to the south. The man saluted, and handed Major Venable a folded message, as he announced, "Sir! General Hill begs to report that he has driven the Yankees back down to the hill by the bridge! He wishes instruction on how far you would like him to go!" Lee raised his hand, indicating for him to pause, and after finding his readers, put them on to read the message. As he scanned the penciled lines, he was immediately struck by the passage detailing the death of General Branch. He had now lost nine generals on this bloody day. Finished with his reading, he handed the message to General Longstreet. Longstreet let out a breath as he read the message and observed, "It is a sad thing to come to know, General. Branch was a good man. Just like all the others!. It will be dark soon General Lee, and we have lost many men. I daresay, if Hill had not come when he had, we would be swimming the Potomac by now." After a pause, Longstreet asked, "How much more do you want from these boys, General?"

Lee stonily stared into the distance towards where he imagined McClellan stood, and stated absently, "We must secure our lines here, before Sharpsburg. Night is coming. It is the Lord's way of making us pause. I think we must pause to restore our lines, General."

Longstreet looked to the courier and directed, "Son, go tell General Hill to fall back to good ground, just south of Sharpsburg and prepare defenses. Tell him to tie into my Division's right!"

The man swiftly saluted and galloped back down the hill. riding furiously off to the south. The sun was low behind the trees as they watched. The firing all up and down the lines slowed, as the men on both sides prayed for merciful darkness.

Lee turned to Longstreet, his eyes were moist, and he ordered, "General Longstreet, please coordinate with General Jones. Have the Provost Guard assemble our ambulances and any wagons they might find. I fear there are many injured sons that could live to fight another day. I should like us to dedicate our energies, on this night, towards bringing as many of them, as we can back to Virginia with us. Please see to it. We shall have much to do before the sun rises, tomorrow!"

General Sykes and General Porter stood with Major General McClellan on the hilltop that had served as his outpost for the majority of the great battle. The men engaged in a spirited debate over Sykes' proposal to commit Porter's reserve in the center while there was some daylight. The news being brought to McClellan, by his signalers, was disconcerting. He had lost three Corps Commanders and nine General officers down below. The prisoner reports he received from interviews conducted by Pinkerton's men had yielded precious little from the uncooperative drawling men. In his mind, he could not shake his belief that General Lee was luring him. Luring him into a trap. A trap upon which he would spring a large withheld reserve. Fitz John Porter had reminded him earlier, "Sir, I am the last reserve of the Republic!" as part of his argument against Sykes' urging.

After much thought, George McClellan succumbed to the concerns of his Army surgeon, his orders simply directed, "Stand your ground until the morrow. Attend to the wounded you can find. Prepare for operations. Attack when ordered."

George McClellan directed a dispatch to be sent to Washington, attention Major General Halleck, announcing a great victory over the forces of General Robert E. Lee. He then announced to his staff that he would get some rest.

4

A VICTORY OF SORTS

The silent guns of Company M sat in the last position of yesterday as the sun rose on the morning of the 18th of September. As the rays of bleak light crept across the still slopes before Sharpsburg, they illuminated a landscape littered with rifles, canteens, broken wagons, crippled caissons, dead horses, and bodies of men, either dead or nearly there. Here and there small plumes of smoke rose from fires caused by the battle. The smoke hung low along with the morning mist from Antietam Creek. Both sides of the lines were eerily quiet.

Joshua, who had slept only fitfully, quietly sat with his arms on his knees as his section woke up with quiet talking. They took their time dressing. Private Wilkins had begun to build a small fire to make coffee. Once they were dressed, Joshua quietly directed, "Go see to the horses before you do anything else! There is a well down behind us." The men from the battery had already begun to move the horses in pairs down to the farm well in a hollow behind their position. They returned, after the animals had been watered, and returned them to their traces. The drivers attended to cutting roughage and grain, mixing it with molasses. They poured the mix into the nosebags for feeding the teams. After the horses were fed, the trusty section frying pan was settled on the coals of Wilkin's fire, and soon lumps of salt meat were crackling. The smell of frying bacon make Joshua hungry, but he continued to sit and watch forward of them, as the sun slowly rose. Wilkins brought Joshua a tin cup of hot coffee, and Joshua, grateful, quietly thanked him.

Lazy smoke emerged from the woods across the broad fields to the west as their opponents also began to wake and attend to breakfast. Joshua studied the wood closely, but could see no movement or sign of activity. He knew they were still there.

Looking toward Captain Haine's tent, he saw the First Sergeant emerge with Quartermaster Sergeant Mills following. They walked towards where Joshua sat. O'Keefe emitted a lazy trail of smoke from his briar pipe as he puffed away on his brisk approach. Joshua, with his tin cup still in his hand, rose when the First Sergeant arrived. After a nod, Joshua asked, "We gonna be movin' soon?" With a wave of his hand, O'Keefe replied, "Nope. The Captain wants to convey to the boys his delight at their actions yesterday. Once you rub their bellies a bit, then set them to cleaning their guns, and reporting what you'll be needin' to Mills, here!" He pointed his thumb towards Mills, who smiled, but said nothing.

Joshua nodded, he had expected this morning to be another day of pitched battle. After a moment he asked, "What is gonna happen next?" O'Keefe grinned, with the pipe clenched between his stained teeth, and laughed, "Boy'O! Can't ya see? We got us two high and mighty Generals who have gone off and scared themselves with all the killin' we done yesterday! It seems to me, they is steeling themselves to see who's to start first, on this fine morning!" O'Keefe turned to look across the expanse before them, he thoughtfully observed, "The Captain said he heard from Hayes last night that nine Generals was shot yesterday on our side, three of them was Corps Commanders! I suspect we will dawdle awhile, until they gets reorganized. Until then, we wait. Stay ready, and attend to yer guns!"

Joshua nodded, and watched silently, as the pair tramped over to Newby's section. Downing the rest of the cold coffee in his tin cup, he then walked over to the fire. Private Wilkins offered him a chunk of fried bacon, skewered on the tip of a knife. Joshua took the hot meat and popped it into his mouth. He had eaten little over the past two days and the meat revived him. After getting a refill of coffee, he found Corporal Page and instructed him to have the men clean the gun after breakfast.

Joshua then returned to his own horse and led the animal down for water at the well. Once he had watered him, he brought him back to the guns and borrowed a nosebag to give him grain. As the animal ate, he carefully checked his shoes and picked out his hooves. The morning sun had risen, and it was going to be another hot day. Joshua checked on his men as they swabbed out the bore of the blackened gun, and instructed the men to clean the fouling from the exterior of the piece as well. The inventory of the limbers and the caisson was now complete and Joshua took the figures from his men and recorded them in a small booklet with a pencil. He would have to find Mills to see to resupply. He knew instinctively, if he waited, Mills would soon be coming by. The men admired their Quartermaster Sergeant, precisely due to his attentiveness. All the good ones were that way.

An hour later, Quartermaster Sergeant Mills rode along the gun line soliciting the Section Sergeants for their ammunition requirements. He advised them, as he collected their shortages, that he had ammunition wagons on the way. Joshua passed him his requirements as he came calling. Mills paused a moment as Joshua passed him his note of requirements, and remarked, "You should be proud, Sergeant Timmonds, you have come a long way since I first laid eyes on you!" Joshua gratefully nodded, adding, "You had a lot to do with it, Quartermaster Sergeant!"

Joshua reflected as he watched his crew prepare their guns. They had been lucky. A twelve-hour fight and none of them had suffered a scratch. He hoped the Almighty would continue to be so kind to them.

After several hours, the sections completed the cleaning of their guns and implements. First Sergeant O'Keefe and the Section Lieutenants conducted an inspection of the pieces. Joshua noticed that Lieutenant Colonel Hayes had arrived, and was in a quiet discussion with Captain Haines, near the rear of their position. It was mid-day now, and the lines remained still and quiet. The heat steadily rose and the men asked to shed their jackets. Joshua refused them. They were doing little and it would not be worth the provocation that asking O'Keefe would bring. Joshua knew that the longer they sat, it would only be a matter of time before Lieutenant Pennington would arrive to the conclusion that a little spell of drill would be a good idea. In order to keep his initiative as the Section Sergeant, he rose and announced to his section, "Alright boys! Fall in! Gun Drill!"

The men groaned and bitched a little, but soon they settled into their paces as Joshua shouted out the commands. As he worked his section, he caught a glance at Newby cursing him. His fellow section sergeant's hand was forced. Newby reluctantly rose and had his crews do the same.

Lieutenant Colonel Hayes stopped his discussion with Captain Haines and watched for a moment. He then asked, "Was this drill your order, Captain?" Haines honestly replied, "Not at all sir, I was planning to let them rest!" Both men watched as First Sergeant O'Keefe returned with his horse from the well below. As he topped the hill, he paused to watch his three sections conducting unordered gun drill. O'Keefe smiled slightly, and looked down, as he silently led his mount past the two officers.

Hayes remarked to Haines as he mounted his horse, "Men like this are why we certainly will prevail, Captain Haines! I congratulate you and them for your actions yesterday! Stand ready for orders, as I have no idea when you shall receive any!" He then carefully descended on his horse back down the steep hill.

After an hour of gun drill, Joshua ordered his section to fall out and make lunch. He then returned to his sitting spot and watched across the still pastures. Looking into the sky above the vast field of battle, he noticed the dark forms of vultures forming in multiple orbiting clusters. The heat of the day carried the scent of death aloft and they had urgently gathered for an anticipated feast. As he sat and studied the far wood, he suddenly noticed a delegation of horsemen with several canvas topped ambulances emerge from the dark woods across the way. The gray-clad rider at the head of the column bore a large white flag. O'Keefe had strolled over to where Joshua sat and silently puffed his pipe. Joshua looked up shielding his eyes from the sun, and asked, "A Truce?" O'Keefe grunted, "I know one ain't been ordered, but I reckon there is gonna' be one, anyhow." He puffed a bit more, and fiddled with his pipe, "A man can only listen to the wounded boys whimper, so much. After a while, the fellows will insist to the officers to do somethin'. You watch them lines boy, in five minutes you'll witness a swap meet a start! Shame we ain't there, we could get more tobacco!"

As predicted, groups of men in blue also rose from their positions and began to move forward to rescue their own wounded. In an hour, clusters of men from both sides began the quiet task of removing the maimed. Some of them shook hands with their foes and stood about talking and smoking. The activity spurred mimicry all up and down the lines as the former deadly foes tentatively met in the midst of yesterday's slaughter. After several hours, the officers of both armies, having satisfied the demands of their men, sounded bugles to cease the fraternization of the armies, and by late afternoon the field lay empty again, except for the still forms of the slain.

They never received explanation for the daylong pause. As the sun hung low in the west, a creaking collection of black-topped wagons arrived. The ammunition supply had arrived. Joshua walked the line, hoping to locate his friend L. G., but this was a different Company and he was not to be found. After they had restocked their limber chests and caissons, the men began to cook more rations for supper. Dark clouds began to form in the north and quickly blotted out the dwindling light of the sun. It would be a rainy night. Rare gusts of strong wind announced the soft smell of coming moisture.

As darkness fell, the men of the section began to find their bedrolls and prepared to call it a night. Joshua rose and walked over to his horse to unstrap his blanket from the rear of his saddle. As he tugged the supple leather straps to loosen it, he glanced once more across the way. Hundreds of small fires flickered in the woods around the battered white structure. He was resigned to the fact that they would certainly fight in the morning. The peace of the day could not be tolerated by the leaders of this war.

The soft rain of the warm September night deadened the sounds of the retreat back across the Potomac. General Lee rode behind his creaking train of ambulances as they descended the hill out of Sharpsburg to the shallow crossing known by the locals as Boteler's Ford. As he approached, he could see General Stuart's cavalrymen sitting on horseback holding torches at the ford's entrance and several more across the way lighting the exit. In the half-light of the night, the ford was filled with wagons. Lee listened quietly; above the clatter of the wagons he could hear the occasional groans of the wounded as the wagons struck stones or deep ruts. He paused by the entrance and watched as long lines of tramping infantrymen descended the hill. They moved slowly and carefully, as the road had become slick in the rain. Many sported black oilcloth ponchos, recently liberated from fallen Union soldiers. Lee momentarily wished for equipage of the quantity that General McClellan enjoyed. He mused at what he could accomplish if he could provide such extravagances to these men. Lee continued to sit and worry. A retreat of this nature put his army in extreme danger. If the ruse of the hundreds of fires in the woods above Sharpsburg were discovered as such, then McClellan could destroy him here, strung out at a river crossing. Lee noticed a rider crossing the waist deep water coming towards him. The rider carefully guided his mount back up out of the water on the Maryland side, and paused to look about, before beginning again. In the torch light by the entrance to the ford, Lee noted that the rider's eyes stared at him. The rider approached and Lee soon recognized Captain Marshall, "Sir! Colonel Chilton, and Major Venable are across with the headquarters baggage and the rest of the staff. They will proceed to Martinsburg and find a headquarters camp there. Colonel

Chilton directed me to remain with you!" Lee nodded, and replied, "Captain Marshall, I shall remain here until my army crosses. It would be most useful for you to ride back up the road to Sharpsburg and relay to my Division Commanders to visit with me here, before they cross. Please do not compel them to leave their units. They shall serve best arranging for their movements, where they are, within the columns."

The long columns of sleepy soldiers, endless wagons, and artillery batteries clogged the narrow and muddy road in their quiet night movement. Lee had moved Traveler into the river up to it's knees, off to the south side of the ford. The road was too choked for him to be blocking it. Lee paused with his Generals, in turn, as they arrived. He engaged each in quiet guidance as they watched their columns wade the Potomac. He still lacked a comprehensive understanding of his losses, and to each he provided instruction to provide him returns, once they had reached Martinsburg. When General Pendleton arrived with the remainder of the artillery reserve in tow, Lee paused with him and reviewed his mission to cover the road to Martinsburg, as a rear guard, until his army was collected again. Pendleton was nervous about his mission. He had never commanded infantry forces before and was uncertain of details they had covered at their twilight meeting. Lee resolved to discuss this with General Jackson when he arrived at the ford. There would need to be a plan to reinforce Pendleton, if McClellan elected to pursue them.

All night they crossed in the rain. Some of the men, recognizing their commander, raised their hats, silently, in resigned admiration for their leader. He remained with them always, it seemed.

As the sky began to lighten in the east, with the coming of dawn, the rain stopped, and mist obscured the bottomlands of the Potomac. The cavalrymen had doused their torches and sat silently on their mounts, sentinels now of their General, who continued to sit astride his horse in the shallow spot in the river. General Walker, at the head of his column, noted General Lee in the mist, and rode over to report, "Sir, I am the last of your Army! Saving those who still lie unburied behind us." Lee solemnly looked Walker in the eyes, and replied in a cracking voice, "Praise be to God! Take them across General! We have little time! I fear they shall follow."

As the last of the wading men exited the ford, Lee followed with an escort of cavalry. As he ascended the steep bank on the Virginia side, he paused by a cluster of artillerymen preparing their 6 pounders on the bluffs of the ford. The young men's faces brightened to see General Lee and he spent a few moments exchanging pleasantries with them. Lee had hoped he would have found his son Robert Junior's battery, but it was not to be. After a while he bid his farewell, and left them with a stern reminder, "Boys if those people dare to cross, remind them that they are in Virginia!"

First Sergeant O'Keefe briskly strode over to his horse and strapped his bedroll onto his saddle, in the dim light of dawn. The Captain had received orders, just moments ago. Once he had returned his belongings to his horse, he reached his foot up to his stirrup and pulled himself onto the saddle. Turning the animal towards his gun line, he shouted in a loud voice, "Limber up! We're movin' out!" O'Keefe watched as each of the Section Lieutenants trotted from the Captain's tent towards their crews. The order indicated that a pursuit of the retreating Rebels was to occur. They were back under the control of the Horse Artillery Regiment, and would accompany General Pleasanton's Squadrons as they pushed forward to regain contact with the Lee's army.

Joshua assisted his section with backing the limber team up to his gun. The others were on detail packing out the tents and baggage into the battery wagon and helping Sergeant Mueller with stowing his tools. They had the guns limbered in a little less than fifteen minutes. They then brought the sections around with limber and guns in the lead with the caissons in trail. After a few more moments the battery wagon and Mueller's forge wagon brought up the trail of the company. Captain Haines sat, waiting until the last of his men were mounted and ready to move. The swallow-tailed guidon hung limply on Corporal Parnell's staff as he sat quietly beside the Captain.

Captain Haines, satisfied that his company was ready for movement, ordered his bugler to sound the advance. Company M then deployed into column onto the broad pasture that led towards a series of roads, feeding into the Hagerstown Pike and on to Sharpsburg. Soon they were making their way through a bumpy stubble field of harvested corn. As he rode, Joshua looked idly to his right. They were now paralleling a sunken road, and to his horror, he saw it was filled with dead Rebels. They had now lain where they had fallen, for the beginning of the second day, and many of the bodies were beginning to bloat from the effects of decomposition and the sun. The wind shifted as they passed, bringing the terrible smell wafting through their ranks. The men cursed and searched for their handkerchiefs to bind over their noses. Captain Haines mercifully moved to angle the battery away from the road. Joshua then noticed that details of infantry were recovering blue clad bodies in rough lines for burial. The men had fashioned meat hooks by bending bayonets and used them to unceremoniously drag the bloated bodies into lines before the trenches being dug to inter the bodies. Clusters of Sergeants, with rags covering their noses, gingerly searched the bodies for signs of identity, while others recorded their findings in small notebooks. He met the eyes of one of the young boys in the nearest detail as he rode by. The young soldier's face reflected a look of both disgust and anguish. Another man beside the boy suddenly turned his head aside to retch. Several others were resignedly digging the beginning of a long trench, into which their fallen comrades would be interred. As they crossed the field, Joshua recognized the ruined caisson that they were approaching, as one they had engaged the day before yesterday. Coming closer, he could see several dead bodies, and two dead horses, still in their traces attached to the singletree of the shot up limber.

As the company drew nearer to the crest of the hill in the stubble, a detachment led by an Officer galloped over to Captain Haines and First Sergeant O'Keefe, as they led the company forward. Joshua noticed that O'Keefe had raised his hand for the company to halt, and Joshua called out to his section, "Hold up boys! Wait on the Captain." The men brought their teams to a halt with low commands to "Whoa." Some lowered their kerchiefs to sample the air; the stench of death remained, trapped in the humid morning air, and most elected to keep their noses covered. Soon the Officer turned and rode back towards the town with the cavalrymen. O'Keefe turned his horse and rode down the line shouting, "Stand fast! The cavalry is clearing the town. Wait by yer guns!"

Joshua decided to dismount to relieve himself. There would be no telling how long they might ride, once the pursuit began. After he had finished, he buttoned his fly, and led his mount over to the ruined caisson. As he approached, he noticed a rebel cannoneer lying folded over, face down on his legs. Flies buzzed angrily around the corpse as he approached. His horse shied nervously off to the side. Forcing himself to look at the man, Joshua could see a great furrow in the small of the man's back. The stark white outline of his lower vertebrae was visible at the bottom of the massive wound. He realized that a solid shot had grazed the man, tearing out a half round channel and severing his spine. Judging from the size of the wound, it had been 12 pounders that had done this work. Joshua felt slightly woozy, but he continued to approach the limber. The horses had grown to nearly twice their normal size from the bloating, and he angled towards the back of the chest, lest his mount become panicked as he led him along. Lettering on the back of the limber chest caught his eye. He then realized he had nearly stepped on another dead Rebel, as he had been looking towards the limber chest. Looking down, he saw in his horror that this man had been completely eviscerated by another solid shot. He lay as open and devoid of organs, as a slaughtered animal. His left forearm was missing, sheared cleanly off by the passing ball. A fine coating of dust covered his features and his vulnerable interior. Joshua shuddered as he stared, fixated. His consciousness was filled with his own mortality. Many such shot had whizzed by him on more occasions than he could count. He gingerly stepped around the corpse and looked back towards the limber chest. His eyes caught the lettering, and his stomach churned as he read the inscription, "Macbeth Light Artillery." The painted letters had been neatly rendered by hand with careful brush strokes. Near the inscription were several splintered holes from case shot shrapnel. His nausea rose to his throat. He was forced to double over, and he vomited painfully. Wiping his mouth with the back of his hand, he weakly led his mount away. Behind him he heard a great voice, "I've said it before, Boy O'! It don't pay to go forward of yer guns!" It was O'Keefe, astride his horse. In a fatherly voice he said, "Come on Boy, leave this shit! I seen the inscription and I don't wonder how it makes ya' feel!" Joshua thought to turn and look at the faces of the dead men, but then he thought better of it, and weakly mounted his horse. He could not know that it was not named for his own home. The Macbeth Light Artillery was not from the Low country at all. Too many years had passed for him to know.

As he rode back to rejoin his section, he wiped his face on his shell jacket sleeve. Corporal Page, shocked by his pale appearance, asked with concern, "Sergeant Timmonds! Is everything alright?" Timmonds grimly replied, "Fine Page, sound as a dollar." O'Keefe's wisdom lingered in his mind, "Never go forward of your guns…"

Soon they received the order to move again. As they passed through the torn up streets of Sharpsburg, the men all looked at the destruction the battle had wrought on the pretty little town. The Rebels had already crossed the river before them and General Pleasanton had ordered the guns to hurry forward to support infantry that would soon be crossing in pursuit.

The heavily loaded mule-drawn wagon closely followed the supply trains of General Pleasanton's last column. The driver was a burly, bearded man and his assistant rode with him on the buckboard seat. The mules drew their load with a choppy churning pace. When they would pause to wait on the advance of the army column, the mules loudly protested. They did not like pulling the load from a dead start. Alexander Gardner was going to do something he had never done before. Around him lay a field of thousands of subjects, for his photographic art. The Confederate dead required no permissions, payment, or copyright. They lay still, bloated, and waiting, for their immortality. Gardner's party pulled up before the shell battered Dunker Church and he surveyed the carnage. Details of Infantrymen were being formed to begin collection and burial of their fellow soldiers, but no details were formed by the Rebels. They had returned to Virginia.

Gardner, seeing plentiful bodies by an artillery caisson, decided that this was a good place to start. He ordered his assistants in his heavy Scottish brogue to extend the tent-like studio shelter from the back of the wagon and establish his dark room. He carefully supervised them as they unloaded his camera and tripod from the tailgate of the wagon. He attended to the assembly of this critical equipment on his own. Once the camera stood securely on it's stout wooden tripod, he stepped back and began to visualize his first shot. Never before had soldiers, dead of battle, been photographed, in this war. Gardner winced at the evil smell that surrounded him, but he persevered. He would need the right composition to frame this shot. He paused and peered through the back of the camera studying the upside down panorama. It just was not right. Once his assistants had reported the readiness of his laboratory, he directed them to drag the bodies about. The men were repulsed, but since Mister Brady paid well, they attended to the grotesque task. The corpses were difficult to move without tearing the bloated skin. Unsatisfied, as he studied the tableaux through his camera Gardner directed adjustments. The men moved the corpses once again, they wiped their hands on their pants each time they were directed to repeat the distasteful task. Finally he had what he needed. He directed his assistants to watch his camera and he walked over to his mobile darkroom to prepare Ambrotype plates. Finding his chemicals neatly arranged on the folding tables under the dark tent, illuminated by a red glass kerosene lamp, he first coated the glass plates with a small bottle of Collodion, pouring the precious excess back into the bottle. He then placed the plate into a small metal rack employed to dip it into a square metal container of Silver Nitrate. The strong smell of ether filled the darkroom. He then inserted his two prepared plates into wooden lightproof cartridges for the camera and rushed out to his camera. He would attempt two exposures before the solution on the plates had time to dry.

Inserting his first cartridge into the box camera and removing the protective lid, he peered upward to assess the light. After a moment's consideration, because of the overcast sky, he changed his aperture to a larger size on the brass lens assembly. He then draped his black cloth hood over his head, and reached out to remove the lens cap to make the exposure. Satisfied with his focus, he ducked away to measure 20 seconds by his pocket watch, then returned the lens cap, and deftly inserted the cartridge cover back into the plate carrier. He handed the carrier to one of his assistants, and after slightly changing the angle of his camera, he repeated the exposure process. Gardner then took his second exposure in it's protective case, back to his portable darkroom. His preoccupation made him oblivious to the ghastly smell of his environment. He hardly noticed that his assistants were wearing rags over their noses and mouths.

Once inside, he took his exposed plates into the dark tent, lit only by the red kerosene lamp. Extracting the first, he gently held the plate as he poured Iron Sulfate over the plate while holding it over a metal tray. He moved the solution over the surface and watched as the silver nitrate transformed into metallic silver, forming the negative image. After he was satisfied with his result, he moved to the next tray and washed the negative with clean water. He held the image of the bodies and the limber up to his red light, and moved into the exterior awning lit by the sunlight. In the better light, he dropped the developed plate into a smelly bath of Sulfur Thiosulfate to fix the image. While he was waiting on the plate to soak, he directed his assistants to heat the bottle of Castor Varnish over a candle. Once the varnish was warm, he gently poured a small quantity over the image to protect his negative. He then set the negative on a wooden rack to dry and returned to develop his second exposure. He reflected on his objective. Mr. Brady wanted graphic images of the dead Rebels. He had arranged to have an exposition in New York to display the shocking photos. Gardner realized that a quality product would enable him to make his name. He had begun to chafe at the reality of Brady always getting the credits for his work. Perhaps he could set out on his own.

Gardner then set out to find other collections of the ghastly dead. At each point he traveled to, he found ample and willing subjects.

Lottie was on her second day of pouring over the contents of the master ledger and making entry categories in her working ledger that she would retain as a traveling record. She had paused to listen as the medical officers that worked in the offices around her discussed a great battle in Maryland. Their topic seemed very distant, as she had no idea of the geography north of Richmond. She resumed her entries as professional diligence required, when she heard a familiar voice, "Miss Markley! You need to prepare a small traveling bag!" Looking up, she smiled when she recognized Henri Tenchant. He gave a noble bow, and continued, "I have volunteered to accompany you by train to Lexington! We are to deliver an emergency resupply of badly needed supplies to a military hospital there! There are many wounded arriving there after the great battle before Sharpsburg! We must make haste. Colonel Johns would like for you to establish a baseline understanding of their stocks!" Lottie was stunned, and stammered, "Captain Tinchant! I have hardly started! Must I?" Tinchant turned serious for a moment, and replied, "Exigencies of war, Miss! We must remain prepared to drop everything for our soldiers! Come now! We have orders!" Lottie nodded, shocked by his sudden businesslike tone. The military curtness reminded her of being scolded by her father.

As she quickly assembled her ledger and spare papers, pencils and gum erasers, she realized she had nothing to assemble them into. Captain Tenchant walked over to one of the nearby work desks and found an empty leather satchel. He then helped her load her items into the leather case. Tenchant then looked at her and in a softer tone, said, "Come with me and I will wait on you while your pack a small bag. We are to meet a military train to Winchester this afternoon. You will need to confirm the inventory while we make the trip, so insure you wear something you don't mind getting dirty." Back at the boarding house, Lottie wished she had found the time to locate a seamstress. What she needed were her rough clothes from home. She packed an extra housedress, extra chemises, and bloomers into a mid sized carpet bag. She would travel light, leaving her hoop skirts, and corsets behind. If she needed something more formal, she would have to clean her business clothes that she currently had on.

After half an hour, Lottie reappeared and apologized to Captain Tinchant

who waited patiently in the sitting room of the boarding house. He smiled as he saw her minimal luggage, observing, "Miss Markley, I congratulate you on your admirable practicality! We may be required to travel rough!"
He then took her bag, and they caught a Hansom cab to the train station. Once they had arrived at the station, Lottie began to walk towards the ticket window of the passenger terminus. Captain Tinchant quickly caught up to her, "Miss Markley, you're off in the wrong direction, our train requires no tickets! It is waiting on the far siding! Follow me if you please." She followed him through the terminal building as he turned right and exited onto the platform. The rail station was bustling with soldiers and very few civilians were waiting for transportation. They crossed several of the tracks out in the sun, using the boardwalks that crossed each successive track, until she made out a rather dirty train of some thirty cars strung out behind. Peering at the train, she saw only two passenger coaches. The rest of the cars were either flatbeds loaded with cannon and mules or box cars. Groups of soldiers and slaves were loading boxed items into several of the boxcars. Captain Tenchant led her to the last passenger car of the train. He turned to her, as they walked, to explain, "Miss Markley, accommodations are going to be harsh on this trip. We shall have to make do with what we find. Such is the nature of military trains!" She nodded, while intimidating in one way, she was fascinated in another.

Tinchant assisted her mount the step to the car and entering within, she saw one vacant bench seat. The rest were full of Officers in a multitude of different uniforms. Most seemed surprised to see a lady come on to the car. Captain Tinchant greeted many of the men as he made his way to the available seat. He motioned for Lottie to take the seat by the window. He placed her bag in the rack overhead and took a seat next to her. The other officers around Tinchant asked him about his destination and he carried on conversation with them for a while. An hour later, the train finally gave several sharp toots of its whistle and the car jerkily began to move.

Henri Tinchant then described the legs of the journey they would take. Since the railroads of the South were all private concerns, the itinerary was complex. Tinchant explained that they were on the Virginia Central Railroad for this leg. They would detrain at Gordonsville and oversee the offloading of their twenty cases of supplies to another train, expected to arrive the next day, on the Orange and Alexandria line to Manassas Junction. There, they would offload again and transfer to the Manassas Railroad to Strasbourg, Virginia. As he talked, Lottie gazed out the dirty glass window of the coach as the train began to enter the countryside surrounding Richmond. She could see earthworks and cannon frowning out from parapets of the fortifications surrounding the city. What obviously used to be picturesque rolling hills, was now scarred with line upon line of disturbed red soil, propping up walls built of chopped logs. The sight made her realize the closeness of the war. The seriousness of her new job began to settle into her consciousness.

The train made several stops and groups of the officers seated with them would rise, and depart, each time wishing their seatmates farewell. Tinchant explained to Lottie that they were usually Officers who were returning to their units from taking leave. For each group that departed, more men would board at the stops. It was dark by the time they finally reached Gordonsville, and after an hour of checking cars, Captain Tinchant found his cargo of supplies. He directed the Sergeant in charge of the Train Guard to have the load transferred to the Orange and Alexandria Station on the north side of town and to have it secured under his name. Tinchant secured his traveling bag from amidst the stores as the soldiers directed several slaves to unload the cargo. He then picked up Lottie's bag for her and walked with her into Gordonsville. After a few minutes of searching, he finally found a boarding house with two available rooms, and secured the rooms paying for them with Confederate paper bills. The proprietress of the house indicated that she still had supper available, when she provided them with keys, and Tinchant agreed. They had a quiet dinner chatting with other lodgers who were already seated at the half filled table. Lottie felt greatly weary, having had to make a long trip with very little notice. After agreeing to meet in morning for breakfast at 7 am, she excused herself and proceeded upstairs to her room. In addition to her fatigue, she felt very far from home and very alone.

She quickly found the numbered door that corresponded with her iron key and entered into the small room. The open drapes of the tiny room admitted enough moonlight for her to find the lamp and some matches on the chest of drawers, and she lit the kerosene wick. Looking around she saw only bare whitewashed plaster. The floor was well-worn and lacking varnish, where the lodgers paced. The bed was clean and well made, and she had water in the pitcher, that sat in its porcelain basin. She peered under the bed and found her chamber pot, and satisfied that she could survive the night, she undressed and settled into bed, drifting off into dreamless sleep.

Early the next morning, Lottie heard an urgent knock at her door. It was Mrs. Adams who was the proprietress of the boarding house, "Miss Markley, your party asked that you prepare to depart!"

Lottie sat up with a start, she could not find her locket watch. She noted that bright sunlight flowed through the crack in her drapes and she realized that she had overslept. She rolled out of bed and groggily poured water into the bowl from the porcelain pitcher and washed her face and hands. Looking into her mirror, she realized that she had bags under her eyes. She washed her face more and briskly rubbed her cheeks with the wash cloth. Looking again, she saw she had produced a baggy eyed visage with red cheeks. Disgusted, she began to dress. She had hurriedly opted to wear the same outfit as yesterday. While slightly rumpled, it would simply have to do.

Captain Tinchant beamed as he saw her descend the stairs, "Miss Markley! My apologies for the rude awakening we have treated you to! Our train will depart this afternoon, and after breakfast, I suggest we visit the hospital at the Exchange Hotel." Lottie was amazed at his countenance, he beheld her as if she were Venus arising from her shell. She felt perfectly miserable and knew she looked shabby, but Captain Tinchant did not seem to mind. They then sat down to a breakfast of tea with ham biscuits. As they chatted over their cooling tea, the Medical Orderly whom Tinchant introduced as Sergeant Major Brooks, interrupted them, "Sir, I have secured you a cab and loaded the boxes of supplies!" Tinchant quickly rose, and announced, "Thank you Sergeant Major! Miss Markley, let us make haste! I assure you it is not far."

After they had mounted the cab and were on their way, Captain Tinchant gave Lottie pointers. He wanted her to simply review their formulary and account for the limited delivery he intended to provide them. He mentioned that he had also brought several rather rare textbooks, which would improve the mood of the staff as she conducted her survey. He explained that the hospital that they were visiting was full of the wounded from the second battle of Manassas, from the previous month. As they rattled along the dirt road, he advised, "Miss Markley, you will most assuredly see many grievously wounded soldiers on your way to the formulary. Try to look the men in their eyes, and their eyes only! To study the wounds on their bodies only brings on horror! It is a trick that we train our nurses in. Many of them are new to this life." They soon approached an elegantly constructed, two-story building. A pole before the porch supported a bright red flag. Captain Tinchant explained that the flag indicated the structure as a hospital. He added that it might soon change to the color yellow, if the prevailing argument that they should fly the same flag on hospitals as the Yankees prevailed, in order to avoid confusion. Lottie agreed that the idea seemed to make sense. As they drew closer, the pastoral appearance of the great hotel was marred by a detail of men digging graves off to the side of the structure. Lottie noted to her horror that a line of dead men lay in rows near the detail. Tinchant explained, "They are dealing with the long term wounded here. It has filled several hospitals to capacity and I fear we are far from done counting the dead!"

Lottie and Captain Tinchant stepped down off the carriage and the Hospital Steward greeted him. Lottie admired how most the men he encountered seemed to know him. Tinchant then introduced Lottie to the man, and asked him to assist her in her visit to the formulary as she was the Confederate States Medical Auditor for the Procurer. The man seemed surprised to see a woman assigned this duty, but he smiled, and led her to the formulary room. As she passed through the hospital, she was shaken by the smells of men in great distress. A dizzying array of stenches assailed her senses as she quickly followed the Steward clutching her workbook.

As she settled in to conduct her assessment in the neat and sparsely stocked room, a party of soldiers brought up the boxes from Captain Tinchant.

Peering at the odd collection of jars and glass bottles she realized that she could not recognize any of the drugs stored within. On the lower shelves she managed to locate several jars of chloroform and one tin container of ether. As she found each of the items she recognized, she entered them into her working ledger. Confused, she turned to the newly arriving boxes being brought in by Captain Tinchant's detail of orderlies and captured the contents of the delivery. The boxes were more chloroform, a small quantity of quinine, camphor, morphia, and a box full of jars of Laudanum. The sudden appearance of Henri, and another older Officer, gave her a start. She rose and greeted them, "Gentlemen, forgive me, but you startled me, so absorbed was I in my duties!" Captain Tinchant, ever courteous, replied, "Miss Markley, the duty of apology is mine! I am pleased to introduce you to Colonel Caldwell. He is the general surgeon of this hospital!" Colonel Caldwell gravely nodded, and observed, "Miss, It is a rare sight to see a lady sent here as a representative of the government. Surely the state of our struggle has not come to the point where our ladies are required to do the work of men!" Lottie gave a slight curtsey, and replied in a strong voice, "Colonel, it is my duty to serve as our country sees fit. I hope that I am an instrument of assistance to you! I would be happier to fight alongside our brave boys, were I assured I could be of some use in that regard!" Colonel Caldwell laughed, "Well Miss, you certainly are a pistol! Pray tell what are you about?" Lottie explained her duties as the auditor for Colonel Johns, and expressed her confusion at the unrecognizable stores that she had found. As she spoke, Colonel Caldwell listened intently. After several moments thought, he replied, "Young lady allow me to respond. You see, while I admire what your purpose is, I should like to advise you that any effort to pursue conservation is lost on the magnitude of our task here. Please advise the purveyor upon your return, that placing limits on our respective consumption is fruitless! The shortage of medications has forced us to review the folk arts of ages past." He reached for a bottle of brownish water, with dark clumps within, and said, "This concoction, Miss, is red oak bark that has released it's tannin into the water, that it soaked in. It replaces bicarbonate of soda, which proves to be in short supply, as an astringent for disinfecting wounds! We have taken to growing poppies in our garden to extract our own opium! Please advise Colonel Johns of this! Recipes are in greater demand than the rare boxes of small portions that you supply! I have nearly 2500 gravely wounded men here!" Lottie listened attentively as the enormity of his requirements sunk in. He smiled, and continued, "Young lady, you are but the messenger, that I understand. Please relay to your masters that your task would better serve us by relaying our plight! Reports of our extravagance ignores our specific challenge! I am loath to instruct my surgeons to scrimp in their fight to relieve suffering from wounds and fever! I am burying nearly 30 men a day, and it sickens me that I am so ill supplied. Now there is news of another multitude of wounded coming from Maryland! Each great battle is yet another medical catastrophe! Please ask Richmond to realize the demand. Record that in your ledger." Lottie sympathetically nodded as Captain Tinchant looked on. She quietly replied, "Good Sir, I shall make it my purpose to communicate your great needs! I am but a novice in this pursuit, but am able to communicate your concerns. Forgive us for delivering so little! This is but our first stop to many places. I fear we have little to offer you." Colonel Caldwell softened his countenance a bit, and softly replied, "Forgive me as well Miss, I understand you mean well. I am frustrated by my daily challenges, and am grateful for the books and the supply that you have delivered. Please understand that the books mean more than any small supply of the precious contents within the boxes. We are resigned to create medications from what nature provides. These boys are young and strong, and that helps them! Your care in traveling this distance to help us is encouragement in itself, and that is what matters!"

Colonel Caldwell spent the next four hours explaining to Lottie the remedies that the hospital had arrived at homeopathically. She carefully recorded each home remedy in her ledger. His frequent mention of the value of Doctor Porcher's work on Southern Flora and Fauna of the South, gained repeated entries in her record. Surely practical education was the answer. She resolved herself to become the messenger for this staff, back to Richmond.

Catherine Burkhart nimbly rolled another paper tube on her wooden mandrel to form the outer skin of the cartridge she was making. Sticking the wooden peg into a hole on the work surface of her work station, she quickly tied off one end with strong thread and gave the excess paper a quick twist, forming the tail of the cartridge. Laying the formed case aside, she selected a slightly smaller wooden rod and rolled the smaller diameter interior insert that separated the powder charge from the ball inside the outer casing. Catherine nimbly twisted the end of the insert and snipped off the excess with small scissors on the bench. She then removed the larger outer tube from the wooden dowel and inserted the inner tube halfway down into the larger case. Extracting the smaller dowel, she then reached over to the wooden bin at the head of her workstation and filled a copper dipper with powder, pouring it into the inner paper tube. With a swift twist of her fingers, she twisted off the top of the charge and tucked the excess paper into the larger outer cartridge tube, leaving room for the .69 caliber lead ball along with three .32 caliber buckshot, atop the large round sphere. Once the balls were inside the paper outer tube, she placed the assembly into a wooden block with drilled holes that held the partially finished cartridge upright, in order to tie the balls into a tight package. Moving quickly, she wrapped thread around the buckshot and the larger ball at the bottom and tied the thread off. With another quick snip of her scissors, the cartridge was finished and she began to make another. After each was finished, she had placed the paper cartridge into a box of finished rounds. She then began to roll another outer case. She wiped her brow with the back of her sleeve to clear the sweat from her eyes. It had been unseasonably warm all week for September, and thankfully, Mr. Edmunds, who supervised the Cartridge Laboratory, had opened the windows to allow the cooler outside air to blow into the sweltering interior. Catherine could hear the older girls quietly conversing about an upcoming cotillion that was planned in Lawrenceville on Saturday. Catherine pondered if she could convince her mother to allow her to attend. Many of her co-workers at the Allegheny Arsenal were busily making plans for what they would wear and who they would meet there. Catherine daydreamed about a ball gown she had seen in the Seamstress store window in town, that she would be able to purchase with a portion of her pay, due to her on Friday. While she quietly thought, her hands swiftly completed the steps and she laid another finished cartridge into the rack with the rest. Beginning on another cartridge, Catherine pondered whether she could convince her mother to let her buy the dress. She had frowned on her daughter's spendthrift ways and there was often an argument over her spending when she had come home. Being only fifteen also made her mother frown, when she asked to go out.

In her peripheral vision, she could see one of the male laboratory assistants coming around to pour more of the black powder into the wooden bins at their workstations. They had been intructed to change out barrels of powder by Mr. Edmunds, so they were distributing the remainder of the barrel they had opened in the morning to bring in a fresh supply from the warehouse magazine across the Arsenal grounds. Catherine and several of the other ladies looked up as the men opened the wooden door to move the empty barrel out onto the wooden loading dock. The opened door caused a pleasantly cooler breeze to waft through the building. Catherine paused to look at her hands. After working all day on cartridges, her fingers were a uniform gray from the dust of the loading. She hated to go home dirty each day, but the money she was earning made the marring of her beauty worth the the sooty work. She was one of 158 women employed in one of four cartridge laboratories at the Arsenal. Women were the preferred workers as their nimble hands quickly adapted to the intricate work required to prepare them.

Outside the low brick building, an arsenal worker slowly approached in a wagon drawn by a two mule team that made deliveries from the magazines. In the bed were two barrels of gunpowder. Seeing the men on the loading dock with an empty cask, the driver pulled up close to enable them to assist him in off-loading a full barrel, in exchange for an empty one. The Arsenal was required to return the empty barrels to the factory in New York for refilling and reuse. The practice made the barrels leaky, and the men could see small dry streams of powder fall onto the newly laid cobblestones beneath the wagon. The road bore a distinct grayish tinge of powder dust in the dry hot afternoon. As the men heaved the heavy barrel onto the dock, they did not notice a horsefly alight on the leg of one of the team mules. As the hungry insect bit into the tough skin of the mule, the animal quivered its muscles, and failing to stop the pain, it gave a quick stamp of its foot. As the iron shoe on the mule's hoof struck the granite cobblestones of the Arsenal road, several sparks flew from the point of impact. Mr. Edmunds walked over to the open door of the laboratory just as an enormous cloud of white smoke emerged around the team. The last thing he beheld was the stark image of the barrel in front of him expanding away from an orange ball of fire as the staves were shoved outward by the ignition of the powder within. Catherine became immediately aware that the entire room had become white hot and filled with smoke. She felt a terrible burning sensation and a violent churning and tearing force that pummelled her senses. Then there was peace, as she rose towards a bright light.

Colonel John Symington had just finished blotting his signature on a memorandum for the War Department, detailing the recent expansion of the Arsenal, when the window before him burst inward, scattering glass all over his home office. The shock wave of a great series of explosions knocked him from his chair. As he staggered back to his feet and began to brush his hands through his hair to remove the shards of glass, the ground shook as another enormous explosion erupted. The shock wave of this explosion caused a strong wind to blow into the shattered window frame. Through the dense white smoke that covered the grounds, he could distincly see red and white flares arcing across the wooded grounds. The glow of flames could be seen where Laboratories 1, 3, and 4 stood. Symington knew as he watched that his tenure as the superintendant was now finished. Filled with dispair, he found his hat and ran out of his quarters towards the burning buildings. Out of the smoke, a staggering figure approached him. His clothes were torn to shreds and dangled from his body in strips. As he staggered toward Colonel Symington with his hair still smoking, the Colonel recognized him as Mr. Finch who drove the transfer wagon. Finch collapsed, and Symington rushed towards him. Finch, in shock, muttered, "The laboratory! " Symington recoiled in horror at the scorched flesh of his face and arms. The skin sloughed off at the slightest touch. He turned, and screamed for someone to help as men hurriedly ran towards the Laboratory from the various shops. Choking white smoke filled the air and the sound of screams and shouting men could be heard above the cracking of the burning buildings.

Lucius McCray, a long serving clerk of the Pittsburg Post, deciphered the telegraph message that urgently arrived late in the afternoon of the 17th. As he wrote out the letters coming across the rapidly tapping key, he began to realize that a terrible accident had occurred at the arsenal in Lawrenceville. He quickly recorded the report and forwarded the message to the newsroom via another clerk, to be hand-carried, as it was local breaking news. After he had finished, another message began to come in. He attentively began to record it's content on a clean sheet of paper. This next message was more complex, proving to be a lengthy description of a great battle emerging in Maryland. The dispatch was being transmitted by a special correspondence of the Post. The message revealed that many Pennsylvania Regiments were involved and that the casualties were enormous. McCray feverishly recorded the text of the message. He realized that this battle would dominate the news for days, as the lists of the dead would soon follow. Such unfortunate business caused a clamor to purchase the editions and was of immense interest to the Editor. After recording the latest dispatch, the wires resumed minor reports of the mundane. It would be another day until a list of dead from the arsenal would be received. The editorial board, deciding the final determination of the next day's news, opted to tell the story of the Battle in Maryland. The accident at the arsenal became a buried story in page three of The Post.

Adilade Burkhart was given only a very light black laquered casket for the burial of her daughter. No one from the Coroner's office could guarantee the identity of the corpse within. Too little remained to determine much, and a thin, stern faced assistant had advised her against attempting to remove the lid. Catherine was with God now and awaited the ressurection, when she would be whole again. Mrs Burkhard wrote a long letter to her husband, who was serving in a Pennsylvania Regiment under General Meade. She had no idea that he was busy at that time burying hundreds of dead comrades near a creek known as "The Antietam."

President Lincoln studied the reports that had been brought to his office in the White House. He had the reports of the battle in Maryland recently transcribed from telegraphs collected at the War Department from the scraps of reports that had dribbled in over the past few days. He was dismayed to learn that George McClellan still sat on the liberated town of Sharpsburg. At least Lee's Army had retreated to Virginia. Nowhere within the reports lay indication of any sort of pursuit. It was a victory, in an unsatisfying way. Despite it's overall lack of decisiveness, and it's horrible cost, he resolved to use it. The time was right. He rose from the wooden chair and the clutter of reports and turned to the secretary against the far wall and rummaged through the tangle of papers stacked haphazardly on the wooden work surface. He wanted to review the Constitution again. He finally found the cheaply printed copy and read it again. He rubbed his bearded chin as he read and struggled to imagine why the forefathers, so careful in their crafting of the document, never mentioned the word "slave." To him it seemed it was a point they preferred not to give the dignity of a mention to. He pondered if it was a deliberate omission, like discussing a shameful thing. He absently returned to the central table in his office with the copy of the founding document. An outside observer would not recognize his office as such; it bore more the resemblance of a meeting room, where jurors might argue the points of a trial. He then reached to a pile of letters he had received in response to his own to various members of

Congress, whom he admired. In each he had posited a case of the wisdom of an executive order expanding the Contraband of War issue regarding slaves within the states in insurrection. Presidential war powers remained an unsettling concept for him, yet he clearly realized that the great fight in Maryland afforded him a window of opportunity. He would not squander it like George McClellan so often did. He then returned to the draft document he was preparing. It constituted a refinement to an earlier draft he had read to his cabinet in July. His improved version of what he had titled "The Preliminary Emancipation Proclamation" would be released to the public in a fortnight, the 22nd of September. The document would give the States in insurrection 100 days to rejoin the Union or forfeit their slaves on the effective date of the signed Executive Order. He planned to sign the document to mark the first day of the new year, January 1, 1863.

If Seward's advisories had merit, the distribution of the proclamation would signal to the world that the elimination of human bondage was now a war aim of the Union. No modern nation would mar their morality by siding with a nation that stood upon slavery as an institution. Lincoln pondered the words as he scribbled the construct of the document. He hoped Postmaster Blair's gloomy projection of massive Republican losses in the next election, due to outrage over the document, would not be the sole outcome. The point of the politics of the document had indeed concerned him, and the compromise of continuation of the status quo in pro-Union States cast a pale of hypocrisy, and "Half-measures" to the document. Lincoln had accepted the compromise as a political reality. He realized this was not a law, but an Executive Order "given on account of military necessity."

He studied his draft, and reflected on the impact it would have in the South. He imagined a mental image of the word spreading across the land. He could imagine slaves laying plans to escape their masters, of tasks left undone, of empty factory floors, and idle machinery of war. The argument remained in regards to what the final disposition of the slaves would be. Perhaps repatriation or colonization in Haiti. That argument remained to be made. As he finished the draft, he found that reading the document made him smile and he felt a rare peace within.

One of his secretaries, John Nicolay appeared at his office door, "Sir, the hour is late! You should seek your rest!" Lincoln laughed softly, "John, judging from the hour, I should say it is quite early! Come look at this final draft. I shall apologize in advance for it's slovenly nature! I would very much like a more appropriate and readable version drawn up for signatures by myself and Secretary Seward!"

Nicolay took the scribbled pages and glanced at them. He realized it was the Emancipation Executive Order. Silently he mused over the consternation Seward's co-signing would create within the restive cabinet. He quietly asked, "Sir, when do you desire it to be ready?"

Lincoln calmly directed, "By this afternoon, in time for my cabinet meeting." He then looked Nicolay in the eyes, and surprised him with a prescient observation, "John, by way of explanation, Seward must sign as well, as my intent is an international communication as well as a declaration to the people! Your whispers to that effect should calm the cabinet."

PUNCH, OR THE LONDON CHARIVARI.— October 18, 1862.

ABE LINCOLN'S LAST CARD; OR, ROUGE-ET-NOIR.

Lincoln felt a great wave of relief as he crept quietly towards his bedroom, not wanting to wake Mary. He reckoned that many would howl at the radical proclamation, and that it might very well damage the Republican Party in the upcoming elections. The main portent of the message would surely bring his desired end. The great moral statement it made, put right on the side of the Union. Surely England and France would see that, and be forced to remain neutral in this fight. It was the only political reinforcement he could lend to his struggling armies. It was the right time, and the right place for a radical move.

5
STANDING THROUGH HELL AND HIGH WATER

It was proving to be a very pleasant September morning. Soft breezes off the ocean cooled the warming air and gently swayed the Spanish Moss hanging from the branches of the trees shading the dirt road leading to Stoney Landing. Edward Markley had grudgingly agreed to meet again with Theodore Stoney and Dr. Ravenel to discuss the boat project. It being the midst of the harvest season, Markley was distracted. He missed having Tom around to assist him, and E.J. run the plantation. Most of the operations in Old Berkeley County were now short field hands, due to government levies for laborers around Charleston, and from runaways that seemed to increase with each passing day. The slaves all knew the Yankees were close by and many had begun to slip away in the night. The Dupre' family had taken to arming their task masters and had warned the slaves that runaways would be shot. Markley reflected that it was foolish to threaten them. He reckoned, as he rode towards the Stoney House, that them having homes and families and a gentler hand in directing their tasks would serve better to keep them on the plantation. As it was, he was short handed and it had slowed the rate of harvest. He resolved to remain patient and trust in the course that he had adopted. He resolved to proceed to Moncks Corner, following his meeting to check his account at the bank and to intercept the mail rider. Elizabeth was extremely anxious to hear from Lottie, as they had only received one letter from her since she had traveled to Richmond. He shook his head and smiled as he reflected on her stubborn ways. She had obviously inherited his spirit and Elizabeth had commented on that fact often.

Arriving at the pretty home of Theodore Stoney, Edward noted that Dr. Ravenel and two other men were sitting on the porch enjoying the morning breeze. The day showed promise to grow warm. Stoney warmly greeted Edward as he handed the reins of his horse to a young house boy.

"Edward! A good morning to you sir! Please grab up a chair. I am pleased to introduce Mr. Samuel Easterby and Mr. John Chalk. They are recently hired on to direct the Negros in completing our craft!"

Edward smiled and shook hands with each of the men. He had heard of Chalk from David Ebaugh and knew he was a mechanic of some renown in the region. Taking a rocking chair from the far end of the porch, he slid it over and took a seat with the others. Markley leaned over and asked, "What news have you from the Navy? Have they agreed to buy it?"

Stoney quickly replied, "Edward, Lieutenant Glassell remains our lead negotiator in that matter. Unfortunately he has been temporarily assigned to Wilmington to assist in fitting out a ship for their harbor. He should return next spring. But I have assurances from Captain Lee that there remains high interest in this design." Stoney relayed to the assembled men the tale of a test performed by Glassell that he had received in a letter. Glassell had affixed a device to a small rowboat, employing a wooden spar attached to the bow of the vessel. The tip of the spar carried an explosive charge called a "Torpedo." The device had been designed to explode upon contact. Employing an old hulk, Glassell had practiced an attack and successfully sank an old hulk on the Cooper River. Stoney explained further that Glassell had then attempted a real attack on the *USS Powhatan* on the Edisto River, a month later, but it failed because his oarsmen lost their nerve. He had come to the conclusion that a fast, steam driven vessel was the answer. Doctor Ravenel's concept was the obvious low cost option, and Navy interest remained high in the project.

Edward was reassured. His participation had cost him much in time and travel so far, as the operations of the plantation demanded his attention. He expressed his concerns to Stoney and the older man understood. Stoney explained that this was the reason for the introductions. David Ebaugh was also preoccupied with repairs to gins and rice mills all over the county with the harvest season. No additional funds were required at present to hire Easterby and Chalk. The two men would continue the construction through the winter. Edward agreed to release the marine engine to John Chalk, and the two men coordinated for a time for him to load them onto freight wagons. Edward knew the operation would cost him a day of labor, and he mentally began to calculate when that time would be the least disruptive to his harvest and ginning. John Chalk offered to assist him in moving bales of harvested cotton to the landing, as an additional incentive, and the two men agreed on a date in October for the transfer.

Edward rose and bid his associates a good day. He had to proceed into Moncks Corner, before the mail rider would depart the post office, near the train depot. After crossing the Santee Canal via the Biggin Bridge, he swiftly rode up the hill towards the hamlet of Moncks Corner. He noted that the bales of processed cotton were beginning to accumulate by the cargo lot of the Northeastern Railroad depot, awaiting movement to Charleston. The sight reminded him of how much work remained for him to accomplish. September was nearly through and the wet weather of October would prove disastrous to his processing and baling. The morning cool was burning off, and Lucy was beginning to lather where the leather straps of her martingale rubbed against her hide.

Edward spied the mail rider loading satchels into his large leather saddlebags, and asked, "Mister Harvey, have you any mail for the Markley family in the Macbeth pouch?" Wade Harvey grinned and replied, "Funny you should ask, Mr. Markley, I have an odd letter here, addressed to you, specifically!" Harvey rummaged through the canvas bag marked "Macbeth" and extracted the letter. Edward, in his haste, only glanced at the return address written vertically on one end and did not recall the name. He did not know a "Captain Henri Tinchant" so he pocketed the unopened letter without further ado, and rode to the bank. He was anxious to determine how good his credit remained. He soon would have freight expenses to move his cotton to Charleston.

After spending an hour at the Farmers and Merchants Bank, in discussion with Mr. Endicott, Edward felt better. His credit was good for another season. Cargo was leaving Charleston, slowly but surely, as the profits from cotton encouraged enterprising blockade runner captains to accept the great risk. Business in the 500 pound bales remained brisk, despite the hazards, and the government had encouraged the banks to assist the planters. Untying Lucy's reins, he quickly mounted and began his ride back to Somerset to check on the progress of the picking. Arriving back to

Somerset, he continued past the main house and made his way to the back fields, where slaves picked the prickly bolls of ripened cotton, depositing the plucked bolls into large burlap bags that they drug behind them down the rows of waist high plants. The midday sun made for hot work. Markley questioned the overseer about the progress. He indicated that they would have the field harvested by tomorrow, if all the hands met their tasks. Edward pondered on what remained to be picked. He estimated that he had nearly a hundred acres to harvest. The progress was proving to be painfully slow. Turning to his overseer he directed, "Make sure you are letting them drink and have breaks to eat. If you misuse them, they will only work slower!"

Edward decided to ride over to the blacksmith barn and talk to Old Mose for a few minutes, before returning to the house. As he approached the overhang of the smithy, Mose came out, "Good day to you Mister Markley, you gots needs fo' your hoss?" Edward shook his head and simply asked, "How are your people doing Mose?" Edward often talked to Mose as the man served as a barometer of his slaves. Mose nervously replied, "Massa, they gots freedom in their minds! I know you know dat!" Edward Markley nodded, it was something he knew and had pondered on since the war had begun. In his own estimation, he knew the South would be unable to prevail in this foolish war. Markley slowly replied, "Mose, that I understand. I simply ask them to consider their homes and families before taking off. I can do little to stop them, but make sure they understand that if they are caught, they won't be returning to Somerset. The government is using all runaways to build forts around Charleston these days! I promise that I will not abuse them, and so long as they stay, they will have homes and food!" Mose sadly nodded, "I will pass it on Boss, jus' know they is a strange magic to that notion of freedom."

As Edward Markley rode back to his home the often visiting idea of selling Somerset and settling in the summer house in Pinopolis, entered his mind again. Life could be so simple then, but that would mean breaking up the families of the slaves through sales and leaving little or no land to the boys and Lottie. He was trapped by the war, economics and his own morals. He would have to have faith that better days would come. Until then, he would work his cotton and hope for the best.

He rode Lucy to the stable and removed her saddle, carefully stowing it in the tack shed along with the saddle blanket, bridle, and bit. He then currycombed her swiftly and released her into her paddock. He reached into his coat and retrieved the letter from his pocket as he ascended the steps leading to the great porch of Somerset, and opened the door. He carefully hung his coat, and hat by the door. He then paused to look at the envelope. He realized then it had come from Richmond, and fearing bad news he went into his study and opened the letter. His apprehension turned to a rather odd feeling as he studied the neat script.

"General Hospital
Gordonsville, Virginia

Esteemed Sir,
By way of introduction, I am Captain Henri Tinchant, a surgeon of the Confederate States Medical Corps. I have the pleasure of working alongside your daughter Charlotte as a frequent military escort, thusly entrusted with her safety, as she performs audits of Army hospitals for the national government of the Confederate States. Over the months of our association, I have found her to be a woman of great character and determination and have observed her great effectiveness in performing her duties in the most demanding of circumstances. You have every right to be very proud of her service.
I take the pain to correspond with you in regards to a very delicate subject. In my observation of your daughter, I have found myself captivated by her great charm, and beauty. I have, at great risk to your perception of my own character, decided to write to ask your permission and blessing to court her. I do not take this request lightly as the exigencies of war prevent me from properly securing said permission in a socially acceptable way. I assure you that I shall continue to maintain my distance and maintain my professional detachment while assuring her safe passage in her travels of Virginia. I await your response, prior to any decision on my part to change my demeanor towards her. If refused, I pledge to perform my duties as I have to date without prejudice and with the professional attention that my calling demands.
For your edification, I submit my brief curriculum vitae for your study. I am 30 years of age and serve as Surgeon Inspector under Surgeon General Moore of the Confederate States Medical Department. I am the 2nd oldest son of a rice planter from the vicinity of Lake Ponchartrain in Louisiana. I received my degree in Medicine at Boston College having graduated with a MD Degree in 1858. The war precluded my establishment of private practice and I have been in the service of the Government since the beginning of the war. I shall be happy to provide additional references as to my character and standing as you might require.
Charlotte is in good health and spirits, and remains dedicated to her service, which is proving to be substantive to our great cause. Many a suffering soldier has been cheered by her attentive dedication to her duties. I remain determined to look after her safety as she performs these duties. I only ask that you withhold this request from her knowledge until you have tendered your decision.
Sincerely yours,
Captain Henri Tinchant, MD, CSA"

As Edward finished the letter, Elizabeth entered the study, "Oh there you are dear, I thought I had heard you enter. Did we have mail?"

Seeing him reading a letter, she asked, "Is it from Lottie?" Edward slowly replied, "I suggest you read this, it may cause you joy or concern, depending on your optimism."

Elizabeth snatched the letter away from his hand and paced the library, as she read. Suddenly, she dropped her left hand holding the letter against her dress and exclaimed, "Dear, she has a genuine suitor! Have your heard of this family?" Edward shook his head, although inwardly he was relieved to see her pleased. He hoped this development would cause her to forget her pointless fixation on Joshua Timmonds. After a moment of thought, he asked his wife, "Should I reply?" Elizabeth quickly nodded her head. Edward sighed, and secured a clean sheet of paper from his writing desk, found a quill, and his inkwell. As he deliberately crafted his response, Elizabeth paced the floor. He absently listened to her as she held an excited discussion with herself, "He is from the same region as General Beauregard! And he is a Doctor! I must query Mrs. Dupre'!" Edward smiled, it was a certainty that all of Old Berkeley would learn of this development within the week. Noting the return address, he folded another sheet of vellum into an envelope, and applied the address provided. He inserted the folded letter, sealed the envelope with wax, and announced, "Elizabeth, I have agreed to his request, and will post this tomorrow."

⚓

Lieutenant Roswell Lamson quickly dressed for his morning watch aboard the *USS Pawnee* . While he remained wistful over his former exciting days aboard the Admiral's flagship, the *USS Wabash,* this assignment had come with a promotion in both rank, and responsibility. He paused to admire the new stripes on his sleeve before pulling on his coat. "Lieutenant" had a nice ring to it and he had delighted in signing his name and adding the rank below in his frequent letters to Katie. The Sloop of War *Pawnee* was a compact and agile three-masted warship with a storied history, thus far in the rebellion. She had seen action from Baltimore, in the beginning, to the great battle to seize their current harbor at Port Royal. Lamson was the newest sailing master of the trim screw-driven steamship. He was responsible to the most skilled and experienced crew of tars whose job it was to furl and unfurl the vast yards of canvas that drove her by windpower. Despite her modern steam engines, sails still enabled economy and great speed in the open water. The complexities of operating in both modes on the open ocean required much knowledge and training of both leader and crew. Lieutenant Lamson also served as the Forecastle Division Gun Captain, and as such, commanded the bow mounted swivel gun, a great hulking 100 pounder Parrot Rifle, capable of throwing explosive shell and solid shot nearly five miles. He commanded 40 sailors at various tasks assigned to his division, and reported directly to the Executive Officer. *Pawnee* had been an integral part of the South Atlantic Blockading Squadron for the past year, and now they had a new and daunting mission. Captain Drayton had met earlier in the month with Admiral DuPont and had received orders to patrol the tidewaters of the Stono River as part of a new concept termed the "Inner Blockade." When Captain Drayton had returned, he was accompanied by the now famous Negro pilot, Robert Smalls, who had taken a vessel out of Charleston Harbor to gain his freedom. Smalls knew the tidewater rivers better than any man alive in the Union Navy, and the knowledge he would impart was invaluable. Their new mission was to prowl the inland waterways, that formed numerous barrier islands along the South Carolina coast, and hunt down small boats and steamers that waited for opportunities to transfer cargos of cotton bales out to awaiting blockade runners at prearranged rendezvous points. Their mission was also to discourage rebels from establishing shore batteries along the coastal rivers to protect this activity. The mission offered a break from the monotony of sitting on station outside the blockaded harbors.

Coming onto the busy deck, Lamson noted that the morning had already grown warm. The humid heat of the deep South made him long for the open ocean. He made his way towards the stern to find Lieutenant Hansen, the Executive Officer, to review his assignments for the day on the Watch Bill. As he swiftly made his way past the trim and neat guns along the starboard quarter, gangs of sailors holystoned the deck in two separate groups. There was much to tidy up, as they had coaled the *Pawnee* yesterday, and there still remained the stubborn soot in odd places. The master of arms threatened the tars with the loss of their breakfasts as they scrambled about to straighten up the ship. Lamson hurried along to get his division orders, it was apparent that Captain Drayton intended to conduct a mid-day inspection. He would need to hurry and conclude his meeting with the Executive Officer, before the men broke from morning chores to have their breakfast. Hurrying abaft, he finally located Lieutenant Hansen, who was in conversation with Captain Drayton at the Binnacle. Lamson quietly stood by while the senior men finished their conversation. Captain Drayton then resumed his rounds, giving Lamson a mild nod. Lieutenant Hansen filled him in. Hansen explained that they were to proceed up the Stono once the tide came in. He planned to poke about upriver to discourage trade boats from making a dash to sea with their precious cotton cargo. They had just received orders that intercepted bales of cotton could be taken for prizes, as cotton was the underpinning of the economy of South Carolina, thus contraband of war. The crew would share the prize money of seized cotton. Hansen explained that Mister Smalls was going to show them the intricacies of navigating the tidewater rivers. The man knew the Stono well, and they were to pay close attention to his advice as they proceeded up river. Lamson learned that the Captain intended to depart with the tide from Port Royal and sail up the coast to the mouth of the Stono. Once there, they would proceed up river fully reefed and under steam alone. He expected to contact Rebel defenders on James Island, so the men were to remain alert. Hansen paused, and then added the instruction to keep an eye on the 6 new contrabands that the Captain had brought on board to assist on the ship. If they showed talent, he had planned to enlist them into the crew, with the rating of "Boy" as it was the only rating available for the contrabands for now. White men started out as "Landsmen." This arrangement meant the Contrabands were starting out 2 dollars a month pay, less than the lowest rating for normal sailors. He advised that the men would likely shun them, so the officers would have to press the men to show them the ropes. Lamson, eager to begin his day, saluted and departed towards his division. He took the advice of the Executive Officer to heart, as he was keenly aware of the two Contrabands he had gained in his division from yesterday.

When he arrived at the Forecastle, he saw the men in his division having their breakfasts, seated on sail cloths spread on the deck. He summoned the captain of the tops, the senior enlisted man of his division, and directed, "Mr. Watkins, after breakfast, advise the topsmen to prepare to go aloft! The Captain will be making way to the Stono at noon. We are to make way under full sail and steam to rendezvous with other ships up the river." Watkins nodded, and replied, "Aye Sir!," before returning to his unfinished breakfast. Lamson was in awe of the quiet tall man, who while quiet on deck, could be heard across the boat while aloft, directing the topsmen in their dangerous work of setting and adjusting the sails. Lamson had grown fascinated by the hybrid work of choreographing the ancient technology of sail with the emerging science of steam. The combination of the two required much of a Sailing Master.

Deep below decks, the black gang finished their quiet breakfast. Reid Markley had only been on board the Pawnee for a week, having signed on board with six other contrabands. He recalled when he had signed on, that two names were required to do so. All of his life he had only one name, "Reid." Being befuddled, as what to use, he had said it was "Markley." The officer recording it, made it so. It took him a while to get used to the crew using that name for him, but he was getting better at responding to the second name when he was called. He and another former slave, Isaac, were assigned to be firemen, with the dirty work of feeding coal to the firebox of the boiler in the cramped mechanical compartment of the *Pawnee*. Yesterday, he had been delighted to receive a visit from "Captain Smalls," as all the contraband sailors called him. Smalls had quietly encouraged him to do his best to learn and please the officers in the engineering department. Reid did not know what "Engineering" meant, but he resolved to do his best. He and Isaac did as instructed, and kept to themselves, quietly talking as they performed the myriad tasks, all very dirty and tiring, that they were directed to perform. The other sailors spoke to them little, except to correct them or mock them. Smalls had whispered on his visit that acceptance by the majority of white crewmembers would take time. Reid remembered his words, "They won't take you into their company until they see you is worth somethin' and you gotta prove you is worth somethin'." Reid put away his mess utensils and rose in the cramped and hot stoker hold, and opened the firebox door to check on the banked coals, glowing red in the firebox. They would occasionally add a small volume of coal to keep the hot bed alive. The other firemen of the crew were above decks enjoying the cool air. The lowest ranking of their division, the new contraband sailors, holding the rating of "Boy," enjoyed the privilege of remaining below in the heat to monitor the boilers and watch the fire. Reid was happy nonetheless. He was free, had joined the Union Navy, and held a rank, despite it being the lowest one. He had been provided fine uniforms and equipment and was being trained to fight. The feeling of belonging to something as a freeman, rather than belonging to somebody, was exhilarating and different to him. As he quietly attended to his duties, he hoped the great ship would be headed north. He still dreamed of the magical place called "Boston."

Captain Percival Drayton watched his crew move to their places after directing Lieutenant Hansen to get the *Pawnee* underway. He was pleased by the efficient response of the jacks to the shouted commands. Soon the topsmen were aloft, and the sheets were released creating shade over the decks from the warming mid-morning sun. The ship was alive with activity and a glance at the great iron stack indicated the increasing smoke as the firemen stoked the coals under the boilers. Drayton resolved to drill the gunners on the movement north to the Stono. His orders from Admiral DuPont were to move to the Stono Inlet to join the *Pembina*, *Ottawa*, *Unadilla*, and the *Huron*, for an expedition up the Stono River. *Pawnee* was a larger gunboat of deeper draft than the rest of the expedition, and Drayton was to test the navigability of the Stono for larger vessels. As he had studied the charts the evening prior, he began to understand the purpose of the mission. The Stono River offered access to James Island and the southern segment of Charleston Harbor. The difficult salt marshes that dominated the area, made attacking and defending the vicinity of James Island difficult for Rebel and Union forces alike. DuPont had begun to realize that James Island and Morris Island were key to the defeat of Charleston's defenses. Such an attempt, however, would require the Army and Navy to work together. After the conference of last month, Drayton remembered being pulled aside by Captain Rodgers, who shared with him the incredible pressures Admiral DuPont was under, by the government, to take Charleston. Rodgers had explained that the signal victory at Port Royal had convinced Secretary Wells that Charleston could be taken just as easily. DuPont had tried to explain to all who asked, why Charleston was different, but none wanted to listen. The Admiral was under a deadline to take Charleston.

Drayton felt the freshening wind, as Pawnee headed for the open water beyond Port Royal, under full sail. It was good to be heading back out to sea with something meaningful to do. The crew quickly settled into the routine of ocean travel and the divisions began to review their drills. Drayton expected action on the Stono and directed the gun divisions to commence live fire crew drill as they made the heeling turn to the north.

Commodore Duncan Ingraham took his place on the bunting covered wooden dais beside Major General Beauregard, and Commander John Rutledge. The Navy bandsmen played the Sumpter Light Guard March. The ladies, who had raised nearly thirty thousand dollars to support the project, excitedly chatted away on either side of the platform. The day had come to christen the *CSS Palmetto State* at the graving dock of the James Marsh Shipyard. Owing to its proximity to Broad Street, a large crowd of onlookers from Charleston had arrived to observe on the sunny September day.

Beauregard was accommodating and pleasant, as usual. The bitter arguments between him and Ingraham over the iron required to finish her, seemed past them now. Ingraham marveled at how quickly the yard had been able to add the casemate rails, once they had arrived. The critical shortage had been broken by General Beauregard's insistence on Blockaders bringing in loads of the iron from scrap iron, brought over from England. It seemed that the Trenholm purchasers in Liverpool had been able to secure an agreement for obsolete English Vignoles type rail iron that arrived on several ships in 38-foot lengths. The shipwrights, and blacksmiths had been able to armor the casemated superstructure in a little over a month. Ingraham stared at the great pile of sawn off ends, that littered the yard. The artificers had labored day and night to apply the material, and then apply the finishing armature of straps that covered the rough seams of the makeshift armor. Looking over to the *Palmetto State*, Ingraham thought her appearance odd, adorned with drying blue gray camouflage paint. The ladies below had begun to comment on her "Bonnie Blue" color. They had failed to appreciate the choice of shade. All the blockade-runners had begun to apply the low visibility, blue gray paint. It provided an enormous advantage in stealth, at distance. Particularly for a ship without masts or sails. The Palmetto State was the first of two Ironclad gunboats to be similarly finished. Her sister ship, CSS Chicora, lay several wharves down at the James Eason Shipyard. Artificers there were still hard at work applying her armor. That christening was scheduled for October.

After a few more stanzas, the band ceased their music, and General Beauregard was invited to speak. The crowd politely applauded. Charleston was happy to have the petite Creole General back in town. He would remain a hero to the city that began the war, and the citizens were comforted by his presence. Following the general's speech, the editor of the Charleston Daily Courier read a poem written by the Ladies Relief Society. Following the reading, he offered thanks to the ladies of Charleston who had raised a full fifth of the total cost of the gunboat. They had achieved it through the solicitation of donations, and the sale of quilts, to defray the cost of the project to the State. Commander John Rutledge was then invited forward to lead a selected lady of the society to a small gangplank in order for her to smash a bottle of rare Bordeaux on the iron ram of the vessel afloat in the flooded graving dock. The crowd cheered and applauded as the bottle smashed, staining the gray blue paint of the semi-submerged ram. Commander Rutledge then helped her back up the gangplank as the band began to play. Once she was safe, he returned to the gunboat and ordered his crewmen, who had stood lining the roof of the casemate, to remove the gangplank in order to make way.

Ingraham and Beauregard watched as her stack began to emit heavy black smoke. The ironclad backed out of the graving dock, now officially a warship of the Confederate States Navy. As he watched the trim ship ease into the channel, General Beauregard turned to Commodore Ingraham, and remarked, "Commodore, I am happy to see this great project come to completion. It has cost us dear in material and effort. I ask you to turn your attentions, now to the torpedo boats and torpedo placements in the harbor. I am receiving word that the Union Navy plans a major assault on this harbor, within the year. The harbor obstructions to shape that battle are now the priority! Word is that they are assembling a fleet of ironclads at Port Royal and will arrive here in force. Insure the Captains of these gunboats train hard and well. We may need them badly soon!"

The myriad of tidal estuaries, coves and marshes that formed the southern half of Charleston harbor, worried General Beauregard deeply. It would remain the greatest weakness of all the defenses, and concerted effort would be required to secure it against Union penetration.

Lieutenant Lamson inspected the Parrot rifle after his crew had swabbed the bore clean, following their gunnery practice on the cruise north towards the bar of the Stono River. They had been required to pause their gunnery on the trip up to allow a large paddlewheel troop ship to pass off to Starboard.

Lamson had found it a grand sight to see the ship bearing more Army troops for Port Royal. He thought it a portent of larger things to come, and had waved to the soldiers lining the rails. The sun had begun its descent into the west when the mouth of the Stono hove into view. After directing the 14-man bow chaser crew to haul up the Parrot rifle to the Port bow, he secured his telescope and peered ahead. He could see four smaller gunboats in the broad river, riding at anchor where the charts showed a junction with the Folly River channel. Captain Drayton had indicated earlier that these ships were the *Pembina, Unadilla, Ottawa* and the *Huron*. As they entered the Stono, the Executive Officer shouted out orders to furl sails. Lamson echoed the command and watched as his topsmen scrambled up the ratlines, to bring in the sheets. The remainder of operations would rely on steam and limited use of the spinnakers and spanker aft. The nature of the river, from this point forward, would require the crew to remain alert on the guns and remain prepared to assist the Marine Division in defending the ship from boarders.

Pawnee pulled up behind the other gunboats at anchor, and Captain Drayton instructed his signalers to send orders for the Lieutenants commanding the *Unadilla* class gunboats to come to the *Pawnee* for a conference. Once he had assembled the officers he would transmit Admiral DuPont's orders for the flotilla. Lamson looked forward to meeting Lieutenant Downes, commanding the *Huron,* as they had been classmates at the Naval Academy. As *Pawnee* dropped anchor, the gigs from the gunboats began to make their way towards her, the oarsmen pulling hard against the current of the incoming tide. As the sun began to set on the western sky, Lamson watched as the saw grass reddened. The thick grass was slowly submerging as the tide covered the mud in which they sprouted. There was a strange and dangerous beauty where they had moored. Lamson could not get over the feeling that they were being watched. Captain Drayton warmly greeted the Lieutenants commanding the Unadilla class gunboats, as they came aboard. Lieutenant Lamson only had a few moments to converse with Gabriel Downes, before Captain Drayton asked them to assemble in his wardroom for a quick conference and some supper. Drayton had earlier directed Lieutenant Hansen to tack up the incomplete chart of the Stono that they had obtained from the Captain of the Revenue Cutter *Vixen.* Much data in regards to the depth of the Stono River channel still needed to be ascertained, and one purpose of the mission of this flotilla would be to fill in the gaps of knowledge. The commanders took seats at the table and mess stewards brought in a tureen of stew. The Lieutenants helped themselves to bowls of supper as Captain Drayton explained his concept. Tracing his finger along the chart, Drayton briefed the officers, "Gentlemen, our express purpose is to press the Sloop of War *Pawnee* as far up the Stono as feasible. Your vessels will support this effort, and the *Pawnee,* in the event she runs aground. It will be essential for her to lead as she possesses the best battery of the flotilla. Each vessel will take soundings with leadsmen, all the way up, and determine the width of the channel." Drayton paused a moment, and with a motion of his hand, he indicated to Robert Smalls to stand. After the small black man was on his feet, he continued, "Some of you gentlemen have met Mr. Smalls. He will serve as my pilot for this expedition in order for us to come to know these waters. Be alert to my signals, as I may take maneuvers as advised by Mr. Smalls. Understand that *Pawnee* drafts more deeply than your ships, so be alert to our grounding. I shall need you to stand ready to pull us off at short notice." Drayton then motioned to Smalls to sit, before continuing, "Expect the Rebels to fire upon us from those points where he has elevation to engage our force. There is also rumor of submerged torpedoes in these waters. I cannot give you descriptions of their appearance, but have reports of their use in the harbor before Charleston. In any case, keep lookouts aloft and alert, for anything odd. If you are fired upon, do not hesitate to return that fire. Do your best to record the locations of those batteries you encounter! It is the intent that we come to understand the defenses of these waters. We may soon support a general effort by the

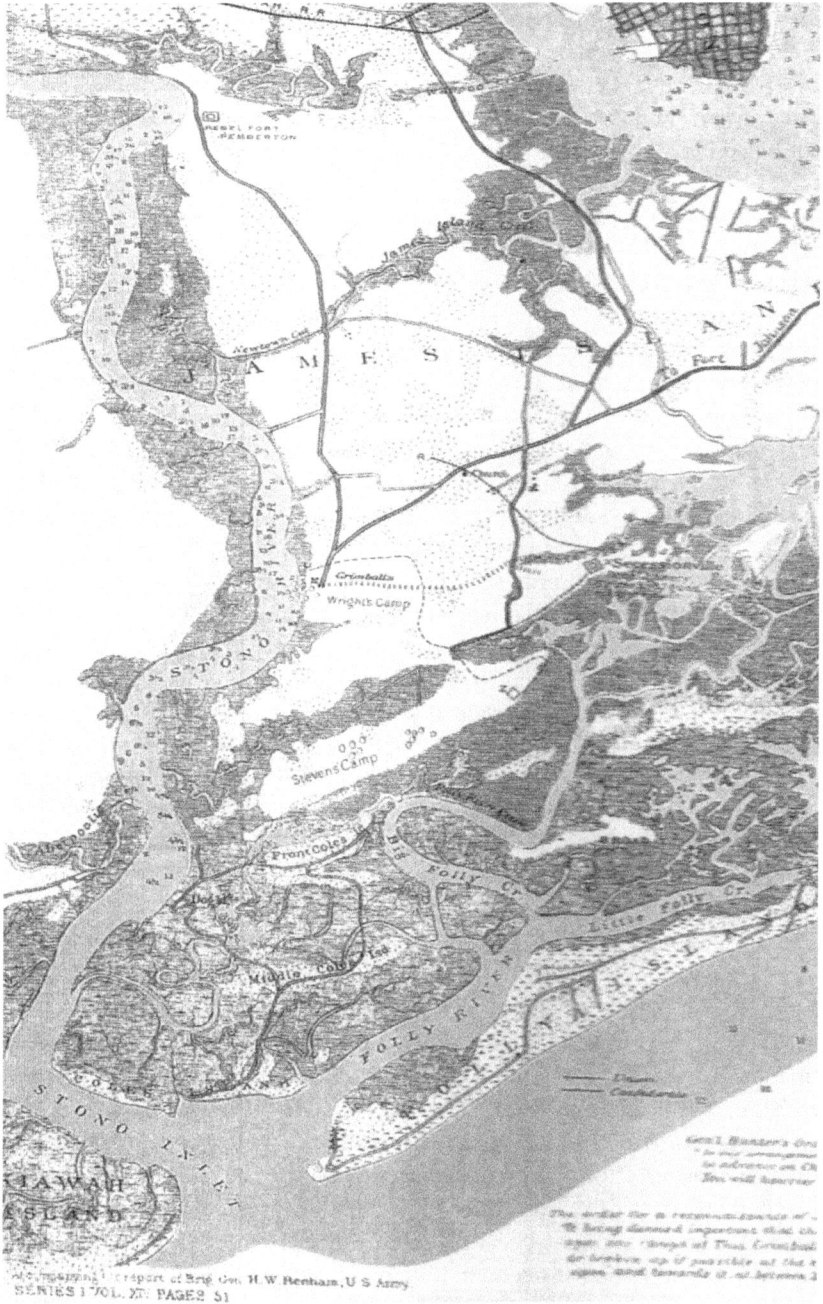

The Stono River

Army to take Folly and James Island. Our understanding of these waters will prove key to that endeavor." Captain Drayton then answered questions from the other commanders, before releasing them back to their ships. The appointed time that they would proceed would be a quarter past six in the morning, when the tide came in. Drayton did not relish the notion of being aground deep inside rebel territory, and worried greatly over this mission.

The next morning at dawn, the *Pawnee* came alive with purpose, as petty officers roused the crew not on watch, shouting, "Show a leg!" The crew quickly rushed to their stations as the drummers beat to quarters. Shouts of "Man the Capstan!" filled Lieutenant Lamson's ears, as the ship prepared to weigh her anchor at the mouth of the Stono. He watched as his division positioned men with stout bars inserted into the capstan. The Master of the boat shouted out, "Man the Bars! Heave taunt!" The sailors in unison pushed hard to remove slack from the anchor chain line wrapped around the drum. The Master of the Boat continued his orders, "Take off the stoppers and heave around!"

Lamson paid close attention; the management of a naval vessel was a complex and interconnected thing. One action quickly affected another and officers had to maintain a close watch to preclude accidents. The crew quickly retrieved the anchor and released the chain lifting tackle from the heavy links outside the chain locker hawse pipe. Lamson looked on as his division placed topsmen aloft to act as lookouts. The Engineering Department, stoked the boilers in the engine room below, increasing the smoke that emerged from the great iron stack, amidships. Soon the throbbing vibration of the great screw shaft could be felt as *Pawnee* began to make her way up river with the current of the returning tide. Captain Drayton and Mr. Smalls stood together on the bridge that crossed from gunwale to gunwale, across the quarterdeck, peering forward up the river. Lamson could see Mr. Smalls pointing out features from time to time, and Lamson wished he could hear the conversation. The morning light came slowly and began to light the tops of the dense trees, beyond the dark green salt marshes. Lamson shouted out to the 14 sailors manning the 100 pound Parrot rifle, that pointed towards James Island, to look sharp and stay alert. They had yet to load the heavy gun. Lamson would wait until the Rebels decided to engage. Nothing could be seen amongst the saw grass, waving in the gentle breezes of the morning. The air was humid and warm, despite the breeze, and the sunlight began to illuminate the dense marsh grass and glittered on the water. A movement above him caught his eye, and Lamson realized it was a flight of Pelicans gliding off towards the Folly River to his right in their never ending search of fish coming in with the tide.

As the *Pawnee* cautiously inched up the Stono, Lieutenant Lamson could hear the leadsmen calling out soundings from their stations just behind him. Each man was lashed off, outside the gunwales tossing their lead weights, attached to marked cords to report water depth under *Pawnee's* keel. The sailor on the port side, shouted out his report, "Mark three deep!" A second later, the starboard leadsman provided his finding, "Mark three deep!" The men had been instructed to provide constant soundings, and Lieutenant Hansen carefully marked each on his chart as they made their way upriver. Lamson noted that the Stono was much wider, and vast than he had imagined it to be. Occasional dolphins surfaced ahead of them as they hunted the tide for fish. Once they had passed Coles Island, the river jogged slightly to the north from its northeasterly trace. Looking behind him, Lamson could see *Huron*, and the *Unadilla*, following them slightly staggered in the broad channel. Ahead, the wooded edges of Johns Island and James Island grew nearer.

Lieutenant Lamson continued to watch over the Starboard rail, towards a dirt path that approached the bank of the river. Off in the distance, he could see a tall tower that marked Fort Lamar, but the top seemed to be unoccupied. The river was eerily quiet.

Near Wright's Camp, just south of Grimball's Landing, Lieutenant Tom Markley led his patrol of 30 troopers from Company G, 5th South Carolina Cavalry on the shady road that led to Coles Island. Just after breakfast, the Captain had rousted them from their coffee and cards to investigate a report of runaway slaves, believed to be holing up near the landing. Jacob Timmonds and Tom's brother, Louis, rode behind him. Louis was joking with Jacob about their recent furlough to Charleston. The teasing had been continuous since they had returned yesterday. Tom occasionally would remind the two to remain alert, but there was little in the way of orders that would contain Louis. He did mostly as he pleased.

Tom pulled his reigns to guide his mount to his left to follow a path through the tangled woods that marked a gully where the salt marshes formed from a small creek, when Tom smelled something strange. Turning to Louis, he commanded, "Shush ya'll! Can you smell that?" Jacob asked, "Smell what?" Tom impatiently waved his gloved hand, "It's coal smoke, burning coal!" The wind was quartering from the southwest, which meant the river. After a moment, Tom announced, "Gunboats! The Yankees are coming up the river! Follow me!" He spurred his horse to ride towards a spit of high ground that overlooked a turn in the Stono from a grove of live oaks. He remembered the spot that he had used before to look out over the great river. With whoops and yelling, his platoon followed, riding skillfully through the thick woods. They made it to the point after 10 minutes of cantering through the woods. Through the tangle of trees, the greenish blue river could be seen. They arrived in time to see the *Ottawa,* and *Pembina* pass. The sailors perched upon the high masts and those who lined the rails with muskets at the ready, could not see them. The wakes ahead of the two gunboats indicated others, so Tom directed them to retrace their steps back to a point further up the river where he could see what else the Yankees had on the water. They rode due north, along the slight ridge to another point where Tom knew one could see the far bend of the river as it flowed around the prominence. Arriving there, he could make out the masts of *Pawnee* and those of the *Huron* following. Turning to Louis and Jacob, Tom exclaimed, "We need to get to Fort Pemberton right away! Jacob, I need you to ride as fast as you can to Fort Lamar! Pass the word that we got 4 Yankee gunboats comin' up river!" Jacob nodded, and turned his mount without hesitation, and rode off to the east. Tom, and the rest of the platoon of horsemen, wove their way swiftly through the dense trees, north to Fort Pemberton. Once they reached Grimball's Landing they could get on the Wapoo Creek road and get the warning out.

As the sun began to climb into the midmorning sky, Robert Smalls turned to Captain Drayton, alongside him on the ship's bridge, and asked, "Sir, you say the draft on this here boat is 12 foot, right?" Drayton looked at him and silently nodded. The portside leadsman cried out as he nodded, "Mark 1 shallow!" There was now only 1 fathom between the bottom of the channel and the keel of the *Pawnee.* Smalls looked at Drayton, and explained, "Boss, if I was you, I would drop anchor right here and have a nice lunch! This here river gets shallower up ahead, and then the ground opens up to the right, by Grimball's Landing up yonder. If I was the Rebs, I would be waitin' there with cannons for you to run aground. The tide will be runnin' out shortly." Drayton was anxious to get as far up the river as he could, but he realized he was hearing sound reality. After a moments thought, he called out to his Executive Officer, "Mr. Hansen, heave to and set anchor! Keep the topside watch alert and keep the men at quarters!" Hansen, hearing the command, nodded and began to shout out orders of his own to the divisions. Soon the rattling of chain marked the release of the anchor. *Pawnee* drifted slightly backwards as the current of the outgoing tide pulled her taunt against the anchor line.

Reid was busy banking the hot coals in the firebox when he received a rare order to report to the galley to pick up pots of White Bean stew to deliver to the messes. The thought of leaving the dark and hot coal bunkers and the boiler furnace, to go topside, was like a gift from heaven. He quickly stowed his shovel and pulled on his uniform top, placed his pork pie hat atop his head, and scampered up the gangway to the galley. There, he was greeted by surly cooks who gave him six tin mess buckets to hoist to the gun deck. The cooks instructed him to go, "Bow to Stern" and then return. As he emerged upon the weather deck, he immediately was pleased by the gentle breeze and he could feel his sweat cooling his body. The sailors on deck had taken their tops off and were in their shirt sleeves by their guns, complaining of the great heat of the day, and Reid was pleased by the cool. Such was the temperature difference on a steamship. The men had their mess cloths down and eagerly took the hot tins of food from Reid as he made the rounds to each mess. The men seemed to appreciate his speed of delivery, and several thanked him. He had not received any positive comments from the crew before. It signified the tiniest inklings of acceptance. He finished his initial set of deliveries, and rushed back below to get the rest of the mess tins. After retrieving the second set of six tins, he finished the deliveries and decided to peer over the high gunwales of the boat from the bow. To his horror, he realized exactly where he was. While he dreamed of going north to Boston, the navy had returned him to Charleston. He realized that to leave this boat now, would mean a return to slavery. He found himself filled with resolve to work as hard as he could, to do his own tiny part to keep his ship safe. He was too close to what he had escaped.

As Reid hurried about his second set of deliveries, he was unaware that the Captain and Robert Smalls watched him work. Smalls turned to the Captain, and said, "Sir, I hope you know that boy yonder is a good one! He ran my engine room all by his self on the *Planter* when we made our run! He didn't have no clue what he was doin', but he faked like he did." Captain Drayton smiled, and replied, "I do believe he is a collier at the moment, but I shall keep that in mind. Maybe he could learn more about the boiler and the valves." Drayton began to realize the potential of the contrabands. With the increasing demands of the Navy, more willing hands could never hurt.

The crew of the *Pawnee* maintained their tense watch in the wide estuary until nearly 4pm, when the return of the tide gradually submerged the black pluff mud at the root bases of the saw grass. The reports from the leadsmen confirmed the increasing depth under keel. Captain Drayton gave the orders to prepare to make way further up the river.

Colonel Robert F. Graham, commanding the 21st South Carolina Infantry, had been in consultation with Colonel Gregoire of the South Carolina Volunteer Engineers at the site of a works under construction to guard the tributary meandering across the northern edge of James Island to the Ashley River. General Beauregard had become increasingly concerned with the network of waters around James Island, and had applied urgent directives to fortify more, and more of the Island. Colonel Graham had dispersed his regiment along several hasty fortifications, fronting the Stono, and had come to visit Colonel Gregoire who currently supervised a large number of negroes detailed to dig works at the northwestern point of the island. As the men talked at the incomplete works, a detachment of Cavalry approached them at a gallop. They paused as the rider at the head of the detachment reined his horse. Graham noted that the young man was a Captain, most likely from the Cadet Rangers, "Sir, there are at least 4 Yankee gunboats working their way up the Stono!" Graham nodded, and asked, "How far up were they when you saw them last?" Tom Markley breathlessly replied, "Sir, they was about a mile shy of Grimball's Landing! They ain't moving fast on account of the tide!"

Colonel Gregoire, only recently assigned to Charleston from Virginia, interjected, "Colonel Graham, my boys back at camp have been working on a project to deny these waters to incursions. This might be an appropriate juncture to give the idea a test!" Graham nodded, but turned to Tom and asked with urgency, "Have you sent a rider to notify General Symington?" Tom shook his head at the question. Graham then sharply directed, "Get word to him this instant! There is no time to waste!" As Captain Markley and his detachment wheeled their horses to make the ride to Fort Lamar, Colonel Graham turned back to Colonel Gregoire, and asked, "Please tell me more about your idea, Colonel." Gregoire nodded and indicated for Colonel Graham to follow him to the Engineer encampment.

As the two men came into the camp, situated under several sprawling live oak trees, Graham noted a party of men, gathered between two white canvas tents. Around them lay several oak salt pork barrels that had what looked like, shortened muskets inserted into the bunghole of the barrel. The men were whittling on odd shaped wooden forms, that appeared to be all the same basic shape. Colonel Gregoire introduced his officers to

Graham, "Colonel, I should like for you to meet Lieutenant Walter Collins and Captain Todd Edgar." The officers quickly stood when they saw Colonel Graham. Gregoire continued, "Captain Edgar, please be so kind as to explain the concept to the good Colonel!"

Captain Edgar motioned the Colonel over to the collection of barrels and containers they had accumulated. He demonstrated with a barrel, that had a shortened musket inserted into the bung, how the trip plates worked. Colonel Graham understandingly nodded, and he asked the Captain, "How quickly can you make a few of these devices? Captain Edgar proudly exclaimed, "We have two already prepared. We were going to seek permission to test them, but Colonel Gregoire could not secure permission from General Symington!

Colonel Graham quickly replied, "Captain, consider a test permitted! I will take full responsibility. Get the devices to the water, as soon as possible. I want them to be allowed to drift with the receding tide, out towards the sea." Colonel Graham remembered reading accounts, from the Richmond newspapers, where similar such devices had been experimented with on the James River. The employment of the so-called "infernal machines" had horrified the Yankees. He realized they needed to discourage the expedition approaching them now. There was little time. Captain Edgar and Lieutenant Collins quickly formed a detail of several slaves and had them secure a Jon boat for their mission. Edgar, and Collins then selected two of the oaken barrels, that they had already coated with tar, and began to fill them with powder from small demijohns of rifle powder they had secured from Fort Lamar's magazines. The barrels required a surprising amount of the rifle powder to fill them. After they had emptied all the demijohns, Lieutenant Collins had been forced to borrow artillery powder from the quartermaster camp, nearby. They employed a wooden wheelbarrow from the engineer digging party to roll the now heavy barrels over to the boat. Edgar secured the two 1817 percussion conversion muskets that they had cut down to serve as firing mechanisms, and loaded them, along with 8 of their fabricated trigger paddles into the boat as well.

Lieutenant Collins secured two 32-pound shot, and a goodly length of sisal rope, and tossed it aboard the Jon boat, as well. The two officers decided that it would be easiest to assemble the dangerous devices in the water. Edgar advised Collins, rather nervously, that they would have to remind each other to cap the muskets, as the "very last step," to insure their own safety. The large wooden trip arms resulted in a hair trigger for the jury rigged musket and would trip it at the slightest touch. Once afloat in the rising Stono, they first fumbled with coming up with a method of tying the 32 pound shot into a hastily fashioned sling to provide ballast to keep the barrel of powder submerged at two thirds of it's length. Once they had devised a workable system of securing the solid shot to the end of the barrel, they lowered the first barrel into the water. Taking care not to splash water into the open hole in the end, they then carefully inserted the loaded musket into the hole, taking care to seal the space around the barrel with some tallow. Captain Edgar then pulled back the hammer on the lock plate to full cock. While the slaves held the boat steady, with terrified looks on their faces, Captain Edgar and Lieutenant Collins carefully assembled the trip arms to the linkage they had devised for the trigger. Edgar then carefully walked the entire floating explosive towards the bobbing stern of the Jon boat, and gingerly extracted a musket size percussion cap from his vest pocket. After giving it a slight pinch to make for a tight fit, he capped the exposed nipple of the upended musket. Turning to the slaves, he whispered, "Row away now, as smoothly as you can!" They paused a moment as the jury rigged torpedo slowly and imperceptibly began to drift in the gentle channel towards the sea. The incoming tide retarded the normal current and the device moved away with painful slowness. After gaining distance from the first, they began the assembly of the second. Captain Edgar's mind was filled with improvements that their next variants would require to make this part of employment easier the next time. After carefully releasing the second device, they quietly rowed back towards the shore and pulled the boat back in.

Reporting to Colonel Graham, he directed them to return to their duties with the fortifications of the growing ramparts of Fort Pemberton. Graham then returned to his headquarters tent and wrote out a dispatch for General Symington, reporting that he had placed two torpedoes into the Stono to stop the Yankee gunboats from coming up the river. Folding the dispatch, he called for a courier and had the message delivered to Fort Lamar.

General Symington had summoned for Captain Legare, commanding the Light Artillery company, when the new dispatch came in from Graham. He had ordered Captain Markley to return to the Stono and send reports back in regards to the progress of the gunboats. Symington hoped to intercept the boats with field artillery, somewhere north of Grimball's Landing. He realized that the Yankees would need a hot reception to buy time to complete the fortification of James Island.

⚓

The afternoon was growing late as the *Pawnee,* and her escorts moved up the river with the tide. Lookouts above Captain Drayton began to shout out sightings of Rebel cavalry as they neared what Drayton's chart indicated as "Grimball's Landing." A quick glance rearward indicated *Ottawa* and *Huron,* a hundred yards aft on his Port and Starboard quarters, and Mr. Smalls was quiet as the leadsmen reported a fathom under his keel. Just to be safe, Captain Drayton ordered the bow chaser gun to be loaded and set on the Starboard quarter of the bow, in the event that the Rebels were readying guns ahead.

Lieutenant Lamson lowered his glass and echoed the Captain's command to load the 100-pound Parrot rifle and orient it to Starboard. The crew quickly snatched the charge run up by the powder boy, and followed it with the heavy Parrot shell, which two men brought up to the muzzle with a wooden tray. The spongeman assisted the rammer in driving the heavy shell home. They then stowed their implements and assisted in running the heavy gun truck out of the gunwale cutout on the Starboard bow. The gunner's mate extracted his sight and set it into the breechring socket, and awaited a target. Satisfied with his gun crew's execution of their drill, Lieutenant Lamson shouted back to the Captain, "Bow Chaser loaded and ready, Sir!" Captain Drayton nodded and replied, "Stand ready!"

Lieutenant Lamson stood forward at the root of the Bowsprit in order to see ahead. He lifted his glass to peer up river and off towards James Island. The coal smoke from the iron stack quartered in the tailwind with the ship, slowly drifting across James Island. The smoke occasionally obscured his view. The winds hinted at poor weather soon. As he continued to scan the river, the late day sun glittered on the water, making it hard to see ahead. Suddenly a lookout in the rigging overhead cried out, "Object in the water ahead!" Lamson, from his perch on the Bowsprit, peered ahead with his glass. Through the bright reflection of the sun on the glittering water he began to make out a dark object jutting out of the water several hundred yards up river. While he studied the odd object, which seemed to be a buoy of sorts, a Pelican swooped by in his field of vision for a moment. Removing the glass from his eye, he could see that the bird now circled and landed on the object. The fishing bird was employing the perch to rest in its hunt for a fish. Lamson peered again through his glass, and with the sea bird providing some sense of reference, he noted that the bird seemed to be standing on the butt of a gunstock, or at least what looked like such. Captain Drayton called out from his place on the amidships bridge, "Mr. Lamson, can you ascertain what the object is?" Lamson intently peered at the object and the Pelican, when another bird arrived, circled, and attempted to land by his companion. Suddenly Lamson's field of view in his glass was obscured. Removing the scope from his eye, he saw a large spray of water and smoke emerge from the glittering surface of the water. A shower of feathers gently descended to float on the disturbed surface of the river. The lookout above cried out, "Torpedo ahead sir!" The low boom of the explosion reverberated across the quiet salt marshes. Lieutenant Lamson swiftly trotted to the bridge to describe what he had seen. Arriving below the Captain, he looked up and explained, "Sir, It appeared in my glass to be a contrivance that used the firing assembly of a common musket to fire the charge! It has a contact trigger of some fashion that causes the musket to fire!"

Captain Drayton wasted no time. He shouted out to Lieutenant Hansen, "Put the skiff into the water ahead with oarsmen and Marines! If you see another object, fire on it with muskets! Load the Starboard Battery! Load Grapeshot!" The crews began to shout and assemble on the guns to Starboard, and prepared to load the four heavy 9-inch guns.

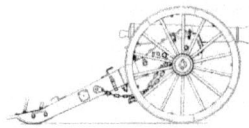

Captain William T. Legare hustled his men as they hitched 4 of his 6-pound guns to their limbers and teams. He had mentally debated bringing all six guns but he currently did not have enough horses to bring caissons with him. Never having fired at Yankee gunboats before, he was not sure how he would do it. His anger at the affront of the abolitionists attempting to attack his hometown, made him anxious to do something to hurt them, something to drive them away. Once the teams were hitched, he drove them from Fort Lamar as fast as the teams could pull the guns. He intended to occupy a spot of high ground, under the trees, that everyone had taken to calling "Battery Tynes." As he rode alongside the cantering teams, he reflected that the term "Battery" was an exaggeration. The site had only recently been surveyed, and no work had been accomplished yet. It occupied a good spot, but much timber still had to be cleared to improve the fields of fire and no works had been erected yet. The moneyed interests of the Grimball family had still required the slaves to continue the harvesting of the cotton, growing in fields reaching all the way to the salt marshes by Grimball's Landing. Their participation in building works would not be realized until the harvest season was finished.

As they skirted the broad cotton fields, still full of slaves picking the final task assignments, the pungent smell of coal smoke filled his senses. The gunboats had a distinctive smell, and judging from the intensity of the smoke, there were more than a couple coming up the Stono. Legare directed Lieutenant Prentiss to quarter off to the north towards the woods above Grimball's Landing, he noted the cavalrymen working the woods south of him, across the cotton fields. Hopefully, they had seen his approach and would apprise him of the location of the gunboats as he set his guns. He suddenly found himself hungry for information about what was coming up the river. The men of the battery quickly unlimbered their guns amidst the slash piles of red oak and scrub brush, that had been recently cleared and partially burned by the survey crew, tasked to locate and mark the future fortification. The Stono was visible through the cleared areas, despite several tall gum and pines that still needed to be cleared. Legare liked the spot as it would mask them until they fired.

As the men led the teams of horses back through the tangled underbrush, a loud boom echoed across the water and the salt marshes. Captain Legare could see the smoke drifting across the wide water of the Stono, just to the north of them. Thinking it was possibly a gunboat from up river, Legare ordered his men to load solid shot. It seemed to him to be the best load to shoot at a ship.

As the crews waited over the barrels of their four bronze guns, the first sight they observed was sailors in a skiff, paddling deliberately up the river. A man in the bow of the skiff stood and peered forward as he braced himself with a long grappling staff. The entire boat of men seemed intent on looking up river. Legare sharply whispered to his sections to hold their fire. The men patiently waited in the afternoon heat, many swatting the myriad of mosquitos that had found them. Soon the gunboat's jib boom and complex rigging could be seen emerging from the trees, followed by the huge black hull. Legare found himself astonished by the size of the ship. No one in his right mind would attempt to move such a huge ship up the Stono. Captain Legare turned from looking at the gunboat to face his gunners; he noticed that all of them were watching him. He shouted at the top of his lungs, "Fire!"

Lieutenant Lamson had been peering dead ahead through his looking glass when the cluster of trees on the right bank, suddenly exploded in smoke. Instantaneously, following the booms of the cannon, the sickening sound of impacting shot thumped into the hull beneath his feet. Another hollow gong-like sound, accompanied by sharp snaps and whirrs overhead, marked another shot ripping through the great iron stack, shearing rigging overhead. Lamson turned to direct his crew to correct the aim of the Parrot rifle towards the source of the smoke, when he heard Captain Drayton calmly shout, "Mr. Lamson, give that battery a shell, if you please!" After a pause, he continued with orders, "Mr. Hansen, have the Port anchor dropped! Helmsman, bring my Starboard battery to bear on the wood!" The crew quickly released the anchor and the Helmsman, telegraphed to the engine room to make all ahead slow, as he tugged on the great ships' wheel to bring her stern around. *Pawnee* slowly began to turn sideways in the river channel, until the Starboard broadside guns bore on the woods. Drayton hoped the maneuver would not cause him to run aground. As he maneuvered to bring his guns to bear, *Ottawa* fired her bow gun at targets off to her Starboard flank. Lieutenant Lamson's crew yanked the triphammer on the 100 pounder Parrot and the huge gun roared, skidding back on its truck, until the breeching tackle pulled taunt, halting its recoil. Through the thick smoke, Lamson could only make out a great spray of water, accented by a deep black cascade of pluff mud. The percussion shell struck low and threw up an enormous portion of the salt marsh. Lamson realized, at these short ranges, that grapeshot would be the best choice, so he ordered the crew to reload with grape. As the men swiftly attended to their duties, he could hear the Captain cry out to the Gun Captains on the Quarterdeck. *Pawnee* then released a great roaring broadside, into the woods ahead of them. All eyes were on the location of the masked Rebel battery, awaiting a reply. No one watched the river ahead as a second jury-rigged and ungainly device crept downriver with the main channel current of freshwater, fighting the tide, to make its way to the sea.

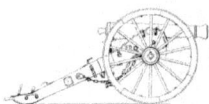

Captain Legare was learning a great deal about the firepower of a Yankee Sloop-of-War, as he cried out to his crews to limber their guns and pull back. The volley from the four 9-inch Dahlgren guns felled entire trees and giant limbs from overhead, filling the air with spraying dirt and wood splinters as the multitude of solid grapeshot from the heavy guns tore through the woods. Legare had no idea if he had lost men, or horses, or guns; he only knew he was too close, and he was definitely outgunned. The gunners did not need to be told twice, they feverishly extracted dead horses from harnesses, and lifted large limbs from the guns and limbers, and attached teams to what remained of their battery. They hurriedly pulled away towards the open cotton fields behind them. They had gotten three guns free of the woods into a clearing out of sight of the Stono, when the Yankees fired another volley of heavy grapeshot into the woods. Captain Legare took stock of what remained of his command. He had taken 4 guns, and caissons along with 34 men and 48 horses to this place. He now found himself with 3 guns, 2 caissons, 30 horses and 22 men. He directed his First Sergeant to see to the wounded men, and he prepared his battery to withdraw to Fort Lamar. They would require bigger guns to deal with these Yankee ships, 6-pounders were no match for them. Legare was unaware of his inanimate ally, slowly drifting towards the wooden bow of the gunboat he had attempted to attack. Across the wide cotton field to the south of them, a smattering of musket fire elicited heavy gunfire from more boats, further down the Stono. Legare could only assume the cavalrymen had decided to fire on the men on the gunboats.

As the late afternoon sun peeked over the tops of the trees of the mainland, the tarred wooden barrel with its awkward superstructure of the trigger boards, and the shortened musket, picked up speed in the Stono's natural current. The great vessel that blocked most of the channel had already begun to cause the channel bottom to shift, as the sluggish yet heavy current dug down to sand, through the unstable mud. The heavy 32 pound shot dug into a spot of pluff mud long enough to cause the entire barrel assembly to spin, and the current pushed the barrel towards the dark wooden bow of the ship, as it lay anchored across the current. The barrel bumped the mud again, and the shot caused it to sway pendulously. After striking the bottom, the top of the barrel angled towards the copper sheathed wooden hull, tapping one of the wooden trip plates. The movement triggered the sear of the musket, which released the heavy hammer to strike the musket cap it had been primed with.

⚓

Lieutenant Lamson, and most of his crew were knocked off their feet as a great explosion shoved the bow of the *Pawnee* tight against her anchor line and sent a high column of white smoke and water vertically in the air by the Starboard forefoot of the boat. Lamson quickly scrambled to his feet and checked on his men. He instinctively knew it was another of the infernal devices, like the one he had seen, before they had been fired upon. Captain Drayton ordered Lieutenant Hansen to send men below to check her bow and assess if *Pawnee* was holed. The party was below decks for a while before a petty officer returned to report, "Sir, the explosion has cracked the planking down low by the Keelson at her forefoot! It has jarred the limber strake upwards and we are taking on water along a quarter of the devil at the fore part of her keel! We can caulk her, but it shall take a spell to get to the keel! We have to move stores in the hold and the ballast blocks to caulk her tight. Sir, Pumpsmen need to go to work!" Hansen had them continue to check, and sure enough, another hole made by a 6-pounder solid shot, was found right at her waterline. They would have to plug it and apply a lead patch to the exterior of the hull. When Lieutenant Hansen brought his report back to Captain Drayton, it shocked him. Drayton calmly observed, "Mister Hansen, if my hull is damaged by her keel, we shall have to get to a yard for proper repairs! Was that caused by a shot? I heard no gunfire!" Lamson shouted out, "Sir, we saw no shots by the bow. I suspect it was another of the Rebel's torpedoes!" Drayton nodded at the report, he ordered the crew, "Raise the anchor and prepare to back down this river! Signal the boats behind that we are coming back out!"

Amidships, the Pumpsmen had taken positions at the bilge pump and began to rock the heavy rocker arms, that lifted 4 pump head plungers connected to a crankshaft, that drove long iron rods into the bilge well below. As the men cranked, great spouts of water gushed from the hydrant heads onto the deck. The water rushed away across the smooth deck planking and drained out the scuppers along the gunwales. The leak was slow and manageable, but the Pumpsmen realized that they would be required to continue their labors until the carpenters and repairers could stop the flow. Captain Drayton realized that his problem was at the worst part of his vessel. He had no choice but to return to Port Royal. He ordered the starboard broadside guns to fire their guns towards James Island to empty them, and then stow them for sailing. He gave a nod towards Robert Smalls, saying, "Mister Smalls, at least we understand that we can get this far with a ship this big. And we have an understanding that the Rebels are sensitive to us coming up this river. Thank you for your assistance sir!" Smalls graciously nodded. He would never let on how scared he had been by the decision to anchor mid-channel to stand and fight the Rebels and their cannon. He was not accustomed to being shot at.

Down below, in the well-lit stokehold, Reid had survived his first naval battle. He had been alarmed when a solid shot had penetrated the *Pawnee's* hull, several feet behind him. The engineer who occasionally came by to supervise them, advised him that they might find it in the next coalbunker.

Reid was sweaty and tired from the constant stocking of the furnace. He had learned from the shouting, that they were now drifting back down the river. The huge jolt that flowed through the boat had caused a leak, and the Engineers had left them to their stoking to go forward to have a look. The eldest of them, an officer, came back, and advised, "Boys, stay at your stations and keep her running, but if I call you to come up on deck, you come at the run! Do you understand?" Reid nodded; he had earlier noted the floorboards of the deck seemed wet and he had not thought much of it. Looking down after the officer's instructions, he noticed nearly an inch of water sloshing about, under his feet. He was suddenly apprehensive. He asked one of the white sailors, "Is we sinking, Boss?" The burley man laughed, "Not much boy! We are just sinkin' a little!" The sailor moved off laughing to join his mates at the boilers above. A little later Lieutenant Hansen came below. Reid was fearful of the stern officer, but he never ridiculed or shouted at the "Contrabands." He would quietly watch them work and ask the Petty Officer following him, soft questions. Reid looked up from his constant shoveling, and said, "Good Evening Sir!" The Lieutenant only nodded, but Reid noticed approval in the Officer's eye.

Coming back into the darkening deck, Hansen reported to Captain Drayton, "Sir, we have crews caulking the keel forward, and the pumps are keeping pace with the flooding below. At this instant, there is an inch of water at the stokehold, no more! Once we can turn, I would recommend making all possible speed to Port Royal!" Captain Drayton nodded. He had remained worried, if the flooding drowned out his fires he would have to put *Pawnee* under tow in a hostile river. The signalmen had reported that the *Ottawa* had been receiving gunfire from the north bank of the Stono just prior to sunset, so the Secesh were still about out there. Drayton calmly replied, "Mr. Hansen, keep the men at quarters, but have them take their mess at their stations. We will keep moving at reverse speed until we reach the Folly River, we can turn about there. We need to make haste to keep with the tide!" Drayton watched the men manning the pumps as they rocked the handles, bringing the bilge water up in spouts from the pump spigots. He reflected that he had not proceeded as far up the Stono as he had desired. The infernal torpedoes, laid by the Rebels, made the expeditions into the tidewater difficult, but he had seen enough to understand what sort of warships would have to be used to conduct this sort of warfare. The next time he would bring the Army as well. Operations in these waters would have to be combined. Drayton swatted his hand as the buzzing sounds of mosquitoes became apparent to him; they always flooded in at twilight, it seemed. It was high time for a cigar; he had found it to be the only way to thin out the swarms of hungry insects that bedeviled the sailors on these waters.

It took Captain Tom Markley several hours to find his scattered troopers after the Yankee gunboat had shelled them in the woods. He was still seething with anger. Their only mission had been to observe and report back to Fort Lamar, where the boats were. Louis had decided to attempt a pot shot at one of the sailors, acting as a lookout high in the mainmast of one of the gunboats. Jacob Timmons had been more that happy to join in with his shotgun, and the reply from the gunboat had been shockingly intense. The detachment fortunately had been able to escape the hail of heavy cannon fire and musketry from the gunboat, but the retreat had scattered his detachment throughout the thick woods covering the southern side of the Island. In the dark woods, Tom hailed the clusters of horsemen as he found them often by the sound of their low talking or the snorts of their horses To each group, he directed them to rally at the Grimball plantation. Tom finally found Louis and Jacob coming back across the cotton field from where the cannon from Battery Lamar had fired upon the boat. Both were shocked by their finding the dead from the barrage of return fire from the Yankee gunboats. Louis blurted out, "Tom, the woods yonder are full of dead men! They are terribly torn up!" Tom nodded and replied, "Well, think on that the next time you decide to fight a gunboat with a revolver and a shotgun! We're damned lucky we don't look the same!" He looked over his shoulder in the deepening darkness; the men at the rendezvous point had begun to make coffee. He could see several small flickering fires. Tom quietly commanded, "Go on, and join the others. I reckon we'll be sleepin' at the Grimball place tonight. Louis, go knock on the door and let the overseer know what we is up to. He might have some eggs to spare." Tom looked towards the Stono through the trees. The water was barely visible in the half-light and the gunboats were gone. He realized that the next time they came, it likely would be to land Yankee troops. General Symington would be smart to get more infantry on James Island. It would also do to have heavier guns. The fact that they had come made him realize that they would return, having learned the way up the Stono.

Amidst the din of the carpenters and repair parties attending to the holes in the *Pawnee,* as she lay at anchor, Captain Drayton paced the deck, observing the repairs in the company of Lieutenant Hansen. Hansen provided the Captain with a folded paper and said, "Sir, this is a sketch from Mr.

Lamson. He saw the first object, prior to it exploding and I daresay it was likely an identical device that we encountered. We showed it to Smalls and he recognized the design. He said there are much better types in the harbor of Charleston. He said these are the first types that were laid, after the battle of Port Royal." Drayton nodded, he paused remembering the battle, then replied, "Not having much of a Navy, it makes sense that they should resort to such desperate and indiscriminate methods. It should be classified as a violation of the rules of war! They are devices of indiscriminate murder!" Drayton raised his arms momentarily in frustration before resuming, "That being said, we need to come up with a means of countering the damned things!" Lieutenant Hansen nodded, "The officers are discussing exactly that sir! They have a concept they would like to brief the Admiral on, when we get back!" Drayton nodded, as they paced the deck. He stopped to look down over the gunwale, at men working by lantern light nailing a lead patch over one of several 6 pounder shot holes in the hull of *Pawnee*. Looking back up to Hansen, he observed, "That Island up the river is a key to Charleston. Next time I come up this river, I want the Army with me. If we own James Island, Charleston has no defense!"

6

THE RAPPAHANNOCK

The dying sunlight made the leaden sky a deeper gray as the steady rain continued to fall. Sergeant Joshua Timmonds directed his section to retrieve the canvas awning they had found in Sharpsburg from its new special spot on the axle of the number one caisson. Following his directions, the gunners erected the shelter between two pines in the rough brushy woods they had been directed to occupy. It was now November and the night promised to be cold and miserable. Joshua had noticed that water in buckets were beginning to develop a skin of ice on them in the early mornings. Winter was coming, after a long delay. As his men erected their precious shelter from the merciless rain, Joshua reached under his oilskin poncho and fingered open the buttons of his shell jacket to retrieve a Cheroot cigar he had bought from the horse artillery regiment sutler. He walked over to the company cook fire to light it. He was all out of matches at the moment. Arriving there, Joshua noticed to his satisfaction that the Quartermaster Sergeant had arranged to have a large kettle scrounged up. Lieutenant Pennington, now commanding, since Captain Haines had been snatched up to Colonel Hayes' staff, had ordered company feeding when the weather was bad. Joshua smiled and nodded to Sergeant Mills as he retrieved a burnt kindling end to light his cigar, "What's fer supper Quartermaster Sergeant?" Mills grinned and found the dipper, raising up a chunky sample for him to observe, and replied, "Secesh beef, onion and desecrated vegetable stew!" Joshua blew a puff of smoke up into the rain, and laughed, "Sergeant you sure you classified that beeve as "Contraband" before you cooked it?" Mills nodded. Joshua, and the rest of the company loved Mills, ever imaginative, and ever dependable. They all felt they had the most efficient Quartermaster in the Army of the Potomac. They had never wanted for anything, thus far. The smell of the thick stew was intoxicating, and Joshua reluctantly walked back over to supervise the picketing of the team horses. He knew he would have to force his cold, wet and hungry men to attend to the painstaking care of the harness leathers, particularly in this wet to keep them from cracking. He shouted out to his drivers, "Ya'll bring them harnesses under the awning wit ya! I want you oilin' them after supper!" To his satisfaction, he noted that all the horses had their nosebags on and munched noisily as they ate the contents. They were content to be able to rest, rain or no rain, and the only thing that kept a horse warm in weather like this was feed. After checking the security of the picket ropes and insuring the halters were properly hitched to the picket line, Joshua returned to his guns, to give the wheels a quick once over. As he inspected the muddy carriages and limbers, in the rapidly fading light, he marveled at how messy everything now was. A month of marching behind General Pleasanton's cavalry had ruined the fine polish they had produced earlier, for President Lincoln's Grand Review after the battle at Sharpsburg.

They had been surprised at the official name of the huge battle after reading about it, in Harpers Weekly. It took Joshua and the other Sergeants some time studying the printed map, to realize that the creek that played little part in the fight, was called "The Antietam." Now the thing was the "Battle of Antietam" despite the fact, that no one would have fought over a creek. The boys were in good spirits; they had been lucky in the last great fight. Luckier than many a soul they had witnessed as they crossed the ruined field, after it was over. Now they were beginning to chase General Lee and his Rebel army back through Virginia. Joshua liked to envision that they were nearly finished; perhaps after one more great fight they would surrender the foolish notion of breaking the country in two. Joshua, remembering his bedroll, quickly made his way to where he had laid his saddle and unstrapped the tightly rolled blanket. His section cannoneers had already begun to claim their respective places under the dripping canvas awning. Nobody wanted to sleep in the cold rain and nothing stood anymore in the tumbledown woods they had occupied. Soon the Virginia roads would get bad with the soaking rains and the campaigning would likely stop.

The sound of an approaching horseman caused Joshua to look up. Judging from the artillery insignia on the rider's hat, Joshua imagined the man was a courier from regimental headquarters, it was hard to tell when everyone wore oilskin ponchos. The rider paused before Lieutenant Pennington's tent and extracted a piece of paper from a leather case, which he handed to the Lieutenant. After a few words the courier saluted Pennington and rode off down the dark muddy path to find the next unit.

Soon First Sergeant O'Keefe's booming voice rose above the pattering roar of the rain, "Bring all yer men over to the Commander's tents boys! We gots us a solemn pronouncement! On the double quick dammit!"

Joshua quickly strode up behind his men, Sergeant Newby sidled up beside him and bummed a dheroot. Since he had matches, Joshua produced two and they shared a rainy smoke while they waited amid the crowd of soldiers. Jim Page turned to Joshua and whispered, "Sarge, we heared it was about the General!" Joshua looked at him quizzically and asked, "What General?" Before Page could answer, Lieutenant Pennington came out of his tent, and stood under the awning with a printed broadsheet in his hands. The men were busily talking amongst themselves, until First Sergeant shouted, "At ease! Listen to yer commander!" O'Keefe held up a lantern so Pennington could read the script.

Pennington addressed his company, "Men, we are directed to read this message to all ranks by the express directive of Brigadier General Hunt! I assure you, this is news to us all! This address to you is from General McClellan and is marked Headquarters Camp, Rectortown, Virginia, dated 2 days ago, the 7th of November." Pennington glanced down and O'Keefe raised the lamp a little to better illuminate the paper. The Lieutenant then continued, *"For the Officers and Soldiers of the Army of the Potomac. An order of the President devolves upon Major General Burnside the command of this army. In parting from you, I cannot express the love and gratitude I bear to you. As an army you have grown up under my care. In you, I have never found doubt or coldness. The battles you have fought under my command will proudly live in our nation's history. The glory you have achieved, our mutual peril and fatigues, the graves of our comrades fallen in battle and by disease, the broken forms of those whom wounds and sickness have disabled, the strongest association which can exist among men, unite us still by an indissoluble tie. We shall ever be comrades in supporting the Constitution of our country and the nationality of its people. Signed George B. McClellan, Major General, United States Army!"*

Joshua and his men were stunned. Some asked, "Who is Burnside?" A low murmur rose from the men as they digested the news. Lieutenant Pennington interrupted the discussion, one more time, "Men, I understand this is disturbing news, but remember that our army is a composite of how prepared each of you are! They have changed the leadership at the top, but the Horse Artillery Regiment has not changed, nor has the Artillery Reserve! Now go get your mess tins and cups, and get some hot food. We are to pause for a while tomorrow, so stand-to will be late in the morning!" The wet men gave a great cheer. Joshua smiled, only in the army could you be happy and sad at the same time. He noticed the men talking as they stood in line. Each man had his own theory of President Lincoln's logic or General Halleck's opinion, of the relief of General McClellan. The tattered copies of the Harpers Weekly and other papers were re-examined for evidence, or indicators of why "Little Mac" was let go, but they revealed nothing to the curious men. Later that evening, in the Sergeant's meeting after dinner, First Sergeant O'Keefe shared with his leaders what the Captain had heard from the officers at Regiment, "They says the pursuit of the Johnny Rebs from Sharpsburg was too slow. There was loud claims from the Congress that there is a conspiracy o' Democrats, that are allowing the Secesh to win. Those o' you lads that don't know, General McClellan is a Democrat, through and through. Word is the elections last week ain't a goin' so well for Mr. Lincoln, him freein' the slaves and all, so high generals of the Democratic persuasion, is likely to get the old boot!" The sergeants laughed heartily, at his take of world affairs. After another sip from his tin cup of whiskey, he continued, "Make yer boys ready, this travelin' we are doin' is a pursuit of Mr. Lee's army! He is believed to likely stop, and start to diggin' along the Rappahannock River. It makes sense map wise as it's gots lots of high ground on either bank and cannot be easily forded. Mark me well, with a new commanding general we won't be goin' into winter camps, just yet. There will be a hell bent effort to please Mr. Lincoln! Keep ready for another fight! I can feel it in my bones." Joshua nodded, as he listened. He made his mind up to focus closely on what was being said as he would repeat the news to his men. It made them feel important to be "in the know" and they would clamor for the latest news.

After a few minutes of small talk and banter, O'Keefe turned to more practical matters, "You all might o' heard, but if you ain't, you'll hear it now. The army is now critical short on horses of all kinds, right down to mules. Keep a close eye on yer teams and their feet! Don't be drivin' them hard. Any animal we lose on this pursuit will be replaced by your personal mounts! The cavalry is short as well! We are also running short on forage, since we are strung out, so we are going to slow our pace. When we halt we will allow the animals to browse for an hour at each stop. Mills is bringing up cracked corn for feed, so adjust yer quantities accordingly! Since we are stoppin' for the sake of our horses, you will use that time to drill yer crews! See to it each time we stop!" After the session of instruction, O'Keefe told Joshua to remain behind as the other Sergeants departed. Joshua sidled over to catch the warmth radiating off the conical Sibley stove that heated the First Sergeant's tent. The chill November rain threatened snow at any time and it had become difficult to stay warm and dry.

First Sergeant O'Keefe poured more whiskey into Joshua's cup and asked,

"So what hear ye from that girl down south? I'm notin' you ain't seeing much mail lately." Joshua took a sip, and shook his head, "Nuthin' Top. I'm thinkin' she imagines me dead. The way most of our fights have been going, I don't reckon she believes otherwise." He thoughtfully took a sip, and continued, "It don't much matter anyhows, we got nothing but war in front of us. We'll all be lucky to live through it!"

Billy O'Keefe nodded sadly, and replied, "Son, you may be right on that score. We are becoming engines of killing, and they still keep comin' and fightin' us. It is amazin' the amount of conviction we see in them Secesh. Sacred honor, and that sort of thing. Like the disease that inflicts the Irish!" Joshua nodded, and growing slightly impatient, he asked, "First Sergeant, you asked me to remain behind. Is there news for me?" O'Keefe nodded, and put his hand on Joshua's shoulder, and replied, "Yes Boy'O there is. I have recommended you to replace me when I receive orders to go to regimental headquarters! It seems that General Hunt has asked me to assist Colonel Hayes as his Sergeant Major. Mills turned down the offer, flat out. Mueller is a dirty German laborer and Newby is still half a private. Lieutenant Pennington is mighty partial to you since you was his section Sergeant, and as the commander, he is apt to have his way."

Joshua suddenly felt weak and sputtered, "Hell, First Sergeant! Why me?" O'Keefe laughed, "Because that's what I asked when I got the same job, Boy O'! Be mighty wary of any asshole that wants to be somethin'! You earned it by duty son, simple duty. You ain't never failed the Company and ain't never questioned your duty. Even when it meant fightin' according to yer oath in a war between brothers!"

Joshua looked into his cup, suddenly sad to realize the mentor he knew as the only stable thing in his existence was soon to be leaving. He asked, "When do you leave?" O'Keefe shrugged, "Don't rightly know, Boy O.' I imagine when the army comes together again. Bein' put out front with the Cavalry like we are, at the moment, don't offer much opportunity for reorganizin'. I suppose once General Burnside figures out where we is a headed!" Joshua nodded, and asked, "Where are we headed, Top?" O'Keefe looked him in the eye, and solemnly replied, "The Rappahannock River! I am betting we will hit Rebels there in force. General Pleasanton told the Captain that yesterday. It ain't for settin' up winter camp, that's for sure. Note we have been following this rail line off to our right for two days on! It leads to a town called Fredericksburg. That's where we fight, say I! Bank on it, son. Get on now, back to yer men! From this day on, each time I hold a Sergeant's meetin,' you pause afterwards for some words o' advice. Don't tell the boys just yet. We'll see how soon they catch on."

The drizzling rain had turned to stinging grains of sleet as the wintry gusts whipped the shoulder panels of Joshua's overcoat about. In the darkness, he could see the team horses bowing their heads against the stinging ice as they stood silently along the picket ropes awaiting the cold dawn and warming feed. Joshua felt both elated, and sad, at the same time. He could not envision being the replacement of O'Keefe. His were enormous shoes to fill, and at the same time, he knew he could do it. Returning to the canvas awning established by his gunners, he silently located his bedroll and turned in. He used his greatcoat to augment his blanket against the growing winter chill.

Joshua shucked his wet boots, and placed them carefully beside his bedroll and settled under his blanket and overcoat. His nose was uncomfortably cold in the chill of the evening. He lay a while in the darkness and thought of Lottie; he wondered if she did likewise.

Lottie glanced up from the gaily-lit table in the dining room of the White Sulfur Springs Hotel and Resort. The brightly lit and ornate room illuminated fleeting flakes of snow falling beyond the white trimmed windows of the veranda on the dark and cold November evening. They had arrived at the former resort, now a hospital full of wounded from the recent battle at Sharpsburg, mid-month after a rather arduous journey from Winchester. The enterprising hospital staff had enjoyed the generosity of the proprietor of the resort and the hospital was a rather cheerful place, despite the suffering of the wounded. She took another sip of dry sherry from the crystal wineglass before her and gazed at Henri as he solemnly explained a detail of medical advancement with Colonel Trimble, the surgeon responsible for secondary amputations at White Sulfur Springs Hospital.

Lottie studied Henri's handsome features and animated eyes. Only two days ago he had informed her of his intent to court her and shocked, she had assented. And while he fascinated her with his charm and dashing nature, she felt oddly removed from the reality of his proposals. Inventories of the formularies had taken on the aspects of a sad joke as most stores proved to be the home remedies and captured Yankee supplies, of which they seemed to have in abundance. The Confederate States

Government supply system provided a trickle compared to what the army could scrounge and the doctors could improvise. She had found it remarkable that the local people would gladly deliver up cases of remedies they had manufactured themselves in exchange for food or whiskey. The only shortage to this newfound system of medicines was the bottles to hold them, and a thriving trade in old bottles had emerged around the hospital as suppliers would often trade their wares, for the glass containers.

The staff had gathered this evening, to celebrate the Thanksgiving feast on the schedule that Virginia held it, rather than what the Yankees had taken to calling "Thanksgiving." The Surgeon General of White Sulfur Springs had arranged for soldiers to hunt down the flocks of Geese that frequented the ponds and the resort cooks had fashioned a grand dinner for the staff and the ambulatory patients at the hospital. The worsening weather hopefully signaled the end of campaigns until next spring. Lottie surmised that the shaggy and exhausted appearance of the soldiers guarding them was a clear indicator of their weary state. She often would offer soft prayers that the Lord would grant them a little peace. It broke her heart to study the wounded boys in the wards. While not as awful and bloody as the forward hospitals had proven to be, the General Hospitals often were quieter but the men within continued to die, and she feared getting to know any of them, because of this fact. She glanced again out the window and noticed that the falling snow had become quite thick.

Henri, noting her gaze, remarked, "Tis a beautiful sight is it not, my dear?" Lottie absently nodded, "I can never say I have seen such copious snow in Old Berkeley!" Henri laughed, "Yes Miss Markley, we rarely see such weather in New Orleans as well! These Virginians are definitely a hardy mountain people to endure such weather continually!" Colonel Trimble, a Lexington native, nodded and proudly observed, "Yes Captain, we are a proud Mountain People! Distinguished gentlemen of Appalachia! I certainly hope those Yankees come to appreciate that!" The discussion turned to the progress of the Small Pox vaccination orders and the progress achieved so far. The conversation then turned to Henri's proposed visit to the General Lee's surgeons, assembling in Fredericksburg. This next visit would enable Charlotte to see the medical supply system at the Field Army level, and it would provide Henri a chance to call on old friends who had remained afield for over a year. Lottie listened intently. The notion of visiting the historic and storied city of George Washington's youth was interesting. To see General Lee in person would also be a thrilling experience.

As Lottie took another small bite of the roasted goose, she felt Henri's knee brush against hers. The simple and suggestive touch caused her heart to race. She remembered that he had taken her hand, as they walked in the chill evening yesterday, and it had caused a flutter within her stomach. After all the hard travel and exhausting work, she found it a comfort to have someone near. She resolved to write her mother tomorrow. The fleeting notion of writing Joshua crossed her mind but a cloud of doubt, erased the temptation. Working for the government had made her pensive to the notion of surreptitious letters to the North. She mentally imagined him dead, anyway. The news was full of Yankee defeats and disasters. She immediately felt a pang of regret as she imagined him dead. Glancing at Henri again, Lottie realized she was losing her ability to think clearly anymore.

Soon a local collection of musicians began to play a soft Mountain Waltz with instruments more suited to a gospel sing in the Appalachian Mountains than a cotillion, but the tune was catchy and Henri invited her to dance.

His elegance and strong embrace was intoxicating. She noted the admiration of the nurses, and the senior staff as they danced to the lilting mountain music, that while jarring to her senses, still maintained a romantic charm, unique to Virginia. Lottie finally felt like she was within a place where she comfortably belonged. It all felt honorable and upright. Momma and Poppa would be proud of her at this very moment. Looking again at Henri, as she danced, she realized that she was in love. Whether it was with him, or the comfortable feeling, she was not sure. She felt safe.

Major Ira Spaulding studied the well-traveled hand-written order, signed under the authority of General McClellan, that he received from a courier on the night of 12 November. It was dated 5 November and had been relayed via courier overland via Rectortown, through Washington. There could not have been a more time consuming way to deliver a message of such urgency. He had just arrived from Berlin, Maryland on orders from General Woodbury. He paused to listen to the heavy rain and sleet as it pattered on his tent in the darkness. He currently was camped adjacent of the Navy Yard in Washington, awaiting the arrival of 56 of the bateaux from the bridge they had just disassembled. The boats were coming via the

C&O canal and the Potomac, to arrive for transfer across the Potomac, to Virginia, aboard a chartered train. He had a partial set of wagons to carry them, but no animals to draw them. His frustration had grown over the passing of the day after he had received instructions by General Woodbury, just this morning, that no bridges were required. Now, he had received another order, from the newly installed General Burnside, that bridges to cross the Rappahannock were urgently needed to coincide with the arrival of the Army before Fredericksburg by the 17th of November. Specifically, four to five bridges of 400 feet would be needed for the Army to successfully cross. Studying the message, his mind raced. He mentally calculated how many pontoon boats, balks, rails and chess planks, would be required to cross the 400-foot Rappahannock River in 5 places. Listening to the rain on the canvas above him, he was reminded that the river would be running high in the wet weather of the fall. Depending on where the General wished to cross, would hold yet another uncalculated challenge.

Later in the evening he would receive a telegraph from the War Department, reporting the news that Major Magruder had rafted 48 boats down the Potomac a week ago and had them stored at Belle Plain. Magruder apparently would be preparing to move overland to Falmouth. Spaulding ran his hands through his hair as he digested the import of his orders. Pulling out the earlier dispatch, he realized that they were due to receive the horses on the morrow, and he still did not have enough of the specialized wagons for the bridge trains. The sheer impossibility of his orders impaired his ability to think. He currently possessed enough rolling stock for an Army standard bridge train, which consisted of 34 boat wagons, 22 Chess wagons, 2 supply and 2 forge wagons. He summoned Lieutenant Falley, the quartermaster, and informed him that they would go to the depot in the morning to attempt to draw horses. The confusion created by the conflicting guidance was creating within him a great urge to entrain and leave Washington, as soon as he could. He resolved to visit the War Department again in the morning to get clarity and to request additional wagons to carry the bridge, floating down from Berlin.

After Lieutenant Falley had departed, Captain Brainerd, who had arrived earlier to set up the camp, arrived at his tent. After a short greeting, he informed Major Spaulding that General Woodbury had arrived in Washington and was staying at a boarding house across the street from the War Department. Major Spaulding pulled out his watch, it was nearly 1030 pm. He eyed Brainerd for a moment, and announced, "Let us secure two horses and call on him!" Brainerd was hesitant, and asked, "Sir, the hour is late!" Spaulding quickly responded, "The entire mission will be late, to God knows what impact, if I cannot get clear orders! Find us two mounts as quickly as you can!" Spaulding grabbed up his greatcoat and carefully tucked the new order from General Burnside in the breast pocket and threw the coat on. In his current mood, he cared not a whit if the General was displeased. There was too much to do. As he waited on Brainerd and the horses, he imagined that General Burnside fully expected to have a bridge to arrive on the 17th at Falmouth, nearly 50 miles away, in a scant four days and he could not envision how he would make that timeline. He currently had only 250 of the men of the 50th New York in camp, with the remainder enroute, either on the C&O canal with the rafts or driving the remnants of the trains cross country to Washington. He also held two clear orders from two different Generals that were countermanded by another. Surely the War Department could clarify. Upon Brainerd's return, they mounted their borrowed horses and rode through the driving rain to the War Department.

After a short visit with the night clerks, they located the boarding house where General Woodbury was staying and rode there. After much persistent knocking, Major Spaulding was able to wake the proprietress, who was greatly displeased, and after much discussion, she resignedly went to awaken the General. He appeared at the door several minutes later, before the two soaking officers on the uncovered stoop. Major Spaulding presented the newest order from General Burnside, stating, "Sir, I need confirmation on this order as it seems to differ from your earlier order of this morning!" General Woodbury's anger was rapidly displaced by the portent of the newest information and he allowed the two men in, out of the rain. After a moments study by the lamp on the hall end table, he remarked, "Major, come back in the morning around 9am. I will go to General Halleck first thing. Have you received the boats yet from Berlin?" Major Spaulding silently shook his head. He paused as this sunk in, and asked, "The horses? Have you been able to get more?" Spaulding resignedly replied, "Sir, we have no horses, not enough wagons, and the remaining men of the Brigade are still enroute. As it stands, there is no earthly way we shall be able to meet General Burnside's intent! I stand ready to do what I must, but the War Department needs to work out these details and give us priority! I promise you that a 50 mile movement across Virginia in this weather will prove difficult at best!" General Woodbury wearily replied, "Come see me tomorrow morning, Major."

The noise of hundreds of hooves awakened Major Spaulding the next morning. He emerged from his tent half dressed to meet Lieutenant Falley as he arrived to report. Spaulding noted something odd about the animals; it was the ears on them. The emerging braying, confirmed his suspicions. He looked at Falley, and asked, "Mules?" Falley dourly replied, "Yes Sir, no less than 250 green broke mules, sir! We got harnesses and collars too, in boxes, and yet to be assembled! None of these animals have ever been trained as teams, nor worn a harness or collar!" He broke into a small sick smile, and continued, "Good news though, is they are shod." Major Spaulding swore and returned to the shelter of his tent to finish dressing. He shouted back to his lieutenant, "Start breaking them, and try to train at least one leader per team!" He hurried his dressing for his ride back to the War Department on his borrowed horse. He realized he had many long days ahead of him.

The chill morning wind blew in gusts through the bare limbed trees in the barren woods south of Winchester. Corporal Billy Cross, and his close friend Gene Gerrard, drew their blankets closer about their shoulders as they warmed themselves at their mess fire. Gene had arranged a fine stew of fresh beef, onions, and some cabbage he had traded Yankee coffee to a farm wife for, at the ramshackle house near their camp. Their reverie was disrupted by Sergeant Dennis, who shouted across the camp, "Alright ya'll get on your feet and form a line by the Quartermaster wagon! The Surgeon is here! Billy Cross stood, and asked, "What's this all about Sergeant?" As the men reluctantly rose and muttered small protests, Sergeant Dennis replied, "Small Pox vaccination, Corporal! Orders direct from General Lee his self! Every man in this army is to get it before we start the march! Cross nodded, and motioned for his men to move over to the line. Word had spread throughout the camp that General Jackson was ordering a move south along the Rappahannock to keep the Yankees from crossing. Mention of Small Pox made him nervous. Rumors of outbreaks since the fight in Maryland were widespread. Many men, including George, had placed the blame on contact with Yankee soldiers coming out of the big cities of the north.

Billy got in line first, behind his men, and the medical officer told him to strip off his blouse and shirt. As he shed his uniform top, he called out for the remainder of his mess to do likewise, which pleased the older medical officer, whom Billy noted, wore the rank of Lieutenant Colonel. The doctor quickly grabbed his left arm and made three swift cuts with a lancet, causing Billy to wince at the stinging pain. The officer then scraped the blade of the lancet across some powder in a small tin container and rubbed it into the cuts with the flat of the blade. He then placed a small square of newspaper onto the fresh wound with the brief instruction, "Don't peel it off, let it fall off with the scab! Next!" Billy stepped away from the procedure and put his shirt and blouse back on. Seeing Lieutenant Carson, he asked, "Sir, is this gonna make me sick?" Carson shook his head, "So far no, Corporal. Just report any man that gets the fever and send him to sick call. Winchester has quite a few cases among the people there. Tis far better to endure this step, than to have an outbreak. Expect that arm to get sore."

The men of his mess returned to their fire, each complaining of sore arms, but they rapidly began to form a more concentrated interest on the progress of Gene's stew. The rations had been vastly better since their return to Virginia, and replacement clothes and shoes had also begun to materialize to the delight of the weary men. Most were overjoyed to see the arrival of the cold, and the wet, as it was a sure symbol of the end of campaigning. Billy wondered though, as the Cavalry seemed to be extremely busy passing to, and fro through the lines at a gallop most of the time. There was much talk of the Yankee Army on the move towards the south; which reinforced the mystery of the orders, just this morning, of a movement tomorrow to Front Royal and across the mountains, south. The word from the officers was that General Lee was to concentrate the Army back together again. Billy mused on that bit of news, it only meant one thing.

General Lee appreciated James Longstreet's wise choice of the roomy wood floored barn as the field headquarters of his recently formed Corps near Culpepper. He had returned from Richmond a week ago and had grown increasingly concerned by the activity of General Burnside, all up, and down the piedmont, south of Harpers Ferry. There had been much speculation in regards to how aggressive Ambrose Burnside would be upon taking control of the Federal army. Initially he had moved only in a limited fashion, which Lee had correctly attributed to reorganization and those activities common to a new commander getting a feel for his new responsibilities. Recent reports of Union troops landing at Aquia Creek and establishing a supply base there, resulted in a deeper suspicion driving this visit to Longstreet's headquarters.

Lee quietly listened as James Longstreet apprised him of developments, over a map laid across a rickety table in the center of the barn. Water from the constant rain pattered in puddles outside the open door of the barn, and the occasional gust of wind would ripple the edges of the map, causing aides to place round stones on the edges to keep it still. General Longstreet moved his hands on the map of Virginia, as he talked, "Sir, I had fully expected them to attempt to come through Culpepper, as a natural circumstance of it laying astride the Orange and Alexandria Line. General Jackson and I have been diligent in adhering to your orders to tear up the lines leading to Winchester, and here, to prevent their use by Burnside, but the establishment of a supply base at Aquia Creek must mean an effort aligned on the Richmond and Alexandria rail line. That ain't as good a rail system as the one I control, but it leads straight away to Richmond. Them people keep crowin', "On to Richmond!," and I am sure that Mr. Lincoln presses for that daily. Burnside is new and is likely under great pressure to do somethin' before the weather makes it impossible."

Lee nodded, and thoughtfully replied, "General, that is also the opinion of President Davis. Those people fixate more on our national capitol than they do this Army. I, for one, remain grateful that they do. Would you, if you were in my place, bring this army together?"

James Longstreet paused a moment as he looked up from the map, and thoughtfully replied, "Sir, I would, but only when I could ascertain his point of concentration. I cannot help but think that they fear using the Shenandoah Valley, based on General Bank's experience there. I should think they would stay as close as they can to the water, for ease of supply. General Stuart continues to report a general trend of their movement, since they started moving again, that suggests the whole army is swinging like a door to the southwest; like a door with its hinge at Washington."

Lee paused and looked out the barn door behind them. He noted white flakes of snow now mixed with the falling rain; the weather was turning worse. Turning back towards General Longstreet and the map, Lee asked the question he already had the answer for, "What divides us then?"

General Longstreet quickly answered, "The Rappahannock River, Sir! We are seeing Yankee cavalry at every crossing with each passing day. There are reports of them moving bridging boats to Belle Plain, across from Aquia creek. They got a river on their mind, and it has to be the Rappahannock. She is running high now due to the rain and every bridge is being looked at. We just got a report this morning that Yankee cavalry crossed at Fredericksburg yesterday and took some of our men prisoner. The rail trestle and the road bridge from Stafford Courthouse are still in place there. I just cannot help but think that General Burnside is seeking the quickest route to Richmond. He presses us all along our front, but refuses to press at any one point in a concerted fashion. It is merely poking by small detachments of cavalry and limited elements of infantry, here and there. What I find interesting is each passing day, reveals a new appearance

FREDERICKSBURG CAMPAIGN
Scale of Miles
WINCHESTER
JACKSON
LONGSTREET
PLEASANTON
McCLELLAN
WASHINGTON
Leesburg
Fredericksburg
Culpeper C.H.
Warrenton
Gainesville
New Baltimore
Manassas Jcn.
Centreville
Fairfax C.H.
Alexandria
Falmouth
Orange C.H.
Gordonsville
Madison C.H.
Stafford C.H.
King George C.H.
Port Royal
POTOMAC RIVER
RAPPAHANNOCK RIVER
RAPIDAN RIVER
BLUE RIDGE MTS.
BULL RUN MTS.
Salem
Upperville
Union
Aldie
Middletown
Millwood
Sperryville
Amissville
Woodville
Little Washington
Front Royal
Chester Gap
Ashby's Gap
Thoroughfare Gap
Warrenton Jcn.
Orange & Alexandria R.R.
BAYARD
Beverly Ford
Kelly's Ford
Rapidan Sta.
Berlin
Barnesville
Rockville
Charlestown
Skinker's Neck
Belle Plain
Marlboro Pt.
Spottsylvania C.H.

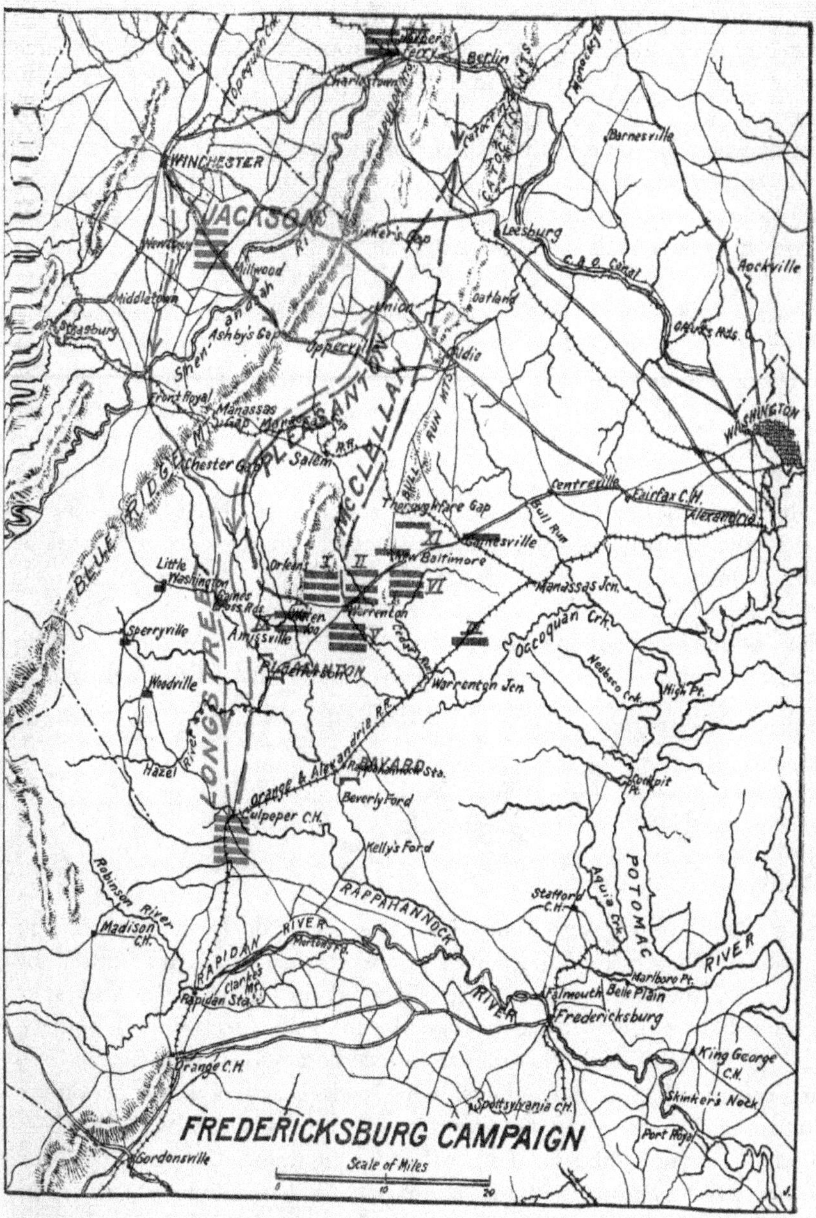

of his cavalry further, and further south." General Lee studied the map for a few moments, and assumed a directive tone, " I shall order General Jackson south. I will suggest you do likewise and spread your Corps that direction as well, for now. Do this in increments as I do not know where Burnside will want to cross the Rappahannock. Destroy all the crossings as quickly as you can. We should avail ourselves of the advantage of this weather and the state of the river. Reinforce Fredericksburg with a Brigade for now, but take a look at the heights there."

Lee turned, and summoned Colonel Chilton, who had silently watched the proceedings. When Chilton came closer, Lee asked, "Colonel, do you require any additional information to draft an order to General Jackson?" Chilton quietly responded, "Sir, only a destination. What town would you like him to move towards?"

Lee thought a moment and glanced back at the map, "Have him move to Spotsylvania Courthouse as a destination. Direct him to leave only a token force in Winchester."

Chilton nodded and left the barn to find Major Taylor. It would take time to draft the orders, and dispatch couriers for delivery. Telegraph means were no longer secure, due to the Yankee advances.

The snow fell in huge wet clumps and made seeing down the road next to impossible. The noise of the guns and limbers was dampened entirely by the snow on the dirt track. Only the labored breathing of the horses, as they pulled their heavy loads through the mud and deep snow could be heard. With each breath, the animals exhaled a cloud of vapor from their flaring nostrils. Joshua rode alongside his section, coated with snow on the shoulders and sleeves of his great coat. He could hear Lieutenant Pennington shouting ahead, "Turn off to the right ahead!" They had been following a road, a poor road, that led to Stafford Courthouse. So far most of the dwellings and farms they had passed were cold and deserted. The Virginia countryside presented an unwelcoming and war decimated tableau. They had not seen a civilian all day and the weather certainly did its part to discourage that. Outriders from the cavalry squadron, riding hard off to their right, would occasionally come by to update them on their progress. Joshua had asked one Corporal who had happened by, "Where you reckon we are going?" The young man had tersely replied, "The Stafford Heights is all I have heard! We are supposed to capture a rail trestle there! The Colonel says we got to find a bridge that is still up! We ain't found nothin' so far! Them Rebs have been mighty busy!"

Joshua shouted out to Jim Page to turn off, when he saw Lieutenant Pennington's tracks on the road ahead. Being the lead section made it difficult to see which way they were headed. After a while, they came upon their commander as he sat beyond the intersection with the First Sergeant and the color bearer. First Sergeant O'Keefe shouted out, "Keep them movin' on this road, there is a spot we will camp on up ahead!" Joshua nodded and waved his arm, motioning for his section to continue their movement. He really had no clue where he was and had no apprehension of danger. No one could see anything in this weather, so it was unlikely the Rebs would be up to much on a day such as this.

The long column of horses and guns pressed on through the wet snow for another hour. Private Page shouted out to Joshua, "Sergeant Timmonds! These horses have about had it! We need to stop soon." Joshua nodded and trotted ahead to find First Sergeant O'Keefe. As Joshua came along side the First Sergeant, O'Keefe turned to him and remarked, "Yep boy 'O I know, you is all cold and such." Joshua quickly retorted, "That too, Top, but the main issue is the horses are spent. We keep pushing them and they'll get sick in this weather!" Joshua knew there was great concern over the animals in the increasing cold. The horses would get cold soaked, and could come down with Pneumonia, if pushed to exhaustion. With no remounts available to the Artillery, it could stop them for days if they wore them down. O'Keefe thoughtfully nodded, muttering, "Makes good sense, not real useful for the army, but it makes sense all the same." He then shouted out to Lieutenant Pennington up ahead, "Sir, we had best find a spot to lay up for the evening; we gots to rest these horses!"

Another half mile down the torturous track, Lieutenant Pennington turned the column off into a sheltered stand of pines. The snow was thinner underneath and the standing trees afforded a break from the gusting winds. As the guns, limbers and caissons were pulled in, the Sergeants shouted out for the men to unhitch the teams and attend to the horses, first. Great care was paid to picket the animals upwind from campfires so they would not be treated to the smoke as they rested and dried out. Joshua had his crewmen brush and curry them and attend to their feeding. Turning to Jim Page, he instructed, "Check them tonight after we eat. Let me know right off, if any of them ain't drying off or shivering. He had become greatly concerned. They had been pulling the teams hard, following the cavalry and the wet weather bode ill for the animals. After the men had laid out the harnesses and saddles, they began to prepare bedding. As they settled in, Sergeant Mills announced the bad news as he and his assistants dropped four Army cracker boxes onto the snowy pine needles, "Search your haversacks for left over meat, boys! The Regimental ration trains ain't made it up yet! Sorry boys, maybe tomorrow." The men complained a little, but still managed to find enough salt pork to make sloosh with the hard tack. Fortunately, plenty of coffee was found and boilers were made ready. Soon, dozens of cook fires lit the woods. The snow stopped falling after the sun had set and groups of men continued to see to the team animals into the night, by lamplight. Over at the picket line of 3rd section, a commotion became apparent; Joshua listened intently, as men talked loudly as they gathered around a horse that whinnied loudly in the cold night. He then heard the loud voice of O'Keefe calling out, "Sergeant Timmonds! A moment if you please!" Joshua quickly pulled his boots back on, that he had been in the process of removing. Since he was summoned by the First Sergeant he pulled his shell jacket back on, buttoned it properly, and put his leather pistol belt back on. Wearily he rose, and trotted over to the commotion.

As he arrived in 3rd Section's area, he saw and nodded to Sergeant Callaghan, who had recently been promoted to Section Sergeant. He and the First Sergeant stood by while several of the drivers attempted to calm a sweat soaked horse, that clearly was in pain. O'Keefe explained, "Timmonds, Mueller went back to the Regimental trains with Mills! Assess this horse and tell me if he can be fixed!' Joshua nodded and moved closer to the struggling animal. While one driver held tight to the halter, another maneuvered the oil lamp closer to the animal's front feet. To his alarm Joshua noted that the snow was red with blood where the horse had stood. In the poor light, he noted that the skin above the top of the horses hoof appeared to be wrinkled. Joshua placed his hand on the animal's foreleg causing it to struggle again. The driver holding him barely kept the horse's head down. The disturbing feel of the skin moving along the horse's canon bone, confirmed his worst suspicion. Joshua quietly commanded the driver, "Hold him real tight, gonna lift this leg." Joshua gently rubbed the horse on its' shoulder as he ran his hand down the sweaty upper leg, down to the hoof, and lifted the leg firmly. In the dim light of the lamp, he could clearly see the canon bone and the metatarsal bones protruding beyond the hoof wall. Joshua gently lowered the horse's hoof, and announced, "First Sergeant, there is only one fix now! He's foundered bad and pushed the canon bone through the sole. I'm surprised he moved this far with that." O'Keefe quietly nodded, and commanded, "Do what you gotta do then."

Nodding quietly, Joshua looked to the drivers and said, "Lets lead him slowly into the woods, over behind us. I want to get him out of sight of the other animals." They slowly walked the limping animal into the deeper part of the woods. Joshua stroked the suffering horse along its mane as it limped along. He had learned years ago, from Old Mose, that the mothers of young colts groomed them that way and it soothed the animals. The drivers were amazed that Timmonds could calm the frantic horse so quickly. When they had reached a satisfactory distance, Joshua instructed the man holding the lamp to adjust it off in front of the horse's nose, to distract it. He drew his Colt revolver and shakily cocked the pistol. He noted the nervous eye of the horse rest on him for a moment. Taking careful aim he pulled the trigger and heard only a snap. Angry, he cocked the gun again; his percussion caps were likely soaked. Aiming again, level with the animal's eye, he pulled the trigger again. The loud boom echoed through the woods and the animal fell quickly, like a sack, and lay twitching on the snowy forest floor. He then looked to the two drivers, and said, "Make sure you get the halter off him. Somebody in your section ain't ridin' no more." Holstering his pistol, he quickly strode back towards his camp. When he was sure no one could see him, he wiped his eyes with his hand. It was a task of the Sergeants, and it was a task he hated.

That night, Joshua dreamed of home. He could vividly see images of Lottie riding her hunting pony, out behind Somerset. He dreamt of a warm place that was quiet, save the soft noises of peaceful industry, and of nature. The urgent call of bugles awakened him with a start on the newly dawning winter day. Opening his eyes he could see the morning moon, brightly shining through the bare trees. He already knew it would be another torturous day of winter marching.

The vast camps of Federal soldiers encircled Warrenton, Virginia. The thousands of marching troops, wagons and horses had churned the road network in and out of the town, into impossible mires of mud and melting snow, while endless columns continued to pass through on their way south. A vast camp of white tents surrounded a stately farmhouse, on a tree-covered hill overlooking the rail depot. There, Major General Ambrose Burnside, had established his field headquarters. Couriers and messengers in their hundreds came and left, bringing reports of the movements, reports and requests, of the vast army slowly beginning its' move after weeks of inaction, around Warrenton. The leaden sky above carried skiffs of snow in a light and indistinct fashion. Brigadier General Jonathan Parke, General Burnside's Chief of Staff, stomped the mud from his boots as he ascended the wooden steps of the estate house. Inside the warm parlor, General Burnside sat at the map table, dictating a telegraph to Lieutenant Comstock, his staff engineer. Parke was returning from the Signal Corps detachment at the rail depot and carried an expected message. Burnside warmly greeted him as he came in the parlor, "Jonathan! I was wondering what took you! Is there news from Halleck yet?" Parke unbuttoned his great coat and reached into the breast pocket, nodding, "Yes Sir! It has just come in." He handed the folded form to General Burnside. Burnside motioned for Comstock to wait as he unfolded the form to read the message,

"Washington, DC November 14, 1862

Maj. Gen. Ambrose E. Burnside
Commanding Army of the Potomac:
The President has just assented to your plan. He thinks it will succeed if you move rapidly; otherwise not.

H.W. Halleck
General-in-Chief"

Burnside found himself having to reread the second sentence of the message in order to completely comprehend it's meaning. Looking up to Parke, he remarked, "Well General Parke, it begins. I almost think Halleck wants me to fail. Damned bureaucrat!" He turned to Comstock, abandoning his previous message, "Lieutenant, see if you can find General Woodbury! Bring me the news on the 50th New York!"

Parke silently reflected on the import of this summons. The plan developed by General McClellan and his staff, earlier, was designed to spread General Lee's army on a wide front, awaiting an offensive by the Army. By consolidating the Army of the Potomac at Warrenton in the very center of all possible approaches to Richmond, astride the very best rail line in Virginia, General McClellan had hoped to force Lee to spread his army thin. A rapid movement south would then cross the Rappahannock at Fredericksburg for the shortest route to the Rebel capitol. While that rail line was of lesser capacity the approach to the south was close to multiple landings on the Potomac, that would enable naval support and ship borne resupply. It was a decent plan, albeit a plan that Henry Halleck, and President Lincoln did not favor. They did not favor it, because it could not happen right away. General Burnside had managed to assume command in a reasonably efficient manner, despite the army's dismay at the loss of a favorite General. Burnside had proven to be a man of common sense and practicality, and he had instituted swift reforms, creating a formation composed of three "Grand Divisions" comprising multiple Corps, each. This configuration empowered the overall commanders, providing them far more latitude than they had possessed before. Burnside had assigned one "Grand Division" each to Generals Sumner, Hooker, and Franklin. It had taken weeks to get each command to understand who worked for whom, but now the army was geared to move to Fredericksburg, if the weather would permit it to do so.

General Burnside had wisely pushed General Pleasanton's cavalry to all points of the Rappahannock to find bridges still up, but they had soon come to realize that General Lee had destroyed them all, in an equally efficient manner. The latest reports from Fredericksburg had revealed the last remaining spans had been only recently burned, making portable bridging a high priority item. Only one Brigade in the Army of the Potomac had these, made up of the 50th and 15th New York Volunteer Engineers. The problem was, these bridges had been used last month to cross the Potomac, following the Battle of Antietam, and no one had ordered them removed. The assumption had been that there were "always more" to be had. Parke mused that the War Department was fascinated by many things; rifles, cannon, horses, and iron clad steamships, as items that immediately came to mind. Odd things like pontoon bateaus, did not fascinate the contractors and bureaucrats in the District of Columbia. Now an entire plan was coming to rely on these odd, unfascinating things. Yet now, 3 days from the anticipated crossing date, no one was totally sure where they were. The entire staff hoped that General Woodbury had news. Parke looked out the window for a moment; the light snow of the early afternoon had just become a heavy one. He realized the end of campaigning was not far off.

A rather brawny Engineer struggled to hold the frantic mule by the halter as the teamster sergeant fed the harness collar over the animal's snout. He jokingly commented, "Jenny here, will grow accustomed to her new attire! Just you wait and see! Now, I'll hold this bitch, while you stretch the crupper back to her tail! That'll fix this harness on the topside!" The engineer did as he was told and reached to lift the Jenny's tail, to run the crupper strap underneath. This affront to the mule's dignity resulted in an evil foreleg kick to the engineer's shin. The man howled and limped away as the animal reared, breaking the grip the teamster had on the harness collar. The mule ran down the dirt street of the Navy Yard braying maniacally, kicking her hind legs high in the air as she hopped and reared in a vain attempt to escape the collar.

Major Ira Spaulding watched disgustedly as this scene repeated itself throughout the morning. He had been issued untrained animals, harnesses still boxed, and unassembled, horse teamsters unaccustomed to mules, mules instead of horses, and an impossible deadline. He dourly reflected that this morning was the 15th of November and he had just received orders to be at Fredericksburg to lay in a bridge on the 17th. He was interrupted in his mental rant by Lieutenant Collins, new to the Brigade, "Begging your pardon sir! I have a telegraph message from General Woodbury! He would like an update on when you will move!" Spaulding turned and stared a moment at the Lieutenant, before sourly asking, "You graduated West Point with an Engineering Degree?" Lieutenant Collins nodded. Spaulding continued, "And you are formally trained in making assessments of problems, and finding solutions, yes?" Lieutenant Collins again nodded. Spaulding again asked, "So Mister Collins, what pray tell is *your*, educated opinion?" Lieutenant Collins swallowed, and responded, "A few more days, Sir?"

Major Spaulding nodded his head, and exhorted, "Yes! Perhaps a few more days! You are catching on Collins! Please draft a response back in my name, if you please, expressing exactly that!"

Major Spaulding then strode over to his horse, tied off to a tree near his tent, and rode over to the wharf on the Anacostia River, maintained by the Navy, to check on the progress of the raft of pontoons to be towed to Aquia Landing. There he was greeted by Quartermaster Sergeant Adams, an old hand in the 50th. He had served in the Engineers in the War with Mexico. The raft consisted of 36 pontoon boats, lashed together in nine rows of four boats. Atop the boats, the bridge chess planks had been lashed down to form a continuous deck upon which were piled stacks of balks, and chess planks equivalent to fit out the package of boats. Other engineer soldiers were lashing all the stacks securely to the makeshift deck. Sergeant Adams saluted Spaulding as he approached, and gruffly announced, "Good day to ya' Sir! We are about complete here, and I have word that the tug will be arrivin' within the hour! How many of the lads do you want to go on the tug?" Major Spaulding thoughtfully paused and looked up into the misting rain soaking everything, before he replied, "No more than ten with a good Sergeant. Seeing as how I do not expect easy going cross country, I will need most of the men for the march overland. We have only two days to cover 50 miles and judging from this weather, we shall be lucky to achieve that. Get the rafts under tow and send a dispatch on the Navy's telegraph that teams from the 15th Engineers will be necessary to pull them up to Falmouth!" Quartermaster Sergeant Adams nodded, and rendered a resigned salute, before turning back and shouting out instructions to the men tying off the load.

Spaulding then rode over to the Navy telegraph station himself to post an update to General Woodbury. He wondered how all these disparate pieces would actually be brought together in the Virginia countryside. His men had been working non-stop for a week, everyday, all day, since receipt of the orders to pull up the bridges at Berlin, in Maryland.

Colonel Chilton pulled the canvas flap of the General's planning tent aside, and looked out at the mixed snow and rain. He had heard a horseman arrive. General Lee was busy in consultation with General Longstreet in regards of his progress to reinforce Colonel Ball at Fredericksburg. The general feeling had become the belief that a major Union attempt would occur at the colonial town, but the army remained scattered and the cavalry reports were spotty. Yet the general consensus remained, a concerted Union movement south along the east bank of the Rappahannock. Fortunately, the weather had all the rivers in this part of Virginia at flood stage, making all the customary fords useless. A young courier wearing a Yankee oilcloth poncho and a soaked slouch hat dismounted, and saluted, "Sir, I have a dispatch from General Stuart for General Lee!" Chilton took the folded paper that the courier pulled from his leather pouch, and commanded, "Stand by until I confirm there is no need to carry a reply." The young man nodded and waited by his horse in the rain. Chilton briefly read the note and then brought it in to General Lee. As Lee looked up, he announced, "Sir, General Stuart reports Union cavalry have crossed at Fredericksburg and entered into an engagement with Colonel Ball's force there! He was able to drive them back across the river and has taken several of them prisoner." Lee thought for a moment and looked at General Longstreet with a knowing glance; he then asked, "Has Colonel Ball destroyed the railroad trestle there?" Chilton quickly responded, "Sir, I have heard it mentioned in other reports, but not from Colonel Ball directly." Lee curtly directed, "Have the man report the destruction as soon as possible!" Colonel Chilton solemnly nodded and turned to find his staff to draft a message for the waiting courier.

Lee returned his gaze to James Longstreet, and solemnly directed, "General Longstreet, move your Corps, all of your Corps, to Fredericksburg. It has been some years since I paused there last, but I recall there are heights there, they have a name I do not remember at this moment. Those heights afford excellent control of the town and all the approaches from the Rappahannock. I should imagine you will need to fortify those heights, as swiftly as you can. Place your forces in such a fashion to guard the approaches at Falmouth, to where the Alexandria and Richmond railway crosses the river. I shall hurry General Jackson along to connect his Corps to your right flank. I am now certain, that is where General Burnside intends to come."

As General Longstreet nodded and rose, General Lee had one final instruction, "General, the small village of Fredericksburg has a storied history. I was engaged to Mary Custis, there. Please avoid causing a battle in its streets. It would be unconscionable to cause harm to the good people there or to destroy such a historic place." Longstreet quietly nodded. He rushed out to provide orders to his commanders. Lee sat in the quiet tent and reflected on the old town they were rapidly moving towards. It had been no stranger to the Union Army. They had rested there and moved through its cobbled streets on several occasions, but never had anyone been compelled to fight there. He decided, after several moments of deep thought, that it would be best to secure permission from President Davis to order it's evacuation. He hated the thought as the poor citizens would be pushed out in their Harvest Thanksgiving holiday, and the weather was monstrous. He sadly realized that many would have nowhere to go. They naturally would turn to the army for assistance and the army could hardly feed themselves. He muttered to himself, "War is terrible, terrible to them particularly..."

The sky, while heavily overcast, refused to release the threatened rain for most of the morning as the 50th New York Engineers crossed the Long Bridge and turned off onto the Telegraph Road, enroute to the Occoquan River. As they ascended the hills out of Alexandria and left the hardened roads of the settlements on the outskirts of town, the sky opened up with a fury. Vicious gusts of wind tugged at the marching men's greatcoats and the heavy rain obscured their vision forward. The long train of heavily laden wagons creaked along the increasingly muddy track and Major Spaulding began to notice that the wheels were sinking deeper with each passing mile. Soon he had dispatched orders, through Captain Brainerd, to assemble teams of men with each of the Bateau wagons to give the braying and muddy mules a hand at difficult points. Each time one of the heavy boat bearing wagons would become mired, teams of Engineers would lay muddy hands on spokes and the body of the wagon bed to manhandle the load through the clinging yellow mud.

The men quickly became coated in the mud, and the driving rain did little to wash it away. It seemed to Spaulding that the trains were in a constant condition of sinking into the mire. By noon, the rain had turned to a heavy wet snow that quickly melted as it came into contact with the ground. The muddy, miserable struggle continued. To Spaulding's amazement no one complained, or shirked their difficult work. They were determined to make their destination. The men ate hardtack crackers as they marched slowly alongside the slithering wagons and teams, up and down the hilly Virginia countryside in the alternating snow and rain. The dense forests of bleak and leafless trees offered little shelter from the punishing rain and howling winter wind, but the engineers did not ask to stop. The ceaseless braying protests of the mule teams, mixed with the constant stream of curses from the frustrated teamsters, provided the march music for the movement. Spaulding mused as he rode alongside, soaked through and through, that this was definitely a "Napoleonic Struggle."

He would periodically ride ahead to the lead wagons carrying the balks and chess planks to pause the head of the column, allowing the Bateau wagons to catch up. The bridge trains covered nearly a mile in length, keeping normal interval, and now they were getting badly stretched out. Prudence dictated keeping the trains in tight interval as the woods about these parts were known to be full of Secesh "Bushwhackers." The sun had begun to set deeper into the half shadow of the bare trees, and the rainfall slackened. The lead wagons came to a shallow ravine housing a raging creek at flood stage. Captain Brainerd returned from giving the stream a look, and he pointed off to the east, "Sir the town of Colchester is about five miles from here, bearing to the southeast. This creek marks the north side of the ridge that flows there! We are still 30 miles from Fredericksburg!" Spaulding disgustedly shook his head. He pulled out his watch and looked at it, it was nearly 5 pm. He quickly calculated that they had pulled out of Anacostia at 5 am and it had taken them nearly 12 hours to go 12 miles. Spaulding put his watch away, fearing the wet, and asked Brainerd, "Can we cross the stream below?" Brainerd quickly replied, "The bridge was burned that supports this road, but we can rebuild a corduroy one tonight. It will take a few hours, but we can get it done. The banks are too steep, otherwise, for the wagons, particularly the Bateau wagons. It will be less of a struggle to rebuild the bridge."

Spaulding directed Brainerd to proceed, and rode back to have the Sergeants pull up the train tightly together, feed and water the mules, and post a picket guard. He then had them form details and directed another detail to build fires at the bridging site. It would illuminate the work and afford hot coffee for the weary men. Spaulding finally dismounted near the bridging site while the axe men filled the dark and dripping woods with the sound of trees being felled. The enterprising engineers had quickly secured enough dry deadfall to build two roaring bonfires that stoutly resisted the drizzling evening rain. Spaulding could see multiple shiny tin cups and mucket boilers lining the edge of the fire as the men heated water for coffee, while they labored.

As he sat and observed the work, something that always caused him to marvel, a pair of horsemen approached him from behind. Leaning around the tree trunk that he used for a backrest, he spied their white faces in the light of the fires. The taller of the two asked him, "Sir, would you be Major Spaulding of the Engineer Brigade?" Spaulding dryly responded, "In the flesh." The man handed him a folded dispatch, "Sir, this is an urgent message from General Burnside, via Lieutenant Comstock! They anxiously desire to know when you will arrive! He insisted that I inform you that your men are two days behind schedule! The entire army awaits you!" Spaulding stood and quickly indicated for the pair to follow him. He walked them over to the nearest of the mud spattered Bateau wagons. Arriving at the nearest wagon, he turned, and explained, "Gentlemen, you know, as well as I do, how far we are from Fredericksburg! These pontoon boats you are looking at weigh nearly 1800 pounds as a load for this wagon. With the conditions we are experiencing, I am moving at less than one mile per hour, and that is with constant struggle to keep that pace. Consider what you are asking for and do your own mathematical estimations!" He then had them follow him back to where they found him and pointed towards the rapidly forming bridge, "I am additionally compelled to make my own road, from time to time, so therein lies the source of more delay!"

He looked at the two men for a moment, having no idea of their rank and asked, "What news do you have of the 15th Engineers and Major Magruder?" The tall man replied, "The Major is still with his bridge

236

material at Belle Plain where the steamers left him. He has no teams or wagons, yet!" Ira Spaulding spit and cursed. He realized that General Woodbury would likely regret staying in Washington. Things were going badly awry. He turned to the two, and directed, "Tell Comstock that I should be at Falmouth in three days. It is my best estimate at this point."

Major Spaulding took his spot against the tree again, and Sergeant Ellington of the Decking crew brought him a cup of steaming coffee. After thanking him profusely, he took a careful sip of the comforting hot beverage as rainwater drained from the brim of his waterlogged Hardee hat into the cup. The men had spanned two large pine trunks across the ruined abutments and were now placing smaller diameter trunks across those to form a corduroy floor. The Abutment teams were shoveling the wet dirt onto the trunks to form an even road surface. A quick glance at his pocket watch, which he had to angle towards the bonfires to read, indicated half past midnight. Soon they could resume the march. Sleep did not seem to be a practical consideration at the moment.

The military train eased to a stop in the Fredericksburg depot. Henri and Lottie had found seats in the single coach car, while the rest of the train consisted of open flat cars carrying Mississippi troops from General Barksdale's Brigade. As the gray clad soldiers tumbled off the cars and formed hasty ranks on the cobbled street, Henri assisted Charlotte with her bag. Henri had decided to visit General Lafayette Guild, General Lee's chief surgeon and provide him with the remainder of his supplies from Richmond for the army at Fredericksburg. After some searching, Henri was able to locate a carriage. Fredericksburg had been ordered evacuated by General Lee and the rain soaked brick town was now full of soldiers, rather than civilians. Captain Tinchant instructed the driver to proceed to a house number on Caroline Street.

Turning to Lottie, he said, "We must call on Mrs. Elliot Lacy. She has lived here for many years and is a dear friend. I fervently hope she has not been evacuated. Her home would be excellent quarters for us during this visit!" Lottie gave a quizzical look, and Henri seeing it, explained, "Mrs. Lacy's son is a colleague of mine from Medical College. He is currently assigned to duties with the Army of Tennessee. We used to visit her home during the Christmas season as Louisiana unfortunately was too far for me to travel to."

Henri was concerned by the military activity he was seeing. Soldiers were establishing barricades along the riverfront and moving timbers to stack them along the alleys, leading up from the river.

Moving towards Caroline Street, he noticed a bright yellow flag flying on a pole above the Tobacco Warehouse on the southeastern side of the town. He mused aloud, "We must visit that next. I assume that is the forward hospital for General Barksdale." Lottie was taken with the beauty of the town as they proceeded down Caroline Street, observing, "It is such a charming little village, it reminds me so of Charleston!" Henri, sensing the urgency of the troops, quietly replied, "It might very well become a battleground shortly, my dear. I will remind you to keep me in sight, always, while we visit here." Soon they arrived at the house number and Captain Tinchant asked the coachman to wait. He then ascended the brick steps and smartly rapped the bronze knocker on the bright red painted door.

After a few moments, a Negro woman, the house servant, answered the door. Seeing Captain Tenchant's gray uniform, she smiled and asked what he wanted. Tinchant explained that he was calling on Mrs. Lacy. The house servant invited him into the parlor, saying, "I shall notify her that she has guests." Lottie admiringly looked at the fine furnishings and books that adorned the cases in the parlor. Henri winked at Charlotte, and whispered, "Hopefully she will remember me."

Elliot Lacy stepped into the parlor and Lottie was struck by her elegant beauty. She looked to be near 70 years old, but possessed the rare timelessness of the well-born Southern ladies. Seeing Henri, she exclaimed, "Well my word! Henri Tenchant! I am so very pleased to see you here! It has been years, and look at you!" Henri gave a small bow, and replied, "Ma'am it is my honor to see you once again! I should never be able to forget your kindnesses to me when I was but a struggling student, so very far from my own home!" Elliot Lacy looked to Lottie, and asked, "Henri, where are your manners, who is this radiant maiden?" Lottie stood and gave a slight curtsey, and broke manners in beating him to a reply, "Ma'am I am Charlotte Markley of Old Berkeley County, near Charleston, South Carolina. I am very thankful for your hospitality on such a cold day." Elliot Lacy smiled, and replied, "Dear, you are a ray of sunshine to an old woman's afternoon! I am so pleased to make your acquaintance." She then summoned Eliza, her house servant, and asked that tea be prepared and brought in. Lottie noted that she kept a small fire burning in the parlor hearth, which offered comfortable warmth. This well established home was also accentuated by an unseen grandfather clock that filled the parlor with soft, yet definite "tick tock" that reminded her of her own home.

As the tea arrived, Henri asked, "Mrs. Lacy, there is clearly a battle approaching this place Why, pray tell, have you not evacuated your home?" She poured a cup of tea for Charlotte, and replied, "Why Henri, I have no where to go! I have made my life here and I have enjoyed a long life, at that. I am resigned to weather this storm, as I have many in this life! Mind you, I fully understand your concern! Why just yesterday the Abolitionist General across yonder river had the presumption to summon Mayor Slaughter to Chatham House to demand the surrender of Fredericksburg to him or face cannonading, by their guns from across the river! General Lee has established an order telling us all to leave, but he has not provided us with any alternatives! I have many friends that would suffer my presence, of that I am sure, but I do not wish to be a burden on any soul in these hard times. Besides, Eliza and me have a stocked cupboard and a good winter garden out back. We shall endure."

Henri then asked her of news from her son, William. She responded, "According to my most recent correspondence from him, he now works in a General Hospital in Vicksburg. It would seem that they are heavily fortifying that city, so I worry daily about his well being." Henri thoughtfully nodded, "Mrs. Lacy, I would ask you to send my best regards to him in your next letter. It has been some time, since I saw him last." After a short pause, he asked, "Mrs. Lacy can you recommend a decent boarding house, here in town? We must see to our duties at the nearby hospital and I have a cab awaiting outside." Elliot Lacy formed a shocked face, and exclaimed, "Why Captain Tenchant, I should do no such thing! You two shall stay here, with me! I have 3 empty rooms in this house! I must insist that you stay!" Henri quickly folded, and protested little. It had worked out as he had hoped. He left Lottie to chat with Mrs. Lacy, while he went out to retrieve his bags and dismiss the cab driver. As he tipped the driver, a rather dirty and disheveled Major from the Mississippi Infantry regiment hailed him, "Captain! Has that home been evacuated?" Henri began to notice the acrid smoke that filled the streets as men on the river bank below were setting fire to hogsheads of tobacco that sat along the river wharfs. Turning to the Major, he replied, "No Sir, this home is occupied by an elderly widow who is a close family friend of mine! She has stated that she refuses to leave." The infantry Major spit, and shook his head, "It's on you then! General Lee gave specific orders to clear everybody out of town! Explain to yer widow friend that this here town is gonna see a fight! The whole Yankee army is coming to Falmouth, on the double!

They is bringing bridges with them and we expect them to cross here!" Henri nodded and took a moment to introduce himself and explain his duties. The grimy major smiled, and commented, "Drop off them carpet bags to the ladies, and come on back out. I take you to see Doc Laschicott at the Tobacco Warehouse!"

Henri quickly ducked in and excused himself to Elliot Lacy and Lottie, who were deeply involved in conversation of a rather serious nature. Noting their patient nods, he quickly exited the house back onto the street.

As Henri trotted back out, the Major extended his hand, "The name is Frazier, Jonathan Frazier. I am Lieutenant Colonel Luse's adjutant, 18th Mississippi! Follow me!" Henri had a difficult time keeping up with the lanky, fast moving officer, he barely paused to look or fuss with details, he simply shouted out orders to details of men digging rifle pits in gardens at cross streets or men stacking boxes and barrels to form street barricades. Moving down to Sophia Street, which fronted the Rappahannock, Major Frazier turned, and hissed to Henri, "Look lively here Captain! Move quick-like, from cover to cover, as we move down this road! The Yankee pickets have taken to shooting at us from time to time." As if on cue, shouts emerged from the dark brush, on the far side of the Rappahannock, and a single musket shot illuminated the twilight. Henri heard the angry whiz of a near miss. Major Frazier pulled him into the basement door of the Variety Store, which they were near. Frazier chuckled, "Sorry Doc, they knows we is up to somethin,' and we knows they is up to somethin.' They've getting' mighty trigger happy, since we showed up." Henri noticed, as his eyes adjusted to the light in the dark basement, that there were nearly 20 men within. Some had small cook fires burning in the dirt floor of the storeroom, while others were knocking bricks out of the wall with axes to create loopholes in the brick wall of the structure.

Major Frasier explained, "We got it on good authority that the Yankees plan to bridge the river here and attack directly into town. They see the way we is fortifying the heights above town, and this here town is the only cover they have! General Barksdale's orders say we are to stop that from happenin.' Us, the 17th, and the 21st Mississippi, are all doing the same thing." Henri nodded and watched as the men slowly slid a musket out of one of the loopholes to test the size. Major Frazier, noting the same, sternly ordered, "Nobody takes no potshots from them loopholes! Let them Yankees find out about them once we can shoot a bunch of them!" The grimy and weary men nodded, while others laughed softly. They appreciated quartering inside, out of the drizzly weather. After a nod to the Sergeant, Frazier motioned to Henri to follow him. Frazier paused, and turned to the Sergeant again, "Make sure these boys ain't wandering upstairs to the store! I'll shoot the first man I catch looting the property of good Southern folks!" Frazier then exited out the far side door and led Henri to the next block. There, they entered a stoutly fenced garden, behind another building. The men within, hailing from I Company, the "Beauregard Rifles" from Madison County, Mississippi, were digging rifle pits behind the stout planks of the fence. Some of the men were busily chopping away the bottom quarter of the fence boards to make low loopholes, through which they could fire. Major Frazier quickly nodded, and asked the men, "Who is your officer, boys?" One of the men digging looked up, and answered, "That's Lieutenant Ratliff, Sir! He went over to the Tobacco Warehouse!" Major Frazier thanked him and motioned for Henri to continue to follow him. At each point where they paused, the men were converting the basements of all the homes and stores that faced the water into positions for riflemen to fight from. Looking across the Rappahannock in the fading light, which reflected off the swiftly moving water, Henri realized that it really was not a very wide river. The Yankees would certainly lose many men attempting to cross here.

Following Major Frazier's inspection tour, the two men made their way back up to Caroline Street and walked the two blocks south, to the Tobacco Warehouse near the rail depot. Fredericksburg's streets were dark that evening as the gas plant had shut their valves and sent the lamplighters away with the general evacuation. Houses, here and there in the town, belied the presence of those who had ignored the order as the glints of candlelight emerged from random windows. Henri looked up and noted, that the clouds had parted somewhat, and a dark, clear sky highlighted with stars, could be seen. He imagined the night would get cold.

In the dim light, Tinchant could make out the silhouette of an Ambulance, and he could see to his delight that the Mississippians were employing a Federal Yellow hospital flag at the Tobacco Warehouse. Dim light played through the loose weave of the burlap placed over the ground floor office windows to mask the light. Tinchant and Major Frazier worked their way through the throng of lounging soldiers on the cobblestone road as they made their way to the rough door that led inside. As the two men entered the creaky door, they found themselves in a well-lit room, filled with tobacco smoke. Inside, Henri Tinchant recognized Doctor Lafayette Guild reclined in a wooden chair, puffing on a cigar. He was engaged in conversation with a pair of medical officers. Spying Tinchant, he exclaimed, "Henri! It is indeed a pleasure to see you again! How is General Moore?" Henri quickly removed his Kepi, and replied, "He is quite well sir, albeit quite busy! He has dispatched me to deliver supplies to your army!" Guild smiled, and nodded. After another puff on his cigar, he asked, "What brings you to the front? I anticipate we shall have a sharp action here soon!" After Henri had explained the purpose for his trip, Colonel Guild replied, "Henri, allow me to introduce Lieutenant Colonel Jones, the regimental surgeon of the 17th Mississippi, and Major Richardson, the regimental surgeon of the 21st Mississippi!" As Major Frazier and Henri shook hands all around, Colonel Guild continued, "As I mentioned, we expect the Federals to attempt a forced crossing here. General Barksdale's Brigade has orders to stop them at the river. He has spread his regiments thin along this bank of the river, and we are shy a surgeon. Would you find it possible to assist us here?" Henri quickly nodded, "I would be delighted to assist sir! I have also had supplies brought here from Richmond. I have arranged their storage at the depot." The men engaged in conversation about the state of medical supplies for a moment, before Henri asked to excuse himself in order to arrange for his orderly to secure delivery of the badly needed formulary items to the hospital. Colonel Guild instructed him to report to the hospital early the next morning.

Lieutenant Colonel Porter Alexander sat astride his horse, watching as the 6-pounder crew of the 1st Company of the Washington Artillery, dug in their pieces on the hillock just south of the Orange Plank road. They had selected a spot above the positions of a North Carolina brigade, east of them. He was anxious to insure they had sufficient elevation to see the majority of the ascending slope before them. He turned to Lieutenant Samuel Johnson, who rode with him, and observed, "As we check each spot, insure that you know what the gunner can see. General Pendleton wants us to have no blind spots on that ground, below. We have to be able to withstand the Yankee counter fire! Instill in them the necessity to dig in deep!" He paused, and lifted his glass in a vain attempt to see the silent Federal batteries across the way on Stafford Heights; he sighed, and realized that it had grown too dark. Turning around, he could make out the cook fires in the camps about the woods behind Mayre's Heights. Only solitary pickets manned the rifle pits and positions along the stonewall and the sunken road. The regiments would only come forward, once the Yankees came. There was no use helping their artillery with their targeting. Alexander had paid careful attention to the placement of the various batteries. Instead of simple direct positions, he took great care to angle their placements to mask them from the Stafford Heights. He instinctively knew the Federals would avail themselves of the higher ground, on their side of the river, and that they possessed plentiful numbers of rifled pieces. By angling his batteries, and insuring they were dug in, he maximized the opportunities for enfilading fires on the infantry formations, that would undoubtedly be forced to approach Mayre's Heights, on the perpendicular. Turning to Lieutenant Johnson, as he put his useless field glasses away, he observed, "Artillery is the business of sheer murder, Lieutenant. Let us take great care to insure we provide as much discouragement into them, as we possibly can. There is an entire host of enemies piling up over there!" As he watched the men preparing the empty positions, he wished he had more of the rifled Parrots and the heavier weight 12 pounders. They would need the same advantage as the Federals to keep pace with this war. He recalled how he had advised General Pendleton of the wisdom of turning in the old 6 pounders for recasting into 12 pound pieces. While it would equal fewer guns, it could make the difference, if they possessed the range and payload of the Yankee guns. He hoped that his advice would reach General Lee. He had heard from General Longstreet that improvements to the artillery of the Army of Northern Virginia were slowly becoming a priority to him.

As they rode back to camp, Alexander tasked Lieutenant Johnson with a review of their stocks of ammunition for the variety of guns, that supported General Longstreet's Corps. As they rounded the rough trail leading to the backside of Telegraph Hill, towards their camp, he emphasized, "I anticipate with the reported size of General Burnside's army, we will need reloads for our caissons at about three hours of fighting. See to it that the Quartermaster turns wagons back towards our supply trains to speedily resupply us as we expend the loads in our caissons. I expect this to be a problem that I can only immediately patch with a reserve."

Alexander was anxious to return to his camp, he still had much to do. There was the order to establish a battery to act as a signal element to let the defenders know when the Yankees came across the river. It would be a task that he would have to coordinate with the cavalry, if he could find them. He had also heard that General Lee would likely be inspecting the defensive preparations, tomorrow. While he was anxious to be in the company of the General, he was apprehensive about the General's satisfaction with his choices. He resolved to get an early start in the morning, yet he still had reports to write and requisitions to sign. The duties of the Corps Artillery Battalion Commander were beginning to make him weary.

Major Spaulding nodded as Lieutenant Falley shouted out, "Sir, that is the last of them!" He watched impassively as the last empty Chess wagons rumbled across the bridge that they had borne to the Occoquan River. They had lost too much time struggling with the muddy Virginia roads and now, the loss of time had been compounded by the necessity to employ their precious cargo to cross the swollen river in order to reach a landing whereby in-bound steamers could tow rafts of pontoons and supplies back down the river to round the peninsula to deliver the bridge to the landing at Belle Plain. He paused to listen to the shouts of his Sergeants as they hurried the men to unlash the rails and begin stripping the Chess planks back up for transfer to the south side of the river. Establishing the bridge had cost him six hours. He was now a full week late from his ordered time and he could count on another set of couriers reaching him today with urgent inquiries about the status of the bridge.

The men did not complain, each task was attended to, in a well-drilled, and expert manner. In fact, he had observed them accomplish their tasks much faster, than specified in the manuals, which had been the object of great study, and drills back in the early days of their initial mustering. He mused that having well drilled men made a great difference. Once the bateaux were stripped of the load of the decking and the connecting balks were unlashed, and removed, the crews poled the bateaux to the south bank where the engineers tied them off in preparation for the construction of rafts. Towing the empty wagons overland would make up for lost time. Once they reached Belle Plain, they could then reload the wagons for one last struggle to Falmouth and then to those places directed by General Burnside for the crossings. Spaulding wondered how his reputation fared. Being over a week late certainly would not glean him a medal.

He grimly watched the men as they rapidly disassembled the bridge. They were masters of their craft, and highly trained and experienced. They had over a year of training and they amazed him with their ability to surmount problems. Nobody needed a pontoon bridge, until they needed one badly, and this collection of bridging material was just that, at the moment.

Quartermaster Sergeant Adams found Spaulding and urged, "Sir, we gots to get these men fed! They've been bustin' their asses all the livelong day and they ain't thinking clear! Request yer permission, Sir, to break out a field kitchen, and make them some rations!" Spaulding tore himself away from his preoccupation to study them for a moment; he imperceptibly could see certain clumsiness, and the occasional missteps of exhausted men. After a moments pause, he assented, "Yes Quartermaster Sergeant, see to it! But break them down into details that can begin the assembly of the rafts while you cook. We have a deadline to meet, an entire army awaits us!" Adams nodded with a concerned look on his face, adding, "Sir, when we get the food cooked up, I'll be bringing you a plate. You can't run forever, no matter who is waiting!" Spaulding wearily nodded. The rain began to fall again, at least the empty wagons would travel faster.

An hour into supper, the 50th was met by the arrival of the steam tug, that Captain Brainerd had summoned. The food was intoxicating and Major Spaulding fought the temptation to sleep. Helping himself to another cup of hot coffee from a blackened mucket near the cook fire, he then walked over to supervise the securing of the rafts to the tug. He instructed Captain Brainerd, and a detail of 10 men to accompany the raft to Belle Plain. Turning to find his horse, he spun back around and shouted out, "I'll see you in two days, Captain! God Speed!"

By 8 pm they had begun the march with the empty wagons, while the men had hoped for a pause to camp, and rest, Major Spaulding urged them on. They still had over 20 miles to travel with two more streams to cross. He worried that the flood conditions would cause additional delays and he had willfully abandoned the remainder of his bridges. The only option available to him now, if he encountered flooded creeks, was to ford higher up and further away from Falmouth. These were all additional delays, he could ill afford. They would have to push like hell, in order to be very late. It was a hopeless feeling he could not overcome, but come hell or high water he would bring General Burnside his bridges. He had no idea that his Brigade Commander had been placed under arrest for the delay. He only knew the urgent imperative to get to Falmouth, as quickly as he could. Spaulding wondered when the next courier from headquarters would arrive.

Near a copse of trees that partially concealed Fredericksburg, Joshua peered through the Lieutenant's field glasses at Confederate troops across the river.

Lieutenant Pennington asked, "Timmonds, what the hell are they throwing into the river there?" First Sergeant O'Keefe had summoned him, as the "token Southron," to explain. Joshua peered at the butternut clad men as they tipped another large burlap bundle over the wooden wharf by the lower part of the quaint little town across the way. With his eye still on the glass, he muttered, "I would say it is hogsheads of tobacco. I suspect they know we are coming their way!" O'Keefe muttered, "Damn! Tobacco, such a waste of a fine substance. We should offer them a trade for some coffee, Lieutenant." Lieutenant Pennington was mystified, and asked, "Why would they throw away all those goods! I should think they would evacuate their valuables, if we posed them a threat! Virginia tobacco would be worth a mint to the English!" Joshua opined, "Sir, maybe we came onto them too fast. I reckon we are someplace that they did not expect us to be." He turned, and handed the expensive field glasses back to the Lieutenant. Pennington took the binoculars and secured them into his leather case. He paused a moment, and said, "Sergeant Timmonds, I expect orders for the First Sergeant to come anytime now. I would like for you to spend as much time as possible with First Sergeant O'Keefe. I intend to promote Corporal Page to your position as soon as I can, in order to relieve you of your duties as section sergeant. From this point forward, I would like you to shadow O'Keefe. Colonel Hayes says we will be in reserve anyway, as the Horse Artillery Regiment will have no role in this fight, until the infantry crosses the river. Mind what he does and insure you can assume his role once Hayes takes him away!" Joshua silently nodded. He turned and saw that First Sergeant O'Keefe gave him a broad grin and remarked, "Hell of a thing ain't it, Boy O'!"

They had sat in a hollow, just beyond the view of the Rebel pickets along the river below Falmouth, for over a week. Each day had seen nothing but gun drill, three times a day. The men kept circulating rumors that they would soon abandon campaigning and establish winter camps, but Joshua could feel something in the energy of the officers. There was going to be a big push. The electrified nature of the army indicated that, despite the fact that little was revealed through orders. They were waiting on something, and he was not sure of what it was.

Returning to his section as the sun set, Joshua called Jim Page off to the side, out of earshot of the men. Looking his favorite gunner in the eye, he calmly said, "Jim, get ready to be promoted to Section Sergeant." Page's eyes grew wide, and he stammered out, "What? What the hell are you saying Sergeant? I just got gunner down! What are they doing?" Joshua shook him by the shoulders, and sternly said, "They are moving me! And not a word from you to the men, they will see it when it happens! Just you be ready to take my place!" He paused, and waved his hand across the silent guns, and cook fires, before continuing, "You have been a part of every fight, and have seen every action we have taken part in. You don't feel ready, but you are! Never mind what you don't know! Drill them like I have and you will be fine! That is all there is to it! And don't worry, I won't be far off. Just remember, not a word to the men! They will find out soon enough." Jim Page shook his head, he understood, but yet could not. The familiar rhythm of the company was being disrupted by change. In some units it came through death and destruction, but with the Artillery, they often delivered this disruption and they had been unaccustomed to change. Joshua noting the confusion in his eyes, realized that he would do well. He cared enough to do well, and that was why Jim Page was his choice. He reflected in that instant that it was probably the same thing that Billy O'Keefe had seen in him. Leaders who could do, but did not feel ready to. Company M had a major shake-up coming and the men would have to adjust.

Down below their urgent discussion, life went on. One man had broken out his harmonica and was playing a soft tune. Sergeant Newby was starting out a new game of cards with select members of his section. The picketed horses were finishing off the crumbs of their cut fodder in the bottom of their nosebags and the battery pickets were silently peering through the brush at the riverbank with their dangerously loaded carbines, at an equally wary and invisible enemy, only 400 yards away across a swollen river. Low hanging clouds scudded across the early December sky, threatening more snow. Joshua imagined Generals above them in fine tents near great houses, poring over lithographed maps, planning great moves of hosts of men in a battle to seize this next hill, that next ridge in a great battle to settle the rebellion. He realized that they again were a small part of a great thing. He had lost all identity except for his affiliation with his unit and the men who looked up to him for guidance. For him, it no longer was a struggle of State against State, or idea against ideology, it was his men against someone else's men. He aimed to insure that his men would prevail; they had become his life, and his cause. Nothing else mattered.

Pausing and looking up, he could make out the quarter moon as it occasionally emerged from the clouds. For a moment he wondered on Lottie, and where she might be. It had been so long since her last letter. He remembered the warmth of home. Even this late in the year, it was warm at home. Shivering a little, he pulled his greatcoat around him and resolved to visit his horse. The animal had become a source of comfort to him. They did not judge and seemed to give love despite their ignorance. He found it was something he did from time to time to gain comfort.

As he stood by the quietly attentive horses, he smelled tobacco smoke and realized First Sergeant O'Keefe was making the rounds, "You should be warming yourself by a fire Boy O'! Yer scarin' these horses hangin' about them." Joshua gave a chuckle and asked, "First Sergeant what are we doin' here?" O'Keefe puffed pensively on his briar, before replying, "We be waitin' for a set o' pontoon bridges to come up. At least that's what I heard Colonel Hayes relay to the Lieutenant. They were supposed to be here right after we showed, so's General Sumner, and his Grand Division could employ them to take that little village across the way. Problem was them bridges still lay across the Potomac after we left Sharpsburg, and nobody ordered them up to match what we was a doin'!"

He chuckled a bit to himself before continuing, "We have a great army, see? It is so great and vast that the fookin' left hand don't know what the right hand is a doin'! I heard the officers call it "coordination." It seems we lack some o' that at the moment. The Rebs are diggin' like gophers across the way! They're diggin' like devils and once we cross, I assure you we shall have the devil himself to pay. Look to yer boys and keep them drillin'! God knows when the bridges will show, but it is clear that Mr. Burnside is in a hurry to get over this river, and when he does, he is gonna throw us at them Rebs! Don't let the boys assume no winter camp, it will make them slow and lazy." Joshua nodded and turned to look across the rippling river as it gleamed in the partial moonlight. The town was full of Rebel troops and it was a very narrow crossing. He wondered how the men would fare who had to put the bridges in. To him, any notion to cross here, made little sense.

Brigadier General Henry Hunt rested his left hand on Major General Burnside's map and used a pencil in his right to point out the positions of his Artillery Reserve, once the order was given to roll them up. The three Grand Division commanders all silently watched. General Sumner seemed to pay rapt attention, General Hooker seemed bored and angry, and General Franklin seemed focused on where he intended to go, rather than what he was saying. General Burnside would pause to ask him questions centered on preventing Rebel observation of his preparations. Hunt had his private doubts of the value of deception at this juncture. Everyone on both sides knew what was developing. Both armies had sat motionless for over a week. While each had not shown their hand, the disposition of each army was clear. Fredericksburg and the commanding heights beyond the town were the common focus. The Rebels could be seen daily, improving their positions on the heights beyond and within the town. The much-ballyhooed activity to the east, by Port Royal, was fooling no one. Hunt remained resigned to crush them with the weight of fire from his massed guns on the Stafford Heights. It was all he could do for General Burnside. After Hunt had finished his update, General Burnside called for Lieutenant Comstock to come forward to brief the Engineer operation. At the mention of his name, General Hooker seemed to become more attentive as it would be his two Corps who would cross directly into Fredericksburg. The intent of his attack would be to pin General Lee's forces down behind Fredericksburg while General Franklin would seek out his vulnerable right flank. General Sumner would cross in the middle and support whichever side achieved the most success. Comstock droned through his description of the 5 bridges that they would emplace across the Rappahannock. General Hooker interrupted him with a blunt question, "When will these bridges arrive, Lieutenant?" General Burnside interjected, he frowned on Generals bullying the Lieutenant, and he had grown protective of Comstock, "I have it on good authority, Joseph, that the remaining material has just arrived at Belle Plain. I expect them here, tomorrow. The date of our crossing will be the 11th instant! So prepare your men for movement then. They are to commence throwing the bridges across after midnight, so I need you and General Sumner to support the engineers with a Regiment of infantry at each crossing construction site until the bridges are complete." He rose, and pointed at the heights beyond Fredericksburg on the map, "Focus your energies on these heights, gentlemen! They are known as Mayre's Heights. You must attack them vigorously and simultaneously while General Franklin works his way towards the Rebel right. If he can push into the wooded areas beyond the railroad tracks, here, then he can begin to unhinge their defensive plan! We must press them with audacity! We are receiving reports that they are exhausted, and poorly supplied. I should not think it would take much of a push to get them moving back towards Richmond." The assembled generals silently nodded; no one had much optimism, so much already had gone wrong. They were hoping for a surprise that was long gone by now. Just as the meeting was beginning to break up late in the evening, Lieutenant Comstock returned in the company of a very muddy and exhausted Major Spaulding. Entering the tent, Comstock exclaimed, "Sir! The bridges have come up! The Engineer Brigade is here!"

Major General Burnside wanted to be angry, but his rage melted when he beheld the state of Major Spaulding and simply said, "Major, the army has anxiously awaited your arrival! I must say I am happy to finally have you here. How long will it take to prepare and throw the bridges in?"

Ira Spaulding rubbed his reddened eyes and slowly responded, "Sir, I have details removing the bateaux from Colonel Haupt's train now, but there are still twenty Chess wagons due in from Belle Plain, with the rest of the components. As soon as I find Captains McDonald, Brainerd and Ford, I will have my commanders available to give orders to! Brainerd came up with me, McDonald and Ford are supposed to be coming up with the wagon trains!" Spaulding paused and asked, "Sir do you have any coffee?" Burnside, surprised at the odd request from the exhausted man, nodded and motioned to an orderly. The man quickly found a tin cupful and provided it to Spaulding. He gratefully accepted the hot drink with a nod and after puffing on it a few times, he cupped the tin between his hands, and took a sip. Refreshed, he continued, "Sir, my apologies, I am quite frozen, we have been at it for nearly eleven days! Sir, if you could show me where you want them I can begin to plan."

Major General Burnside, and Brigadier General Parke took him to the planning map as the Grand Division Commanders rose to leave. General Burnside indicated the bridging locations on the map. Spaulding could feel the urgency of his commander in his motions and the clipped manner in which the directions were provided. After he had been shown the locations, which spurred him to complex thought, Spaulding asked, "Sir, what supports shall I have?" Burnside quickly responded, "I have directed a Regiment of infantry at each crossing site and all of Brigadier General Hunt's artillery along these heights to be in your direct support!" Spaulding looked back down at the map, pausing as he studied Fredericksburg, itself, and asked, "Are the Rebels in the town?" General Burnside gravely nodded. Major Spaulding asked, "Sir, what day is tomorrow?" General Parke replied, "The 10th of December." Major Spaulding nodded, and then slowly replied, "Sir, give me the day and then I will be ready after midnight on the 11th. I need to feed, and rest my men!" Burnside nodded. He instinctively knew this man was not like his leader; he wore the grime and visage of a soldier doing his best against all odds.

Major Spaulding, now equipped with a map showing his bridging locations, found Captain Brainerd and directed him to send the Lieutenants down to the river at the selected sites to conduct a reconnaissance of the approaches and estimate the work of the abutment crews to prepare the departure landings on their side of the Rappahannock. Once they had found select spots, he could direct placement of the Bateaus in preparation for movement to the river. While he wished to do this work in daylight, and after his men had rested, there was too much to do tonight. Spaulding mused; it was better to do this at night anyway, since Rebels were on the other side of the river. Occasional shots from shouting pickets reminded him of that through the early morning as he awaited their reports. At midnight, Lieutenant Falley reported the completion of the unloading of the rail cars and the arrival of the trains of Chess wagons from Belle Plain. Major Spaulding breathed a great sigh of relief. His bridges were finally with the army. He paused to look up at the early morning sky. A cold and distant waning moon was visible through breaks in the clouds. The night was growing colder now that the rain had stopped. He imagined it would become very cold by morning. Spaulding arched his back; the straps of his haversack, canteen and map case dug into his shoulders and made his back sore. He desperately wanted rest but still had much to do.

Captain Brainerd found him and in the manner of all good company commanders he blurted out, "Sir, the abutments crews want to begin preparations straight away for the proposed entry points! May the work begin, tonight?" Major Spaulding shook his head, and replied, "They are supposed to rest. What is their hurry?" Brainerd quickly responded, "Sir! They have too much to do! There is a large gulley at each site! The surveys indicate that we have yards and yards of fill to throw in to create a usable approach! I must insist that we begin immediately, otherwise there will be no usable access to the bridges!" Impressed by the younger man's passion, Major Spaulding assented sternly intoning," There remains still much to do tomorrow. Meter out your men's time carefully, Captain! This will be a demanding day, coming! Insure that they are quiet!" Captain Brainerd nodded impatiently. Spaulding instinctively knew that the Sergeants were behind this entreaty, they in their innate practicality saw what had to be done in the light of the announced timeline. The Sergeants had wisely sent their Captain to clear the work.

Brigadier General Henry Jackson Hunt spent the evening checking with his Battery Commanders along the line of guns in parks, along the lee of the Stafford Heights. He rode alongside Colonel Hayes, as he visited with each. The orders had been to stay out of sight until just before dawn. There was no use exposing their positions to the Rebel artillerymen across the Rappahannock. As they rode the track behind the Chatham House, Hayes explained his logic to place all the rifled pieces of the artillery reserve on the heights, "Sir, it is nearly a mile to a mile and a half to the observed Rebel works that we can make out from the heights. The smoothbore guns are best suited for the close support fight. The best I can do is strip away the Rebel artillery as our boys cross!" Hunt nodded as his deputy explained the logic. He had grown concerned that the time that Burnside had given to General Lee would make for a bloody affair in the morning. The prospect of Rebel troops in the town itself made him even more concerned. The bridging operation, scheduled to commence before dawn, would require the infantry to cross in the face of an awaiting enemy. Responding to Haye's assessment, he simply stated, "William, keep a keen eye to the Rebels doings in the town, as well. We may very well have to support the crossing! This is not something we have done before! I do not envy our Engineers on this morning." Hunt extracted his pocket watch, and glanced at the face, as he held it up to the pale moonlight to examine the time. It was nearly 1 am; the bridges would be put down in scarcely two hours from now. Returning the watch to his pocket, he peered across the misty river bottom beyond the trees. He could make out various fires in the dark and silent town. Most appeared to be waning and growing smoky. The builders had obviously drifted off to sleep. Much waiting had made cynics of their enemy across the way. Word of trading between pickets had been of large concern to General Burnside and he sternly warned his commanders of the danger of soldiers talking to their enemies. All elements of deception had evaporated over a week ago, and the activity in the town was a clear indication that General Lee expected an attack there, as well as south of the town. Rumors also indicated that General Jackson had repositioned his forces to join with General Lee. Hunt reflected on the quandary that General Burnside was in now. He was a man trapped by a plan. All Henry Hunt could do at this point was to support a bad plan, to the best of his ability. Colonel Hayes interrupted his reverie by intoning, "The Horse Artillery is not going to be involved in this one much. They can't see much more than the town itself, based on the ground the General gave to Pleasanton. Their role will be to cross behind the army to exploit whatever success they achieve in the morning." The mention of Pleasanton caused General Hunt to ask, "When do I get my Sergeant Major?" Colonel Hayes smiled and replied, "Tomorrow Sir! He has been preparing the new First Sergeant to assume his duties." Hunt stopped his horse for a moment on the dark road and asked, "Whom did Lieutenant Pennington choose?" Colonel Hayes paused a moment to remember. After a few moments thought, he replied, "I think the name was Timmonds, Sir." General Hunt silently nodded and observed, "I gave that man his oath years ago. A good choice I would say. I recall he is actually from South Carolina! Tis a good thing he did not go "Secesh"! He is a damned good gunner, could determine ranges like no other! In any case I want O'Keefe by tomorrow!

We are in for some hard work!" Colonel Hayes nodded, unseen in the darkness, and quietly responded, "I will see to it, Sir! We should be approaching Captain Kusserow's New York Battery, next."

Down below, in a hollow behind a grove of trees, the fires of the cannoneers of Company M smoldered. First Sergeant O'Keefe could not sleep. He was soon to leave the Company that he had been "Top Sergeant" of for nearly 9 years. He felt it his duty to find Joshua Timmonds, and wake him up. Such was the lot of a First Sergeant. He was pleasantly surprised to find him dourly staring at a dying fire with his back to a tree. "You ready for this, Boy O'?" Joshua looked up silently. O'Keefe chuckled and took a seat in the grass beside him, pulling his pipe from his greatcoat pocket to prepare a smoke. Joshua sullenly observed, "Ain't ready for this First Sergeant." O'Keefe found his leather tobacco pouch, and dug out a finger full of the precious tobacco and responded, "You never will be lad. Remember you got to be watching the Lieutenant all the time! You gots to be thinkin' ahead for him! Ask yourself now, where will ye be after the mornin'? Where is your next position, once that bridge is in? If I was you, I would get my horse and cross over, after the infantry crosses and get a feel for the ground across this river as soon as you can! No worries, we ain't got much to do tomorrow. We are to be the reserve to the reserve, in the morning! That, Boy O' is the task of a leader! You gots to be thinkin' ahead!" Joshua nodded and pulled his great coat tighter around him. The night was growing cold. He asked, "First Sergeant, are they for sure, crossing tomorrow?" O'Keefe struck a match and lit his pipe, replying, "Bet yer life on it Boy O'! The Engineers is stagin' pontoon boats on the heights behind us, now. They've got crews making roads leading up to the river too. The woods above us are full of Regiments, all nervous and such. Word is from the Lieutenant that everybody and his uncle are crossin' in the morning!"

Joshua, enjoying the smell of O'Keefe's pipe softly asked, "Do ya think we are gonna get far?" The question elicited a laugh from the old Irishman, "Shit no, Boy O'! This whole affair is gonna be a goddamned disaster! I can feel it in my bones. We is crossing in the face of a well-prepared enemy! They has been watching us gather here for nearly two weeks! If you think General Lee ain't been makin' ready with everything he has, then you was born yesterday! My wager is this is just like Malvern Hill was for us, exceptin' that we is the Rebs, for a change. They know the ranges and have all of the ground covered with Infantry supports! You just look out for your boys! That is yer job Joshua!"

Joshua was startled to hear his first name from the First Sergeant. He had only heard him use his first name when he was drunk in New York. He felt O'Keefe's hand pushing something to him. O'Keefe was handing him the diamond of a First Sergeant, "Here Boy O'! Get yer housewife out and procure a needle and thread. I'll say I'm sorry that you'll have no fine ceremony. You'll be needin' this diamond on yer sleeve in the mornin! I am off to General Hunt, first thing! Good Luck, son!" O'Keefe then rose with a grunt and made his way back to his tent, leaving behind a lingering cloud of pipe smoke.

Joshua looked up at the night sky and noted the clouds breaking and the pale moon. It seemed terribly far away and offered little light. He wearily rose to his feet. He needed to find some light to sew his new rank on.

7

THE GAPING MAW OF HELL

Sergeant Adams reported to Major Spaulding atop the dark road that led down to the old ferry landing where his bridges would go in, "Sir, the abutment crew is nearly finished and the bateaux are up and off the wagons! May we proceed?" Spaulding pulled out his pocket watch from his vest pocket and held it up to the pale moonlight, it read 3:00. He looked to Adams and asked, "Have the decking crews positioned the Balks and Chess Planks?" Adams nodded, "They will be done soon, Sir! The damned boats will be a struggle to slide down this hill!" Spaulding bluntly replied, "There will be no helping that Sergeant! We can ill afford the mules making a racket by the river! Throw the bridges, Sergeant! I will report back to General Woodbury." Spaulding glanced across the misty river. Hopefully, the pattern of early morning fog would repeat itself again, as the sun rose. He could see the dim glow of the fires that the Rebel pickets had warmed themselves by. He hoped they were sleeping across the river; they had never laid a bridge in the face of an enemy. He mused that this would be an interesting day.

As Major Spaulding ascended the hill to find General Woodbury, Captain Brainerd motioned to the teams of boatmen who stood by their heavy craft lined along the bluffs that sloped towards the river. With hoarsely whispered orders of "Heave Ho!" the Sergeants urged their teams of twenty men each, to lift and slide the heavy wooden pontoon boats down the slope. The tangled scrub brush and saplings actually eased the passage of the thousand pound boats. The Sergeants sternly whispered, "Keep it as quiet as you can boys!" Unfortunately the wooden boats boomed like drums each time they came to rest on the ground. Surprisingly, the opposite bank was quiet and eerily still. The first crew of boatmen reached the river and they pushed the bateau into the water. To their surprise, the heavy boat slid easily across what they discovered, was a sheet of ice. The surface of the Rappahannock had frozen and the ice was nearly an inch thick. The crewmen climbed into the boat and the extra weight caused the bateau to crunch through the ice, making alarmingly loud crunching and cracking noises across the frozen surface. Once they had broken through the ice with their oars and poles, the engineers maneuvered the first boat adjacent to the abutment which the abutment crews were still shoveling fill into to make a road surface. The boat crew tossed out an upstream anchor on a rope and to their disgust, the first cast resulted in the anchor skittering along the surface of the ice sheet. After retrieving the anchor, the Corporal tossed the anchor high in the air and penetrated the ice with his second throw.

Once they were aligned, the balk crew quickly ran first two then two more balk beams to attach the first pontoon to the abutment. The boat crew inserted the ends of the balks into the pegs on the gunwales of the pontoon boat and adjusted the slack out of the anchor line. The planking crew then began to fetch the chess planks and began to lay the heavy planks down on top of the Balks, to make the road surface of the bridge. The wooden boards made hollow bumping noises as the men laid them down. Their Sergeant harshly whispered, "Keep it quiet boys!" The next boat crew heaved their bateau into the water and battled the ice to establish themselves twenty feet from the first boat.

Captain Brainerd watched the crews begin the bridge in the dim half-light of the early morning. His concern over the noise of the bridge going in, was rising. There really was no quiet way to erect a pontoon bridge and he was amazed at the initial progress the crews were making. Glancing to his left, he could barely see the adjacent Company beginning to put boats into the water. They were twenty yards distant and the mist seemed to be increasing. He mused that was a good development. Across the river, nothing stirred and he was grateful for the quiet. Looking back to his company, he was pleased to note that two bays were in and planked, and the men had begun to lash the top rails down over the chess planks on each side of the roadway. A well-trained company could put in a 20-boat span in a little over four hours, but the ice was an unexpected development. The men, despite little rest, worked with quiet urgency. Hearing clanking noises behind him, Captain Brainerd turned and could make out the supporting infantry iegiment arriving. While they were nearly 30 minutes late, he was grateful for their presence. At least they had security now. The commotion caused a barn owl off in the distance to call with its haunting hoots in the early morning. Fredericksburg lay still across the river and he noted that the picket fires were no longer visible. Major Spaulding came alongside him on his horse and inquired as to his progress. After a few moments of quiet discussion he rode further down to check on Captain McDonald's bridge. His primary order had been to keep it going "Fast and quiet!"

The hooting of an owl stirred Private Del Wainright, of the 13th Mississippi Infantry from his boredom with picket duty. He gently leaned his Enfield rifle against the wooden storage shed he had leaned against for the past 3 hours. He adjusted the thin blanket draped around his shoulders, like a cloak, against the bone chilling cold. He suddenly heard a noise that sounded like a long board being dropped onto a wooden surface. Del picked his rifle back up, and peered into the cold fog. Realizing he could see nothing through the damp fog, he turned his head to hear the noise. He thought he could hear talking across the river. After several moments, he heard more noises like those made by a boat when the oars were banged against the sides. The Yankees were definitely moving across the way doing something in the water. He decided to go to where Sergeant Blanchard slept on the sidewalk on Sofia Street. Finding his Sergeant asleep with his back against the wall of a brick Liquor Store, Del squatted and shook his shoulder.

Sergeant Blanchard awoke with a start, "What the hell is it Wainright! You got the duty until sunrise!" Del blurted out, he was prone to stuttering when he was nervous, "S-Sergeant! Them, them Yankees are doin' somethin' yonder across the, the river! They is, they is making a ruckus over yonder! Come listen!" Sergeant Blanchard wearily sat up and pulled his ruined boots on. Private Wainright helped him to his feet with his free hand, then led him to his picket post by the storage shed. Arriving there, he silently pointed in the direction of the noise and insisted, "S-Sergeant just take a listen!" Sergeant Blanchard muttered, "Damn! Ain't nothin but fog tonight!" He then turned his head and after a moment he thought he could hear voices.

Private Wainright began to speak but Blanchard shushed him, the sound of another board being dropped made it clear to Sergeant Blanchard. He turned to Wainright and sternly whispered, "Load that rifle boy, if'n you ain't already, and stand fast right here! I gotta get word to Colonel Carter! They is a comin' straight across, right here!" Sergeant Blanchard jogged back up Hawke Street towards the Livery Stable where the Colonel and Captain Archer were sleeping. After he had awakened the Captain, who in turn shook Colonel Carter, they sat up to listen. Sergeant Blanchard described the noises on the river. Captain Archer lit a match and ignited a nearby candle, so he could see his pocket watch. It was 5am, looking outside he could clearly see a heavy fog shrouding the street outside. Colonel Carter stood up and directed his groggy orderly to saddle his horse. He needed to report to General Barksdale at the Market house, four blocks away. After a few moments noticing that his orderly still had yet to finish dressing he decided to make the move, on foot. At the door of the stable he turned to Captain Archer and directed, "Roust yer boys, Captain and have them fall in on the rifle pits at the river! I'll be back directly. Pass the word to the rest of the Companies, if you would be so kind!"

Colonel Carter met General Barksdale's aide de camp at the wooden table, the General had set up under the porch of the Market House as his field headquarters. Barksdale summoned Carter inside after the aide de camp had awakened him. The General patiently listened to the report. Barksdale had harbored doubts that the Yankees would be foolish enough to come directly across the river into Fredericksburg, but it now became clear that it was their exact intent. He quickly ordered, "Colonel get your men into their positions! I will alert the rest of the brigade!" Turning to his aide he directed, "Quick Major, ride up to Telegraph Hill and report to General McLaws! Tell him the Yankees are coming! Tell them to fire the signal guns!" After the men had departed, General Barksdale began to dress. Once he had attached his sword belt over his sash he checked his French pin-fire revolver to insure he had loaded it. Looking at his writing desk, he realized that it was the 11th of December. Today would be a day of battle and he intended to make General Burnside's army pay in blood for each yard of street in Fredericksburg.

Captain Brainerd leaned out of the way of the chess plank crew as two men trotted down the bobbing roadway of the bridge, carrying another 20-foot long deck plank. He had been notified by Sergeant Adams that Major Spaulding was looking for him. As he reached the finished abutment, he could see Spaulding in the mist near the stockpile of Balks on the overgrown riverbank. Upon reaching his mounted commander, he saluted, and reported, "Sir we have the tenth bay going in now! We are halfway there!" Returning the salute, Major Spaulding looked up and noticed the emerging glow to the east. The sun was coming up. Before he could respond to Brainerd's report, the boom of a distant cannon was heard from beyond Fredericksburg. After a few seconds, a second boom reverberated in the river bottom followed by the pealing of bells from a church steeple, across the river. Looking at Brainerd, Ira Spaulding directed his Company Commander, "Captain, no need to worry about noise now! Tell the men to get to it as fast as they can! We are surely discovered!" Major Spaulding turned his horse and rode through the rough brush to Captain McDonald's Company. He would need to deliver the same order to him before ascending the hill to report to General Woodbury.

Captain Brainerd looked beyond the stockpiles and noted that the officers of his supporting infantry regiment were forming the soldiers into ranks again. He turned and ran back onto the bridge, dodging the returning crewmen of the decking crew, to find Sergeant Adams. He had to tell them to hurry now. Time was of the essence. Reaching Adams, he shouted, "Those shots were the Rebels alerting their army that we are coming! Tell the boys to hustle! Noise ain't the object any more!" Sergeant Adams quickly nodded as he looked at the men around him busily lashing the last set of railings to the chess planks, "Thank God for that Captain, now we can work like we are used to!"

Across the way the sound of a "Long Roll" of drummers was heard. Also shouts were emerging as the Sergeants of an unknown Rebel Regiment was being ordered into positions. Captain Brainerd tried to see what was going on across the way, but the thick grey fog obscured the town, only 200 feet away. Captain Brainerd emphatically directed, "Sergeant! Make sure they understand. This is a race! We must reach the far bank before this fog lifts!" Brainerd noticed the bobbing of the bridge intensifying as the next balk crew came forward at a run, carrying the long timbers to link the next bateau. The boatmen were throwing out their anchor downstream to alternate anchors for shifts in current. The men swiftly hooked the timbers onto the pegs of the last bateau as the boat crew adjusted the wooden boat to hook the timbers to the corresponding pegs for the next bay. The sun had now risen above the horizon making the fog pure white. Looking up, Brainerd could see the slate rooftops of the topmost homes on the ascending slope of the city. He realized the fog would burn off soon. There was little time.

The second reverberating boom of the signal cannon caused Henri Tinchant to awaken with a start. He knew the meaning of the signal from his day spent with the Mississippi surgeons. As the church bells began to ring, he hurriedly dressed and put away his traveling items into his satchel. Once the battle got underway, it would be a good idea to remain thoroughly mobile. He knew that many times battles meant no going back. As he pulled his boots on, he heard a gentle knock on his door. It was Mrs. Lacy. She held a candle lantern in her free hand, as she asked, "Captain Tinchant do tell, does that firing mean the Yankees are coming?" Tinchant solemnly nodded, "Yes Ma'am, it surely does! I will shortly be required to go to the hospital and I am afraid that Miss Markley has a duty there, as well! Would you allow me to assist you with leaving this place? This town is a military object at this point and it will not remain a safe place for a proper lady!" Elliot Lacy assumed a firm visage as she placed her hand over her heart. She announced, "Well my word, Captain Tinchant! This is not the first time those Yankee hirelings have visited our town. I shall not leave my home and belongings to them to paw over! I shall not abandon this house for General Lee nor shall I abandon it for you! Just come check on me once this foolishness is concluded."

Henri Tinchant chuckled, and replied as he stood on his booted feet, "Yes Ma'am, I shall and that is my solemn promise! I should advise you to take some provisions, blankets and pillows down into your basement and shelter there. They have already threatened the town with their cannon once and you can assume that the presence of the Mississippi Regiments shall relegate these streets to the status of a battleground! Please stay inside and in your basement." As Henri took his bag downstairs, he heard Elliot Lacy softly knocking on Lottie's door, "Make haste dear, the Captain will need you to follow him to the field hospital!" She descended the stair, holding up the hem of her house coat and asked Tinchant, "If you have time, I shall make you some breakfast." Henri glumly shook his head, "No thank you, Ma'am! It will be standard rations from this moment on at the Hospital. Please have no worries. Myself and Miss Markley are quite accustomed to a Soldier's fare."

As Lottie descended the stairs, she moved with a purposeful air. He proudly noted that she, too, had possessed the foresight to pack her bag as well. In an instant, he regretted having her so far forward in what seemed to be a coming great battle. He felt differently about her now, recalling many tender moments. Hopefully, the yellow flag over the hospital would be sure protection from the battle. He was grateful for General Barksdale's decision to use it. Lottie beamed as she saw Henri and playfully exclaimed,

"Captain Tinchant, I have never seen a battle!" Henri softly replied, "I am afraid you will not admire it, once you have beheld it. Quickly Miss Markley! We had best be on our way." Henri paused to offer sincere thanks to Mrs. Lacy and he repeated his instructions to remain in her cellar. Lottie paused and thanked her as well, and quickly followed Henri out the door into the dark and foggy street.

The forward hospital was a hive of activity by the time they had arrived. The regimental surgeons had arranged several stout tables on the main receiving floor of the Tobacco Warehouse. Orderlies were busy preparing the upper loft for the wounded that had been treated and had laid out burlap sacking from the hogshead materials in the warehouse to form rude beds. The loft had ramps that made it ideal for stretcher-bearers to transport the wounded to the upper level. Henri and Lottie arrived just as Doctor Lachicott was briefing the Regimental Surgeons, "Myself and Captain Tinchant will attend to amputations! Thoracic and pelvic wounds will be the purview of Lieutenant Colonel Jones and Major Richardson will focus on head and face injuries. All this planning will soon go to hell anyhow so remember to amputate conservatively! We have seen how many soldiers die from second amputations so do it bold the first time!" Henri nodded at the sage advice as Doctor Lachicott turned to Lottie, "I hear you work for the Purveyor, young lady, is that true?" Lottie eagerly nodded her head, Lachicott continued, "Excellent, you can assist Orderly Sergeant Willis with pharmaceuticals! You just make double sure you bring us the right items!" Pausing to look at each of his Doctors, Colonel Lachicott continued, "I plan on us being overran as General Barksdale's orders are merely to delay the enemy here. I expect the entire Yankee army to fill this town once they get across that river! That is the singular reason we are flying a Federal style hospital flag. Our stretcher-bearers are limited in number, so we may have to help them, if necessary. We shall treat all the fallen regardless of what Army they serve. I suspect it will help General Burnside's mood if he observes us treating his wounded, as well. Hopefully they will respect this flag and this hospital and treat it according to our common practice. Just remember our main goal is to give our boys a fighting chance to survive this crucial mission!

The doctors busily organized their instruments as orderlies began to fill empty barrels with water from the river using buckets. Lottie rummaged through her traveling bag and found a regulation apron that she normally used when doing inventory. Catching Henri's eye as she tied it around her, he gave her an approving nod. Walking over to her, he put his hand on her shoulder and softly said, "Be strong Charlotte, this is going to seem like hell. Just remember to look the men in the eyes, never fixate on the

261

wounds. Do that and you will keep your wits." Lottie felt a knot growing in her stomach; she tried to remember the days of helping her father after his hunts. She desperately needed to come up with visions of gore and blood. It would make this easier, if she could.

Sergeant Roy Cobb of Company A, "The Confederate Rifles" 17th Mississippi Infantry Regiment, directed his men to prop their muskets along the barricades of timbers and barrels on the north edge of Sophia Street. The Rappahannock River lay obscured by mist, just beyond their makeshift works. Seeing the men nervously peering over the barricades into the dense early morning fog, he chuckled, "Ya'll settle down boys, wait on the officers! Ev'rybody knows they kin see a dang sight further than us'ns, so just wait on the word! After sitting down on a large beam with his back to the barricade, he produced a quarter of a fine Virginia ham. He had found it in a garden shed in town, behind a house on Hawke Street. Pulling out his wicked Bowie knife, he carefully carved several slices off the chunk and tenderly returned what remained into the shelter of his canvas haversack. Turning to a young private crouched by him, he suggested, "Son, you help me build a little fire here and I'll give you some ham." The young private scrambled about finding bits of wood residue and soon had the makings of a cook-fire. Sergeant Cobb rented a half-canteen frying pan from Corporal Gaines, at the cost of another slice of ham and proceeded to fry the treasure while he waited.

Private Orr hungrily watched the progress of the small meal, but he could not settle down. Across the way, in the midst of the fog, the Yankee engineers could be heard shouting and laying boards down. Looking anxiously at Sergeant Cobb he asked, "Sergeant, ain't this foolish? Them Yankees will be on us at any minute!" Cobb gave a great grin, and replied, "Best waitin' you will ever have boy is when they roust you to wait on a battle to start! It don't never happen so fast as the Officers think. Go ahead and settle down!"

Sergeant Cobb carefully attended to the ham slices as they gently browned over the small fire. As he stirred the pieces, the smell of the cooking meat drifted down the line of waiting men, causing them to curse and make offers of items in exchange for a nibble. An officer in the distance called out in a low voice, "Don't nobody load their muskets until we tell you! Stand fast and wait for orders!" From the noises on the river, Sergeant Cobb guessed that they were nearly half way across. When he was satisfied with his breakfast cooking, he lifted the pan and stomped out the tiny fire with his foot. He wished he had been able to find some coffee. He provided Corporal Gaines with his payment on the point of his knife, then he did likewise to Private Orr. Sticking the remaining 3 slices onto his knife, for portability, he returned the dirty pan to Corporal Gaines. Gaines remarked in mock horror, "Why, you ain't washed it!" Sergeant Cobb grinned as he bit into the slices of cooked ham, and muttered, "Left you some gravy there, just add some water! 'Tis my gift to you!"

Cobb leaned out and studied the faces of his men. Many looked over their shoulders from time to time, and when they noticed the thickness of the fog, they quickly looked back. The noises on the river drew closer, yet they waited. Others used the early light to re-read letters from home or to study the small pamphlets of salvation that had been distributed by the Chaplain.

Captain Rankin walked the line with Lieutenant Boyd. They would pause and lift field glasses towards the river. Boyd commented, "Sir, I can hear them clear as a bell, but I cannot make out anything visibly of value!" Rankin lifted his glasses again, peering fruitlessly into the fog. He lowered his glass and replied, "If this isn't burned off soon we shall have to engage the sounds of their work! We won't accomplish much unless we deliver tight volleys! When they give the word, we will form lines of battle like we was in the open." Lieutenant Boyd nodded. Turning around one more time frustrated, he raised his field glasses and looked into the fog for a last attempt. As he peered through the fog, he suddenly could make out the lighter wooden surface of the bridge as the sunrise made the yellow, unfinished deck planks lighter than the surface of the Rappahannock. He blurted out, "Captain, I can see the bridges!" Captain Rankin quickly turned and raised his field glasses as well. The sun had emerged from the trees to the east illuminating the surfaces of the bridge. While he could not clearly make them out, he could see where two incomplete spans were reaching towards their side of the river. He quickly shouted, "Run and notify Colonel Holder!" Lieutenant Boyd rapidly nodded his head and trotted to the house on Hawke Street where the Regimental Headquarters had been established. Captain Rankin then looked at his men and shouted, "On your feet boys! Form two ranks!" The eager young drummer began to sound the long roll. Captain Rankin initially wanted to order him to stop, but upon reflection, allowed him to continue. He hoped the drumming would unnerve the Yankees across the way. Once his men had stood and formed their ranks, he shouted out, "Load!"

Captain Brainerd made a conscious effort to stay clear of the men as they rushed Chess planks forward to complete the 12th Bay. Their running made the bridge bob lazily in the still river. He noticed to his amazement, that most of the ice was no longer visible. Brainerd quickly paced the bays, checking the lacing of the rails to insure the lashing teams had been thorough. The bridge would take a pounding from the long lines of waiting infantry and artillery, and any incorrect preparation would cause the intricate system of interlocking timbers to fail. Looking up, he noticed, to his horror, that he could now make out the row of homes and shops that lined the river on the far side. The fog was burning off. The noise of drumming and an odd movement caught his eye; he then realized it was a long row of arms in the air, moving up and down. Looking closer, he realized it was a regiment of Rebel infantry loading their muskets.

He turned and looked at his men, they were completely preoccupied with the "race" to the far bank. In the distance, he heard the cry, repeated several times by numerous commanders, "Ready...Aim!" Brainerd caught Sergeant Adam's eyes, before he shouted, "Get down, men!" Those nearest him heard him and hesitantly laid down on the plank tread way, while others further back continued to come forward with planks. They did not comprehend his shout. He desperately motioned with his arm as the shouts of "Fire!" emerged from the thinning fog.

The crackling roar of the Rebel volley was earsplittingly loud and filled the air with angry whizzing noises as the hundreds of Minie balls struck the water and planks of the bridge. Their impacts threw splinters from the deck planks into the air. Captain Brainerd saw several of the decking crew fall between him and the north bank. One man fell into the water and slowly drifted under the bay between the pontoon boats. The supporting Infantry behind his lumber stockpiles had loaded, and on the orders of their officers returned a heavy volley back to the south over their heads. Captain Brainerd shouted over the noise of the return volley, "Keep down men!" Raising his head for a moment, Brainerd noticed that the smoke from the volleys had made the obscuration of the thinning fog thicker. He rose to his feet and shouted, "Get back to it, boys! Clear off the wounded and get back to work!" The shocked men looked around and at each other, until Sergeant Adams shouted, "Ya heard the Captain! Get crackin! We got 7 bays to go! Get off yer asses!" The men quickly rose to their feet and several paired up to drag the wounded and dead back to the north bank. While dreading the next volley, Brainerd stayed put as he shouted encouragement to the next pair of decking crewmen, bringing up the next set of chess planks. Behind him, he could hear the Rebel commanders shouting orders. They were reloading and another volley was soon coming. He had to continue building the bridge.

The sounds of firing drew Major Spaulding away from General Burnside's forward headquarters, back to the river. As he rode down the hill from Chatham Manor, he realized to his horror that the majority of the fog was gone. Now the river bottom was filled with powder smoke instead of mist. Pausing for a moment, he could see one bridge was just halfway across and the other was only a quarter complete. Stunned, he watched as a Balk crew was shot down to a man by well-aimed fire from Rebels behind barricades along the south bank. They were no longer firing by volleys. They were deliberately shooting as his men presented themselves. The remainder of the crews had sheltered behind the stockpiles of material they had neatly stacked by the bridges.

Realizing he needed help, he turned his horse and rode back to General Burnside's Headquarters. He was met there by Lieutenant Comstock, who asked, "Major, what is the progress on your bridges? The southern bridges are finished and they have crossed a regiment to secure the far side." Major Spaulding lost his composure and shouted back, "Lieutenant! The firing you hear is the sound of well-trained men being murdered by the enemy! We need the Rebels driven from the far bank or you will never have a bridge here! Unless you want to run a deck plank forward yourself! I need fires brought upon the far bank!"

The shouting brought Brigadier General Hunt out of the planning tent, where he had been meeting with General Sumner and General Burnside. Listening to their conversation for a moment, he returned to General Burnside and asked, "Sir, is it your desire to fire into the city? I appears to me that the enemy have stopped the bridge erection here!" Hunt clearly needed the senior man to make this decision; he personally harbored great distaste at the notion of shelling a town, which might still contain women and children. General Burnside paused; Hunt perceived that the decision paralyzed his commander, for a moment. Fredericksburg was one of the older towns in the country; it was a landmark full of historic portent. Finally, Ambrose Burnside blurted out, almost as if he was justifying his action to himself, "That damned Mayor assured us that the town would not be used to aid the rebellion! He gave his solemn word as a gentleman!" He looked around desperately to his subordinates, asking, "You all heard the content of the agreement, did you not?" The officers silently nodded, and he turned to Hunt and reluctantly ordered, "General Hunt, order your guns to shell the town! Drive those troops away from the river! I need all my bridges up, before I will commit this Army!" General Hunt silently nodded and strode purposefully out of the tent. Passing Major Spaulding and Lieutenant Comstock, he returned their rapid salutes, and directed, "You two get a means arranged to communicate with me! I will be up with the guns for awhile. I will need some reporting in regards to my effects on the Rebels!"

General Lee and Lieutenant General Longstreet sat in tapestry upholstered folding chairs underneath a loosely rigged canvas awning. Longstreet was bringing his commander abreast of the dispositions of his regiments as they formed along their works on Mayre's heights. Lee had grumbled about the positioning of the artillery by Lieutenant Colonel Alexander, but General Longstreet had brushed those objections aside with a respectfully argumentative statement, "Sir, I have looked at all of those positions, myself! Hell, Sir! A chicken could not walk unmolested along the front of these works! Young Alexander has been thorough and diligent in his placement! You cannot expect linear battery positions in the face of such amassed Union rifled pieces!" General Lee held his hand up in tacit surrender; he realized Longstreet had become passionate about the competency of the young officer. The tension was lifted by the arrival of Lieutenant General Thomas Jackson, both Longstreet and Lee were awestruck by his appearance. Somehow he had procured an elegantly tailored frockcoat with all the trappings of a Confederate Lieutenant General. James Longstreet yelled out, "General Jackson, what has become of your attire! We nearly shot you for a spy!" General Lee softly intoned, as close as he would ever come to joviality, "My my, he dresses the part of a fine officer." Both men were unaware of the commotion that his new uniform had caused on his lengthy ride to the headquarters and General Jackson blushed a bright red. He hurriedly stammered, "It seemed fitting, Gentlemen, to represent the proper image of a Corps Commander! This was General Stuart's notion, I did this only after protest!" General Lee softly chuckled and rescued his Corps Commander with the question, "General Jackson, how goes your movement to our flank? Those people are showing clear intent to come this way!" Before Jackson could answer, Longstreet was far from done with his teasing, "Say General, all them

Yankees coming this way doesn't frighten you, does it?" General Jackson removed his hat and slowly answered his boss first, "General Lee, my men have made good time as you should expect and are in place overlooking the rail line between the wood and the river. A swamp bisects me on my Corps front but I have placed General Gregg in a position of stout reserve, should that become a concern. What troubles me most sir, is there is shelter for them south of that rail line as it is erected on an embankment! They will shelter there, I am sure. With your permission, I should like to ask General Stuart to enfilade that shelter with his horse artillery battalion, that is, barring any missions you may have assigned them." Lee softly nodded and replied, "No General, I have no additional plans. General Stuart has already closed the Rappahannock to any attempts by them to employ gunboats in support, so feel free to make arrangements with him as you please." Jackson nodded, and then turned towards Longstreet, "General, I fear no Yankee hirelings and I have prayed that they may enjoy easy crossing of the Rappahannock. We shall see who fears whom when they receive the greetings of my brigades!"

General Lee turned serious for a moment and emphasized to his two commanders, "Gentlemen, Colonel Chilton has developed some studies of the pass times that General Burnside will require to cross the four bridges we have seen them putting in. His guess is that it will take him nearly 8 hours to cross his 100,000, unless he finds another ford, or gets more bridges in. Keep your positions and your men out of sight of their artillery until the very last minute. I expect General Hunt has placed his long-range pieces on the Stafford Heights and I do not doubt their capability to impair us if they are given the chance. I would expect them to make a general assault by morning tomorrow." As he finished speaking, Colonel Chilton interrupted him with a message, "Sir, this is just in from a rider dispatched by General Stuart." General Lee took the dispatch and read it. After a moments study, he looked up to General Jackson, and said, "General Jackson, you should return to your Corps! General Stuart reports that they have put in three bridges at the bend! Look to your men, Sir!" Jackson, smartly saluted and briskly strode out. James Longstreet watched him go and remarked, "Sir, I surely think he has high anticipation of them coming!" General Lee curtly replied, "It is because he has the soul of a soldier, General Longstreet! We could learn a thing or two about his peculiarities."

Their conversation was interrupted again as the entire Stafford Heights erupted in smoke. Colonel Chilton rushed in a few moments later and announced, "Sir, they are firing their artillery into the town!" The men rose and watched from a small knoll forward of them that overlooked the town. Great plumes of white smoke rose in the air above the Stafford Heights and

267

the roar of the massed cannon was like a non-stop thunderstorm. Plumes of dark smoke rose from the town as several homes had begun to burn from the effects of bursting shells. The occasional round would burst over the slate roofs and fill the air with white smoke. As General Lee watched the bombardment, he solemnly observed, "Those people have no regard for the inhabitants of Fredericksburg or their property. This, gentlemen, is the way of war for the abolitionists. Use this example as a guide when they march upon our works! I have every intention of destroying that army, if providence gives me that chance." Turning to General Longstreet, he directed, "See to your men, General Longstreet! Insure they are well prepared."

Colonel Charles Tompkins needed no additional orders from General Hunt. When the clatter of Rebel muskets reverberated across the misty river bottom, and he saw engineers falling wounded and dead on the bridges below, he shouted to his orderly to summon his bugler. His commanders and their guns were waiting in a park by the Phillips house, back away from the crest of the heights. Those commanders knew their positions and knew the signal. The young bugler rode up on his mount and saluted. Colonel Tompkins directed, "Sound "To Horse" then sound "To Battery!" Repeat the same calls twice, I'll see if they remember." Turning to his orderly, who followed the bugler, he sharply directed, "Find General Hunt! Inform him I am bringing my guns up to support the Engineer Brigade. Inform him that I shall fire on the town!" The young man nodded and rode down the road that led to Chatham Manor.

The teams of guns on limbers and caissons emerged before the bugler had finished the second iteration of the call. Thomkins knew that they had heard the firing and implicitly understood what it meant. He felt confident he could drive them back. He controlled twelve heavy Parrot Rifles and twenty-six Ordnance Rifles and his ranges were short. As the six Companies came up to occupy their positions on the Stafford Heights, he peered down into the river bottom. The action below had devolved into an exchange of general musket fire between the supporting infantry regiments on his side, and firing from the houses and barricades along the Rebel side of the river. The engineers had sought shelter behind stacks of bridging material near the bridge sites. He noticed that the mist of the morning was largely being replaced by the smoke of the firing. The smoke hung thickly over the surface of the water in the still of the morning.

He watched as his 4 batteries of 3-inch Ordnance Rifles swiftly unlimbered and established in battery. The Captains and Lieutenants commanding shouted out ranges and loads, while studying the town across the river through their field glasses. The Sergeants shouted the men through their paces as they had constantly drilled. The first Battery fired their initial shots, by file, before their caissons were set the regulation distance back. The rifles spit long tongues of flame and billowed white smoke as the guns recoiled violently over the frozen ground. With each discharge, Tomkins could hear the shriek of the bolts as they flew at high velocity towards the houses and shops bordering the river. Lifting his own field glasses to his eyes, he could see two large sprays of dark brown dirt as the shot ricocheted off the cobblestones of Sophia Street and plowed into the basement floors of the buildings lining the river. He watched as the impacts from the batteries, further east of his line, collapsed brick walls from upper floors and showered bricks into the alleys leading down to the river from Caroline Street. He could occasionally see small groups of gray clad figures leaving houses, seeking better locations, as the solid shot passed through multiple shops and dwellings. Tomkins motioned to his Adjutant. When the man approached on horseback, he tersely directed, "Major Walker, ride down the line and inform the commanders to switch to shell! We need to drive them back from the river! Focus their fires on the buildings along the river!" Major Walker saluted and galloped off down the gun line.

Down below the heights in the river bottom beneath the hill that housed Chatham Manor, Joshua Timmonds spent his first morning as Company M's First Sergeant studying the progression of the battle around the bridges being put in, 400 yards to the east. The cannonade from the Stafford Heights made for a hell of a show. Fredericksburg looked to be a very pretty town that had obviously housed very wealthy people, but now several fires burned uncontrolled, and the screaming shot and shell tore great holes in the masonry structures lining the river. The gunners on the Stafford Heights were firing in a very deliberate fashion and he could tell by the tempo of the firing that they were sensing their shots. As he watched, the shelling paused and he could see the engineers as they rose in teams to resume construction of the bridge. The running men got another pontoon boat positioned and attached it to the end of the bridge with long timbers. More men ran the length of the bridge with long boards to make a road way. They had placed several down when musket fire emerged again from the ground floor of the buildings along the river on the Rebel side. Several of the engineers fell on the bridge and the others dove into the boats to seek shelter from the rifle fire. A great cloud of gun smoke from volley

269

firing regiments, on his side of the river, indicated the return fire from the supporting Regiments behind the bridges. Joshua could tell things were going badly and he wondered how the generals were going to change things to get the bridges across.

Joshua turned from watching the battle over the bridge site when he heard Lieutenant Pennington calling for him, "First Sergeant Timmonds! We have orders!" Hearing the title seemed strange to Joshua. He turned and shouted out to his section Sergeants in a loud voice, "Stand to! Get your teams hitched!" He could not see wasting the men's time while he talked to the Commander. He purposefully strode over to Lieutenant Pennington and provided him with a quick salute, asking, "What are our orders, Sir?" Pennington read them from a dispatch he had received, "This is from Lieutenant Colonel Hayes. He directs us to find ground by which we can engage the Rebels along the waterfront of Fredericksburg in order to support the engineers with the emplacement of the pontoon bridges! The Colonel urges us to make haste!" Joshua quickly answered back, "Sir, I have walked the ground all around this area. The best we can achieve is a section behind you to the right! There is a small flat spot that we can employ, but we'll have to use our prolongues to get to it, there is no room for horses or limbers there!" Pennington quickly replied, "Very well then. See to it First Sergeant!" Joshua hurried away to Sergeant Newby's section. Once he got there he informed Newby to limber up his two guns and drag them to the small knoll to the right of their camp. He was curt in his instructions, "Unlimber below that knoll! I will have 2nd Section form a detail to help you haul the guns up with prolongues! Leave the limbers below and have your number 5 run the charges up." Newby nodded, glad to have some action. Joshua then made his way to 3rd Section and informed Sergeant Armstrong, "Assemble your drivers and gunners and have them secure their carbines and cartridge pouches! You will provide support for Newby's section! Make it quick, I expect the Rebels to start shooting at them as soon as they show!" Armstrong nodded; the novelty of employing their carbines was an interesting and different task. As Joshua continued to shout out his orders, the men scurried about searching for their little used accouterments.

First Sergeant Timmonds then mounted his horse and followed Sergeant Newby's section and watched as the men unlimbered at the base of the small knoll. Joshua quietly instructed, "Wait on the detail of helpers and the supports before you pull the guns up!" After they had unlimbered, the crewmen removed the prolongues from the trail hooks and attached them to the lunettes of the heavy guns. Looking up, he could see Sergeant Armstrong and Sergeant Page hurrying their men across the sheltered camp to the low knoll. Joshua could hear the increasing intensity of the Rebel firing at the struggling engineers. Looking up, he could see the sun rising above the trees to the east. The morning was growing warm and the frozen ground had begun to melt. Lieutenant Pennington also rode over to watch as Sergeant Newby directed the men as the rolled the heavy guns up the slippery and muddy slope. The cannoneers slipped and swore as they heaved the first gun up onto the knoll and oriented it towards the town. The men rushed down to run up the second gun as Rebel minie balls began to clip through the trees around the stationary piece on the knoll. They knew that the gun there would become a significant threat to their hold on the riverbank. Lieutenant Pennington shouted to Sergeant Newby to order his gunners to carry canister rounds from the limber chest up on to the knoll, as First Sergeant Timmonds directed Sergeant Page's men to find spots overlooking the far side of the river. Joshua directed them to load and the men quickly pressed the levers that opened the compact Smith Carbines, folding open at the breech. As the Rebels across the river continued to fire at the engineers and the supporting Regiments, Sergeant Page's men dug the gutta-percha cartridges out of their pouches and loaded the carbines. Peering through the brush at the riverbank, Joshua estimated the range to be nearly 400 yards. He hurriedly instructed Page, "Just shoot at their muzzle smoke! Keep them busy while we get the guns ready!" When he returned to the base of the knoll, the cannoneers had just finished manhandling the second gun up the muddy slope. It had been a struggle and they were red-faced and sweaty. Lieutenant Pennington ordered the men to their places and shouted out, "Load canister! 400 yards! Advance the charges!" Sergeant Newby's section quickly fell into their places and Joshua watched as the carbine-armed artillerymen below began to engage the rubble-ensconced Rebels across the river. On the heights beyond, General Hunt's guns of the artillery reserve began to resume the pounding of the city. The warmth of the mid-morning sun had transformed the frozen earth into a muddy mess as the crews began the loading and aiming drill. Lieutenant Pennington directed each of the gunners to focus at the base of the structures lining the Rebel side of the Rappahannock. Once the pieces were loaded and primed, with the number four crewmen on the lanyards, Lieutenant Pennington shouted, "Fire!" Both of the 12 Pounders roared and blew a great cloud of smoke across the river. The carriages recoiled violently back as the trails dug a shallow trench in the half frozen mud, marking their passage rearward. Joshua watched as the twin charges of canister blew portions of wooden barricades to splinters across the river. Puffs of red brick dust marked the impact of the murderous balls as they struck the foundation level of the structures. Lieutenant Pennington shouted out again as the crews ran the pieces forward, "Load canister! 400 yards! Advance the charge!" The crews continued their well-drilled movements and had the section guns reloaded in under a minute. Looking down to his left, Joshua noted that Sergeant Page's men were firing at a rapid rate and he hoped that their ammunition would last as each man only had 20 rounds each in the tiny carbine cartridge pouches. Listening for a moment, the odd bullets whizzed overhead from time to time, however, the majority of the firing was still directed at the Engineers on the bridges. First Sergeant Timmonds then made his way to Sergeant Page's positions and looked across the river through the scrub brush on the riverbank. Fredericksburg was enduring a pounding from the artillery on the heights and he stared transfixed as an entire sidewall and chimney of a house tumbled down from the detonation of a shell. He wondered if anyone had been inside who wasn't fighting.

Sergeant Roy Cobb and his trusty Corporal lay on the dirt floor of the Mercantile store sub-basement with his hands over his head as the burst of a Yankee shell exploded on the floor above them. A great plume of dust filled the basement as the chimney of the establishment collapsed outside with a great clatter of chalky clinking noises. Cobb looked up for a moment, trying to gaze through the dusty air that was illuminated in beams by the morning sunlight penetrating through the loopholes they had knocked out in the basement walls. Another round tore through the upstairs with a great crashing and breaking of multiple items as the projectile tore through the structure on its way elsewhere. In the darkness he could hear a sobbing voice, "Make it stop! Dear God! Make it stop!" The murmur of the men was interrupted by the loud clatter of canister shrapnel impacting on the wall that faced the river. Sergeant Cobb shouted out to his men, "No worries boys! Just lay low! Get ready for when it stops! That means they will get on the bridge again!" The distant roaring of the cannons in the distance was punctuated by the loud claps of exploding shells around them. Despite all the racket, and the disturbing nearness of the destruction, Cobb had yet to lose a single man. After another unnerving hour of explosions and near misses, the shelling stopped. Cobb quickly rose to his feet and reached down to pull up Corporal Gaines. He shouted, "Get to them loopholes double quick boys! They is a comin'!"

The men clumsily scrambled to their feet in the dark basement. Since there were limited loopholes, Sergeant Cobb selected his best shots to use them. The others would load and pass muskets to them. Private Orr, as one of the select marksmen, slid a long Enfield rifle out the bright hole in the brick and peered down the long barrel and aligned his sights. He aimed at a pair of men trotting towards him across the incomplete bridge carrying a long timber. The smoke from the shot obscured his vision for a moment as the recoil of the rifle gently pushed his shoulder back. Pulling the rifle back out of the loophole without looking back, he was handed another and he slid it back out and cocked the hammer. The first man he had shot at, was down. As he refined his aim, another marksman hit the second man and he fell, arms outstretched into the river. Three more men, carrying nothing, ran from the Yankee side onto the bridge. Two of them picked up the timber and continued forward, while the third checked on one of the fallen men. Orr took careful aim and dropped the hindmost man carrying the timber. As he extracted his second rifle from the loophole he saw that the ranks of supporting infantry on the Yankee side had fired a great volley at them. The smoke from the discharge obscured the far side of the river. Orr leaned back away from the loophole as the rounds impacted on the wall outside in a series of loud smacks on the bricks. Peering back out with another rifle, Private Orr could find no more targets on the bridge. He decided on longer work, instead. Pulling the rifle partially back out of the loophole, he adjusted the rear sight for elevation and aimed at the blue-clad men in ranks as they reloaded for another volley. He estimated them to be nearly 200 yards distant. Orr carefully took aim and noted that the other marksmen were also concentrating on the supporting infantry as he saw several men fall as they struggled to reload. He slowly pulled the stiff trigger and the rifle bucked familiarly into his shoulder. He said aloud, to no one in particular, "Seems them Yankees ought to have more sense to be doing what they are doin' here!"

Soon the loud thunder of the guns on Stafford Heights began again. Sergeant Cobb ordered the men to retreat back to the root cellar portion of the basement. The familiar shriek and rumbling impacts of the Yankee shell and solid shot resumed. Cobb wondered how long this exchange would continue. He hoped the Yankees would abandon their fight here.

Five blocks east of the battle over the unfinished bridges, the Surgeons of General Barksdale's brigade began to receive their first customers. Litter bearers from the three Regiments defending Fredericksburg made their hazardous way through the nearly constant shell fire with their ghastly cargo of wounded men to the tobacco warehouse by the destroyed railroad bridge. The structure had taken several hits from the inbound shot, leading Doctor Laschicott to direct the orderlies to erect the yellow hospital flag vertically at the peak of the building, so it could be better observed by the gunners across the river. Fortunately, the wooden construction of the warehouse did little to delay the heavy projectiles as they made their way through the structure. Lottie still flinched as each wayward round made its ripping flight through the upper floors of the building. She noticed the strong tobacco smell grew in intensity each time the building was hit.

Henri assisted Doctor Laschicott with a badly wounded man that the litter bearers brought in. He directed Lottie and Sergeant Waverly, the senior Medical Orderly, to assist. Henri quickly gave Lottie a list of items to retrieve as Sergeant Waverly delivered a bucket of water. Then he assisted the Doctors in lifting the wounded man on the table. Lottie noticed that the soldier had a terrible wound where his knee had been and his butternut pants were soaked in blood. The injured leg was floppy and had to be aligned on the table by Sergeant Waverly. Henri directed, "Miss Markley, please find the chloroform and a Chisholm Inhaler, if you please!" She hurried to procure the items and placed them on the small table beside his surgical kit as Sergeant Waverly expertly tore the soldier's pants away from the bloody and mangled knee. Waverly then took the can of Chloroform and poured a small quantity into the cup of the inhaler and handed the device to Doctor Laschicott. Lottie noticed that the young soldier was very pale and he quivered uncontrollably. Seeing Doctor Laschicott, he plaintively begged, "Please Sir, save my leg! I cannot work without both my legs!" Laschicott soothingly said to him, "Son, I am more worried for you life than I am your leg. Lie still and when I place this device in your nose, I should like for you to breathe deeply through it." The frightened young soldier nodded and did as instructed, soon he was unconscious. While remembering the advice from Henri, Lottie could not help but to stare fascinated as the two men addressed the amputation.

Doctor Laschicott matter of factly discussed his technique with Henri as he directed Sergeant Waverly to pull the soldier's leg up into an upward angle and pull down on the skin of the man's thigh. "Captain Tinchant, assist me please in affixing the tourniquet low on his thigh, near the hip." Henri quickly attached the device and tightened the compression. Laschicott continued, "I shall amputate mid-thigh as this wound has likely shattered the lower extremity of the femur. The method I prefer, is that of Doctor Bromfield. Please hand me my large scalpel. Sergeant, please pull down on the skin as hard as you can." The senior surgeon quickly cut through the skin completely around the circumference of the man's leg. Watching the procedure caused Lottie's hair to stand on end and sent a shiver through her, but she continued to watch, transfixed. There was less blood than she expected. "Captain, you will note that I have only cut through the integuments. This procedure is not a flap method as you obviously can tell. I also shall not dissect the fascia under the skin as is commonly believed to be necessary. It is simply injurious and wastes time." Trickling blood ran over Sergeant Waverly's fingers as he stoutly held the leg. Laschicott continued, "Please closely observe as I cut the exterior layer of musculature. Sergeant Waverly, please release your firm pressure on the leg and adapt a gentle hold."

Henri leaned in to watch and as the Sergeant did as instructed, the outer layer of muscles reflexively pulled back towards the soldier's hips as the severed tissues contracted. Laschicott then made a second cut down to the bone in a quick circumference of the man's leg. He then asked for water and quickly dipped his hands in to wash away the sticky drying blood. Turning to Lottie he directed, "Young lady, please take that piece of linen and tear it in half, but tear it only half of its length, if you please." Lottie, without understanding why, did as she was instructed and handed the cloth to the Doctor. Laschicott took the cloth and handed it to Sergeant Waverly, while saying, "This method employs this linen sling to pull all the musculature back from the area of the bone to be cut. This technique prevents further injury to the muscle and allows for a higher cut."

As Sergeant Waverly quickly affixed the sling against the cut flesh, and pulled, nearly three inches of thick femur was exposed. Doctor Laschicott retrieved his saw and observed, "Doctor Tinchant, note that I do not scrape away the pereiosteum in any manner. That is another time consuming step that elicits no positive benefit." He deftly aligned his saw, while holding the leg with his left hand, and starting with a backwards motion he began to expertly saw the through exposed bone. In a matter of minutes he was nearly two thirds through the femur and he then slowed down his motions, "I fear I rarely achieve a completely clean cut! I am always leaving a spiculae. Miss Markley please retrieve my bone nipper." Lottie quickly found the nipper and stood nearby as he finished the cut.

Henri picked up the lower leg and pulled it away as Doctor Laschicott put down the saw and cleaned up the bone end with the nipper. He then procured a small rasp and quickly beveled the sharp ends of the sawn bone. Laschicott then turned to Sergeant Waverly and said, "You may lower the leg and release the sling." Laschicott then retrieved his forceps and began to probe the stump for the end of the femoral artery, saying, "In the event that you have not done such an amputation, Doctor, it is imperative to separate the anterior crural nerve from the femoral, or the patient will experience continual pain. I always take a moment to find it and dissect it away from the point of ligature." With deft and rapid movements, greatly admired by Henri, Doctor Laschicott quickly tied off the femoral artery and the femoral vein. He then turned to Henri, and continued, "Now you must watch for a moment for any hemorrhage from the other vascular locations within the stump! Most of the time, clotting will suffice, but to be forced to resect again after bandaging invariably will bring on the fever!" Laschicott them swiftly brought the excess skin together over the end of the now tapered stump and sutured the edges of the skin together over the wound. Before he closed the stump entirely, he inserted a copper tube, and closed the stump around it. He simply remarked, "For drainage. Insure the orderlies bandage around the tube."

Leaving Sergeant Waverly to the bandaging of the stump, Doctor Laschicott and Henri quickly dipped their hands in the bloody water and moved on to the additional wounded that were flowing in. The shelling had stopped again and the sounds of musketry came up from the river below.

Brigadier General Hunt sourly watched as nearly four hours of shelling Fredericksburg seemed to have no effect on the Rebel marksmen along the Rappahannock. Sergeant Major O'Keefe had brought him the news from the east that two bridges were in and a Brigade of Franklin's men were across to secure the other side. Aside from limited artillery fire, the Rebs were showing little inclination to attack that crossing. Hunt extracted his watch and looked at the time, it was nearly 2pm and he could see the two partially finished spans below. He realized that no progress had been made since the fog lifted early in the morning. The plan, so carefully laid by General Burnside, was rapidly collapsing. General Hunt decided to go have a look for himself.

Guiding his white horse onto the road that descended from the Stafford Heights down to intersect Telegraph Road, he found a very agitated General Woodbury, who commanded the Engineer Brigade. Woodbury was in a heated discussion with a very dirty and weary Major. Hunt recognized him as Major Spaulding, whom he had addressed earlier in the morning. Their discussion was hard to hear for the noise of the continuing bombardment of the town. Hunt stopped by them and asked, "Gentlemen, what guidance have you received from General Burnside?"

Both men stared at him for a moment, and Major Spaulding blurted out, "Sir, none whatsoever! Everyone seems perfectly content to watch my men be slaughtered attempting to bridge across a river with a hostile force sitting astride my far abutment! The bombardment is a waste of ammunition, General!" General Woodbury attempted to silence his angry Major, but Spaulding insisted on being heard, "Sir, we either have to abandon this site or put Infantry across in some other manner to clear the town! I do not have enough skilled men to spare to continue pushing them into certain death to erect this bridge!"

General Hunt grimly nodded, "Major, I have arrived at the same conclusion, myself! I shall go to Burnside and consult with him. General Woodbury, it would be helpful if you were to accompany me!" Woodbury glumly nodded. The two rode swiftly up the road towards the Phillips house, where General Burnside had his forward headquarters. The day was growing pleasantly warm and the sky was clearing. Small traces of snow still remained in the areas under shadow.

Arriving at Burnside's headquarters tent, the two found the General and his Engineer in consultation over a map. General Hunt removed his cap and greeted his commander. There was an urgency in his voice when he suggested, without solicitation, "Sir, we need to get Infantry across to finish the upper bridge! I am afraid my artillery is having little to no effect on the Rebels and your two bridges to support General Sumner's approach are no further advanced than they were early this morning!" General Burnside angrily snapped back, "The problems before Fredericksburg is an issue I am well aware of General Hunt! I thought you were confident that your artillery could drive them from the town! Why has that not occurred?"

General Hunt reigned in his anger, and deliberately replied, "Sir, I have watched my guns collapse entire structures and then have observed firing continuing from the basement floors of those same structures! The piling of rubble is making their positions impervious to my guns! I remind you sir, we have never attempted this sort of effort before!" Burnside then asked, "How do you suppose I am to get Infantry into the town to clear them out? I remind you that I have no near bridges to the town." The question gave Henry Hunt reason to pause. Lieutenant Comstock helpfully interjected, "Gentlemen, I still have nearly a dozen pontoon boats that have yet to be used on the bridges!" The idea became clear in Henry Hunt's mind at that moment. Looking to Burnside he offered, "General we could ferry Infantry across the Rappahannock and clear the Rebels from the waterfront!" General Burnside thought about it and replied, "That too would be suicide! I could never order someone to do that! If we are to embark on such a mad idea, then I must insist on volunteers."

General Hunt was amazed by his commanders lack of drive. He quietly asked, "Who has the closest Brigade to the crossing?" Brigadier General Parke, Burnside's Chief of Staff, quickly responded. "That would be Oliver Howard's Division. They are camped all about us here. I do believe Colonel Hall has his men closest to the river." Hunt's eyes lit up, "Would that be Colonel Norman J. Hall, late of the 7th Michigan?" General Parke nodded, "He just assumed the Brigade Command he passed the 7th over to his Adjutant, Lieutenant Colonel Baxter."

The revelation gave Henry Hunt an idea. Hall had originally received his commission in the First Regiment of Artillery when the war had begun. Hall had witnessed that beginning at Fort Sumpter, where he served under Anderson's command. Hunt remembered his dismay, upon hearing the news of Norman Hall accepting a volunteer commission as a Colonel of the 7th Michigan. The young officer had shown great promise as an artilleryman. Unfortunately for the artillery promotion was too slow, stymied by the rigid regimental structure of the United States Army's artillery arm. Hunt turned and started out of the tent to find his horse. General Burnside, disturbed, called out, "General Hunt! Wait! Where are you off to?" Hunt called back, without turning, "I am off to find some Infantry to volunteer to cross the river!" To General Burnside's additional dismay, Lieutenant Comstock rushed out behind him.

Colonel Norman Hall shouted out the order to fire as his subordinate Regimental commanders had closed their interval, reloaded, and made ready with their muskets. With a great roar, the muskets of the 7th Michigan and the 19th New York Infantry delivered a hail of minie balls into the lower floors of the buildings across the river. Hall noted that the Rebels continued to fire on the bridge, despite the nearly constant impacts of solid shot and exploding shell into the buildings. His only hope, at the moment, was to continue delivering heavy volleys into the rubble to discourage their firing. Hall had earlier discussed the situation with the grimy Major of Engineers, who was charged with the right wing bridge. He reported the loss of 20 of his skilled men and two of his officers. The situation was beginning to look hopeless.

As his regiments reloaded, Hall watched, frustrated, as puffs of rifle smoke emerged again from the houses and stores along the river front. Splashes in the river marked the strikes of the minie bullets. The Rebel marksmen, having no Engineers to shoot at, were focusing on the Pontoon boats. They apparently hoped to sink them. Their constant sniping was suddenly answered by the heavy boom of a cannon, low and off to his right. As Hall watched, a solid shot suddenly made a larger hole in a wall that one of the puffs of gun smoke had eminated. He then saw several men clad in gray, run out of the building and enter another. Turning to his Sergeant Major, he asked, "Who's artillery is that off to our right?" Sergeant Major Jennings paused from his scruitiny of the 19th New York in closing their ranks, shouted back, "Sir, I presume it is the Horse Artillery with General Pleasanton!" Hall nodded and shouted back, "Send a runner to them! Tell them to keep up the good work!"

As he commanded the Brigade to fire another volley, he was hailed by Lieutenant Abbot, "Sir! General Hunt and Lieutenant Comstock from General Burnside's headquarters desire a word with you." Hall, hearing Hunt's name, smiled and replied, "Very well then! Lead me to them." Abbot replied, "Sir, with all the firing going on, I strongly suggest we go on foot! They are currently talking to Major Spaulding by the bridge!" As Hall followed his adjutant, he distinctly became aware that they were targets. Three times he heard the angry singing whizz of near misses as he ran crouched behind his Lieutenant. They found General Hunt huddling with Major Spaulding behind a stack of Chess planks. They consulted, crouched together, as heavy lead bullets smacked into the timbers. The low boom of the Horse Artillery guns puntuated the discussion from time to time.

General Hunt had little time for greetings, and spoke with urgency, "Norman, I am seeking volunteers from your regiment to cross the river in Major Spaulding's pontoon boats! Can your Michigan boys find the courage to do this?" Hall nodded, he would do almost anything for Hunt. Hunt then explained, "Colonel, my artillery is accomplishing nothing to further General Burnside's plan! I believe that only a concerted effort by Infantry can clear the far bank to enable the completion of the bridges. I can continue my general bombardment up until the moment you cross, then I will have to cease firing! Hall, again nodded and replied, "Sir, you have one battery off to our right and down by the river that is doing good work. I will assemble my men as you ask, but I would be more comfortable if they continued their fire as we cross!" Hunt gave a puzzled look, "What battery is that? All my guns are on the Stafford Heights." Hall flinched as a minie ball grazed the top of the timbers and whirred overhead, "Sir, I have been informed that it is the horse artillery attached to General Pleasanton!" Hunt nodded with a knowing look, "I'll see to it Colonel!" As he rose into a low crouch, preparing to leave, he looked to Spaulding and directed, "Major, assemble your boat crews and boats! Norman, God speed to you and your men! Get as much of your brigade across as you can!"

Bidding farewell to Lieutenant Comstock, who had elected to assist with the assembling of the boats and oarsmen, General Hunt ran in a crouch back up to the intersection where Sergeant Major O'Keefe waited with his orderly and the horses. Mounting his gelding, Hunt remarked, "Let's ride up-river to General Pleasanton's camp. He is firing the Horse Artillery guns from his position to some good effect. We shall need to find out who it is and get them coordinated with our plan!" Sergeant Major O'Keefe pointed to the star over his chevrons and crowed, "Sir, I'll be bettin' you this star that it is Lieutenant Pennington and the old company! They hates sitting out a fight!"

The two men rode down the sheltered ferry landing road that led to the hollow where General Pleasanton had been assigned to picket his cavalry brigade and the horse artillery. The loud boom of a cannon, with the unmistakeable throaty roar of a 12 pounder, drew General Hunt in. The crackle of musketry then emerged, following the sound of the cannon. Rounding a corner that was sheltered by bare Willow trees, General Hunt could see two guns amidst more Willows on a small knoll. Greasy, muddy tracks up the steep bank of the knoll, indicated the struggle the men had endured to pull the guns up. Despite the warmth of the air, the ground remained a muddy and soggy mess from the melted snow.

General Hunt was astonished by what he beheld. Artillerymen, employing the break open Smith carbines, were fighting as infantry amongst the thick brush on the east bank of the Rappahannock, while a section of guns engaged Rebel positions, singularly, across the river. While shocking to General Hunt with it's lack of doctrinal precedent, it did appear to be gradually pushing the Rebel marksmen out of their positions. Hunt and Sergeant Major O'Keefe found Lieutenant Pennington busily pointing out targets for his ad hoc infantry. The artillerymen were soon joined by a small detachment of Pennsylvania cavalrymen who had become bored and wanted to join in. Pennington quickly found them a spot and explained the concept. General Hunt pulled him aside, and directed, "Lieutenant! In a few moments, a Regiment being led by a good friend of mine will be ferrying his men across the river in the engineer's pontoon boats!" Hunt paused as a particularly intense volley was fired, before continuing, "Their Colonel has requested that you provide them with support as they cross! It is beyond me where you developed these tactics, but by God they are working! Continue your firing until they arrive at the far bank! You are only to employ shot, once they are upon the water!" Lieutenant Pennington quickly nodded, and promised, "I shall see them across, Sir! I will not let the 2nd Regiment down!"

Sergeant Major O'Keefe stared in wonder at the section of guns on the small wooded knoll. He appreciated the effort that had been made to occupy the difficult position, employing only man-power. He could see First Sergeant Timmonds closely instructing the crews and the gunners, often correcting their aim and closely observing his effects. The firing was deliberate and effective, and the men were non-plussed by the constant musket fire directed at them. O'Keefe proudly remarked, "That there, General, is a fookin' thing o' beauty there! That boy there didn't know shit, when I first laid eyes on him! Look at them go!"

Henry Hunt nodded, pausing only momentarily before sternly ordering, "Come! We have to get back up on the heights. The batteries on top have no idea what we are up to!"

Private Orr stared transfixed at Corporal Gaines. His corporal had decided to take a turn at the loophole, and had no sooner fired, when the wall collapsed in a great mass, by something large and fast. Only Gaines' face and shoulders were visible in the dust and the piled bricks. His eyes stared darkly into nothing and he worked his mouth in breathless gasps, like a freshly caught fish. Orr could only stare, not knowing what to do. Around him, he could hear curses and shouts in the dusty basement. Feeling a firm hand on his sleeve; a strong hand that pulled him towards the door, he heard Sergeant Cobb's deep voice, "Come on boy, he's dead! It's time we skedaddled!"

Cobb wanted to do something about the Yankee guns off to his left. This was the third basement he had been shot out of. The Yankee bastards were waiting on the smoke of his sharpshooters and engaging them singly. He thought to himself, "It were'nt sportin! It was plum murder!" The next house they entered was filled with protesting men from another company. Their Lieutenant was ordering the men not to fire out of the loopholes. He ordered them to wait for more activity on the bridge.

Suddenly an unknown voice from one of the men watching at a loophole shouted out, "Sergeant! They're putting men in boats! Lots of them are getting into them boats!" Sergeant Gaines glanced at the Lieutenant. The young officer nodded and commanded, "Boys! Lets spread out a bit! Get some men into the upper floors here and into the other houses up the street! Don't shoot until they are halfway across!" The Lieutenant then pulled on the shell jacket of another of his privates, and ordered,

"Ellington! Go find the Captain! Tell him they are sending infantry across in the bridge boats! Be quick about gettin' back!" The young man nodded, and smiled, "No worries Lieutenant, I'll get back real quick like!"

The report of the Private was promptly relayed by the Captain to his Regimental Commander. Colonel Luse, commanding the hopelessly scattered men, rose from his protected basement and made a hazardous trot on foot up Caroline Street to General Barksdale's command post.

Luse grinned, as he noted that the General had moved his table into a side alley. The previous location was now a pile of tumbled bricks. Barksdale looked up as Luse arrived. His uniform and face was dirty, but he was clearly pleased, "Well Colonel! Good to see you ain't buried yet!" Luse smiled broadly, "Sir, I suspect I lead a charmed life! Begging your pardon sir! My men are reporting sightings of Yankees loading infantry into their bridging boats, near where I have the 17th Mississippi! I got two Yankee guns across the river at eye level! Their fires are accurate sir! They are driving the boys from their cover each time we fire!" They were interrupted by the shouts of men around the corner on Caroline Street, followed by the loud crack of an exploding shell. General Barksdale nodded, "Colonel look here." Barksdale pointed to his map, which Luse noted was a real estate platt map, obviously borrowed from the Assessor. The general had marked up unit locations with a pencil. "I am little surprised that they are using their guns close like that. General McLaws is trying to get Pemberton to shift some of the guns to help us, but it looks like General Lee may pull us out of the city! Hell! I could hold them off for days, but he don't want to totally destroy the town." Barksdale then quickly pointed out intersections with his finger, "Get your boys back off of Sophia Street and get them into the houses so they can fire down Hawke Street and Caroline Street. I will direct the other Regiments to do likewise! I want to tangle them Yankees up in town here for as long as they will let me!" Colonel Luse nodded, "Sir, we will need to move them quickly! I expect them to quit their artillery as soon as they start to make the crossing." Barksdale gave Luse a hearty slap on the shoulder, creating a small cloud of brick dust, "Very well! God Speed Colonel! Be sure to make them pay for every cobblestone!"

Private Eliza Fanning presented his Springfield musket to the First Sergeant to have it "rung" by the senior Sergeant's inspection rod as he filed with the rest of the Company into the 30 foot bridge boat. First Sergeant Virgil

Banks, repetively droned the instruction, "Step up boys, make sure your muskets are unloaded!" Slamming the ramrod into Private Fanning's barrel the steel rod bounced with a ringing noise and the First Sergeant rapidly caught it and extracted it, shouting, "No loaded rifles! You'll play hell clearing a wet charge! Step lively boys!" Fanning peered through the mist of gun smoke that blanketed the river. The musket fire from the far side had tapered off, but the pounding of artillery filled the air with thunder. The men were very nervous about the prospect of rowing the wooden boats towards the Rebel held far bank of the Rappahannock. The officers were shouting commands as the men of the 7th Michigan loaded into the ten pontoon boats, "You men on the sides will use your musket butts as oars! The engineers do not have enough oarsmen!"

Colonel Hall intercepted a young drummer boy, who was attempting to follow the first company into the boats. He gently led the tow headed youngster back to cover, "You shall cross when I do, son! We shall need every rifle at first!" Hall then found Lieutenant Colonel Baxter at the loading site, "Henry! Make sure Spaulding gives you enough oarsmen for the returning of the boats! If you lose an oarsman, you will need to insure your Captains understand that we have to speedily return the empty boats to pick up the following companies! They will have to detail men to replace the oarsmen, if you take fire." An errant friendly shell burst over the river, causing both men to hunch over. The crack of the explosion was ear-splittingly loud and the fragments of the projectile kicked up splashes of water on the surface of the river. Colonel Baxter shouted back, "Sir, I trust they know to stop firing once we start!" Hall smiled and shouted back, "No worries Henry! You'll only have to worry about the Rebel artillery by then! Make sure you get across no later than the first couple of companies! I cannot advise you on what to do, I recall no instruction on how to fight in a city!" Baxter nodded, and added, "Well Sir, if the good Lord spares me, I shall be happy to author such a text!" Hall turned serious and shouted back over the intensifying thunder of General Hunt's bombardment, "Drive them back from that bridging site, Colonel! I will bring the 19th and the 20th Regiments across the bridge to reinforce you the instant we get the damned thing finished! Take good care Henry!" Lieutenant Colonel Baxter smartly came erect and saluted his Brigade Commander. He then turned and strode to the rivers edge to watch the departure of the first boats.

Private Fanning struggled to stand as several of the men in the back shoved the boat towards the far bank. An engineer near the front shouted out, "Point her towards upstream! Row like hell boys!" The four engineers that manned the boat had proper oars, while the soldiers standing near the gunwales only had their musket butts. Eliza dipped his rifle butt into the water and attempted to assist, but the resistance he felt in the water was light and seemed meaningless. Glancing up, he could see the silent buildings across the river. The smoke drifted through the empty streets like an uneven fog. A loud boom from behind them, and off to their right, was immediately followed by a high pitched whizz over their heads. Fanning could see a large hole made by the impact of the solid projectile in a brick house, across from them. The men in the middle of the boat tried to move towards the side to help row, but there was no room. Fanning noted, through sweat stung eyes, that they were nearly halfway across. The exertion of rowing was soaking his undershirt, under the hot woolen sack coat. The Engineer called out, "Keep rowin' boys! Row like hell!"

Fanning looked back up at the structures, only to note multiple puffs of new smoke emerging from various windows of all floors of the buildings. With angrily high pitched buzzing noises, the carefully aimed minie balls smacked into the men packed into the first four boats on the river. Fanning heard a man cry out, forward of him. The falling man caused a mighty jostle amongst the closely packed standing men. He saw in the corner of his eye, a man in an adjacent boat drop his rifle into the water, before falling out of the boat, as if to follow it. Shouts of "Row! Row men!" emerged from the boats. Two more booms reverberated across the river as the cannon from the friendly side punched two more solid shot into select houses. The number and locations of the puffs of smoke from the distant houses seemed to increase on the far side. Some of the rounds hit the water throwing up tall splashes of river water. Other bullets struck the wooden hull of the boat, sending a slight shock through the heavy craft. A spray of warm wet liquid struck Private Fanning. He had no time to wipe his face as he rowed. The sweat rolling off his face, mixed with the fluid and ran down to his lips. The tinny taste told him it was blood. He hunched over and pushed the ineffective musket butt through the water. He rowed like a man possessed.

The far side seemed to take forever to reach as more gun fire punctuated the grunts of the straining men. Soon, booms from further off could be heard, followed by large columns of water that flew into the air around the boats. The Rebel artillery had begun to fire upon them. After the first series of booms, the entire sky around them erupted in thunder as the artillery on Stafford Heights fired at the far off batteries. Eliza felt the boat slow with a grating slide as they beached on the far side. The men jostled one another in a desperate bid to abandon the boat and find cover to tend to their muskets. Two men ahead of Eliza ran with the end of a rope and tied it off to an overturned wagon on the landing. After he jumped out of the boat himself, he could hear his Lieutenant shouting for the men to clear their muskets. Private Fanning hunched behind the overturned wagon with several other men. He clumsily dug open his cap pouch and capped his musket. Pointing it to the ground he cocked the hammer and pulled the trigger. The muffled hollow pop, indicated a clear channel. Beyond their cover the volume of Rebel musket fire aimed at them, seemed to increase. As he looked up, he could see the boats nearly halfway across as the engineers quickly rowed the lighter craft back to the rest of the Regiment. Cries of "Load!" echoed along the waterfront as the men, huddling behind whatever cover they could find, found their cartridges and loaded their weapons. A voice Fanning could not recognize, directed, "Fire at the windows boys! Fire as fast as you can load!"

To Private Fanning, it felt exhilarating to be giving it back to his enemies after the helpless terror of the river crossing. He loaded and fired as fast as he could from behind the ruined hulk of the wagon. Each stout shove of his rifle was a comforting feel. As he loaded his fifth round, he noted that more boats were coming. Each was full of blue clad men. A rumbling noise from beyond the town was marked with more heavy splashes among the approaching boats.

The next lift of boats carried his Company commander, Captain Thomas, and the remaining half of the 157 men that made up Company B of the 7th Michigan. With his Colt revolver drawn, he shouted out to the men huddled behind their various points of cover, "Stand up boys! Fix bayonets and move off this landing! Move! Move at the double quick!" Many of the men paused, still knee deep in the river, to follow his commands. Private Fanning fumbled to find the sharp burnished weapon and extracted it from its scabbard to affix to his musket. He then ran as fast as he could towards the first brick wall he could find on the far side of Sophia Street. He was vaguely aware of several near misses as they struck the cobblestones near his feet.

As the additional men climbed up the river bank, Captain Thomas urgently directed them to spread out and find cover. The volume of fire from the Rebels in the houses above them had intensified and several men fell, hit as they climbed out of the water. Thomas studied the scene. One small group of men had taken cover behind a small mound of dirt and were firing their rifles while laying behind the cover at windows of a house on a side street. Many had reached the wall and stood with their backs to the bricks, holding their muskets nervously and unsure of what to do. Spying Lieutenant Collins, Captain Thomas called out, "Collins! Find the other Lieutenants and come to me!" He then turned to his men cowering along the wall, and

directed, "Fix bayonets men! Gather with your messmates and your Sergeants! If you can't find them, then try to!" The men, suddenly having achievable directions, began to leave their fear behind and searched to find their friends and rearrange their positions. Captain Thomas sprinted from group to group, repeating the instructions. He noticed that the Rebels were firing at the next group of boats making their way across. New soldiers in this tight location would pile them up hopelessly. He had to begin taking houses from the Rebels.

As his Lieutenants assembled, Captain Thomas hastily instructed them, "Gentlemen, here is my plan, listen close! We need to take this first row of houses and stores along this street from the Secesh! Break your men down into messes with their Sergeants! They all know each other, therefore, they should be able to work together better. Take each floor with the bayonet! Remember how they shot at you when you were helpless in the boats!" The young officers quickly nodded, as he continued, "Save the cartridges for engaging the Rebels in the adjacent buildings! I also do not want the men shooting one another in the close quarters of the dwellings. Let us take this first row of houses on this street!" Captain Thomas then assigned two structures to each Lieutenant and then sent them on their way.

Private Fanning and his messmates were quickly huddled by Lieutenant Alston and given their instructions. Sergeant Watkins returned to the gathering after making a hazardous reconnaissance to find the nearest door to the basement of the store that they sheltered behind. He breathlessly informed his Lieutenant, "Sir, there is a door behind us on the left side of the basement! You will need to get the other messes to fire at the house that overlooks the alley! They nearly got me! They look to be on the second floor." The Lieutenant nodded and assured him, "Very well, I will get Sergeant Collins to have his men fire at them as you move towards the door. Shout out to us once you have the basement floor!"

Following Sergeant Watkins' instructions, the five men of his mess stood along the back wall nervously holding their bayoneted muskets. Once the Lieutenant had Collins' mess firing, they rushed to the door. Sergeant Watkins gave the wooden door a great kick and it crashed open. He shouted to his mess, "Get after them boys! Show them the bayonet!" Private Fanning followed his messmates into the dark ground floor. There was much shouting and from the upstairs stairwell a musket shot filled the cellar with a deafening boom and dense smoke. Confused, Private Fanning tried to point his bayonet into a direction that would not impale his messmates in front of him. The men in front of him began to shout and there appeared to be a struggle. He saw Private Lindstrom make a sudden sharp motion with his musket and a blood curdling scream filled the cellar. Another shot emerged from the dark off to Fanning's right and he instinctively jabbed in the direction of the orange flame as hard as he could with his bayonet. He felt it strike something that gave and he could feel the blade entering something as another loud scream emerged. Pulling his rifle back, there was suddenly shouting all around them. The voices called out, "We've had enough! Boys don't shoot us! We'll give up!" He realized what the officers were always saying about the application of cold steel. Few men could bear the prospect of being bayonetted. Sergeant Watkins found the boards that held the stout cellar shutters and pushed open the shutters flooding the dark basement with light.

To their surprise there were nearly a dozen Rebels in the basement, holding their hands up. Watkins, thinking fast, ordered, "March them out behind the building and hand them over to the Lieutenant!" He then shouted out one of the open windows, "Lieutenant, We got prisoners coming out! Tell the next mess we got the cellar!"

All up and down Sophia Street, the men of the 7th Michigan cleared the first row of houses and stores, floor by floor. Some of the Mississippi troops fought stubbornly for each level and each corner of the street. In other places, they surrendered when they realized their enemy was coming at them silently with cold steel. After an hour, Captain Thomas realized he had nearly thirty prisoners under guard at the shelter of the landing. The remainder of the 7th was assembling on Sophia Street and occupying the houses that marked the toehold of the far side bridgehead. The increased firepower of the Regiment's muskets reduced the volume of fire aimed at the bridge. After a short visit to several of the houses where his troops were firing from windows on every floor, Colonel Baxter decided to release the boats back to the engineers.

Major Spaulding received the news as the fourth lift of boats returned back across the river. Finding Captain Brainerd, who now had his arm bandaged, he directed, "Captain get the crews back up and organized. Start placing the bateaux as soon as the crews recover them! We have a bridge to complete!"

Lieutenant Compton came to visit as the crews began to pole the returning boats out to the end of the bridge to begin installation of the next bay. Compton sought out Major Spaulding and issued a terse instruction from General Burnside, "Sir, you must make haste! The army needs to cross." Spaulding gave him a weary nod, "Lieutenant, I trust this day will be remembered by the Army as it crosses. I hope you shall also remember what it takes to perform such engineering when you develop your next plan!" Spaulding wordlessly walked away from General Burnside's staff officer and began to talk to and encourage the busy men. Their progress was slow and balky at first as some were promoted by death into new responsibilities. A half hour into the resumption of throwing the bridge, they suddenly gained their rhythm and the bays were completed in faster, and faster fashion. Musket fire punctuated the far side as the isolated soldiers of the 7th Michigan fought from house to house along the riverfront. Spaulding quietly watched as the stack of chess planks dwindled down to the spares and he heard Captain Brainerd call out, "Sir, we have a landing!" Spaulding looked towards Sergeant Ellerson on his side of the river and cried out, "Sergeant! Send the Abutment crew across at the double quick! I will notify the Infantry." Spaulding then turned to find Colonel Hall. He found him nearby as he was giving orders to the other Regiments of his Brigade, "Sir, you have your bridge, you may put your men across! We have some refinements to make, but we can work around your men!" Norman Hall gave a serious and solemn nod; Major Spaulding could see his worry over his isolated Regiment. The Massachusetts Regiment led the column of men that formed into column of fours with shouldered muskets behind their Colonel. The young drummer began to beat the march, but he was silenced at the abutment by Sergeant Ellerson as he shouted out, "No drumming! Go to Route Step and go slow! The damned bridge ain't so tight or proper yet!"

Spaulding watched as the blue clad men carefully crossed the bobbing and shaky bridge. He could see the need for much tightening and refinement, and it looked like one of the Bateaus was taking on water. Looking east, he could see the second bridge beside them was two thirds complete as the men there hustled to complete the second span. The increasing crescendo of musketry attracted his attention. Looking up, he could see the Massachusetts men running up the alleys that led into the town. The streets were full of smoke. He realized that a significant force still held the town.

As he beheld the chaotic scene, he was interrupted by Captain Brainerd, "Sir! Come quick!" Major Spaulding, becoming annoyed, asked, "What is it?" Captain Brainerd blurted out, "We found Sergeant Adams, Sir! Please follow me."

Mystified, Major Spaulding hurried down the bridge behind his Captain. He noted men working on the loose lashings and tightening the anchor lines to steady the bobbing bridge. "We found him here, Sir!" Brainerd pointed towards the bow of the last boat, marking the bay where they had been forced to stop because of the Rebel firing. Spaulding looked, and was shocked by the sight of his trusted and oldest engineer. The Sergeant had been hit multiple times by minie bullets. One arm he had obviously bandaged himself, the other strikes were in places he could not attend to. Major Spaulding noted multiple pegs driven into bullet holes in the bateau. As he studied the horrifying scene, he realized that Adams, his Mexican War veteran had remained behind, to repair holes in this, the last Bateau of the last bay, until a shot to the head had stopped him. The hammer from the plug kit was still clutched in his hand. Spaulding, wiped his eyes his exhaustion made him maudlin, "Captain, it is men like this. Men like this, will insure that we win. It is the heart of our soldiers! What you see here, Captain, tells me that we shall prevail! See to him, please. Get him out of this boat! I want him returned to his family! I will pay for it!"

Colonel Luse, his pistol drawn, decided to peek around the corner down Caroline Street to catch a glance at the landing area where Platte Street intersected Caroline Street. Poking his head around for a second, he noted many blue clad men forming on the landing from the bridge. Suddenly he heard shouting and muskets firing. A blinding cloud emerged from the brick wall, inches from his exposed face. He rapidly ducked back, spitting the red brick dust out of his mouth and rubbing his eyes with his free hand. His adjutant, standing beside him, calmly observed, "You should'a let me look boss. It won't be right or proper you getting' yerself shot, today!" Luse smiled, and replied, all business, "Major, put our companies in the cross alleys off Caroline Street! Have them load their muskets and wait. Each time they form troops in the street, I will order one company to rush to form a line of battle. Your men shall greet them with a volley! Insure the Captains understand they need not make a stand! Deliver a volley and retreat back to cover. When they pass their respective alleyways, then have them deliver a volley into the flank and leapfrog back towards the rail line. We can make their day a living hell. Keep details of men in the upper floors all along this street. Tell them to shoot officers if they can!" Major Frazier nodded, "Sir, begging your pardon, I will get going. They are scattered all about and I shall need some time to find the Captains!"

Colonel Luse wiped his eyes with his hand again after he poured some water on his hand with his canteen. The brick dust stung and irritated his eyes. Turning, he walked back uphill towards the next street. On his way, he heard a tapping above his head. Looking up he saw a white haired woman at the first floor window of the house he had sheltered behind. Once she had made eye contact, she opened the window, "Young Man! Are the Yankees here now?" Colonel Luse exclaimed, "Ma'am, why have you not evacuated as ordered?" Elliot Lacy shot back, without pause, "Young Man, I am an old woman with nowhere to evacuate to!" Luce grinned and replied, "Ma'am, you are likely to become an old deceased woman if you do not seek shelter in your cellar! We are fighting house to house and the street is filling with Yankees, scarcely four blocks down the street! This is no place for a lady!"

Elliot Lacy smiled back and rather inappropriately offered, "Young man, would you like some soup? It has the breast of my last chicken in it!" Luse tipped his dusty hat, mustering the last of his civility, "Ma'am, while tempting, I have no time for your offer. Perhaps you could take it to the doctors at the Tobacco Warehouse. I am most certain they have hungry men there and the hospital will be the safest place in this town!" As he watched his suggestion register on her face, he decided to add, "Just insure you go out of your back door Ma'am! Nothing will survive a trip down Caroline Street at the moment!"

Elliot Lacy nodded; the firing and the increasing sound of musketry had made her nervous. Henri and Lottie were also at the hospital and she would be most grateful for some company. Turning to Eliza, who had become petrified by the battle, she instructed, "Eliza, please be a dear and pour the soup in my old white tureen. We shall carry it in the potato basket to the Hospital! Put what is left of the cornbread in there as well. It is poor food but it will have to do. As the man said, we shall have to use the alley out back to get there!" Eliza nodded and busied herself with arranging the meal in the wicker basket as Elliot Lacy found her shawl and bonnet. She paused and considered locking the door, but she reasoned the Yankees would only break through a locked door. There was no sense in having it damaged. She sighed and imagined she would be lucky to be left with a stick in the house, if a battle was to be fought here.

Leaving by the back door, Elliot and Eliza cautiously made their way out the back garden gate. They paused in the alleyway as a loud clatter of musketry erupted down the street, towards the river. Elliot listened to the shouts of men as the battle grew and grew. Inwardly she felt sad as she knew every noise she heard meant more death and suffering. Turning to Eliza, she urged, "Come now child, we must reach the safety of the hospital! We can go behind the Assessor's Office on this alley and reach the corner where the warehouse is!" Elliot was thankful that the horrible cannonading had ceased. While the sounds of battle were horrifying, it was nothing compared to the terror of the plunging shells that never had seemed to stop. As they rounded the corner of the city offices, they proceeded down the street that led to the Tobacco Warehouse. Elliot thought it odd that the street seemed dusty and hazy, although no traffic was moving. As they approached the corner where the Old Richmond Stage road led to the railroad bridge, a soldier at the hospital began to shout out to her. At first, Eliot could not hear what he was saying, but as she drew closer, she could hear his shouts, "Ma'am! Stay where you are! It is certain death to venture into Caroline Street!"

Elliot could see what he meant as several minie balls kicked up puffs of dust amid the cobblestone street as errant rounds ricocheted from the exchange of fire further downtown. The soldier peered out as the defending Rebel troops poured another volley into the advancing Federal troops. Motioning quickly, he urged the women to cross. He called out, "Hurry Ma'am! It is only safe to cross when our boys are shooting!" As Elliot and Eliza entered the large wagon bay of the warehouse and her eyes adjusted to the dim light, she beheld a piteous sight. Scores of wounded men lay in rows on piles of straw along the rough wooden walls of the warehouse. The soldier doffed his hat, and addressed them, "Ladies we are grateful for the help, we have too many wounded to properly attend to. The surgeons are fast at it and it is everything we can do to get the wounded off the street! We got wounded in the houses as well, but we have no way to reach them." Elliot, shocked by the condition of the men, blurted out, "My, my, Son! We must see to these boys! Eliza, put the soup down and find me some water and some cloth!" Elliot began to work her way along the lines of the wounded men. Many seemed greatly relieved to receive a cold cloth on the brow and to hear a kind word.

The courier leapt from his horse and announced to Brigadier General Parke, "Sir the bridges are all up and complete! Colonel Hall begs to report that his Brigade has control of the riverfront! He asks for direct and prompt reinforcement to seize Fredericksburg!" Parke held his hand up to silence the man, asking, "Son, do you have a written message? I should like to provide General Burnside something digestible, rather than a shouted report!" The young man, chastened, reached into his leather satchel and produced the written message from Colonel Hall. Parke took the message, and chided the courier, "Son, this is an Army headquarters, there is a certain propriety expected at this level! Please try to remember that, we have nearly 100,000 troops at play here." Parke took the folded message and ducked back under the canvas flap of the tent to deliver the dispatch to his commander.

As he arrived, General Burnside looked up and asked, "The bridges?" Parke replied, "Yes sir! All of them are in. The moment you have desired has arrived! Shall I cut orders for the Grand Divisions to proceed?" Burnside thought a moment, and replied, "I should prefer to visit with each before I compel them to break camp, General. There is much coordination I wish to communicate before they proceed. Please standby until I accomplish that task. The deception still is the direct thrust through Fredericksburg, and I cannot accomplish that until I have that town!" Parke nodded, "Sir, I understand, shall I arrange your orderlies and escorts?" General Burnside nodded, "Yes, the sooner the better. I shall need to consult with the Grand Divisions! Assemble them and prepare them to move at my order!"

Brigadier General Parke summoned his Aide de Camp and directed the alert of the General's entourage, they were to be ordered to move at a moments notice. The young Captain saluted and rushed to deliver his message. General Park's mind reeled. There was so much for him to do. He mentally reflected on the day's requirements. There were ration requisitions to complete and the Navy situation required an update, the General had asked for an update on the progress of the gunboats, currently down the Rappahannock. The issue of when to send the Provost across into Fredericksburg, along with these other concerns, were lodged in his consciousness. All these factors remained without firm guidance. General Burnside seemed to be a man who required prodding to prioritize what came first. The desire to visit the commanders of the Grand Divisions only promised to conspire to generate more delay. He resolved to catch up and write a few more dispatches to the Quartermaster and the Ordnance Bureau while he waited on the reports of readiness of the escort guard. General Burnside remained quiet and asked for no further information, and for that, Parke was pleased. All priorities would change, if he ventured to ask. A young Captain arrived and announced that the escort was prepared to move. General Burnside nodded and pulled on his greatcoat. Turning to Brigadier General Parke, he announced, "I shall see you later tonight, General! We shall create our movement orders then."

General Burnside started off in the direction of General Franklin's Headquarters; he was determined to meet with each of his Grand Division commanders before the evening was done. Burnside reflected on the elements of his plan as he rode into the increasing chill of the late afternoon. For his plan to work, he needed to be able to strike nearly simultaneously across the entire front. He had no idea that it would not be until late in evening until he would return to his headquarters.

Colonel Hall motioned with his hands as he discussed the situation across the river with Lieutenant Pennington and First Sergeant Timmonds. The ad hoc meeting had materialized as Hall had traveled over to visit Company M, after the Michigan troops had crossed. Joshua noted that the General was effusive in his praise of their work. Now they wanted more. Joshua remembered O'Keefe's grumbling in regards to infantry commands misusing artillery, but Hall was an artilleryman. His credibility in this regard trapped Lieutenant Pennington within his proposal.

"Can you pull a section of guns across? We could use them as close support in the town!" Hall was emphatic that they could employ the guns as the army had at Chapultepec on the causeway. The mention of the location of one of O'Keefe's oft-repeated war stories gave Joshua pause. Turning to Lieutenant Pennington, he interjected, "Sir, pulling those guns behind the teams in narrow city streets seems mighty risky to me. There is no room to maneuver to unlimber or turn the teams! Nor is there any guarantee that the enemy isn't in every window above us!" Pennington was unmoved, "First Sergeant, you just witnessed the men employ prolongues to move the guns today! I see no reason why we cannot try this! Prepare Sergeant Page's section to cross the bridge! They will follow the 20th Massachusetts."

Joshua nodded, resigned, he replied, "Sir if it all the same, I should like to accompany the section with Lieutenant Woodruff, he still is a mite green."

After Lieutenant Pennington nodded his assent, Joshua mounted his horse and rode over to find Jim Page. He found Page and his men returning from the brushy riverbank with their carbines. The men were animated by their experience as amateur infantry. Joshua stopped a few feet from Sergeant Page and announced, "Jim, get your section teams assembled and limber up your guns! You are to be attached as a section to the Infantry crossing the river. You will provide close support to the fight in the town. Swap out your shot for canister with Sergeant Mills! I reckon that will be the only kind of ammunition you will need!"

The look on Page's face, impelled Joshua to continue, "I know Jim, that's why I am going over with you. I'll keep an eye on Lieutenant Woodruff for you. This is going to be interesting."

An hour later, four six-horse teams pulled the two guns and two caissons down to the River bank. Long files of the 20th Massachusetts Volunteer Infantry still clogged the two pontoon bridges. The engineers came over to their guns as they waited, and a grizzled Sergeant advised, "You boys need to walk them teams across! No one rides! The horses tend to get spooky as the bays sway and rock under the weight. Keep a tight hold on their reins, this here bridge is held together with rope and pegs. A panicked team can dump you in the river!" Joshua looked at Jim Page and noted his nervous swallow, "I'd worry on the town more than the bridge, Jim!" After half an hour had passed, the engineers finally motioned for the section of guns from Company M to approach the bridge. The grizzled and dirty sergeant shouted out, "Only one team on the bridge at a time! Take yer time boys!" Joshua watched as the first team drawing the gun and limber began to move slowly across the swaying structure. Joshua found it interesting to see how the deck sank slightly under the weight of the gun. He also noted that the horses were skittish and nervous about the unsteady footing of the bobbing and moving surface. He shouted out, "Keep a tight grip on the reins boys! Make them walk real steady like!"

Joshua then elected to cross, after the first gun and limber had crossed and struggled up the muddy far side abutment. He did not want to allow the infantry to detail off a single gun and crew. As he walked his mount across, the volume of musketry in the streets above him indicated a town very much in question. Walking the bridge, several large bloodstains on the sawn deck planks reminded him of the cost of this bridge. Looking up he could see large masses of men in blue collecting on the street along the river. They did not move or act with a purpose and he found that disturbing.

Riding up to the team, Joshua found Sergeant Page fully engaged with an Infantry Major from the Massachusetts Regiment. The officer was attempting to order up the single gun. Joshua swiftly interjected, "Sir, my orders are these guns are to operate as a section! I must insist that you wait on my Officer, Sir!" Joshua studied the very young officer, who was obviously the son of a rich and influential man in Massachusetts. The resistance offered caused his young face to pinch in anger, "You listen to me First Sergeant! I am a Field Grade officer and I shall brook no disrespect from an enlisted man! I shall direct this gun to support my men as I see fit!" Joshua stood his ground, "Major, this gun is under my control at the moment and it will go nowhere until the Lieutenant arrives! My orders are to report as a section to Lieutenant Colonel Baxter. Those orders sir, are from Colonel Hall!" The Major, now infuriated, pulled a small leather journal from his map case and demanded, "Your name and unit, First Sergeant! Provide me that, this instant!" Joshua glanced towards the river, the second gun was slowly being pulled across the bloodstained pontoon bridge, "It is First Sergeant Timmonds, Sir. Joshua Timmonds, Company M, 2nd United States Artillery, attached to Brigadier General Pleasanton's Cavalry Brigade." Joshua then glared at the young Major and spat, before continuing, "And this fookin' gun sits where she is until my Lieutenant arrives!" Behind them, the musketry reached another crescendo, as more and more units of Colonel Hall's brigade began to press up the alleyways and side streets of the smoldering town.

After much struggling and shouting by the drivers, the team pulled the second gun of the section up. They drew it up adjacent to gun number 1 on Sophia Street. The angry Major pulled Lieutenant Woodruff aside and the two exchanged words. Joshua resisted the urge to eavesdrop and turned his attention to Sergeant Page, "Jim, keep a close eye on where you get placed! They ain't got a hold on this town yet! Keep your number 6 and 7 with their carbines close by and loaded. If they put us in a street keep your eyes on the windows of the houses above us. They could be anywhere!"

Lieutenant Woodruff returned, he pulled Joshua off to the side, "First Sergeant, the Major wanted your name. He intends to put you on report for insubordination! I will get word back to Lieutenant Pennington, but we are to follow him for now and go where he directs! LTC Baxter was gravely wounded and that Major is the senior man now!" Joshua silently shook his head. After a pause, he remarked, "Hell sir, that young buck ain't 21 years old yet. Mind where he sends us, Sir. This ain't no place for artillery!"

After receiving their orders, the artillery men readied the teams under the watchful eyes of the Sergeants. The plan Lieutenant Woodruff had arrived at, was to follow the leading company of the 19th Massachusetts in order to unlimber the guns behind their line. Each time a company filled the street, the Rebels would emerge and deliver a volley before retreating to the cover of the alley they emerged from. From what Joshua could observe, the distances were only two blocks or so, distant. He realized that the teams and limbers would have to exit down an alley to the left of the guns, and stand ready to resupply from the left. It would be up to the gun crews to advance the guns, by hand, up the street. The entire plan was consumed by the madness of the moment. The infantry Major had hoped to greet the next Rebel foray into Caroline Street with canister, at point blank range.

It took much shouting between Lieutenant Woodruff and the Massachusetts Infantry Company commander to coordinate the movements of the trotting infantrymen with the two guns. Joshua was becoming concerned as he directed the guns to unlimber. Lieutenant Woodruff had to clear men from the alley to their left in order to turn the teams and the limbers off the street. As the gun crews marked their paces and loaded the guns with canister, Joshua could hear the odd whooping yell of Rebel infantry. Looking beyond his guns, and over the heads of the ranks of the 19th Massachusetts, he saw a mass of brownish and gray clad men pour out into the street from an intersection ahead. As they jostled and hurriedly formed ranks across Caroline Street, Captain Mays of the 19th Massachusetts, shouted, "Now men! Fall back behind the guns!" The Rebels in front of them raised their muskets as their commander shouted, "Ready!" Joshua warily watched as the Massachusetts men rushed past his two guns. Hopefully, they would be clear before it was too late. As the cobblestone street opened up with the parting of the blue clad soldiers, Lieutenant Woodruff shouted to the top of his voice, "Fire!" The two bronze guns roared as one and skidded throwing sparks from the trails as they violently recoiled back down the slick street. The road ahead was full of choking white smoke and the roar of the muzzle blast had been amplified by the structures on either side of Caroline Street. Joshua's ears rang uncomfortably as he realized another lesson, learned the hard way, from this new experience. Joshua urged his horse forward to see the effects of the canister. Peering through the thinning smoke, he could see clumps of prone bodies on the street ahead. The remaining Rebel troops had ducked back to the safety of the corner buildings.

Major Frazier recognized the roar of the guns as soon as he heard the reverberating boom, echoing through the streets. He exclaimed to his orderly, "Damn! The Yankees have cannon across!" He turned to the young Sergeant and directed, "Son, find the Company B Commander and send him to me. We have to deal with this new hazard!"

Frazier decided to risk a glance down Caroline street from his position on the Old Richmond Stage Road. After removing his slouch hat, he furtively peeked around the corner and could see two bronze guns in the distance, near the intersection of Caroline Street and Hawke Street. Resuming the comfort of cover, he reflected on this new development. While ingenious in it's short term impact, the placement of artillery in the midst of the town exposed the very weakness of artillery to his strength. Artillery needed room to maneuver and distance to exploit it's superior range. The Yankee commander across from him had committed a grave error. Frazier determined, then and there, that he would have those guns. They would make a wonderful gift to General McLaws. When Captain Harvey arrived, Major Frazier gave concise and curt orders, "Captain, take half of your force and occupy the second floor of the Dry Goods store and the Rectory of the Church. You should be able to see those guns on Caroline street. When their crews begin to ready them to fire, kill them! I will order Company C to conduct a counter attack behind them down Hawke Street. If they attempt to limber them, shoot the horses! In fact, I wish for you to shoot every horse you see around them guns!" Captain Harvey gave a sly grin, "Sir, it shall be an honor to do this! I do ask that you allow us to get back at that Federal Infantry, once we get this done!" Major Frazier bluntly replied, "Don't fret Captain, it looks as if we shall have all the infantry we can stand shortly. Now be off!" Frazier turned back to look down Caroline Street. As he peered around the corner, he could see more and more blue clad troops filling the street from the landing. He was filled with the unease of not knowing where they were flowing into the town. Soon they would have to leave the wounded in the hospital uncovered.

Joshua cautiously moved astride his horse up to the next intersection. The crews were behind him, moving the guns forward by hand, as Skirmishers from the 19th Massachusetts edged along the sidewalks. They had learned to look up and held their bayonetted rifles at the ready. Stopping at the corner, Joshua leaned forward to peer down the street to his right. Relieved he noted that this intersection was merely a blind alley ending in a rock wall. The alley was empty so he waved the guns ahead. As the sweating crews manhandled the heavy cannon forward, Joshua urged his horse to continue forward to cross the alley. As the crews with the guns and Joshua exposed themselves, the building above them and off to the right suddenly erupted in musket fire from the upper floor windows. Joshua looked up in the direction of the fire as several near misses passed near him with the angry high pitched whirr of the minie balls. One round hit the barrel of the closest gun, causing a bell like tone, as the bullet disintegrated against the bronze. Joshua heard cries of pain and became aware of a round hitting his mount near it's shoulder. Still looking at the building, he reached for his revolver. As he tugged at the strap of his holster, he felt a blinding jolt on his face below his right eye. Everything went white and then black. His last memory was the sensation of falling as his horse collapsed in the street. The blackness and nothingness was warm and comfortable. There was no sense of time, nor worry. He awoke briefly to hear shouting and the firing of many guns. He had a vague sensation of people running past him, over him. Then he drifted off again. After an unknown time, a jolting pain caused him to open his eyes. He was being carried by men. Nothing was familiar and he remembered the smell of body odor from unwashed and sweating men. He felt very cold and the light outside was dim. The firing hurt his ears, which still rung from the roar of the cannons in the street. His head throbbed and the jolting of the litter made the pain come back in waves. He tried to lift his head and the sudden pain brought back the blackness.

A stabbing pain brought him back again briefly; Joshua became aware of being inside. The room smelled strongly of tobacco, reminding him of the smells of home. He was aware of lantern light and he could hear a removed voice, "It is quite remarkable really, almost no damage. While lethargic, the patient appears to awaken from time to time. Watch closely as I demonstrate the path of the projectile." A piercing penetrating pain brought the darkness back. The weariness of the past weeks overcame him and he dissolved into a deep and dreamless sleep.

Melvin Nicholson, of McComb Mississippi, did not admire his new detail much. While fighting Yankees was bad enough, working for doctors as a litter man was worse. Everyone expected you to just get right out there and pick up wounded men, regardless of what else was going on. He had learned on his first two trips that the Yankees down the street shot at everything that moved, regardless of whatever mission of "Mercy" he was up to. Now, to add insult to injury, they had a doctor with them. The officer, who had introduced himself as "Captain Tinchant" was insistent on them finding Yankee wounded. To Nicholson, this made little sense. The Yankees had armies of doctors and money for fine hospitals. Most of the time, it was best to leave them to their own. Little did he realize that they were already technically behind enemy lines.

The Captain peered out into the street from the corner of the building that they sheltered behind. He said, "Down there by the cannon in the street are some soldiers down in blue uniforms! Follow me boys! We are bound to find some there." Nicholson swore under his breath as he tightened his grip on the litter and readied to rise to follow the Captain. Each step onto Caroline Street was an invitation to hell; the Yankees kept sending more troops across the bridges, and the fight now spread all over the town. No one knew who controlled what, anymore. Rushing forward, they found two wounded men amongst the Yankees in the street; one was a First Sergeant and the other a Private. The Private looked poorly, but the Captain insisted that he could be saved, so they loaded him aboard the litter and took him back to the Tobacco Warehouse. Nicholson envied the litter men ahead of him, they were now headed back to safety.

They knelt as Doctor Tinchant checked the prone bodies for signs of life. The street was eerily quiet for a moment as they nervously waited for his next signal to move. Nicholson peered behind for a moment. He could see the afternoon sky beyond the structures of the street, the day was warming, and puffy clouds filled the sky. He tried not to look at the ghastly wounds of the dead. Sometimes it was hard not to, as the streets were covered with gore. Dead men lay in gardens, by stoops and splayed out on the street. Hunger struck him as he had no breakfast. Private Nicholson reached into his tarred haversack and to his disappointment there was nothing there.

The haversack usually had a mystical quality of holding at least one last hard biscuit, but no longer. The idea struck him as he looked at the body of a Yankee infantryman laying on the sidewalk near him. He tried not to look at the man's shattered head as he reached into his haversack. His searching hand closed on several hard crackers and he quickly extracted them, putting them into his haversack. Despite his dread, he glanced back at the man he had robbed. The profile of the man's head was odd. Focusing his glance, he realized that only the face remained. The rest was gone, a tale tell hole in the center of the man's forehead told the story of the cause. Retching slightly and feeling the burning bile in the back of his throat, he turned away, wishing the Captain would direct them to move.

After a few more minutes of watching the Captain feverishly check the dead Yankees, shouts emerged from down the street. At first, he could not make out what was being said, but then he clearly heard a man shout, "You Goddamned dog robbers! Get yer filthy hands off our men!" The sharp report of a musket being fired was followed by an angry buzz by his ear. Nicholson crouched lower, while retaining his grip on the stretcher. The crackle of musket fire that followed immediately produced a hail of minie balls that angrily buzzed near him smacking into the prone bodies around him and into the bricks of the home behind them. He heard several panes of glass in windows on the wall above him, shatter, raining glass shards all around. Above him he heard a voice cry out, "To hell with you! You damned Yankee bastards!" The cry was followed by a volley of musketry from the windows above him. Men from his Regiment had occupied the higher floors.

Taking this opportunity, Private Nicholson picked up a musket laying beside one of the blue clad corpses and deftly extracted several cartridges from the man's cartridge box and ran hunched over to the nearest corner on the friendly side of Caroline Street. Once he had reached the safety of the corner, he hastily loaded the rifle, which was much finer than the smoothbore he had carried. Peering around the corner, as his comrades continued to fire from above, he saw to his shock that the Captain and his other stretcher bearer, who he knew only as "Jason," both lying still in the street. He determined to return to the hospital and report to Sergeant Waverly. They would be upset to learn they had lost a doctor. After firing a token shot back at the blue-clad troops down the street, Private Nicholson made his way back to the Tobacco Warehouse through the narrow alley behind the buildings. The setting sun, increased the darkness of the inner bowels of the town.

Lottie Markley wiped her brow with the back of her hand, unwittingly leaving a smear of blood on her face. The influx of terribly wounded men seemed endless and she was in constant demand to bring this item and that item to the surgeons who feverishly attended to the horrible wounds. Glancing down at her apron, she appraised it to be thoroughly ruined as it was smeared with blood. The aprons of the surgeons were soaked through at the waist and they had resorted to loose rags to wipe their hands on. The sounds of gunfire were gradually being replaced with the tramp of marching feet and drums. Lottie heard the orderlies quietly talking about the development, muttering softly, "the Yankees are here now." To her it felt odd to be now "behind enemy lines," but she did not really feel fearful. Henri had earlier explained that medical staff were considered "noncombatants," and as such, they could focus on treating the wounded, regardless of the outcome of the battle.

As she busily attended to the bloody work of the surgeons, she began to notice that Henri had not come back to the hospital in quite a while. The never-ending flow of wounded trapped her in her duties. She would seek him out, once the surgeons were finished. She had grown quite numb to the horrors each passing soldier brought with him.

On the broad loading dock that ran along the Hannover Street side of the warehouse turned hospital, Elliot Lacy paused by each of the Federal wounded that were now newly arriving. Orderlies had spread more straw on the weather stained boards and they had now started to employ the cobbled surface of Hannover Street itself and the wounded men poured in. Glancing up she could see masses of soldiers in blue marching down Caroline Street. They had a neatness and uniformity that the southern boys lacked. The soup she had brought earlier was now long gone. Doctor Laschicott had procured some beef broth and had the orderlies prepare a large kettle of the comforting substance. Elliot moved from man to man, and, if he were conscious and hungry, she would tenderly spoon the broth to their lips. Some of the young men, many just boys, would ask her to pause; obviously they wanted to hear a female voice. As she looked over the rows of men, she despaired of ever being able to comfort them all. Smiling, she noticed that Eliza had made it a point to join her. She seemed partial towards the blue-clad soldiers.

Doctor Alexander Dougherty walked and conversed with his Administrative Officer, Lieutenant Munro, as they followed the Horse-drawn ambulance across the bobbing pontoon bridge. The gruff engineers had informed them at the abutment, that riding was forbidden as well as stupid. Dougherty, respecting the trade, had quietly complied. As they approached the ruined town Dougherty noted, several structures burning fiercely. No one was attempting to extinguish the blaze. Dougherty reflected as he walked on his mission, "Find and establish hospitals, use what exists, or convert structures to suit. We are to expect high numbers of casualties and we must treat them east of the Rappahannock." General Letterman's words rang in his mind. While not a strategist, Dougherty could see they were approaching dominating ground across the river. Judging from the fight the Secesh had given throughout the day in Fredericksburg, it was clear that a larger fight lay ahead. The increasing chill of the evening coming made him glad he had worn his great coat, despite the fact that the garment hid his distinctive green Medical Service shoulder boards. A slight inconvenience that would require more talking to explain his role as a surgeon. Soon they reached the abutment on the far side, which was still receiving attention by another group of engineers. As Dougherty looked about, he saw groups of soldiers cooking rations along the sidewalks of the cobblestone streets. He found it jarring to see the weary men calmly cooking coffee and beef rations among a multitude of blue and butternut clad corpses that lay all about, undisturbed in their final repose of sudden death. Lieutenant Munro eagerly pointed up the street, "Look Sir! There is a hospital flag!"

Peering up the street, Colonel Dougherty could see the bright yellow flag, still illuminated by the setting sun, atop a large wooden warehouse with a porch style roof over the long loading dock. Men in their shirt sleeves, and women, appeared to be tending to wounded. As he strode up the street to get a closer look, he realized the men were wearing gray and butternut colored trousers. "It is the hospital of the defending Rebels! Follow me Munro! I shall establish capture and negotiate paroles for the medical staff! More hands definitely will not hurt for the coming campaign!" Dougherty increased the rapidity of his stride as he passed the sitting groups of oblivious infantrymen enjoying the simple delight of a pause in the battle. Some of them called out simple taunts in a distinctively Massachusetts brogue, "No worries General, all the Secesh done run off!" Ignoring them, he pressed on, noting the pale and ghastly pile of amputated limbs on the sidewalk, just outside the double door of the structure. Dougherty knew then, with grim certainty, that he had located a functioning field hospital.

Colonel Dougherty briskly strode into the open doors, followed by Lieutenant Munro. He was met by shocked and astonished medical orderlies from the Mississippi Regiment. As the men froze, Dougherty asked in an authoritarian tone, "Who commands this Hospital!" A young orderly stammered in response, "Colonel Laschicott, Sir! He is back yonder in the surgery, Sir!" Doctor Dougherty slowly nodded and peered about as his eyes adjusted to the dim light. To his satisfaction, he saw that the hospital contained wounded from both sides. Looking back to the orderlies he replied, "Consider yourselves interned by General Sumner's Grand Division! I duly recognize your status as non-combatants, but you must reveal to me, this instant, if you are harboring combatants within these premises!" The orderlies quickly shook their heads, and the youngest again responded, helpfully, "Sir, they is all maimed soldiers! I should be happy to take you to see the surgeon!" After he had removed his gauntlets, Colonel Dougherty motioned with his hand for the man to lead him to his commander.

Raymond Laschicott glanced up as he began the initial sutures to close off the artery on the freshly amputated arm he had begun work on only moments before. Seeing the Federal Officers in their dark blue overcoats, he busily muttered, "Welcome Gentlemen. I earnestly hope you are willing to donate us supplies. This fight has exhausted my stocks." Laschicott returned his attention to the delicate work. In the dim light he realized, by the bloody light blue pants of this most recent patient, that he was saving one of theirs. He had found little time to notice much about the hundreds of men he had treated so far.

Doctor Dougherty removed his Hardee hat, and gently remarked, "Such fine work, Raymond! I always admired your work when we studied together in Boston!" Laschicott quickly looked up, surprised, "Alexander Dougherty! Such an unusual coincidence this is! How long have you been an Army surgeon?" Dougherty explained his story in a brief fashion as Laschicott finished the stump. He then reverted to his authority, stating, "Raymond, I am sure you understand that you, your doctors and your men are subject now to our authority!" Laschicott nodded, "Been there once before at Savage Station, Doctor." Dougherty soberly continued, "Have you capacity here for more wounded?" Raymond Laschicott shook his head, "I have nearly 200 here now, I must suggest the church on St. Mary's Street up the hill. The pews are not fixed to the floor and it has a fair bit of space. We considered it ourselves, but the commander objected."

Both men quietly knew that the worst was yet to come. The common bond between the professional medical providers, was the endless rectification of maimed and compromised men. Their respective ideologies mattered little in their line of work. Yet each man deeply resented what each represented to the other. Professional respect, however, trumped every other consideration at the moment. Lachicott did protest one issue, "Your soldiers shot dead one of my surgeons, Alexander! He was seeking out your wounded men! I must protest that atrocity!" Dougherty calmly replied, "There has been much viciousness on this day, friend! I expect much, much more! Surely you understand that these young men have their blood up! It simply cannot be helped!" Dougherty solemnly turned to Lieutenant Munro, and commanded, "Have Sergeant Ames bring up the ambulance! Give them a quarter of our available stocks!" The young officer nodded and strode back out into the darkening streets.

Dougherty looked again at his old acquaintance. As their eyes met, he softly said, "Between you and me, Raymond, I offer my most sincere apologies. I regret I have more sites to find for General Sumner. I shall instruct our Provost that you and your men are to be unmolested." He then returned his hat to his head and started out. Pausing at the rough threshold that opened onto the main floor, he turned and asked, "Who was your surgeon that was shot?" Laschicott quietly replied, "Henri Tinchant. He hailed from a wealthy Creole family in Louisiana." Dougherty sadly shook his head.

Alexander Dougherty then returned to the darkening streets. As he looked about he noted the dark gas lamps. There was no lamplighter present to make the rounds. At the street corner that led up to Saint Mary's Street, he noted a fine brick house that had once been gaily adorned with evergreen boughs, Christmas was not far off. The once ornate door was marred by bullet hole, and the glass panes of the windows were nothing more than shards of glass. One lonely pane remained on the second floor dormer. The distinctive bottle bottom in the center of the pane, hailed back to Revolutionary War vintage hand blown window panes. "Historic and shot all to hell!" he muttered to himself and he made his way up the cobblestone street.

As he topped the ridge that marked the path of Saint Mary's Street, he glanced off to his right and saw the elegant steeple of the church. As he turned and strode towards the door, a voice shouted out, "Be mindful Sir! The Rebs are shooting at anything that moves on the cross streets! They still got some of the town!" Dougherty took the advice to heart and paused at the first intersection he came to. After a moment, he dashed across. Sure enough, the distant pop of a musket, and the smack and whirr of a minie ball hitting the street near him, caused him to run faster. There was much remaining to be done before this site could become a usable hospital. He proceeded into the Church. Entering into the sanctuary, he immediately noted shards of brick and plaster scattered about the floors and pews from a cannon shot that had passed all the way through both walls. He gave one of the nearest pews a shove, and indeed, they were not fixed. He quickly calculated what the capacity might b, and noted the woodstove by the back wall. Heat would be necessary for the wounded in this weather. The footfalls of his boots echoed as he walked forward to inspect the access to the bell tower and steeple. He was resigned that the signalers would want to operate here as well. Compact stairs behind a door near the pulpit told him what he wanted to know. He fully intended to mark the structure as a hospital with a yellow flag, if he decided to employ the church.

8

YONDER HEIGHTS AND HILLS

The dawn of the 12th of December, 1862 brought the tramping feet of the soldiers of the right and left Grand Divisions of General Burnside's vast army. Nearly 80,000 men from General Sumner's, and General Franklin's commands pressed to cross the narrow wooden pontoons across the swollen Rappahannock. After weeks of waiting before their enemy, the great moment had arrived. The heights occupied by the Rebels remained quiet, save the desultory shelling of the bridge locations from time to time.

In tents in front of the Phillip's House, General Burnside reviewed his grand plan with Brigadier General Parks and his Army Staff. Couriers arrived on horseback, frequently interrupting the brief, bringing meaningless reports of units across the river. As General Burnside droned on about the main effort southwest of town, Brigadier General Marsena Patrick's mind wandered. His current duty was as the Provost Marshal of the Army of the Potomac. Once the offensive was underway, his duty would be to secure and police the rear area, sweeping up stragglers and shirkers, and establishing holding pens for Rebel prisoners. Patrick reflected on Fredericksburg, rubbing his bald head with his hand. He had been the Military Governor of the hamlet, once before, when General McDowell had paused there during the Seven Days battles of the previous summer. The inhabitants had been snobby and hostile, but he had admired the beauty of the old town. It held a rich history, particularly from the Custis family, and of George Washington when he was but a boy.

BATTLE OF FREDERICKSBURG

General Patrick listened for a moment as General Burnside began to describe the supporting attack through Fredericksburg itself, towards Mayres Heights. Patrick imagined the Rebels to be firmly established behind the quaint hand-laid stone wall, which marked the boundary of a farm road that dumped into Hazel Run and afforded access to the rail yard below. He surmised that it would be a difficult task to assault those heights and he struggled to remember the details of the ground, west of town. Normally, he would completely ignore the operational aspects of the assault and wait on the coordinating instructions, where he would receive his specific instructions as the Provost. Something bothered him as General Burnside described how the troops would exit the city to form lines of battle and assault the heights. As he suddenly remembered what bothered him, he blurted out, "The Mill Race!" General Burnside paused from his briefing, and asked, "General Patrick, pray tell, what did you just say?"

Patrick, suddenly embarrassed, replied, "Sir, in your supporting attack you must address the Mill Race between the town and the heights!" Burnside, astonished at the interruption, remained silent. General Patrick decided to continue, "Sir, I am quite familiar with this town! As you exit the city, itself, you will encounter the Mill Race. It is nearly 20 feet wide and 5 feet deep. It is, for all intents and purposes, a river unto itself! It supports a paper mill and several other operations! Our men cannot cross it, unless it is drained."

Burnside simply asked, "How do you know this General?" Marsena Patrick quickly replied, "Sir, I was assigned the duty of Military Governor of Fredericksburg, when the rest of the Army was on the Peninsula, last summer." Burnside nodded, and asked, "Can it be drained or bridged?" General Patrick nodded his head, and replied, "I know the location of the main sluice gates, Sir!" Burnside stared for a moment, before responding, "Very well then, General Patrick, see to it once you get across."

Patrick slowly nodded. He was shocked at the disinterest that Burnside had shown to the details and complexities of the ground ahead of them. Patrick had seen war in Florida against the Seminole and in Mexico. He was no stranger to the details. The devil, himself, lay hidden in those details. Patrick made a mental note to assemble his staff after the brief. He then turned his attention to the remainder of General Burnside's briefing. The instructions specifically for him, would soon be coming. Mentally, he imagined they would be the same as always, "Police up the stragglers and establish a collection point for the prisoners." There might also be some controls for the Sutlers and the Embalmists, who eagerly followed the

Army wherever they went.

James Longstreet and Thomas Jackson huddled with General Lee around his map. General Jackson had only just arrived. He had returned from riding his lines. Jackson curtly rendered his report to his commander, "Sir, we have tied our flank into General Longstreet's here, near Bernard's Cabin. I have arrayed my brigades, thusly with General Pender, Lane and Archer's along the Richmond and Fredericksburg railroad line. General Gregg's Brigade is in reserve followed by Taliaferro and D.H. Hill's men. My pickets report the Federals are pushing men across the bridges in a near constant fashion! They have the cover of their guns on the Stafford Heights, so I have ordered my guns to lay in defilade until I order them forward. Sir, I certainly anticipate a fight tomorrow and my boys are ready!" General Lee nodded and after a pause he asked, "General are you sure nothing can turn our flank here at Hamilton's Crossing?" Jackson looked to the map to remind himself, before responding, "Sir, General Daniel Hill can cover that ground, I shall instruct him to deploy skirmishers. I expect General Stuart should be instructed to coordinate with me if he sees any attempt to flank us further to the southeast!"

Lee turned to James Longstreet, and asked, "General Longstreet, has General McLaws achieved the return of General Barksdale's Mississippians?" Longstreet chuckled for a moment, answering, "Sir, indeed they have. We had to place one last Lieutenant under arrest to bring out the last portion of them! McLaws still has pickets along the outer environs of the town. It is fairly filling up with Yankees." The mention of Fredericksburg put General Lee in a foul mood, and he sharply responded, "It is sheer tragedy what has befallen such a beautiful place, General Longstreet! I had hoped only for a tactical delay there. What has resulted is devastation of many homes and businesses belonging to the very people we are sworn to protect and defend! I cannot find humor in an issue I must report to the Governor." Longstreet, undeterred, countered, "Sir, it is the Federals who decided to shell the town. I wonder sir, since it is now full of their troops, would you wish for us to return the favor to them? It is a very tempting target!" Lee sadly shook his head, "General, our ground here is excellent, the positions are well laid and prepared. Let them come. Spare Fredericksburg and let us defeat them before these defenses! That, General, is the honorable way to defeat them."

General Jackson became more animated than General Lee was accustomed to, and he exclaimed, "Sir, this is a perfect opportunity to totally annihilate them! I would suggest allowing their entire Army to cross this river! With their backs to the Rappahannock, we could slay them all!" Lee paused for a moment, somewhat bemused by his Lieutenant's blood lust and asked questions in the realm of the practical, "General Jackson, this point, here midway between your left and right flank, the wood here reaches beyond the railroad line. In fact, the line goes through that point of woods. How do you have that covered?" Jackson, who watched Lee indicating on the map, rapidly replied, "Sir, the ground there is wet and mostly impassable. General Lane covers one side and General Archer has the other. I have Maxcy Gregg on high ground behind that center and his flanks are anchored by my reserve! I intend to keep them close in order to counterattack the Federals when the time is right!" Lee nodded, satisfied for the moment.

General Gregg stretched to relieve the ache in his back from a days riding as his men assumed the positions in the wood, assigned to them by General Hill. After his stretch he rubbed his thigh where the wound from Maryland still ached, particularly when it got cold. His horse patiently stood, occasionally chewing his bit, as he waited on a new command. Looking up into the sky, Gregg could see the stars, far away, as they grew brighter on the crisp and cold December night. How nice it would be to be at home looking at them from his private observatory. Astronomy had been one of his avocations, along with others, but now the situation demanded one of his first, the most. Gregg paused to shout out to one of his Regimental commanders to have the men stack arms as their position was in reserve behind General Archer and General Lane. They would assume the line if those two Brigades of General A.P. Hill's Light Division was driven back. Maxcy Gregg's South Carolinians were carefully placed to be a nasty surprise for the Federals. At any rate, General Hill remained very nervous about the woods where they were. It was the only spot that offered cover to the Federals as they came across the river. General Hill was equally cautious about fratricide in the tangled woods and had repeatedly urged his Brigade Commanders to avoid shooting into the backs of one another at all costs. Too much of that had occurred in the confusion at the Second Battle of Manassas. As he scanned the dark woods, the emerging cook fires of his Brigade began to light the tangled pine and scrub oak that led down to the railroad tracks. The men chatted quietly and some had already turned in under tattered and ragged blankets. The stacked muskets with their long bayonets reflected the scant gleam of the cook fires as the night grew darker and colder.

Gregg sat on his horse in the middle of the "Military Road," a rough-hewn affair, no better than a rough dirt track created by felling the right trees. In some places, disturbed roots still jutted up through the wet soil. The new route was of immense concern to General Jackson as it offered a direct route into the Corps rear. Securing this road was another of the tasks given to him by A. P. Hill. Peering to the east he could see the cook fires of Archers men glowing faintly in the wood. As he understood the plan, they would be aroused from their bivouac near dawn and move to the very verge of the wood to await the inevitable Federal Advance. He hated not being able to see what lay before him; he would have to rely on messengers to know what was happening. A horseman approached him and squinting in the darkness Gregg recognized Colonel Samuel McGowan who commanded the 14th South Carolina, "Good Evening Sir! This is quite the place to spend our time before Christmas!" General Gregg nodded, "There is many a place I should rather be, Samuel." Gregg was convinced that the young Colonel was perhaps the best leader in his Brigade. He could always count on him to find him out. McGowan paused silently for a moment, before asking, "Sir, will they come tomorrow?" Gregg softly replied, "Yes, I think so. At least General Hill is convinced as such. Samuel, try to keep the boys from getting too excitable in this tangle. Our orders are such that we shall have to rely on our ears and our minds, rather than our eyes for this battle. We are to hold this line where we are. We must remain patient as Archer and Lane's Brigades withdraw. That is, unless we are ordered forward. I expect confusion." Colonel McGowan nodded. He appreciated the wisdom of General Gregg. Both had graduated from South Carolina College and both had fought in Mexico. McGowan bid his commander a good evening and rode back over to his Regiment to bed down.

As General Gregg sat still in the chilly night, Colonel Hamilton found him on foot and urged, "Sir, it is late. We have you some supper, if you wish, and have prepared a tent for you." Maxcy Gregg wearily assented. A good rest would help his depressed state, it was nearly Christmas and home was far, far away.

The yearling deer had been startled from its bed by the strange smells and clanking noises of the men moving through the woods. With deft hops, the animal silently moved towards the rail line. The cut afforded quicker movement for the frightened animal, despite the disturbing smell of the treated wooden ties supporting the iron rails. The yearling had traveled for nearly half a mile, before dashing down into a creek bed that afforded more cover. After crossing the boggy creek bottom, the frightened deer paused to sniff the air. Strange noises in the woods above and the smell of wood smoke, drove it to return to the creek bottom and follow it towards the river. As the deer approached the edge of the wood, bounded by open ground to it's left and right, the animal then caught the scent of more men in the open fields ahead of it. The deer carefully listened and sniffed the scent in the air. Soon the alert creature of the forest saw men standing in ones and twos out in the open, looking towards the river. Seeing no safe escape, it slowly backtracked and found a high spot overlooking the creek and bedded down. At least no men were in the creek bottom and the marginal safety of this spot would have to do. The deer settled down and warily rested. The darkness came quickly, but the wind continued to bring the disturbing smells past it's twitching nose.

Brigadier General Marsena Patrick led the compact column of a cavalry troop, and two infantry companies of his Provost Guard, across the Rappahannock on the pontoons on the north side of Fredericksburg. He had been forced to argue his status with a Connecticut regimental commander in order to insert himself into the queue to cross the wooden structure. Patrick was obsessed with the potential failure of the supporting attack, if the mill race west of town was not emptied. He knew instinctively that General Lee would employ every obstacle he could to frustrate an attack on Mayre's Heights and the mill race canal posed a considerable one. It being a hand dug canal, it's flaws would still leave it nearly 3 feet deep in places and the steep banks would require the troops to climb into, and then out of, the canal. Patrick tried to remember where the sluice gates lay upriver on the Rappahannock as he led his mount across the bobbing bridge.

Entering the town, General Patrick became concerned about the density of troops that milled about the streets. No one seemed to be organizing them and many had begun to employ the stoops and front gardens of private homes as collection areas. He surmised this would lead to trouble soon, but he had urgent business to attend to first. The sun had fully set and the night was growing quite dark, but he was relieved, as this would help his mission. The last thing he desired was to be observed from the heights beyond the town. Once he had reached Caroline Street, he summoned Captain Jannito who commanded his Rhode Island Cavalry. When the second generation Italian commander arrived, he gave him a curt order, "Captain, take your Troop ahead of me on the road! Follow Caroline Street until it parallels the river! There is a sluice gate about a mile upstream. Expect it to be guarded by the Rebels! When you make contact with them, send me a runner!" Jannito nodded, and asked, "Just how many Rebels do you expect, Sir?" General Patrick smiled and replied, "Why I have no earthly idea, Captain! That is precisely why I am sending you! Avoid entangling yourself. Just keep them busy until I can send my Infantry up!" Captain Jannito broke out into a broad grin and announced, "Very well, General, just be sure to mention me in dispatches, if I find the damned Sluice gate all by myself!" The Captain waved his arm broadly and the Troop thundered through town on the cobbled streets, causing groups of Infantry to dive out of the way of their movement. General Patrick waited another quarter of an hour for his Infantry to assemble, before he ordered them to follow down the road.

General Patrick and the infantry had only marched a half mile before a rider from the cavalry returned down the dark road. They had departed the cobblestones and now trudged on muddy dirt. Only the slightest hint of light illuminated the bare trees in the open fields and lining the heights to the west. As the rider pulled abreast of the General, he pulled his mount up to a swift stop and saluted, "Sir, Captain Jannito has a report for you! It is a sketch! I am to explain it to you, Sir!" The young trooper quickly unbuttoned his greatcoat at the neck and extracted a small piece of paper, handing it to General Patrick.

Opening the message, General Patrick realized it was too dark to read it. He shouted out to the nearest Infantry Officer, Captain Frye, "Captain! Find us a candle!" General Patrick quickly dismounted and the small cluster of men gathered around the General. Frye secured a small candle from the knapsack of one of his soldiers, and a Lucifer match. After carefully lighting the candle, he held it for the General to study the sketch.
The young cavalryman explained, "Sir, Captain Jannito found this wooden mill, right near the river. It sits at the point where the canal meets the river. The Captain figures there are about twenty Rebs in and around the mill and we saw horses there as well, so we think there is an Officer or two over them. They hollered at us as we got near, but they did not shoot at us. The Captain reckoned it was because of the dark. There are no pickets or skirmishers out." Patrick nodded and turned to Captain Frye, "Move your company and Captain Ames' company up behind you! Move as quiet as you can and when you get 80 yards from the Mill, put your men on line and

give that mill a volley." He then turned to the young cavalryman and directed, "Ride back and tell your Captain to screen with your troop west of the Mill. Move quiet and scoop up any Rebs that try to retreat to their lines." The young man nodded and stood. General Patrick rose as well and relayed to the cluster of Officers around him, "Get your men moving!"

Patrick rode slowly behind the first Company as they marched down the dark road. He could barely see where they were going. The only light visible was a slight glow behind the distant trees on the heights beyond. The Infantry was moving with tolerable silence, marred only by the occasional soft curse of stumbling men and the clink of tin cups, muffled by haversacks. After a short march, Patrick heard a harsh whisper, "A rider is coming up!" Soon Captain Jannito arrived and finding General Patrick, he saluted, and reported, "Sir, the mill is 100 yards up ahead on the right! We are pinched between the canal and the river now, but I have a platoon that managed to wade their mounts across and have positioned themselves to the west of the mill. If your companies will follow me, I can show them where to form the line. The Rebs inside the mill must be asleep, we have seen no movement!" General Patrick and Captain Jannito sat and watched astride their mounts as the Infantry companies trotted forward down the dark path and assembled on line before the barely visible mill. The wooden wheel slowly turned on one side of the structure and the wet paddle blades reflected the scant light. Patrick assumed that the noise of the mill mechanism had masked the sound of their approach. The whispered orders, "Load!" was heard as the Infantry Captains prepared their commands. As the infantrymen fumbled with loading in the darkness, the ground floor double door of the mill was flung open. Men could be seen briefly as they scrambled out, before a lamp from inside the structure was snuffed out. The darkness was filled with shouting as the Rebel troops hurriedly organized to meet the threat. Seeing the development, Captain Frye shouted at the top of his voice, "Ready....Aim!...Fire!" The volley by the two companies erupted in a bright orange flash, accentuated by bright sparks created by still burning powder as the hail of minie balls tore into the confused Rebels. Men could be seen falling in the half-light and the return fire from the southern ranks was scattered and light. Many began to shout and some raised their hands, shouting, "You got us Billy Yank! We're givin' up peaceably!"

General Patrick shouted out curt directives, "Round them up and disarm them! Captain Jannito, secure the rear of the Mill! Captain Frye, form a detail of men, and follow me!" General Patrick drew his pistol and rushed into the doors of the mill. Several men in butternut uniforms lay dead or wounded by the open doors. Entering the dark mill house, the structure was silent except for the ceaseless rumbling rotation of the disengaged mill wheel. After some blind fumbling around, Captain Frye found a match and struck it, providing meager light. The match light sufficed to locate the oil lamp used by the Rebels and once they had it lit, General Patrick scanned the room. In seconds he found what he was looking for. On a clapboard wall to his left, he spied a large iron hand wheel hanging from a stout nail. Pointing to it he directed a soldier, "Son, secure that hand wheel and follow me!"

Rounding the building and risking the compromise of the oil lamp, General Patrick quickly found the sluice gate and noted it elevated and fully open. The large screw that worked the gate had no wheel on the top. Turning to the soldier, following him, he instructed, "Fit the wheel onto that screw, Son, and lower the sluice! Once you have it all the way down, hang on to that hand wheel! It is coming back with us!" Patrick knew from experience that it would take several hours for the mill race to drain. The canal would be passable by morning. Leaving Captain Ames and his company to secure the mill. General Patrick returned with the remainder of his Provost Guard to Fredericksburg. He did not want to imagine what was happening in the town while he had been gone.

The clamor rising in the street caused Elliot Lacy to look up as she spooned broth to a shivering soldier who had lost his arm. The young man sat with his back propped up against the hard wooden wall of the Warehouse loading dock. Elliot could see that the street was filled with soldiers. The sight was accompanied by breaking and crashing noises, punctuated by loud shouts and hurrahs, from time to time. She turned and looked at the young man, sadly noting he was merely a boy. She asked, "Are you warm enough, young man?" The boy nodded, "Tolerably, Ma'am. The arm hurts somethin' awful, though." Elliot nodded, "I shall let the Doctor know, Son." Elliot rose and moved to the next man. This one had dark hair and fine features, including a bushy mustache. His good looks, however, were marred by a mass of bloody bandages on one side of his face. Elliot noted red stripes and diamond sewn on the sleeves of his tunic. He clutched a tattered and worn bible on his chest with both hands. As Elliot leaned closer, she could see him occasionally shiver. With the sun down, the loading dock had grown quite cold. As she adjusted the ratty blanket and burlap hogs-head material tighter about him, she asked, "Would you like some warm broth, Sir?" The soldier numbly shook his head. Judging from the look of his face, he was likely too swollen from his injury to speak. She gently pried the tattered bible from his weak and protesting hands, and asked, "Would you like for me to read a passage to you?" The wounded man weakly nodded. Elliot opened the bible to pages that held a thin portfolio, obviously to protect a treasured tin-type photograph. Guiltily she paused, then opened the photo. The image within, made her gasp. Quickly closing the portfolio, she turned to the 23rd Psalm and read it softly to the soldier. When she had finished, she noticed that he was asleep. Gently returning the bible to the safety of his clasped hands, she quickly stepped back into the warehouse. Upon entering, she encountered Doctor Laschicott in the company of a Federal Medical Officer. Laschicott urgently directed, "Mrs. Lacy, you must see to Miss Markley at once! She is in the office in the back with Lieutenant Colonel Alexander! Captain Tinchant was killed this afternoon!" Elliot could only gasp, "Oh My! The poor child!" She then gathered her skirts and rushed to the back office. Within, she saw Charlotte Markley, red-eyed and stunned as she mindlessly wiped her bloodstained hands on her apron. Colonel Alexander talked softly to her, but she seemed not to hear. Seeing Elliot Lacy caused the tears to well up again and she broke into weeping again, asking "Have they brought him back?" Elliot Lacy, tears running down her cheeks, could only say, "No." Elliot excused Colonel Alexander and sat on the hard wooden bench with Charlotte, soothing her tears. Elliot, hoping to distract her, produced the photo and handed it to Lottie, "Here dear, we have recovered a keepsake you gave him from a Yankee soldier! At least we can preserve some of your sweet memories." Lottie blindly took the proffered photo as she wept. Without looking she muttered, "There were no keepsakes, Ma'am! We hadn't enough time, what with all the traveling required of us!" Still sobbing, she wiped her face and looked down at the portfolio in her hands. Opening the strangely familiar cover, she gazed upon a photograph of herself when she was only seventeen. She remembered that she had been forced to borrow money from her mother, to pay for the token, and had secretively posted it, many years ago, to a boy she now considered dead. Lottie clasped her hand to her mouth to stifle her gasp. She quickly turned to Elliot, who now bore a genuinely confused look, and asked, "Mrs. Lacy, please show me this soldier! I must see him this instant!"

Joshua dreamt that he awoke from a long sleep, and the pain returned. He tried to swallow and his throat felt stiff and wooden. He dreamt that he saw Lottie, hovering over him. She was dim and out of focus, the pain would not go away. Her touch on his face was soothing and he felt peaceful, despite the dull pain. In his dream, he felt like he was in a great crowd of shouting and laughing people. Looking towards her, he felt a great rushing love as he strained to focus on her face. Then the darkness came again.

Major General George Meade intently listened as General Reynolds conducted his council of war. The senior officers of the Corps were gathered under Mr. Bernard's ramshackle barn overhang as John Reynolds explained their tasks. While he had a map, Reynolds preferred to point towards the darkening hills and woods before the seated officers. They had all looked the ground over, earlier in the afternoon, so the landmarks he mentioned were familiar to Meade. Years of service in the Topographical Engineers had lent him a sharp eye for the details of terrain. While concerned with the time afforded to the Rebels to prepare, he saw possibility in the ground assigned to him. The day had already proven busy as his men had taken a small hamlet in a hollow on the west bank, known to the locals as "Smithfield." The Reserves had done fine work, driving a Rebel line of skirmishers back to the rail line that dominated the horizon before them. Now he had received orders to push his division of Pennsylvania Reserves towards a point where the rail line entered and then exited a point of woods some 600 yards away. Reynolds explained that the Pennsylvanians were to drive as hard as they could, to clear the woods and then execute a maneuver to the left and right, to clear the Rebel artillery from their positions. Generals Gibbon and Butterfield would secure his flanks and reinforce his attack as necessary. The order to advance would come in the morning at an unknown time. That would be up to General Franklin as the Grand Division Commander. As General Reynolds turned his attention to Gibbon's specific instructions, George Meade mused on what he would face in the morning. While he was tasked to go after the Rebel guns, he had no idea where they lay as they had remained silent all day. He hoped it was due to a shortage of guns and of ammunition. He knew his men were up to it. They collectively wanted another crack at the Rebels, after the frustrations in Maryland. Meade was glad to have General Reynolds back with the Pennsylvania Reserves. Reynolds had missed Maryland due to his recall to Pennsylvania by Governor Curtin. He had been ordered to plan a defense of the state, following Lee's incursion and had busied himself in training second line troops to defend Pennsylvania, while Meade had fought over the cornfields by the Antietam Creek. The evening briefing concluded with instructions from General Reynolds to wake the men early. Tomorrow would bring the anticipated battle.

The men of the Regiments stacked arms in the soggy bottom lands around Smithfield and unrolled their rubber blankets to lay on the ground to protect against the wet. It would be a cold camp without fire, or warm rations, as there was no wood to be found in the trampled pasture. The soldiers carefully tucked their canteens in their blankets with them to prevent their freezing in the chill of the night. There was little gaiety and most fell fast asleep, following the exertions of the day. George Meade sat under an awning created by draping canvas from a wagon over an A-frame of fence rails. He carefully cleaned and loaded his Remington revolver, taking great care to assure its function tomorrow. He hoped he would not need it. Pulling his overcoat tighter in the late evening chill, he peered up at the bright moon as it emerged from scudding clouds overhead. The momentary brightness revealed the sight of his regiments in their sleep. A few officers moved quietly among their men, smoking cigars. Meade, finally resolved to turn in. After asking his aide de camp to awake him at 5 am, he found his blanket and wrapped it over his greatcoat and drifted off in the bed of the wagon. He had only been down for a moment, when Colonel Sinclair found him to inquire about dispatching out pickets to the front. General Meade wearily assented to the proposal and lay back down. The increasing chill of the night made his sleep fitful.

The morning came quickly and cold. A year of sleeping under canvas had made him sensitive to the slightest light of dawn. Groggily sitting up, he was treated to the welcome sight of Lieutenant Dehon, his aide, waiting with a cup of steaming coffee, making the morning seem almost cheerful. Meade asked, "Where in God's earth did you find firewood?" Dehon grinned and replied, "Colonel Sinclair's boys found a fence last night, halfway up the slope. They brought back rails, Sir!" George Meade chuckled and sipped the reviving coffee. Dehon continued, "Sir, General Reynolds sent a rider. You are to meet him at the Bernard place in half an hour. We are saddling your horse now, Sir." Meade nodded, it could only mean one thing, General Burnside had issued the order to attack. Meade quickly directed, "Have Captain Cox deliver orders to the Brigades to stand to. I will give detailed orders when I return! Have them make ready!"

After a short ride back across the frost crusted pasture, George Meade arrived at the Bernard Farm. The morning fog made it difficult to see very far, so he rode carefully seeking out the General's tent. Seeing a cluster of Officers on horseback, he guided his mount to join the collection of men around General Reynolds. General Reynolds appraisingly scanned the group of Officers, mentally tallying who had arrived. He curtly directed, "Follow me, Gentlemen. I am now in receipt of orders from General Franklin to proceed with the attack. Artillery on the Stafford Heights began to fire across the broad river valley as if cued to his instructions and the howling of shells broke the morning silence as the group of commanders rode forward. After a half mile of riding, General Reynolds reined to a halt at a point where a creek wound its way north along the Bowling Green Road. Reynolds explained as the Division Commanders secured their field glasses from their pommel bags, "This feature is a stream called Deep Run, If you look west you shall see the rail line." A friendly shell exploded short overhead, interrupting Reynolds and causing several of the Officers to flinch, but he continued, "My engineers tell me that the rail line is elevated, so expect the Rebels to employ it! There may already be some behind it now! General Meade, you shall center your attack here! Guide on the trees that approach the rail line and press your attack audaciously! Do not pause for volleys, you must cross the rail line and gain those woods as quickly as you can! With God's help, hopefully this damned fog will blind them to your approach!" General Meade silently nodded, raising his field glasses in an attempt to identify landmarks through the mist to assist in his attack. General Reynolds pointed with his right hand and explained, "Attempt to gain the crest of those heights. I shall need you to establish a point of penetration in their lines! General Gibbon will advance behind your division to your right and General Doubleday will do likewise to your left. Send me runners to report your progress as frequently as you deem fit." General Reynolds paused for a moment, Rebel guns far off to the north had begun to fire into Fredericksburg, clearly focusing on the continuing flow of Federal troops crossing into the town. Turning his horse, General Reynolds commanded, "Gentlemen return to your Divisions! We shall advance at half past eight!"

Father Corby, standing atop a large stone near the Steamboat landing, concluded his early morning sermon with the general absolution,

"Dominus noster Jesus Christus vos absolvat, et ego auctoritate ispsius, vos absolve ab omni vincula, excommunicationis interdicti, in quantum possum et vos indigetis deinde ego absovo vos, a pecatis, vestris, in nomini Patris, et Filii, et Spiritus Sancti, Amen!"

As he completed his genuflection, he noted the unnaturally somber mood of the men. Normally a raucous lot, they seemed lost in reflection on this frosty morning. The word had gone out that they were to enter the general attack, soon. General Meagher, resplendent in his tailored green frockcoat and gold sash, finished his own genuflection, then returned his cap to his head and departed to meet with his officers as the men rose to their feet.

Father Ouellet, the French Jesuit Chaplain from Colonel Byrne's regiment, teased Corby as the men returned to their muddy bivouacs, "You know Father, the Holy See might not approve of these methods!" Father Corby, smirked for a moment as he removed his purple vestment from his muddy frock coat and folded it, "These trying times require practicality, Father." A pair of Rebel shells shrieked overhead and impacted near the pontoon bridges, throwing up great columns of greenish water, "I anticipate many of these boys never returning." Father Ouellet nodded somberly, "Nonetheless, Father, I shall see to as many souls as God permits! I shall endeavor to do that by their sides, where they lay!"

Corporal Alan O'Rourke returned his forage cap on his head, and rose to his feet. Through quick motions, he indicated to the men of his squad to follow him. Rubbing his upper arms through his greatcoat, he attempted to warm up. The town was wreathed in a dense cold fog. The orders had been to bivouac without fires last night. He desperately wanted some coffee, but settled for a swig from his wool covered canteen, the familiar tinny taste settled on his tongue. O'Rourke had an uneasy feeling deep in the pit of his stomach, as his men, the boys of Company C, 69th New York State Volunteers, rolled up their rubber blankets and attached them to their tarred canvas knapsacks. An unsettling feeling filled him, as his instincts told him that this day would be an ugly battle. The Sergeant Major had begun to shout for the Soldiers to "fall in!" and the men scrambled to pack away their belongings. O'Rourke looked on, bemused, as he spotted Private Seamus O'Malley carefully tucking purloined silver spoons and forks into his rucksack. Corporal O'Rourke posed him a rhetorical question, "Busy last night were you, O'Malley?" Private O'Malley broke into a broad grin, "Aye, Corporal! And alas, I have obtained me absolution from Father Corby, hisself! Why with all this absolution, I'm sure to own heaven before long!" O'Rourke sourly replied, "If you don't be paying attention Boy-O, you might be meetin' your maker today! Secure your musket and fall in!"

The roar of guns on the heights beyond the town had taken on the aspect of a great storm. More, and more Rebel shells ripped through the upper floors of the homes along Sophia Street as the Rebel artillery attempted to ruin the pontoon bridges. Frozen bodies from the fight a fortnight ago, still littered the sidewalks and front gardens of the homes along the street.

O'Rourke leaned over and finding his initials carved into the stock of his 1842 Springfield he picked it out of the stack, removed and sheathed the bayonet and brought the weapon to shoulder arms. He then moved with the rest of his Company onto the cobbles of Sophia Street.

Ranks of blue-clad men filled the street all the way through town, nothing seemed to be moving, although the sounds of battle were growing beyond the town. He heard one man ask another, "Why ain't the Rebel cannon shooting at us any more?" First Sergeant Ainsworth shouted back the answer, "They ain't shootin' here because they got better targets! The lead Divisions are attacking! Just pray they capture them guns, before your turn comes!" After a half hour of waiting, the orders to "stand easy," and "ground your muskets," was shouted out by the officers, up and down the line. Corporal O'Rourke looked about and thought the fog was thinning out.

A disruption in the ranks ahead of them caused Corporal O'Rourke and the men around him, to crane their heads to see what was happening. As the ranks parted ahead by the Captain, a man exclaimed, "Well fancy that, Lads! It's General Meagher, his very self!" Meagher and several of his staff officers strode directly through the middle of the column, pausing frequently to greet the men and exchange jokes. O'Rourke saw that the officers carried bundles of cut shrubs. Reaching him and his squad, Meagher looked Corporal O'Rourke in the eye, and proclaimed, "Here Son, take these sprigs of Boxwood and put it on your Caps! We are down to only one Regimental Color, so we need to show the Green!"

A Captain thrust a segment of a bundle of Boxwood sprigs into his hands as General Meagher shouted out, "Adorn your hats, Boys! Show them that Ireland is represented today!" The General's retinue continued through the ranks as the men in O'Rourke's squad broke off segments and tucked them through the Irish harp pins on their forage caps.

The foliage seemed to brighten them up and many began to chat nervously as they waited. Corporal O'Rourke reflexively reached through the slit in the side of his greatcoat and searched his trouser pockets. After digging a moment, his fingers touched the Rosary sent to him by his sister. Just touching the amulet relieved him somewhat, but his stomach still felt as heavy as a stone. The crackling rumble west of them seemed to reach an unceasing crescendo.

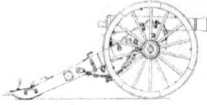

Major John Pelham looked at his gold pocket watch, it was 9am, the roar of artillery and musketry off to the north made the team horses anxious. The drivers of his four batteries, sequestered in the woods along the old Richmond stage road, struggled to keep them still, whispering to them in Creole to soothe them. He reflected on his orders from General Stuart, "Keep your guns masked, until commanded!" As he sat astride his white horse, listening, one of Stuart's cavalry pickets rode up to him, saluted and announced, "Sir, Major Pelham, there is something you have to see! The fog is lifting! If it would please you, Sir, follow me!"

Arriving at the edge of the wood, Pelham was amazed at the sight of an entire Union corps forming lines of battle on the still misty, frost laced pastures that descended to the Rappahannock. Countless blue regimental colors, punctuated by the red, white and blue national colors, made for a grand and awe inspiring display. The early morning sun glinted off the barrels of thousands of burnished muskets and the troops expertly maneuvered to form lines to assault General Jackson's lines. Major Pelham, a mere youth himself, directed the courier, "Son, go find Captain Henry and escort him to this place! Make haste!" The young Private nodded and spurred his horse back down to where the batteries were sheltering in the woods. Major Pelham dug out his naval telescope and, after adjusting the focus, he trained it on the blue-clad ranks. He expertly judged the flanks of the forming ranks to be just under a mile from his location.

When Captain Henry arrived, still attempting to finish buttoning his tunic, Major Pelham exclaimed, "Mathis, behold what lies before us!" Pelham offered Henry the telescope, but the Captain eschewed it's use, "That sir, I can see unassisted! They are totally exposed on their left flank!" Pelham turned to the young courier and asked, "Son, are you aware of General Stuart's location?" The young Private eagerly nodded, to wit, Pelham extracted his field notebook from his map case and busily scribbled with the stub of a pencil. Once he had finished, he awkwardly tore the page from the book and handed it to the courier, "Take this to the General. I beg him to allow us to attack that force while the time is right!" As the young courier turned his horse and rode away, Pelham directed Captain Henry, "Mathis bring up a section from your horse battery! Position them just at the edge of these woods, until we get our answer back! Tell them to be prepared to shoot and move rapidly!"

Pelham watched as his Captain descended into the still dark woods. Turning back to the field, he continued to observe the panoply expanding before him. The Federals deliberately maneuvered as if they were on parade. The faint bugle calls and drumming echoed across the field as well as the shouts of their officers. Scanning the ground between himself and them, he realized that they had deployed no flankers or screen of cavalry. It dawned on him, that they had yet to cross their cavalry on the bridges. Bemused, he reflected on his good fortune. Only 4 days ago he had driven a flotilla of Yankee gunboats back with only four light guns. Today, he would engage a Union Corps with only two.

General Stuart sat on a fallen log beside Wade Hampton, enjoying a cigar and conversation, when the courier found them. The young private smartly saluted and handed the message to the General with a long leaning reach while remaining atop his mount. General Hampton wryly commented, "A true Cavalryman, General Stuart! Death before dismount." Stuart chuckled and unfolded the message. The young Private attempted to explain, but Stuart silenced him, with an upheld hand. Scanning the message, he asked, "Son, did Major Pelham seem sure about what he asks for?" The Private promptly replied, "Yes Sir! He is very anxious to make the attempt!" Stuart turned to Hampton and asked for a pencil. After a moments search, Hampton handed him a nice new one from his map case. Stuart muttered as he scratched out his reply on the back of the message, "Hope he don't get himself killed!" Handing the message back to the Courier he directed, "Inform Major Pelham that he will withdraw on my order! Insure you return at once as I have to report this action to General Lee!" The young Private secured the message in his vest pocket saluted, and galloped off.

John Pelham waited, while looking the ground over, between the wood he sheltered in, and the flank of the massing Federals. As he followed the Old Richmond Stage road, from south to north, he noticed a slight hollow at an intersection. A bushy grove of cedars stood on the east side of the road, effectively blocking observation of the hollow from the east. Perhaps shelter lay there as the grove blocked direct observation from the massed Yankee guns on Stafford Heights. Perhaps. The neighing of team horses and the clatter of the traces indicated the arrival of Captain Henry. Pelham turned and noted that he had brought up a bronze Napoleon and a 12 pound Blakely rifle. Major Pelham nodded approvingly, ready for anything that way. Looking to Captain Henry, he directed, "Leave the caissons here. We shall go forward only with guns and limbers! I do not envision us staying long enough to need a second chest of rounds." Minutes later, the young courier returned with his answer.

323

With whoops and shouts the gunners whipped their teams, driving the horses forward across the pasture with the limbered guns bouncing behind them. Major Pelham raced his mount ahead of the laboring teams as he led them to the hollow he had found. There would be little time to prepare before the artillery on the heights would respond. The teams dragging the guns arrived shortly behind him. The horses in the teams blew great clouds of frosty vapor from their nostrils as the gunners quickly unlimbered their pieces to orient onto the enfiladed Federal flank. The course of the intermittent stream bed opened up in the direction of the assembling Union troops as the rising morning sun cast long shadows across the scrambling gun crews. Major Pelham shouted out, "Load Solid Shot! Range 1200 yards!" He paused to allow Captain Henry to gather his wits, and Henry then called out, "Advance the Charge!" Major Pelham rode forward, off to the left of the guns, to a spot of high ground. Finding a good position, he extracted his telescope and studied the elongated ranks. As he studied the image, he heard Captain Henry shout, "By Section! Fire!" The two guns split the still morning air with a commanding roar.

General Meade watched his Brigades of the 3rd Division form their lines after they had ascended the slopes from the hamlet of Smithfield. He admired the discipline of the men as they executed their transitions from column of fours into lines of battle. The Rebel lines had remained silent and mysterious, but he anticipated that state of affairs to soon change. It was only a matter of his approach getting close enough. He watched as the Sergeants worked the lines of troops to insure none had loaded their muskets, employing ramrods to "ring" the muskets. The bell-like tone of the steel ramrod striking the steel breech plug of the musket was a sure indicator of an empty chamber. The men must resist the urge to stop and fire. It slowed the advance and made them an easy target for the unknown number of cannon the Rebels undoubtedly would bring to bear. Satisfied with his initial alignment, he shouted out to his Regimental Commanders, "Fix Bayonets!" The clatter of his three Brigades of men extracting the wicked spike bayonets from their sheaths and attaching them to the barrels of the muskets filled the air. As he prepared to have the bugler sound the advance, a pair of loud booms echoed off to his left. Turning, he stared, transfixed, at the white smoke emerging from a slight grove of trees far off down the Bowling Green Road.

A sharp shriek followed by a sudden burst of muddy soil and the fleeting glint of light from a spherical object, made him realize what was occurring. He had exposed his flank to a masked Rebel battery. In the instant of his realization, the second projectile, aimed slightly higher flailed through a rank of men, before him, with incredible violence. Arms, legs, entrails, muskets and bits of uniforms and equipment flew in all directions as the terrible energy of the solid shot ravaged more than a dozen men. The first round entered the ranks several Companies down, bowling down men, before churning up another muddy spray of wet earth and body parts. Meade watched stunned for a second, before the Commander within him emerged. Without looking to his Adjutant, who he knew was nearby, he shouted, "Bring up my Batteries and orient them to cover my left! Send a runner to General Reynolds's Headquarters! I want supports from the Artillery Reserve to fire upon that battery!" Two more booms in the distance, impelled him to more furious activity. Spurring his horse, he galloped to find Colonel Sinclair commanding his 1st Brigade. Finding him astride his horse, attempting to rally his men and bring them back into ranks, Meade shouted, "William, make them go to ground! Have them lay down until our batteries can reduce them!" George Meade then turned his horse to find Colonel Magilton to repeat the order. To his great relief he saw many soldiers down the lines, making this common sense move, without orders.

Soon he saw galloping teams dragging guns, swing wide between his huddling men and the distant Rebel held woods, the Battery Commander in the lead with a swallow tail red, white, and blue guidon, borne by the color bearer following. The officer was recklessly exposing his flank to the Rebel lines. Meade asked, "Which guns are those?" His adjutant raised his field glasses and studied the racing battery for a moment, before replying, "Captain Ransom's! They are seeking a position clear of our men!" Meade realized the evil genius of the Rebel artilleryman, far off to his left. Soon, Gibbon and Butterfield would be moving up from the river. The Corps was too tightly clustered as it uncoiled, to properly maneuver against an aggressive attack on the flanks. He suddenly remembered why the stubby short range howitzers, which had been ruled obsolete back in '60, had a use and a clear purpose. It was why they were named "Flank Howitzers." Another pair of booms, of which he finally saw the smoke and location of the distant guns, presaged the howl and cracks of exploding rounds. Watching the impacts among the huddling troops, he realized that his antagonist had adapted a response to his decision to have his men lay down. Now they were employing Spherical Case shot in order to continue the killing.

The distinctive, and diminutive activity from Major Pelham's engagement, captured the attention of Major Pendleton. Excusing himself from General Jackson's retinue, he rode forward towards the point on the rail line where the Richmond and Fredericksburg Railroad line emerged from the wood at Hamilton's Crossing. They had been under harassing fire from the Yankees for most of the morning, but the fog had reduced visibility between the lines. It was clear they had no targets, as the shelling was largely ineffective. Those shells that came close, accomplished little more than scaring the horses. The sight that emerged before him as he cleared the woods was impressive, reminiscent of Sharpsburg. He quickly turned to summon General Jackson. Arriving at the discussion, he blurted out, "Sir, the Federals are approaching in force! You simply must see this!"

General Jackson sat astride his horse for a few more seconds as he halved a lemon with a Barlow knife. He did not respond until he had pocketed his spare half, "Do say, Major Pendleton! General Lane, please accompany me!" Together the men rode the short distance north along the track until they entered the stubble pasture that opened up towards the river. Seeing the thinning effect the rising morning sun had on the fog, Jackson absently bit into the lemon half, and muttered, "Very providential." General Lane gave a low whistle. The lines of blue-clad Union troops covered the entire front of open pasture from Smithfield almost to the outskirts of Fredericksburg. As they watched, the groups on the left were continuing to form lines, while the groups to the far right were beginning to lay down. Two more reports from guns on the far right explained the cause for the disruption to the ranks. General Jackson turned to Sandy Pendleton and asked, "Is that Stuart's Horse Artillery? I certainly hope it is not mine, as I have yet to authorize such action!" Major Pendleton assured him it was not, "All your guns remain silent, Sir! Precisely as ordered." Jackson nodded and watched as more, and more units were affected by the galling fire of the two well positioned guns. General Lane lowered his field glasses and observed, "Sir, that indeed is a very large force! Possibly two Corps of Federals! I pray we are not overwhelmed!" General Jackson watched silently for a few more moments, occasionally biting a bit more from the lemon. He then dryly replied, "General Lane, I welcome their appearance! Indeed I wish the good Lord, in his divine providence, would send me more! I intent to kill them all, here before this river! That, after all, General Lane, is what we do in the name of our holy cause! Go now General, and alert your Regiments! We shall have much work to do!"

A mile below Hamilton's crossing, Major John Pelham began to notice the near misses of Union artillery as several combined batteries attempted to silence him. At first, he mistook the fire for the harassing shots that had soared overhead all morning, but soon rounds began to rip through the grove of cedars that they had sheltered behind. Then, off to his left, a great muddy spray of dirt at the lip of the depression, accompanied by a shrieking howl, convinced him that he was the target of Federal Ordnance rifles. Moving his horse to the far side of the bowl, he commanded, "Captain Henry, limber your guns and displace to me!" The gunners quickly obeyed his commands, they had noticed the closeness of the impacts, as well. It took them mere minutes to reposition and then unlimber the guns. The displacement obstructed his view to the closest ranks of Yankees, but more had obligingly appeared, coming up in column, from Smithfield. No sooner had they unlimbered, when numerous shells impacted and threw clods of wet, half frozen dirt up in geysers of dark earth and white smoke, amidst the ruts of their last location. The Yankees were beginning to find the range. Pelham cried out, "Work your pieces quickly boys! Put more Spherical Case into them!" Captain Henry shouted out commands and then checked the lay on the Blakely gun. He wanted the precision of the rifle applied to its best effect. Stepping back, he commanded his section to fire, and the twin guns roared as one.

Private Frank Gustin of the 2nd Pennsylvania Reserves lay uncomfortably on the wet and muddy ground. The sodden pasture the artillery had caught them in, was cold and wet. He felt the chill wetness soaking into his wool uniform. He already knew that the wonderful greatcoat that kept him warm, now would become beastly heavy as it became soaked. Cannon, which he assumed to be theirs, fired at the far away Rebel guns, directly over him. The muzzle blasts were deafeningly loud and the shells made an angry buzz over his head as they made their deadly way to the east. Looking up, he caught a glimpse of Colonel McCandless's muddy boots as he moved in a crouch, carrying his sword in his hand, shouting, "Stay down boys! Our guns are as dangerous as the Reb's at the moment!" Gustin put his head down and stared at the mud for a moment, when another buzzing whizz, the sound of the Rebel shells, approached. The round hit quite near and exploded only feet from him. Private Gustin opened his mouth to shout, but found his face buffeted with muddy earth. Spitting violently, he cleared the mud from his mouth and shook his head in a vain attempt to stop the ringing in his ears. Near him he saw a pink form that he recognized as a disembodied hand and lower arm. The lifeless part looked pale and small and the bloody ragged end, fixed his gaze. Looking back at the hand, he noticed the fingers twitch a little. Nauseated, he lowered his head and fought the onrush of bile from his stomach. Pulling his rifle up closer to him, he lay his head down on his arms and waited for the artillery exchange to cease. There was no glory here. He could hear the shrieks of the maimed and off to his left he could hear the soft sobbing of a terrified man. The officers and sergeants continued to shout out meaningless commands, more to distract the men than to actually accomplish anything. As he listened he heard the shouts and calls further down the line, in between the howl of crossing shells, of a regiment being maneuvered to face the threat. Soon he could hear drumming, which meant men were marching on the Rebels. As he focused on his very own small piece of earth, he noticed that sunlight was brightening and illuminating the soggy field. It would be a very pretty winter day, were he not in such a horrible place.

General Thomas Cobb paced the muddy sunken road, behind the stout stone wall, where his brigade had been assigned, He had seen the position once as he had scouted the ground with General McLaws, several days before, but had never looked at the ground from the exact vantage of the position, until now. He quietly took inventory of his shattered command. Maryland had been a punishing adventure for the Georgians of his brigade and the past two months had consumed him in striving to replenish his depleted ranks and revive the spirits of his men. They were terribly homesick, and hopes of winter camp and furloughs had been dashed by the new Federal offensive. General Lee had ordered away the Carolina boys the week before, which saddened the men. They had bonded and the North Carolina farm boys had become great friends with their brothers from Georgia. As it stood now, he had Ben Phillips' Legion, McMillan's Irishmen and Ruff's boys of the 18th Georgia. Bryan's 16th Georgia was due to be returned today, but General Cobb had yet to see them. General Longstreet had borrowed them for some duty that was never explained. As he reviewed his thin lines, he wished for them now. Word from General McLaws was that there were "scads" of Yankees in the town below them. Off to his left, Joe Kershaw's South Carolinians filled the remainder of the sunken road, off beyond the Innis house. The width of the road worried him; it crowded the men, and he could not envision how his ranks would have much room to maneuver, if it came to that. The men nodded and softly greeted him as he walked past and he would encourage them with promises of furloughs, once they pushed the Federals back across the river. It always helped to pose the enemy as an obstacle to going home. And many had a score to settle after the losses at Crampton's Gap, in Maryland.

Thomas Cobb recalled the morning so far; they had been rousted from their fitful sleep, well before dawn, without breakfast. A fact that explained the dozens of small fires along the road as the men attempted to warm their meager rations and heat water. They had quietly filed through the fog, down from their camps on Howison's Hill, where he had left his artillery alongside the massive 30 pounder from Richmond. Captain Porter, the Chaplain, had insisted on the men reciting the 91st psalm as they trudged through the misty predawn dark. The quote echoed in his consciousness, "thy shall not be afraid for the terror by night, nor the arrow that flyeth by day." He imagined many an arrow would show itself when daylight came.

The darkness slowly gave way to a lightening gray as the rising sun fought the dense fog of the Virginia bottomlands. The smell of wood smoke rising from the town below filled his senses. He remembered watching some of the houses burning the night before. Colonel Ruff greeted him as he approached his Battalion, "Good Morning Sir! My boys are ready, albeit a might cold!" General Cobb returned his salute and dryly replied, "Not to worry Goode, I hear it promises to become quite hot shortly! General McLaws has relayed to me that those Federals mean to come our way. Make the best use of your space as I know this is a difficult position to fight from. I would suggest relays, have some of the boys load and some fire. God help us if we are to be forced from this road! I also expect the 16th to show shortly, so see if you can assist me in shoehorning them into your right!" Colonel Ruff nodded. He had been thinking of many of the same thoughts, responding, "I shall see to it General."

Moving back in the direction of "Federal Hill," he encountered Colonel Robert McMillan, the elder statesman of the Georgia Legislature who commanded his Irish Brigade. Cobb smiled as he approached, the boys on this part of the line were behaving as if they were on a pleasure outing, with many laughing and joking. As he drew closer, Cobb announced, "Well Colonel! How fares the Irish on this fine morning?" The graying Colonel replied with a smile, "We could be better, particularly if we were in Savannah, or perhaps Atlanta! Other than that, General Cobb, we are most happy to be under your employ!" General Cobb turned and looked beyond the wall, quietly observing, "Expect them to come shortly. Allow the artillery to work them over first, let them get close before you give them a volley! That town will tangle them up, there is no possible way for them to make a concentrated attack! Good luck Colonel!"

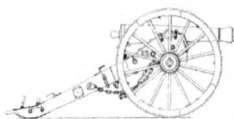

Captain Henry heard the salvo of Federal shells hurtling in and turned in time to see one of them tear into the carriage of the Blakely gun. The spray of splinters of oak and iron fittings shredded the bodies of two of the crew and wounded the Gunner as he was trying to aim. Henry shouted to Major Pelham, "Sir! We have lost the Blakely! We need to return to our lines! This is damned madness! We cannot fight the entire Yankee army alone!"

Pelham turned to him, and calmly directed, "Captain Henry, have the surviving crew assist on the 12-pounder. I shall quote a line from Sir Walter Scott's "Ivanhoe," Captain. I remember it goes, "*all is possible for those who dare to die!*" We are gravely delaying them and the army behind us can use that time! I shall fight here, until ordered to withdraw!" Two more shells from the Yankee battery, near the troops he had targeted, burst near the ruined gun. The impacts sprayed the crew of the bronze Napoleon with wet dirt. Captain Henry shouted over the din, "Spherical Case Shot, 1200 yards, advance the charge!" The well drilled crew lost themselves in serving the gun, despite the heavy firing around them. They repeated the process of loading and firing, ignoring the enemy cannon. The massed troops were the object of their fire and they focused on accomplishing the complex gun drill as rapidly as they could.

Major Pelham studied the effects of his fire as his remaining gun played over the vast line of Union troops. He did not pause to study the Yankee cannon near them. Watching them was only bad luck, better not to see the shot that sends you into the next world. In the background, he could hear the crewmen by the limber shouting to Captain Henry that they were running out of ammunition. So intently did he study his distant foe, that he never noticed the rider who had galloped out of the shelter of the woods to his location. The young cavalryman's greeting caused him to look away, "Message to you Sir! It is from General Stuart hisself, Sir!" Pelham took the folded scrap of foolscap and opened it,

"*Major Pelham*

You gallant fool! Withdraw your battery from danger at once!

Major Genrl J.E.B. Stuart, esq.

Commanding, Cavalry Corps ANV"

Major Pelham chuckled a moment and asked the young messenger, who flinched from time to time as the shells whipped by, "Private, should I obey this order?" The young cavalryman nodded swiftly, "Sir, I would be thinking hard on it. Word has it General Lee wants to talk to you!" Pelham laughed again. Then he turned and caught Captain Henry's glance, before he shouted, "Limber up!"

Private Gustin realized, as he lay on the cold wet pasture, that the shells were no longer howling over his head. Lifting himself up on his elbows and feeling the damp earth soak through both the overcoat and his sack coat, he looked about. He lay in a great tangle of blue-clad men and he could see the cold vapor of their breathing rising from the prone men. He then heard men shouting down the line and the shouting traveled like a wave towards him, until he heard his Captain shout, "On your feet, Men! Fall in and form ranks!" Behind him, the drummer boys began to sound the long roll and the encouraging sight of the dark blue regimental color, rose back into the sky along with the soldiers of the Color Guard as the regiment realigned itself. The officers formed the soaked, and muddy men forward of where they had sheltered from the fire, in part to allow the stretcher bearers space to remove the wounded, and in part to prevent the men from having to gaze at the horribly maimed dead. Many of the men were soaked and shivered in the mid-morning cold. They were happy to be moving about. Ahead of them, the wooded front and raised rail line remained eerily quiet. Frank Gustin felt a fleeting sensation; it seemed that they were under full observation from a waiting and patient enemy.

With the blowing of bugles and the beat of the drums, the long blue ranks begin to pace forward, accompanied by the shouts of the officers and Sergeants. Messengers on horseback galloped, businesslike and hurried, to and fro, between the advancing ranks. The point of woods and the rail line became more detailed as they moved closer. Glancing to his left, and right, Gustin noticed his messmates all possessed a fixed stare towards the woods, and the Captain, ahead of them, kept his gaze fixed straight ahead, not bothering to check alignment of the ranks. The soil was soft and squishy as they paced abreast across the sloping pasture. Despite the morning chill, Private Gustin felt the sweat building up under his Sack coat and his overcoat. Suddenly, the edge of the forest came alive in the form of spaced plumes of white smoke as hidden batteries erupted in fire, aimed at the approaching Union ranks. Loud cracks instantaneously erupted in front of them. Gustin could hear the grunts of men to his right as bursting case shot tore gaps in the formation. The officers screamed simultaneously up and down the line, "At the double quick, march!" Nearly tripping several times, Private Gustin fought to keep up with the rest of his Company. The point of woods they were guiding on looked nearly in musket range when another salvo of artillery again burst in front of their lines, felling more and more men. He heard his Captain shout out over the din, "Don't stop men! If you stop you die! Keep moving!" Gustin felt as if his heart would burst as he heaved breaths into his lungs and ran. The lines were getting ragged, but the men all attempted to keep their interval. Glancing up, he saw lines of gray and brownish clad men beginning to emerge from the woods, off to his right. The bright red flash of a Rebel color caught his eye as he trotted along. He made out an officer on a sorrel horse waving his saber, obviously to have the Rebel troops form up. The long line of unseen cannon spewed another volley of white smoke and more men from the advancing Regiments were stripped away.

The wood seemed much closer now and Private Gustin felt a deep desire to reach the questionable safety of the trees. His fixation on the wood was disrupted by a loud and angry stuttering crackle of musket fire, off to his right front. A sheet of minie bullets slammed into the ranks dropping men to the left and right of him. He briefly caught sight of a shiny Springfield musket flying through the air and landing in the pasture, bayonet down, remaining there upright with the buttstock swaying back and forth. They continued to run at the double quick. The Rebels were off diagonally to their front. Nothing threatened them straight ahead. He heard a distant rumbling and the shreiking roar of shells passing off to the left and right of him. Sharp cracks marked the impacts of the friendly artillery, striking above and before the Rebel troops. Another volley sent another wave of the wicked minie balls lacing into the running men. Gustin heard two rounds buzz past his head, but he breathlessly continued on. After several more paces, the ground began to be marked by taller grass and small bushes amid a brown tangle. His feet were wet and he realized he was trotting across shallow standing water. Seeing his Captain ahead of him with his sword raised, he realized they had reached the edge of the point of woods. After a few more steps, he sank to his knees in very cold water. Sensing high ground to the right of him, he angled towards a brushy area. His legs ached as he slogged through the cold water. After a few seconds struggle, he found grassy and muddy footing. After much slipping and stumbling, he found himself in a tangle of dried and dead blackberry bramble. Gustin could hear his panting comrades following. As he shouldered edgewise through the tangled and wicked thorny brush, a sudden explosive thrashing erupted to his right. He caught a fleeting glimpse of a terrified deer bounding off through the deeper woods ahead. A general shout from their officers echoed through the woods, "Fall in on me! Load!"

The increasing crescendo of cannon fire to his left made Sergeant Augustus Talmadge of the 1st South Carolina Rifles anxious as he made the rounds among his men. Many had rose from their reclining positions to sitting up in order to listen to the sounds of battle. Talmadge was checking cartridge boxes, on order of the Captain. A quartermaster wagon had come up with cartridges and Captain Randolf wanted every man to have forty rounds. Talmadge gave one of his reclining men a playful kick on his shin, and directed, "Waters! Show me yer pouch! How many bullets you got?" Private Waters swished the gum twig in his mouth a bit before tipping his tattered hat away from his eyes as he slowly sat up, "Hold yer horses, Sarge! I got em here somewheres!" Talmadge watched bemused as Waters dug through a second canvas haversack, and replied, "Looks to me like I got 20 shots, Sergeant." Talmadge put his hands on his hips, and asked, "Now why in the hell don't you got a cartridge box, boy?" Waters grinned, and replied, "I don't like em, Sergeant Talmadge! The damned thing just slows me down. I like to snatch them cartridges up, real quick-like! Just like I snatch up them Yankee biscuits!" The remark drove his nearby messmates into helpless laughter, as Sergeant Talmadge fought back laughing himself, "Waters get over to the wagon yonder and get 20 more shots! Get right back, we could fall in at any minute." Talmadge continued to make his way along the Company, whose men rested in rough lines behind the long rows of stacked muskets, along the dirt path. An occasional loud bang would signal another Yankee shell exploding in the nearby woods. The rattling of musketry perked him up a bit, which meant the enemy was not far off. While he did not mind being in reserve, the inability to see what was happening made everyone nervous.

A man on horseback approached him as he walked down the row of stacked muskets and noting the distinctive tricorn hat, he stopped and saluted, palm up, "Good Morning Sir!" General Maxcy Gregg returned the salute. He had seen the Sergeant before, but could not place the name, "Good Morning to you Sergeant! Keep an eye on the men, don't let them wander off! We may receive a call at any time." As the General rode past, Sergeant Talmadge noted that he stopped, from time to time and stared into the empty and misty woods to his left. The General was clearly nervy this morning. As Talmadge trudged back towards his own gear. Shouts of men behind him caused him to turn and look. A Whitetail deer made a panicked dash right through a stand of arms, knocking bayonetted muskets down with a clatter. The frightened animal then leapt entirely over two sitting men and dashed madly through the camp. The men shouted and some laughed, but Talmadge heard one older man comment, "They only do that when something is chasing them."

Private Frank Gustin realized they had become terribly mixed up, when he noted some of the boys from the 13th Pennsylvania in front of him. They were unmistakable as they wore deer tails on their forage caps. Gustin thought they looked a little bit like wild Indians, but as rumor had it, they were the best riflemen in the whole Division. One thin faced man, seeing Gustin, remarked, "Best get behind us son, unless someone told you to be a skirmisher!" Gustin mutely nodded and allowed the serious and quiet men to proceed before him through the woods. They moved noiselessly, and paused often, with rifles at the ready. Glancing back towards the open fields, he realized that he was ahead of his Company and decided to double back. Quickly glancing back in the direction of the "Bucktails," he was surprised to see they had swiftly disappeared. The misty woods, and gray leafless trees nearly matched the light blue greatcoats of the Union infantry.

Returning to the mass of men he took for his Company, Captain Atkinson, shouted, "Gustin! Fall in, dammit! No skulking! Step lively" As Private Gustin returned to the company of his friends, they watched and listened to the discussions of the officers, only feet away. They were momentarily distracted from their eavesdropping by the rattle and clatter of another Company being marshaled closer to them on the right. Clearly they were being readied to advance. A bearded man on horseback came up to the cluster of officers, and while the men recognized Colonel McCandless, they were mystified by the bearded man, until the First Sergeant informed them with a harsh whisper, "You men shush! That is General Meade, the Division Commander!" Colonel McCandless could be clearly heard, "Sir, the skirmishers from the 13th have found a Rebel camp ahead and they have no idea we are here! They are cooking breakfast behind stacked arms! If you can have Magilton tuck into my left, we can make a general assault upon them!" General Meade nodded and raised himself up on his saddle, in a vain attempt to see through the woods and the slight rise before him.

As he studied the ground, he impassively watched as a pair of skirmishers led a Rebel prisoner towards the General at bayonet point. The hapless man held his trousers together with his free hand while he held the other, aloft in the sky. The skirmisher, holding the man at bayonet point, looked at Colonel McCandless and stated, "We caught this one shittin' in the woods, Sir!" General Meade looked down at the muttering man, and asked, "What unit are you with, Son?" The Rebel soldier looked up and glumly responded, "General Gregg's Brigade, South Carolina Infantry." General Meade thoughtfully paused a moment before saying, "Last I knew, Gregg's Brigade is part of A.P. Hill's Division! That means we are among Tom Jackson's force!" He turned back to Colonel McCandless and directed, "Colonel! Stand fast here, I shall collect up Magilton's command and press them to join your left. I shall pass the order to advance once that is done! No drums or bugle calls, have the men move as quietly as you can! Insure they are loaded and have bayonets fixed! Once you get the order, press them hard. I shall go back to General Reynolds and have supports follow us!"

The men stood in loose ranks for nearly 20 minutes until more crashing and trudging to the left indicated the arrival of Colonel Magilton's Regiment. The officers commanded in whispered tones for the men to form into a rank of two rows. They issued stage whispered orders, "Check your loads! Don't cap your muskets! Move quietly!" Private Gustin watched, amused, as Colonel McCandless confiscated all the drumsticks from the drummer boys and placed them in his saddlebags.

Soon the hushed orders floated down the line, "Advance men! Keep it quiet!" Slowly they began to move, breaking ranks frequently to dodge the many trees and bushes that impeded their way. Private Gustin realized that he could hardly feel his toes, so chilled were his wet feet. Based on his mother's advice from childhood, he would "surely catch his death of cold." A bright day had emerged above as he looked up, but it was still misty and dark in the winter woods.

After nearly a hundred yard advance, they approached the backs of the skirmishers who sheltered behind the trunks of trees. The men trotted back to their company, and one paused by Colonel McCandless and held a whispered conversation, with much pointing and gesturing. Private Gustin tried to hear what was being said, but he could make nothing out. McCandless rode the line on his horse and whispered to the Captain, "Have them prime their weapons and place them on half cock! They are 50 yards off! Make ready to advance."

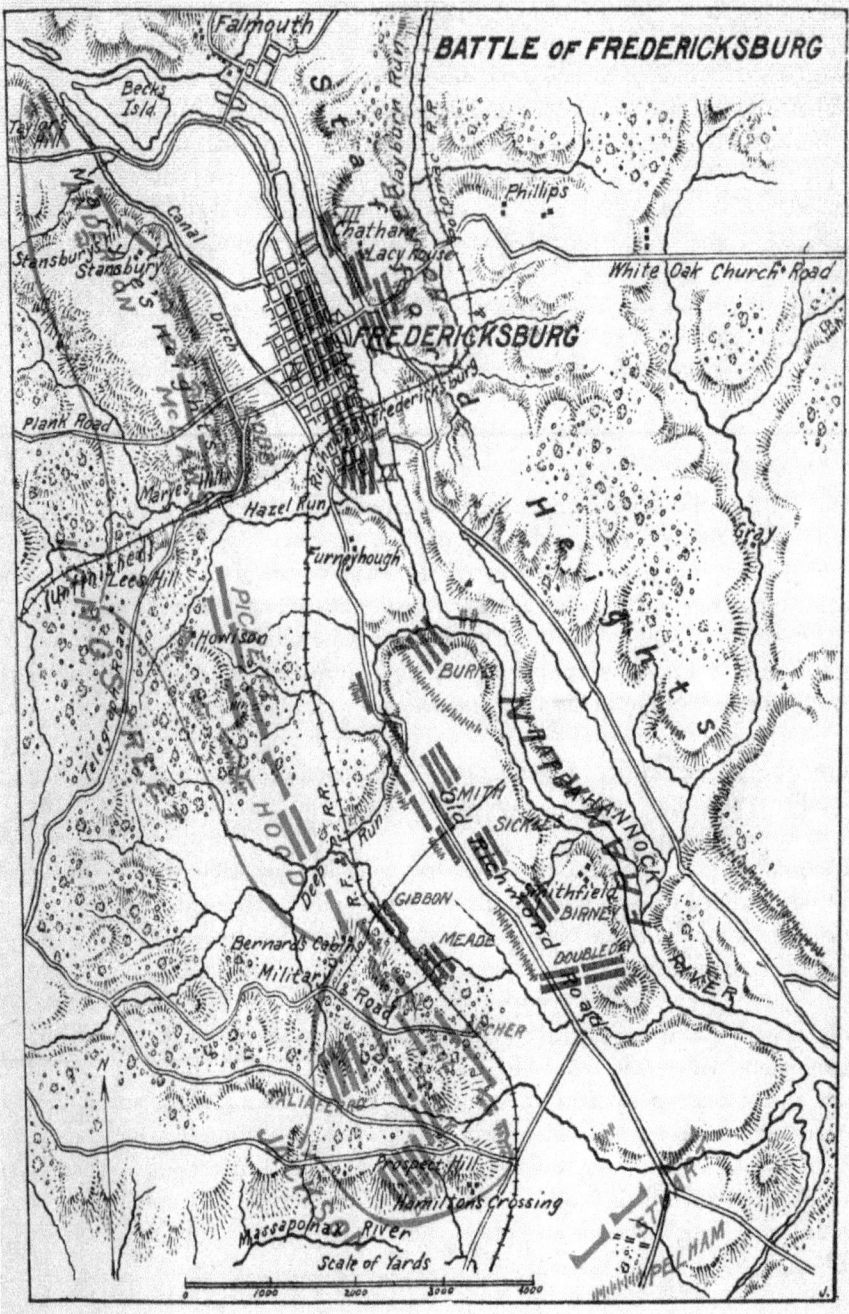

Crashing noises in the wood below, caught General Maxcy Gregg's attention and he turned his mount towards the noise. Beyond, the crackle of musketry rose and fell. Clearly heavy fighting was occurring near where the rail line ran before him. Inwardly he wished he knew this ground better and he instinctively suspected that elements of General Lane's Brigade were employing the wood to fall back through. The crack of muskets discharging nearby meant that his pickets were firing, perhaps blindly into the woods. Spurring his horse, he rode down into the wood, shouting, "Hold your damned fire, boys! That is our own men! Cease your firing!" Gregg rode nearer to a Picket sheltering behind a tree, and challenged him; the shocked soldier turned and shouted, "Sir, get back! Them's blue-bellys! It's a hell of a lot of them, too!" A sudden blast of musketry emerged below him and he could see the rounds shredding the bare saplings around him. A powerful blow struck Gregg in his stomach, doubling him over in his saddle. Instinctively he willed himself to spur his horse, but his legs would not respond. Looking down, he placed his hand on his stomach and stared dumbly at the gout of blood on his glove. His last sensation was his body heavily striking the ground.

The rattle of musketry in the woods, followed by the loud cry of charging men, was enough of an indicator for Sergeant Talmadge. He shouted at the top of his lungs, "On yer feet boys, them's Yankees! The shocked men, scrambled to their feet, upsetting cook fires and coffee pots as they collected cartridge boxes and rushed towards their stacked weapons. The crashing noises in the woods grew louder and they heard the shouts of Officers crying "Ready!......Aim!.........Fire!" The edge of woods was cloaked in the sudden burst of white smoke and orange muzzle flashes accompanied by the deafening roar of the muskets. A perfect hail of minie balls shredded gunstocks, ricocheted off iron barrels and slammed into the bodies of the stunned men with meaty smacks. Sergeant Talmadge was spared by a Private in front of him, who's head exploded in a red cloud of tissue and chunks of skull. Another volley erupted to the left of the first, felling dozens of men around him and striking the bare tree trunks around him with hollow pops. Forgetting the rifles, Sergeant Talmadge shouted, "Run for it boys!" The sudden emergence of the Federal troops caused the men of the 1st South Carolina rifles to run for their lives; most were unarmed. Passing through other camps, he shouted out to the astonished men, "The Yankees are coming!" Unknowingly, they were creating a general panic that would cause most of General Gregg's Brigade to melt away into the cold and tangled woods.

Colonel William McCandless strode purposefully behind his advancing Regiment, with his aide de camp following, leading his mount by the reins. He had found it easier to walk than ride between the tangled trees. Pausing amid the tumbled down stacks of hundreds of abandoned Enfield muskets, he noticed the sun was high, illuminating the forest floor. Great gobbets of blood pooled, and congealed on the brown leaves, and the bodies of dead and wounded men littered the camp. The companies were ahead, and had stopped to reload, with great reaching activity of hundreds of uplifted arms, stroking charges down the barrels of their muskets.

Catching Captain Mealey's gaze, McCandless motioned forward with his gloved hand. The Captain nodded and shouted out, "Charge bayonets! Forward, March!" The companies advanced through more upturned bivouacs, and it was clear that the Rebels were running. McCandless turned to listen, as a great rattle of musketry emerged off to the right. He imagined Colonel Magilton had found more camps, and was driving them as well. Summoning his bugler, he had him sound "Commander's Call," which brought his three Captains, Major Ent and Colonel Biddle, who commanded his understrength regiments. As the officers assembled, he quickly directed, "Gentlemen, you must press forward until we find the road the rebels built through this wood! They should be arrayed along it! Once we strike it, I want Colonel Biddle to secure the right, and make contact with 3rd Brigade, Captain Talley, you must find the right flank of the 2nd Brigade! We must push forward abreast! Keep driving them, and send runners to me! I shall follow the 2nd! Find Captain Mealey and you shall find me!" The men quickly nodded, and hurried back to their commands. McCandless knew the momentum must be maintained, he had no idea what lay ahead. Colonel McCandless then turned, and directed his Aide de Camp, "Send a runner back to Colonel Sinclair! Inform him we have ruptured the Rebel lines! Tell him to send up ammunition and reinforcements!"

General Jubal Early sat on a fallen log, listening to the sounds of battle in the wood before him. Straggling men had been brought before him, and after interviewing several, he learned some were from Gregg's Brigade, some were Tennesseans from Archer's Brigade, and some were North

Carolinians from Lane's Brigade. Despite his instruction to wait on orders to counter attack, from General Jackson, he could feel disaster in the air. Easing up on one side, he extracted a compressed plug of tobacco from his pocket, and bit off a hefty portion of the plug. Ruminating on what he would do next, he savored the tobacco, recalling his days working on the farm at home, growing the crop. His spot on the log was well lit by the mid-morning sun, offering a thin warmth against the cold December air. The sounds of battle through the wood increased in intensity, and soon a rider approached. Early placidly sat in the sun, and spit out a quid of dark juice, as the rider stopped his horse before him, "Sir, greetings! I am Lieutenant Chamberlayne, General Hill's artillery! You must act, Sir! There has opened up an awful gulf between General Lane's, and General Archer's brigades! My batteries are in grave danger, if Infantry is not applied at once, to drive the Yankees back!"

This news caused General Early's eyebrows to raise, he asked, "Where is General Hill?" The young Lieutenant shook his head, "I have no idea, Sir! There is not much time for me to find him!" Early nodded, he had gotten crossways with General Jackson two days ago for misunderstanding of orders, and while hesitant to act now, he could see there was the imperative for a decisive move. General Early stood, spit and pulled his gauntlets back on, turning towards Colonel Walker, who silently waited behind him, he directed, "Go roust Lawton and Trimble! Follow the Lieutenant! Let us rush to General Hill's assistance. He then untied his black gelding and mounted with an agility that belied his aged appearance. Astride his horse he watched as the men quickly and expertly formed into column and began to stride towards the noise of battle with their muskets at shoulder carry. He could hear Hill's artillery firing now, which meant canister at short range. Urgency would be required.

The men were in high spirits and shouted out to the stragglers and wounded who filed past, "No worries boys! We're a coming to help out ya'll's light division!" The glum retreating men could only stare as Early's men guffawed, and laughed.

The woods began to thin out ahead, and Colonel McCandless could see that his men were approaching in ragged lines towards what looked like another Rebel bivouac site. Thinking quickly, he shouted out to his Sergeant Major, "Have the men close ranks! Stop them here and have them load!" As the soldiers. Some from the other Regiments, began to align themselves, he was summoned by a messenger from the Brigade Artillery. The young officer saluted and announced, "Sir! Colonel Sinclair has been gravely wounded! He has directed you to assume command of the 1st Brigade! I trust you are Colonel McCandless!" McCandless nodded, wondering where this had happened. The confusion of the attack through the woods, left him wondering how many men he had left, and what had become of Magilton and Jackson's Brigade. He quickly strode over to Captain Mealey, "Timothy! You are now in command of the 2nd Reserves! I have to replace Colonel Sinclair! Keep them aligned and wait on the order to advance! I must find the Brigade Color Guard!" Walking down the line, he greeted Colonel Biddle of the 121st Reserves and repeated the news, adding, "If they shoot me, Chapman, you must take over from me! Form your men tight as has the 2nd! On my command we shall advance through that clearing ahead!" Chapman nodded, "Don't get shot, Buck. I do not believe I would relish your new job!"

After greeting and advising each of his regimental commanders, McCandless centered himself on the Color Guard, and instructed the young drummer, "Beat common time, Son!" The men struggled to keep their alignment, in accordance with the shouted orders of their officers, as they reached the edge of the wood. As they reached the verge of trees and open pasture, Colonel McCandless raised his drawn sword, and commanded, "At the double quick, March!" The long blue ranks began to trot, some tripping occasionally in the low corn stubble of the field, as they crossed the open place. McCandless began to see men in gray assembling across from them. Forming ranks at the orders of their mounted officers, they appeared to his front in alarming numbers. These Rebs were not running or disorganized. It became immediately clear, that these men were fresh reinforcing regiments. Watching the gray ranks before him growing, McCandless realized he would lose the race, he cried out, "Mark time, march! Form ranks and prepare to fire!" He listened breathlessly, as his regimental commanders echoed the order. Shouts of "Prime!" were shouted up and down the ranks, as the men dug percussion caps our of the pouches on their belts and capped their muskets. He estimated the range at nearly 200 yards distant, and he realized he would lose much of the effect of a volley. There was no helping things now. He rushed to position himself, and the colors behind the ranks, as he shouted out, "Fire!" The roar of the volley drowned out the shouted commands from the regiments, down the line, as his men poured a concentrated volley into the Rebel ranks. Through the cloud of smoke he could see men in the gray ranks fall, but not nearly enough to break them. Without orders from him, the respective regiments were commanded to load, and the men expertly flipped open the leather flaps of their cartridge boxes, extracting the flimsy paper cartridges.

McCandless scanned the men to his front, as they extracted the iron ramrods and rammed the minie balls home over the charges of powder, quickly returning the rods to their channels. It was then that the Rebel ranks delivered their fire. Men before him fell, with shouts and cries, but the determined Reserves closed ranks, and prepared to return the favor. The emergence of firing from an unexpected quarter, off to the left, caused him to order his Adjutant, "Direct Captain Mealey to refuse the left flank with his regiment! Have him move with all speed!" This new development concerned him. The retreating Rebels had led him into a concentration of reserve troops. Without reinforcement, he would not be able to hold out long. McCandless directed his Aide de Camp, "Lieutenant! Get word back to General Meade, we must be reinforced, now!" The end of his sentence was drowned out by his second great volley. He turned to his left, and watched Captain Mealey rushing his men to form new lines perpendicular to the new threat. Another Rebel volley caused many to fall, but the men stood fast, and closed ranks. He was now resigned to slug it out with his determined foe, so long as his men could stand it. He tried to mentally calculate how long the ammunition in the men's pouches would last, but his mind was racing too quickly for him to think clearly. Glancing off to his right, he could see no evidence of Jackson's brigade. They were not tied to his brigade's right. It was then that he realized his mistake. He now had unsupported flanks. They had come too far.

The young courier galloped up from the hollow, behind the Stafford Heights, with a message from the signal tower overlooking the rail trestle. Near the portico of the Phillips house, he dismounted in one smooth motion and handed the folded message form to a Captain standing on the porch. The young officer took the message inside and provided it to Brigadier General Parke, "Message for General Burnside, Sir! It is from Franklin's Grand Division!"

General John Parke unfolded the message and quickly scanned the contents. It seemed that General Reynolds' Corps had gained a breakthrough, fitting news indeed, news worthy of interrupting Burnside and Hooker's meeting. Tapping on the closed door leading into the dingy parlor, he announced, "Sir, begging your pardon on the interruption, but we have received an encouraging dispatch from General Franklin on the left!" General Burnside returned his cigar to his mouth as he stood to receive the message. After scanning it, he announced, "This is capital news, John! Please monitor General Sumner's progress and get me reports! Hopefully, the timing of his orders will pin Lee down!" Parke nodded and moved toward the door. Parke hoped that Sumner was doing as he was told, no messages indicated any action from that front, yet.

Burnside looked back over to Parke and directed, "Send a courier to General Sumner, insist that he proceed with his attack this instant!" Parke nodded and left the two generals. Inwardly, he was disturbed by the detachment of his boss. He should be at some high point, watching this battle. Command via messages received, and messages sent, would never accomplish much. He hoped the Grand Division Commanders were not mimicking this command style. After dispatching the courier, Parke lit a cigar and listened to the sounds of battle from the porch of the Phillip's farm. In between the nearly constant thundering of Hunt's guns, he could hear the heavy musketry rising from the river bottom from his left. Franklin was in it, in earnest, down below. Perhaps the breakthrough would result in a Rebel retreat. It would be nice to have a peaceful Christmas.

General Thomas Cobb studied the message brought to him, via a rider from McLaws, the communiqué directed him to report as quickly as possible, in the event that there was a failure of his command, to hold his position. Folding the message, he handed it to his Adjutant to dispose of, as he replied to the messenger, "Son, General McLaws may find hisself waiting a very long time for anyone backing me off of this ground! Tell the General that I understand, and I shall not hesitate to let him know if my Legion cannot hold this ground!" Cobb then spit and extracted a cigar from his vest pocket. Extracting his jack knife, he cut off the end and dug in his pocket for his match safe. One of his entourage, Captain Taylor beat him to it, producing a lit match. As Cobb sucked on the cigar, Taylor advised, "Sir, this little house shan't be all that safe, once them Yankees come, on this hill and all. We shall prepare you a place down on the road." Cobb nodded, and looked about at the small brick home, halfway down the hill from the sunken road where his men stood. He remarked, "Be sure to clean up a bit, before you leave boys! This is someone's home after all." Suddenly above them, their guns suddenly came to life again, firing howling shells over their heads into Fredericksburg. Cobb and his staff watched, as the bursting, and careening projectiles, brought further destruction to the neat little city of Fredericksburg.

A young orderly had brought General Cobb's dapple horse around to the front of the home, when several men could be heard, crying out, "Here they come!" Taking the reins in his hand, Thomas Cobb turned to look towards town. Thousands of blue uniformed men were exiting Fredericksburg in columns, boiling out of the cross streets, that led towards his position. To Cobb, it reminded him of the result of poking an anthill with a stick. The regimental drummers anticipated his commands, and began beating out the "long roll" as his men rushed to the stone wall, prominently posting their respective colors, and battle flags, along the stout stone wall. The emergence of the Federal Troops, spurred General Longstreet's artillery to furious action, and the discharging guns combined into a thunderous roar, over their heads. Down below, the beleaguered troops gamely began to form ranks, on the outskirts of town, under a hail of shell bursts. Cobb could see large gaps blown in the ranks by the long-range fires, as the Union advance halted before the millrace. General Cobb, observed as the thousands of men crossed the muddy ditch, in great disorder, as the unceasing cannonade continued to pummel their formations. Cobb heard one of his officers comment behind him, "Sheer murder!" Cobb only muttered in response, "That'll teach them to invade Virginia!" Eager for something to do, General Cobb rode his line, hugging the narrow borrow pit along the hillside, from time to time he exhorted his men, "Hold your fire boys! We shall wait on them to come close, before we give them a volley! Wait on my word boys!" He noted that most of the men were firmly gripping their muskets, awaiting release, to destroy the approaching foe. The sight of the host forming below, while awe inspiring, also filled the men with rage. They feverishly awaited their chance to add to the slaughter, being wrought by the cannon. Cobb returned, on his mount to the center of the line. He would wait on horseback by the Brigade battle standard. The Blue and Red color, perfectly square and adorned by a Saint Andrew's cross, adorned with white stars, hung limply in the still mid-day air. He inwardly wished for a greater wind. A wind that would prominently display the symbol of the rights of free States, to their approaching enemy.

General Cobb continued to study the approaching Federals, until he was interrupted by his aide, Captain Barrow, "Sir! The 16th has come up! Where do you want them!" Cobb looked up the hill behind him, and saw clusters of men coming over the top of Federal Hill, he curtly replied, "Guide them to the left of the 24th! You'll just have to shoe horn them into the line! There ain't much room here." Turning his attention back to the approaching foe, he estimated them to be nearly 400 yards distant. After a thoughtful pause, he shouted, "Load and make ready!" The impatient men quickly, and efficiently loaded their thousands of Enfield muskets, with a loud, and continuous clanking of steel ramrods, all up and down the stone wall. Many, after finishing the loading, and priming of their rifles, lay them atop the wall, in readiness for the anticipated command to fire. Surveying their progress, and sensing their impatience, Cobb shouted out, "Wait on my orders boys!" He wanted them close, and the artillery still was busy tearing large gaps in the advancing ranks. Cobb realized that the advancing commander could not accurately sense how reduced his command had become, due to his position, forward of his men. What was left of the advancing brigade would be totally destroyed by an accurate volley. He realized that cold calculating patience was required now. Just let them get close enough for every shot to count. The Union commander approaching him, bravely rode the line at 300 yards distant and began shouting orders to "Close ranks!" The hapless men, still dodging bursting case shot, and shell, gamely readied their muskets. Cobb realized the import of this desperate move. A long range volley, might delay the inevitable, but he was untouched by the feeble attempts of the supporting artillery to defeat his stone wall, and he was being reinforced by an additional regiment. Glancing behind him, he saw the 16th Georgia, beginning to descent the hill above him, in a ragged line. He was still looking up at them when a ragged volley erupted from the advancing Yankee line. Dozens of men fell amongst the 16th, as the reinforcing Regiment was caught in the open, on the steep and exposed slope.

Angry, General Cobb shouted out for Captain Thomas, "Captain! Direct sharpshooters to engage that horseman!" Taylor nodded and selected several men by name on the line, "Get that officer boys! There is a prize for his hide!" The select men, leaned against the wall and shouldered their muskets, adjusting the ladder sights as they did so, employing shared advisories about range from the watching, and waiting soldiers around them. One after the other, several shots rang out along the stone wall, marking it with plumes of white smoke. The third shot hit its' mark, and the dark blue clad officer on horseback, fell hard from his mount. The crazed horse ran, stirrups flailing, back towards the mill race. Captain Thomas then directed, "Reload and bring down the color bearer!" The grim marksmen began to slowly, and carefully reload their rifles, while their fellow soldiers shouted, and jeered them on. Another officer on foot below them began to urge the blue-clad regiment to advance, amidst great gouts of dark earth, thrown up around them by the fire of Longstreet's artillery. They were only around 150 yards distant, when a smattering of shots dropped the national flag, and several men of the color guard around it. The red, white and blue standard was quickly raised as the Federals began to advance at the double quick. The dwindling advancing soldiers gave a great shout as they ran towards the wall. General Cobb, pausing one last minute, estimating 100 yards, before shouting, "Fire!"

The simultaneous roar of thousands of muskets, blinded the men with a great cloud of white smoke. The long line of men behind the wall, quickly lowered their muskets, and rammed home fresh cartridges, then raising their arms to remove the spent percussion caps, to prime with fresh ones from their belt pouches. The officers shouted for them to wait on clear targets, as the haze gradually thinned in the early afternoon sun. Only clusters of men remained standing, who feverishly were reloading from their last volley. General Cobb was in no mood for mercy, and commanded, "Present! Fire!" Again the stone wall was blanketed with the acrid sulfuric smoke, as a second great volley slapped down what remained of the Union Regiment. As the smoke cleared no upright men could be observed. Only the shifting of limbs from the wounded marked where the Regiment had advanced.

As the smoke of the battle wafted away, the distant tremblor of drumming signaled another Division of Federals marching out of town, towards the heights. General Cobb's shouts of "Make ready, here comes some more of them!" was drowned out mid-sentence with the terrible roar of Longstreet's artillery, on the hill above them.

Brigadier General Hunt was becoming increasingly frustrated by the developing situation. Because of his far off positioning, on the north side of the Rappahannock, he had no targets to engage, except for the Rebel cannon, and that set of targets were clearly well concealed, and covered by works, that made for fine work by the rifled pieces. Artillery duels rarely settled great battles, and as the Rebels refused to show their infantry, he could do little to affect the course of this great fight. As he dourly watched a battery of 20-pound Parrots, vainly attempting to silence a stubborn Rebel battery in the woods edge, far away, he was interrupted by a familiar voice.

"I've some grave news on the old company, General!" General Hunt turned and returned the Sergeant Major's salute, "What news?" O'Keefe continued, "That fookin' Lieutenant sent 1st Section across to support Colonel Hall's Brigade, once the bridges was in! First Sergeant Timmonds took them across, and now 5 men is dead! No one knows nothin' about Timmonds, and he didna' come back with the rest of them. I would call him dead, Sir! But I am requestin' to go look into it!" Hunt made a pained face, Timmonds had been one of his favorites, ever since Fort Leavenworth. He asked, "Who are the dead?" O'Keefe rattled the names off by memory, "Palmer, Olson, O'Leary, LaRoache, and Bills, Sir! If I find Timmonds dead, that makes six. Pure stupidity, it is, Sir! Puttin' guns into the town, when she's not secure!" Hunt thoughtfully observed, "Yes, it is sad to lose trained men! What about the guns?" O'Keefe waved his hand, "No worries on that, General! The Provost, General Patrick, has them under guard. Lost all the horses, though!" Hunt raised his field glasses for a moment, as he watched the disturbing events just above the town, below him, he muttered, "That makes the third attempt on those heights!" Lowering his glass, he directed, "Very well Sergeant Major, take some ammunition wagons from the ghost trains across the bridges, they likely will need resupply, once you have done that, you can look into things." O'Keefe nodded and tendered a salute. As he turned his horse, General Hunt added, "If you find him dead Sergeant Major, you must assist Pennington in selecting a new First Sergeant! I suspect Mills is not a bad choice." O'Keefe silently nodded. With a loud "Yah!" he spurred his horse down the muddy track, that led to the river.

In a hollow, just behind the positions on the Stafford Heights, he found a collection of the tarred canvas wagons. Colonel Hayes had positioned them mid-way between the guns, and the bridge. The wagoners huddled around fires, warming themselves, as their mules waited in their traces, occasionally braying, and protesting their plight. Sergeant Major O'Keefe reined to a stop, and shouted out, "Who's in charge o' you fookin' gypsies?" A hatless man in his undershirt looked up and grinned, "That would be Quartermaster Sergeant Bollinger, Sergeant Major! You can find him that a way!" The soldier pointed to a location, further up the road. O'Keefe spit, and shook his head, the sounds of battle raged all around, and the army had so many men, that for some, there was little or nothing to do. The vastness of it all, made little sense. After a few moments he found Bollinger, sitting by a kettle of something cooking, smoking a cigar.

"Must be special to take yer leisure in the middle of a vast battle, Quartermaster Sergeant!" O'Keefe dismounted, and strode over to his old acquaintance from Mexico, many years past. Bollinger looked up, rolled the cigar in his mouth, and spit, "We seem to have more Irish in the Army than I seem to remember, do they pay you fellers more than us?" O'Keefe chuckled, as he lifted the dipper in the pot, to smell the concoction, "I need a favor L. G. I need to get across them bridges, down below. I want you to round up two wagon teams. Make one loaded with 12-pounder, and the other with 10-pounder Parrot ammunition." L.G. mulled the request over for a moment, before replying, "Them engineers ain't lettin' no supply wagons cross over yet, them bridges are reserved for Hooker's infantry!" O'Keefe nodded, "I am bluffin' my way across, using General Hunt's good name. I got soldiers down, from me old company! Gotta find em' and get them back!" Quartermaster Sergeant Bollinger nodded, "I'll line out two teams! Have a sit, Sergeant Major, and help yourself to some stew. Got some of my best mule in there."

Quartermaster Sergeant Bollinger soon reappeared with two mule drawn wagons in tow, "Alright Sergeant Major, here they are! If you ain't particular, I think I will join you. Mind you, these damned jackasses are real particular about crossing them pontoon bridges! I intent to see them across proper like!" Soon the small party was underway, descending the muddy slope. While the sun was up, the air still contained the December chill, causing the Wagoners to raise the collars of their greatcoats, as they rode. As O'Keefe approached the road he recognized the Major there, from their earlier discussion of yesterday. Thinking quickly he announced, "Major Spaulding is it?" Spaulding looked up, his face registering surprise at the sight of the ammunition wagons, "What precisely is this, Sergeant Major?" O'Keefe puffed himself up and replied, "This here is a push of artillery ammunition, Sir! I have in me pocket orders from General Henry Hunt hisself, directing an urgent resupply of the guns forward!" Spaulding gave him a skeptical look, but since those guns had labored so mightily to help him yesterday, he sternly directed, "Very well then Sergeant Major, you need to get across fast! I expect an infantry division to cross, at any moment, from General Hooker's force! Last thing I need is mule skinners clogging up my bridge! Have them dismount all riders, and walk them across!" Bollinger strode over beside O'Keefe's horse and spit, before he muttered, "Won't work so well, gotta have the driver stay right where he is Sergeant Major! Them mules don't brook no change-ups!"

The first driver dismounted, as instructed and attempted to lead the team across. The mules stoutly resisted the tug on their reins, and began to bray loudly. After a concerted struggle he pulled the first pair of animals onto the first bay. The sway and bobbing of the surface, caused the frightened animals to bray louder, and stomp their feet. The team began to strain backwards, to escape the bridge. Quartermaster Sergeant Bollinger then came alive, "Back them goddamned mules off the bridge!" Turning to the Major, he stated, "Sir, jackasses is jackasses! Stand back, and let me do this the easy way!" Before Spaulding could protest, Sergeant Bollinger ascended the drivers seat on the army wagon, and quickly arranged the team leads in his fingers. With a great snap of the leather leads on the backs of the six mules, followed by a great blue stream of profanity, the team lurched forward, careening the heavy wagon onto, and across the 400 yard span. Once across Sergeant Bollinger shouted back, "Alrighty there Cletus, it's your turn!"

The young Corporal driving the second wagon, accomplished a similarly hazardous, and rapid crossing, and the second heavy wagon joined the first. Sergeant Major O'Keefe looked towards Major Spaulding, and grinned as he quickly trotted his mount towards the abutment, "Don't mind them teamsters, Sir. They're all a little touched in the skull, they is."

Once across, they stared amazed, at the piles of chairs, carpets, broken china, and hundreds of other assorted household items in piles by the bridge departure abutments on Sophia Street. A nearby sentry, of the Infantry Provost Guard calmly remarked, "It's contraband Sergeant Major! We have orders to allow none of it to cross the bridges by General Patrick." O'Keefe's quizzical look, impelled him to continue, "Boys was breaking into the houses yesterday, takin' all manner of stuff. Took us all night to get them back to proper order!" O'Keefe paused, and took stock of the town. Troops in waiting, crowded the street above them, while others wandered about in small groups. These small groups were accosted by the officers of the Provost Guard, and escorted back up to Caroline Street. Other small groups of the Provost Guard, investigated the cellars of the buildings along Sophia Street, searching for stragglers and shirkers in the dark cavernous basements. Turning to Sergeant Bollinger, O'Keefe commanded, "L.G. take the wagons up the cross street there, and find a Quartermaster. I care not a damn about which one! Empty the wagons and return to this place and wait on me!" O'Keefe turned and rode up Sophia Street towards the ruined railroad trestle, he had heard reports that a hospital was established near there.

Private Gustin moved closer to Sergeant Balk, a bearded and rough Dutchman, as the whizzing Rebel minie balls cut down two men, to his left. Glancing down, he thought he recognized one of them, a lanky farmer from Beaver whom he had exchanged pleasantries at Smithfield, the night before. Balk uttered a stream of German curses, as he feverishly reloaded his Springfield musket. Gustin felt more comfortable beside the great bear of a man, as he too reached for a new cartridge in his leather pouch. After searching both tops, he realized his top compartments of the cartridge pouch, were empty. Steadying his rifle in the crook of his right arm, he used both hands to extract a tin, for the 5 spare cartridges in the bottom compartment. He then realized other men were shouting, "We need more cartridges!" Some were squatting, and searching the pouches of the dead, and wounded. To their front, more and more Rebels appeared in ranks, the frontages of their Regiments continued to expand, as theirs contracted.. The stimulating rout of the Rebels, was now turning into a determined slug-fest, between two bodies of men, too hard headed to admit defeat, or retreat. Glancing left, as he returned his ramrod to the channel under the barrel, Gustin caught a glimpse of Colonel McCandless, slowly firing his revolver at the gathering gray mass, shouting "Keep up your fire, men!" To Gustin, it seemed that an equal amount of gray-clad men were falling as were his comrades in blue. Through the haze of gun smoke, he began to notice that the Rebels continued to have men to fill the holes. Glancing backwards, he noticed an empty wood behind them. There were no reinforcements for them.

Northeast of the 2nd Pennsylvania, General George Gordon Meade sat astride his mount, and attempted to comprehend the unseen. The intensity of the firing in the wood, beyond the railroad tracks had increased. His experience inferred to him that the penetration of his brigades had finally found solid Rebel resistance. The reports of the couriers had become more and more disturbing. Two of his brigade commanders were wounded, another reported losing contact with his regiments. Now reports asking for more ammunition were coming in. The firing to his left, along the tracks, revealed that Jackson's brigade was still pinned down below the wooded heights. The firing deeper in the woods straight ahead, meant that McCandless, replacing the wounded Colonel Sinclair, was too far out and too deep to have supported flanks. Colonel Magilton was nowhere to be seen or heard from. Wounded men limped out of the woods with bloodied wounds, each bearing tales of hundreds of milling Rebs and shortages of cartridges. Turning his horse and trotting down the tracks to the left, he had nearly reached the flank of Jackson's brigade when another volley from the heights tore through the winter bare trees and brush all around him. Feeling a tug on his hat, he removed it and noted the new musket ball hole in the crown. He quickly backtracked along the rail line to find a path back into the open. Patting his mount on its neck, he realized his hand was wet with blood. Bending over, he saw that the animal had been shot in the meaty part of its' neck. As he digested the chaos around him, a clear vision gelled in his mind. The penetration of these lines would be lost without immediate reinforcement. Suddenly the crescendo of firing to his right increased perceptibly. Trotting quickly out of the wood, he saw Gibbons' men rushing forward towards the elevated rail line through heavy Rebel fire. Meade was encouraged to see that his earlier request to General Reynolds had been finally heard. Still his brigades deep in the woods, were isolated and remained unsupported. Emerging from the wooded railway line into the soggy pasture, he spied another Federal force advancing up the slope. On either side of the formation, newly arriving batteries were smartly swinging into position to cover the advance of what looked to be a new division. Meade turned to Lieutenant Rause who had dutifully and quietly followed him and directed, "Lieutenant, ride to that formation, and inform them to come up! This day will be lost if I am not reinforced!" The young Lieutenant saluted smartly and galloped off, down the soggy pasture.

Looking back to his right, General Meade noted Gibbons' Division bounding over the elevated rail line with a great shout into the hazy gun smoke of the latest Rebel volley from the edge of the wood. He realized that more pressure was needed to carry this effort. Pausing to look behind him, he realized he only had two officers remaining in his entourage. He quickly summoned, Captain Eldridge his engineer, and directed, "Paul, press into the wood and attempt to ascertain from Magilton and McCandless how they fare! Come back to me at once!" He watched as the young Captain disappeared back into the woods. The loud hollow booms of the cannons supporting the flanks of the attack sent shells shrieking by to his left and right, exploding deep in the woods on either flank of Gibbon's attack. The charging men paused to unleash a great volley into the edge of the bare wood at unseen Rebel troops they had pushed back. Opportunity lay here, he thought.

The two officers on horseback conversed in the gray, leafless wood. All around troops moved carefully past them. The soldiers had received the harsh enjoinders to "Move quiet-like." Beyond the hasty council of war, the sounds of a pitched battle emerged beyond the dense wood, punctuated from time to time by the odd popping noises of the nearly spent minie balls, ricocheting through the trees. Colonel Edmund E. Atkinson was a young graduate of Georgia Military Institute and had risen to rank quickly. He was significantly younger than Colonel Stiles, who he was providing instructions to. Atkinson had received the reports that the Yankees had made a hole in the lines, but were now scattered in unsupported and isolated regiments. General Early had little information to pass, in his initial counter attack orders, so Atkinson had determined to obtain as much information as he could, from the wounded men and officers that had drifted past them, through the thick woods. Looking towards the older Colonel, Atkinson directed, "Get your men up behind those regiments in the fight and form up. Keep them quiet! Run your skirmisher company forward, and have the Captain contact the commander of the regiment, to your front. Tell him to tell them to give us one good volley when they hear us start hollerin'! Then have them let us through. I don't want them Yankees to know we're coming! Wait on my command."

Quietly and steadily, Atkinson arranged his brigade behind the embattled defenders of the semicircular wood line, that bounded the western edge of the fallow cornfield. From time to time the ache in his shoulder throbbed with a sharp pain from his wound in Maryland, but the anticipation of the counter attack enabled him to ignore it. After an hour, his six regiments were aligned roughly behind the embattled Tennesseans of Archers Brigade, and the South Carolinians, who had rallied from Gregg's brigade. Atkinson quickly rode down the line, ordering in a harsh whisper to his Regimental Commanders, "Fix Bayonets! Pass the word!" The metallic clatter, from the order followed him, as he repeated it on his ride along the line. Once he had reached his far right flank, he noticed teams bringing up a battery of 6-pounders to support the counter attack. Pleased with this development, he rode back to the center and waited. He wanted to trigger his command the instant the Yankees fired a volley. Listening to the sounds of the firing, he practiced his ear for the distinctive noise of their firing. After several minutes, he felt certain he could distinguish it from the fire of Archer's and Gregg's men. Drawing his short field officer's saber, he shouted the command at the top of his voice, "Advance at the Double Quick! Give them hell boys!"

Private Frank Gustin gratefully accepted half a handful of cartridges from the wounded Sergeant, who moved up and down the depleted line of men. The man had been shot in the arm, but instead of making his way to the rear, he busied himself by picking up the cartridge pouches from the dead and moved along the lines of the regiment, distributing their contents.
Gustin's shin still smarted from a spent ball that had impacted into the dirt before him, before giving him a sharp whack on his lower leg. The German Sergeant had found the incident hilariously funny, despite the grim state they found themselves in. The thinning ranks of the 2nd Pennsylvania Reserves began to slowly back towards the shelter of the wood line behind them, as more and more of their shrinking number fell. A young Captain, that Gustin did not recognize, shouted out for them to "continue your fire!" Gustin, and his companions did their best to comply, despite their dwindling number of cartridges.

At the halfway point back to the woods, a sudden and great volley erupted from the Rebel ranks at the edge of the far wood. Many of the heavy projectiles struck the earth before them and one struck Gustin's canteen. When he brought it up to look at it, he saw a ragged tear in the tin as the remaining water drained out. He then saw that the man who had been beside him was down. The stricken soldier shrieked in pain as he tore at his sack coat and shirt to stare in horror at the oozing hole in his belly. The passage of time seemed to slow as the Sergeant to his left commanded, "Keep steppin' back boys! Keep your faces to them and keep firing!" As they struggled to step backwards while loading their long muskets, an odd noise arose from the smoke shrouded far wood. The sound was an unnaturally loud collection of whoops and shrieks combined with more guttural yelling. Private Gustin, soon realized it was a Rebel charge. He recalled hearing it before, only less distinctly in Maryland in the corn.

He watched amazed as hordes of butternut clad men emerged from the wood before them. The afternoon sun glinted evily from thousands of fixed bayonets. The men of the 2nd Pennsylvania Reserves gamely delivered a well disciplined volley that felled dozens of the charging men but the remainder were on them in an instant. Some leveled their bayonets, and thrust and parried, in the close and entangled merge of men but they were soon shot down by the surging Rebel horde. Gustin heard a gruff voice behind him announce, "Put down that there rifle, Billy Yank! " Turning he saw a grizzled and bearded soldier with an Enfield rifled musket leveled at him. Dropping his rifle, Private Gustin meekly submitted to his fate. In the distance, he saw the remainder of his regiment disappear into the woods.

The heavy fusillades of musketry had now died down to a smattering of scattered shots as sharpshooters dispatched the Federals who rose from the carpet of bodies strewn before the stone wall, in attempts to flee the killing ground. Captain John Berrien had received a summons to consult with General Cobb. He dodged his way past the crowds of men hunkered behind the stone wall, and make his way to the Stephens' house, midway down the sunken lane. Nearly a full division of men had now taken positions along the sunken road and he detected the distinct brogue of North Carolinians, intermingled with the Georgia regiments. The men were in high spirits and they ignored the orders of the officers to, "stay low." They had now repulsed four great frontal assaults and it was clear that their position was a good one. Guiding on the whitewashed brick

BATTLE of FREDERICKSBURG

farmhouse, he trotted through an opening in the stone wall and strode through the shattered front door. The Stephens' house afforded a commanding view of the sloping plain that led down into Fredericksburg, and General Cobb had taken to visiting it frequently, between attacks, to better see when Federals passed more troops through the town to attempt assaults on the heights. Entering the small parlor, Berrien's boots crunched on the broken glass underfoot and interrupted a council between General Cobb and General Cooke. Cobb looked up and was quick to provide direction, "Captain Berrien! I shall need you to promptly get back up to Camp Jeanie and find the quartermaster! We need cartridges! Bring back all you can find! We can hold them for the rest of this year if I have ammunition!" John Berrien quickly nodded and as he attempted to reply General Cooke rose to leave, continuing his sentence from the interruption; "I shall do as you request and bring the remainder of the North Carolina Brigade to this position. You should be adequately situated, then." Just as Cooke had strode to the door a portion of the stout brick wall of the structure blew in, as a Union shell detonated on the wall of the structure, blowing chunks of brick and plaster across the tiny room.

Captain Berrien shoved brickbats and timber fragments from his legs and rose. The room was filled with plaster dust, and he coughed several times, and shook his head, from the ringing of his ears. As his hearing slowly returned, he became aware of the sound of a heavy and distant cannonade. He correctly reasoned it meant another Federal assault. Quickly scanning his surroundings, he saw General Cobb lying on the floor behind him with a great red stain spreading on his pants leg. Looking out the door, he noticed that Captain Butler, General Crook's aide, held the General's head in his arms as he knelt by the prostrate officer. Berrien checked on General Cobb, he was semi-conscious and would not respond to his questions. Rising, Captain Berrien rushed out the front door and shouted, "Send medical orderlies! The General is wounded!"

Despite the approach of the Federal ranks, the men in the sunken road doffed their hats as the litter bearers carried General Cobb down the sunken road past them. Many uttered curses and swore vengeance for their beloved leader. The sight of his wounded body, passing by the men of his legion, filled them with a bitter rage. As he disappeared from sight, the soldiers returned their hats to their heads and grimly bit off the tails of cartridges to charge their rifles afresh. There still remained much killing to be done on this winter day to preserve Virginia and the South.

The officers shouted orders to the men, commanding them to shelter below the wall, as they crouched to peer over the mossy stones. When the blue-clad men had closed to 100 yards distant in the sodden pasture below, they shouted, "Here they come boys! Ready!......Aim!"

As if released from chains, the men quickly passed the long barrels of their muskets over the cover of the stones and took careful aim at the new mass of blue scarcely a hundred yards away. At the cries of "Fire!" the crowded ranks discharged their weapons in a synchronous loud roar of smoke and fire. The heavy white smoke blanketed the field before them and they speedily reloaded. The return volley from the hapless Union regiments spattered harmlessly against the stout stones. Only a few of the Georgia men fell in the ranks more from pure bad luck, than effective aim.

Captain Berrien took advantage of the smoke and spurred his horse up the road towards the crest of the hill. He still had to find cartridges for the troops, below.

Corporal O'Rourke had just finished tucking the sprig of Boxwood under the cheap brass harp on his forage cap, when the shouted orders came. "Fall in and form up men!" First Sergeant Kirkpatrick moved down the column of soldiers in the crowded street, shouting, "Get ready to move, when we tell ye! We are to bypass Caldwell's brigade ahead!" Private O'Malley commented, "Was becoming to like stayin' right here, all peaceful like." He then nudged Corporal O'Rourke, and added, "You think it will be bad up there, Corporal?" O'Rourke studied the Officers ahead for a moment, many were shaking hands and exchanging folded bits of paper, "Look at them! They know it is bad, Jesus! It's no wonder we got absolution again!"

Their gloomy prognostications were interrupted by the command, "Shoulder Arms! Prepare to advance by file!" The crowded nature of Caroline Street made passage of General Caldwell's brigade, milling in the street ahead, a difficult proposition. Colonel Nugent began to shout out orders that indicated a clear urgency, "Count off by the front rank of the column!" The men quickly shouted out, "One, two, three, four!", all through the length of the long column. Nugent then commanded, "Number four file, forward march! Mind the instructions of the guides! No shirkers!" The men to the far right of the column of fours began to step off, weaving their way over to the left of the street to move forward. It took several minutes before the men in the third file began to follow them.

When the order came to move the number two file, Private O'Malley quipped, "Alas my sweet Corporal, darlin', I must be off! I shall try to leave a few Secesh for you." The movement seemed to stir the Rebel artillery as a fresh flurry of shells ripped through the upper floors of the ruined houses lining the street. With each passing, chunks of bricks and slate tiles compelled the crowded soldiers below to dodge the debris. Once his file would began to move only to halt for a few moments before moving again. Officers from the companies lined the path, shouting out to the men to keep moving. The soldiers in Caldwell's brigade shouted out encouragement and cheered them, as they marched past. They were clearly jubilant that someone else would precede them.

As Corporal O'Rourke's file neared the intersection of the cross street ahead he noticed the Sergeant Major ahead with his hand out, "Stop here a moment lads! I'll tell ye when ye can pass!" O'Rourke took in his surroundings. Several bodies clad in blue wool were lying dead in the street, one corpse was hideously mangled. The Sergeant Major nervously peered around the corner, towards the Rebel works, a mile distant. He then turned to explain to the waiting men, "The Rebs you see, have the range to this intersection with their murderin' cannon! Ya cannot cross in column, no mores! They'll toss a shot in here if ya do!" Peering back behind him again he nodded and commanded, "OK boys, you next dozen or so move now! Do it at a run!"

Alan O'Rourke ran as fast as he could, his cartridge pouch and canteen banging against his hips as he ran across the cobbled intersection. Their movement ilicited a loud boom off in the distance. A Rebel solid shot smacked into the cobblestones short of Caroline Street and sent chips of stone and brick rubble flying all around them. As luck would have it, all the men with him got across safely. As he and his companions caught their breath and leaned on their muskets, they heard Colonel Nugent again shouting orders, "Form up boys! Form up by company columns!" The soldiers dutifully fell into column of fours, and soon received the orders, "Come to attention! Left face!"

Looking forward, O'Rourke noted the approach of General Meagher with another senior officer he could not recognize. They slowly rode their horses until they were centered on the boxwood bedecked flagstaff of the regiment. They had no flags, as General Meagher had ordered replacements, that were yet to arrive. The Sergeants had wrapped boxwood boughs around the staff. O'Rourke thought it looked like something the Roman Army would carry, but at least it was green. As the horses stopped and the Generals wheeled to face the men of the Regiment, Colonel

Nugent shouted out in his strident voice, "Present Arms!." The soldiers expertly brought their long smoothbore Springfields up, vertically to their front. After the Generals had politely returned the salute, Nugent commanded them to "Order arms!" The iron buttplates all smacked down on the cobblestones in unison. O'Malley, now behind O'Rourke again, muttered, "Who's the swell with Francis Patrick, Boy O'?" O'Rourke only could shrug, but First Sergeant Kirkpatrick turned his head and uttered in a vicious whisper, "That's your Division Commander, General Hancock! Now shut your fooking yap, O'Malley" O'Malley broke into a broad grin, and exclaimed under his breath, "Jesus! We're in for it for sure! First it's the noble speeches an' then it's another new General!"

As the men waited, General Meagher took his hat off in an eloquent salute to the Regiment and gave the same speech he had just delivered to the 88th Regiment.

'*Officers and Soldiers of my beloved 69th Regiment!*
You are mere moments from entering the fierce battle before us! The fate of our adopted home could very well hang on our actions in the next hour! Remember we have pledged our loyalty to this land of the free! Do your best men! I shall be there with you and if I should fall! Then I shall be grateful that I took part in this great cause! Show them that Ireland is here today! God bless you and good luck!"

When General Meagher was finished, the men raised their hats and gave a great hurrah. The sounds of heavy musketry beyond Hannover Street, leading to the heights beyond, bore witness that another attacking brigade had met the Rebels. The orders came quickly, "Right face! Forward march!" The drummers picked up the beat and the Irish Brigade departed the questionable sanctuary of Fredericksburg. The men quickly became hot marching uphill on Hannover Street, and many loosened the top buttons of their greatcoats as far down as the cartridge box cross straps would allow. Soon they crossed another lateral cobbled street before moving downhill again towards what looked like a treelined creek. O'Rourke glanced around; the homes and sheds in this part of town were a sorry sight, most had great shell holes in the roofs and walls. Looking up, he could see Marye's Heights rising slightly before them. What he took to be the Rebel lines were cloaked in gunsmoke and the roar of cannonading and musketry was a continuous pounding noise. Peering at the muddy pasture beyond the small watercourse, he saw that the pasture was dotted with blue clumps. O'Malley exclaimed, "Jesus! They are leading us to sure slaughter! Look there! Those are dead men!" Soon their ghastly view was blocked by the bare trees lining the mill race as the column decamped the road and started off across another muddy pasture leading to the mill race canal. Reaching the bank of the canal, Corporal O'Rourke could see that many others had crossed prior to them turning all the approaches to a quagmire. The tenacious mud tried to remove their Jefferson boots as they struggled to march in step to the drummers through it.

Colonel Nugent then stepped quickly out to the left of the struggling column, and proceded to shout, "Prolongue to the left! Form a line of battle! We shall cross the mill race in line of battle! Make haste men!" With shouldered arms, the men of the 69th New York trotted out in their well drilled manuevers, to transition from column of fours into a two man deep line of battle. The manuever enabled fewer men to cross each area of the muddy canal. The cries of "Ignore the footbridges boys!" was shouted out to the men as they were compelled to wade through the knee high water. O'Rourke sucked in a deep breath as he plunged into the ice cold muck and forced his legs through the mire.

Rebel gunners had noted the movement of the Brigade and turned their 6-pounders and rifles onto the crossing. Shot and shell tore through the bare trees and burst in the muck throwing mud on the struggling soldiers, as they fought their way across the mill race. Two men near O'Rourke were gutted by a bounding solid shot as they attempted to walk across the ruined frame of a footbridge across the canal. Their bodies disintegrated into a gory burst of meat and limbs. The muddy far slope elicited a great struggle for the men to clamber onto the trampled far bank as the officers shouted for them to form up. The soldiers slipped and fell, in the feverish scramble to form back into lines of battle to resume the assault. Corporal O'Rourke wiped the mud from the lock of his Springfield musket after he joined the ranks with his fellow soldiers. The Rebel batteries continued their hellish fire and an entire cluster of men to his right were blown down by a well timed case shot blast that made his ears ring. First Sergeant Kirkpatrick cried out in a desperate voice, "Stand fast boys! Stand fast!"

The men sought the safety of one another in the ranks, as they had so frequently drilled, the tremendous clatter of musketry upslope from them drowned out the commands of the company officers, who marked the line of battle with their sabers held level at their chests. Corporal O'Rourke focused ahead, through the drifting smoke, he could see nothing but still blue forms lying prone on the ground, as it rose before them. Soon they would be going up that hill. The thought of what the remainder of this day would bring, caused him to quickly genuflect. This might be his last day, he mused, as his heart raced in his chest.

Brigadier General Parke interrupted Major General Burnside and Lieutenant Comstock with a message from Major General Franklin, "Begging your pardon, gentlemen! This dispatch is from Franklin. It would seem that he is enjoying some success on the left!" Ambrose Burnside eagerly stood to take the paper and studied it for a moment. Breaking into a broad grin, he remarked, "Capitol News, indeed! General Parke, please insist on pushing hard on the right! Send instruction for Sumner to press them and keep pressing them! I shall not allow Bobbie Lee to reinforce his right!" Parke silently nodded and left the room closing the door behind him. Despite the import of this message he possessed an anxious feeling, but he could not understand why. He instead busied himself with instructions to the headquarters staff to draft, and deliver the attack orders to Sumner.

Four miles to the south of the Phillips house, General George Gordon Meade borrowed a horse to ride back towards General Reynolds' headquarters. His own horse had decided to lay down, no doubt from its wound and neither he nor his Aide de Camp could get him to rise again. The sight of his Bucktails, retreating in confusion back out of the wood filled him with a great rage. The slaughter of the 3rd Division would quickly become meaningless unless someone reinforced them. All of his couriers had come back with messages of refusal. It was as if the 3rd Division of the Pennsylvania Reserves was the only Union force in the fight. Another great eruption of musketry caused him to look back to the wood. There he saw that Colonel McCandless had seized a color and held it aloft while riding down the railroad track rallying the retreating men behind the cover of the raised embankment. Another cluster of men forming must be the remains of Magilton's brigade. If they could hold there then at least it would not be a total disaster. He bitterly turned the borrowed horse and rode down towards the ranks of stationary troops, several hundred yards below him.

As he approached the mounted Officer, near a farmhouse, Meade turned to the young Captain accompanying him, and directed, "Keep your distance a few paces son, this will not be polite!"" As they approached, Meade noted that the man wore Brigadier Rank and he looked vaguely familiar. Eschewing the courtesy of returning the man's salute, General Meade sharply asked, "Are you General Birney? The same General Birney who has refused two requests I have sent for immediate reinforcements?" The man nodded and stammered, "Sir, Sir, I cannot accept tasks from subordinates of General Reynolds, when, ah, when General Reynolds personally ordered me to secure these batteries with my brigade!" Meade grew red in the face as he released his rage, "You damned sightless scoundrel! You are bearing witness to a victory turning to debacle! What hazard are these batteries under? Are you a goddamned fool? My division is in the process of destruction and you sit here on your damned sorry ass and lecture me on my goddamned lack of authority to order you!" The top of Meade's balding head was becoming hot, so he ripped his hat off and threw it aside compelling his aide to dismount to retrieve it. He continued, " I command you this instant to reinforce me! I am a Major General and you are but a goddamned Brigadier! Rise up off your ass and reinforce me this instant! Your recalcitrance will result in the loss of this battle you shameless jackass! God help you when I find John Reynolds!" Meade then turned his horse and galloped back up the hill to rally what he had left. His Captain followed behind him stunned, still holding the General's sweat soaked and bullet holed hat.

Reinforcements slowly came up, but far too late to effect more or less, of a return of the status quo of bitter close combat along the rail line. The momentum of the 3rd Division had irreversibly been turned.

Corporal Alan O'Rourke fought the uncontrollable shivering that coursed through him. He wanted to think it was due to the cold, but he was sweating under his New York State shell jacket and sky blue regulation greatcoat. The officers seemed to be taking forever to establish a satisfactory alignment of the brigade. And as they waited the Rebel artillery did not. O'Rourke watched horrified, as a skipping solid shot bounced up twice before tearing into a portion of the line off to his right. The sight of arms and legs flying into the air both fascinated and sickened him. He felt the shiver run through him again and his stomach felt hollow. Throwing back the cape of his greatcoat he fumbled for his canteen. Finding it, he tugged out the chained cork stopper and took a sip. Feeling a nudge to his right he noticed O'Malley, who grinned and offered his canteen, "Take a sip o' this one Corp! You find it stiffenin' for certain!" O'Rourke nodded and took a long pull. This was no tin flavored water, it was whiskey and the warmth of it took his mind off his fear. Soon the loud voice of Colonel Nugent, echoed over the rattle of musketry and the roar of the cannon beyond, "Fix Bayonets! Commanders, prepare your companies to advance at the quick time!" The soldiers of the 69th New York, happy for something meaningful to do quickly unsheathed the sharp and shiny steel bayonets and twisted them onto the muzzles of their smoothbores. The men in ranks had grown utterly serious as the body laden fields above them bore testament to what they were about to face. Colonel Nugent then appeared on foot, his sword drawn and carried in his right hand, shouting to the Regiment, "Men, many before us have tried this! You can plainly see what the Rebels did to them! Do not stop! Do not try to shoot! Do not lay down! We need to get on them as quick as we can! Stay in ranks and keep up with your brothers! We are pushing through and you know the word! Let me hear you say it!"

The charged up men shouted the Gaelic battle cry in reply, "*Faugh a ballaugh!*" Which meant, "Clear the way!" The drummers took up the beat for quick time and the men began their passage across the soggy plain leading up to Marye's Heights. Corporal O'Rourke shouted out encouragement to his mess as they struggled to stay abreast of one another. The Rebel artillery redoubled their fire, striking portions of the line each time stripping away several men. The diminishing line of battle continued to contract as they climbed the gradual slope. Colonel Nugent commanded several oblique maneuvers to skirt the boarded paddock of the city fairgrounds and as they bypassed it Corporal O'Rourke noticed scores of men sheltering behind the questionable cover of the bullet-pocked fence.

Reaching a low swale, Alan O'Rourke realized that many of the men lying there were not injured at all, they were merely sheltering in the safety that the dip in the slope afforded. One man cowering there as the 69th clumsily stepped around them shouted, "Don't go up there boys! They whipped us solid! There ain't nothin' to do but die up there!" Several of the men in ranks shouted out, "*Faugh a ballaugh!*" again as they struggled to close ranks after passing over the long rows of prone survivors. Corporal O'Rourke had to keep throwing the cape portion of his greatcoat back over his shoulder. He knew the bulky garment would certainly impede his musket work. Keeping his eyes grimly on the distant stone wall that bisected the heights, he began to notice the spiky aspect that the wall had. It dawned on him that to spikes were all the bayonetted muskets propped against it by the Rebels. The Rebel infantry were watching their approach. The multiple attempts had taught them patience. They seemed content to let the artillery work them over first before committing to musketry.

Stumbling, Alan O'Rourke realized they were now entering the field of the genuinely dead and maimed. He had unwittingly stepped on a dead man's chest and the body gave off an odd croak, as his weight compressed the dead man's chest cavity. He discovered that the fallen muskets were also slippery and treacherous to step on, and many of the men had taken to looking down to avoid bodies and equipment that fouled their approach.

At nearly 100 yards from the stone wall, O'Rourke noticed that the thundering of the cannon had stopped. The continual roar was replaced by a strange and pregnant silence, punctuated only by the drummers, the shouts of the officers and the shrieks and groans of the previously wounded. Looking ahead again, Alan saw the odd sight of thousands of hats, of all types and colors, appearing alongside the bayonetted muskets lining the work. The Rebels were preparing to deliver a volley and all the men in ranks were peeking over the stone wall at their targets. At the urging of the beating drums and the shouts of the commanders the men of the 69th closed another 20 yards. As the long row of Rebels began to stand up, Colonel Nugent shouted out in a great voice, "Load!"

Corporal O'Rourke tugged at the flap on his cartridge box, and swore, as he realized he had forgotten to pull the leather tab free of the brass button that held it closed. Extracting a paper cartridge, he quickly bit off the paper tail and poured the heavy charge down the barrel then swiftly inserted the greased and tied buck and ball projectile into the musket. Whipping his ramrod free, he tamped the charge home, and returned the rod to its channel. As he brought the Springfield up to prime it, he glanced up and saw that the Rebels were now standing and leveling their muskets. He shakily extracted a percussion cap from his pouch and primed the nipple, when he heard distant cries of "Fire!" emerging all along the Rebel lines.

The Rebel volley crashed upon them like the wave of a great storm. The huge white bank of smoke blotted out the horizon, as a great mass of buzzing minie bullets slammed into the ranks, like a sudden summer hail. Screams and shouts emerged from the Irish Brigade's ranks. Nearly every other man seemed to fall. Corporal O'Rourke looked around, magically he found himself untouched but he could see several officers gathered around Colonel Nugent. The men were tearing at his frock coat around his belly. O'Rourke then saw a short Major trot along the front, carrying his short staff officer's sword, "Close ranks boys! Let's give it back to them! Close ranks and prepare to fire!" The soldiers hustled to comply and once they were shoulder to shoulder again, the orders came, "Ready!......Aim!......Fire!" Corporal O'Rourke was shaken from his horror by the stout kick of the smoothbore musket. The buck and ball cartridge contained nearly twice the charge of a rifled musket. Smoothly returning the heavy butt of the musket to the ground, O'Rourke began to reload along with the other men touching him on both sides. They were in a race for their lives and the Rebels had probably finished their reloading cycle. The lazily rising smoke obscured the pale winter sun and as it thinned, O'Rourke could see the mass of men before him, readying their muskets, resting them on the stone wall, taking careful aim. The second round of discharges were measured and aimed fire. He realized then that a frontage of Rebels, nearly three times wider than their own, was converging their fire on the Irish Brigade's narrow ranks. He was not an officer but he could clearly see the hopelessness of their plight.

James Longstreet carefully studied the latest attack out of Fredericksburg through his field glasses. He then lowered them to glance at his pocket watch. It was now 2pm and the attacks seemed to come out of the town every quarter to half an hour. He reasoned the constriction of the streets in Fredericksburg, contributed to the phenomenon, but with his strong positions the Yankees were on a fools errand, if they believed they could dislodge him from this ground. The supply of ammunition was his only worry. He had already received a dispatch from young Alexander expressing concern for the stocks of artillery ammunition. They did not possess the plentitude that the Federals seemed to enjoy. One of his aides had earlier reported of the Yankee batteries across the Rappahannock had at one instance kept up a rate of fire of nearly 50 shots a minute. As he listened, his own guns had slowed down in their rate of fire in order to conserve their limited ammunition.

A commotion behind him caused him to lower his glass, as Major Sorrell announced, "Sir, It is General Lee!" James Longstreet turned, and saluted. He then patiently waited, as Lee slowly dismounted, his heavy wool greatcoat made him slightly clumsy. "General Longstreet! How does your Corps fare?" Lee asked once he had relinquished his mount to his orderly. Longstreet quickly replied, "General Lee, I am holding them! Why, I should think that, providing my ammunition stocks remain supplied, I could readily slaughter everything they have north of the river as well. It seems clear to me that General Burnside is at a loss for imagination at the moment!" General Longstreet paused, reading General Lee's silence. He knew Lee had little use for crowing subordinates, so he more solemnly continued, "McLaws and Kershaw needed help, below us. The unfinished railroad cut below us there, posed a slight concern. I have allocated all, save a brigade of my reserve, to cover that area. General, I am comfortable that

I can hold this place!" Lee silently nodded and paused to look at another Union regiment dissolving beneath the continual Confederate fire, before softly remarking, "General Jackson had a close and concerning fight on my right. Do not be alarmed if I order further shifts from the right and center to reinforce him." Longstreet nodded and added, "Sir, the men are doing well, they are buoyed by the repeated successes at stopping them, but the cost in officers has been grave. Cobb and Cooke are down! The report I received on Tom is grave, he is likely to pass!" Lee gravely nodded, "Such is war, General! It is God's will. We must trust in him as we execute our duty to protect Virginia!" The two generals silently watched, as the battle raged below them. Both studied the battle with sharply attuned senses, as they studied the effects of their artillery and infantry on the struggle below. Lee departed with little spoken, and little ceremony. He had other spots of the battlefield to visit.

Sergeant Major O'Keefe threaded his horse up the street jammed with waiting soldiers. A few moments earlier, he had located the abandoned guns of the section. They had been pulled into a weedy back lot by the top of Hawke Street. He regretted not checking with Lieutenant Pennington first, as none of the section crew was present, and apparently all of the horse team were dead or stolen. A quick assessment revealed that the two guns would need three new wheels due to the splintered spokes. The damage spoke volumes to the old experienced gunner. The multiple bullet holes all over the carriages caused him to imagine a close range ambush by infantry. The pocked gun carriages meant that the gunners were the targets. He shook his head and spit. After pausing to consult with a Provost Guard at the corner of Princess Anne and Hawke Streets, he received the advice to proceed down Caroline Street, as troops were being staged for assaults on Princess Anne Street. Beyond the brick canyons of the town, a great battle was raging, and judging from the volume of musketry, it was an infantryman's fight. He shook his head at the notion of fighting over a river valley. It placed the guns too far back to be of much help against an enemy in works. He did not envy the men waiting in the streets.

He paused to ask an infantry Sergeant Major, who waited and watched over his men on the street, from the steps of a ruined house, "Afternoon Sergeant Major! Where do you lads hail from?" The tall leathery senior Sergeant replied, still clenching a cigar in his teeth, "125th Pennsylvania,

Tyler's Brigade. I been hearin' bad things up there, these boys are all new."
O'Keefe understandingly nodded, as the man continued, "They are all fresh
out of the Reserve Camps back home. I am gonna have a busy day keepin'
them still, I reckon!" O'Keefe dug out his pipe, loaded the bowl, and lit it
with a Lucifer match, before replying, "Well, they has to meet the elephant,
someday! I wish you luck, Sergeant Major." After taking a great puff, he
asked, "Are you aware of a field hospital near here? I am hunting some
wounded artillerymen." After a moments pause, the Pennsylvania Sergeant
Major replied, "The Adjutant made mention of one at the end of this street,
up yonder by the rail line. He said it was a warehouse, so I figure you keep
going the way you was going and you should find it."

O'Keefe gave the man a nod, and continued to negotiate his careful way
through the crowded streets. He was glad to be mounted. Had he
attempted to negotiate the street on foot, he would have never passed. At
least he had enough stripes on his sleeve to protect him from the challenges
of the officers. Soon a large wooden warehouse on the left side of the
cobblestone street came into view. Looking up, O'Keefe noted a tattered
yellow banner flying on one of the vent cupolas of the tin roofed structure,
a hospital. Tying his horse onto a lamp post near a provost guard sentry,
O'Keefe looked the trembling Private in the eye saying, "You let someone
pinch me horse, and I shall fookin' shoot you for it, Boy O'!" The
frightened lad stammered, "I'll keep a sharp eye on your horse, Sergeant
Major!"

Entering the hospital, O'Keefe was shocked by the number of wounded
men it contained. Tearing his gaze from the gore of the maimed soldiers, he
noted that most of the orderlies wore gray or butternut trousers below their
bloodstained shirts. The lack of standard shirts was another indication for
him, that this was a Rebel hospital. It made perfect sense that this would be
the best place to look for his boys. The Rebs still held the town when they
went in.

Cornering a young orderly, he asked, "You! Have ye seen Union men in
here wearing red pipin' of the worlds finest artillery!" The young
Mississippian drawled in response, "Yep, Billy Yank, we put them out thar
on the outside porch, they's got women lookin' after them at the moment.
We ain't got many. Yer Yankee doctors done went and took over the
Presbyterian Church on Hannover Street." O'Keefe bit his tongue and
merely tipped his forage cap in thanks. After looking about, he made his
way towards the wooden freight doors that led to the loading dock. The
Southern orderly frankly spoke out as he departed, "Mind you, Sergeant
Major, all them boys are on medical parole and their names is duly noted!

This thang here today ain't a goin' you boy's way!" O'Keefe only mumbled, "Much obliged, Boy O'." Coming back outside into the chill air of the covered loading dock he noted a long line of blue clad men lying in straw bedding on the wooden dock. As he scanned the row, he saw a young woman kneeling alongside one prone form.

Lottie looked up when she heard a distinctly Irish brogue, "Yer her ain't you?" She beheld a powerfully built, big man with a great bushy mustache and a wizened, leathery face. "Pardon me, Sir! Whatever do you mean by such a question?" O'Keefe looked down again and immediately recognized Joshua, despite the grotesque swelling on the left side of his face.

Turning to Lottie he responded, "Charlotte Markley, that's your name, is it?" Lottie was shocked and asked, "How do you know my name, Sergeant!" O'Keefe laughed and pulled his pipe out of his mouth to reply, "Jesus, Mary and Joseph, girl! I've been that boy's First Sergeant for nearly 9 years on! I have given him every letter, every parcel, from you, since 1856!" Lottie gasped, "My goodness, you are O'Keefe! He spoke well of you in all his letters!" O'Keefe then kneeled by Joshua. Disappointed to see he was asleep, he turned to Lottie and asked, "How is he?" She replied, "He is much better, despite a slight fever. He needs to have something more than broth, but he complains of pain, when he tries to drink! He needs to be taken to a proper hospital! Have you come for him, Sergeant O'Keefe?" O'Keefe nodded, "Can't have one o' me First Sergeants fallin' into the grubby hands o' the Rebels! I suspect this army is soon to depart this side of the river, from what I am hearin'! I have come to take him back."

Lottie incredulously asked, "What am I to do, Sergeant O'Keefe? For years I yearned to see his face and to talk to him! Now I am left with him, wounded and feverish, and you intend to spirit him away again! You and your war are unbearably cruel to us!"

"My war!" O'Keefe roared, "It was your people that started this, Miss! We are simply bringing the States back into the fold, as they should be! Your beau here, said hisself that he never understood it! He'd always say it overran him and denied him a chance to go home!" Noting her tears and somewhat struck by her beauty, even as dirty as she was, O'Keefe softened, "Perhaps you should consider crossin' that river with him?" At first Lottie was shocked, exclaiming, "My goodness! Never! My father would never understand!" O'Keefe understandingly nodded, adding, "Then you must resolve to wait for this war to end. Of course at the pace o' things I've seen, that could take quite a while!" Replacing his forage cap back upon his head, he turned to leave, "Miss Markley, tis a fortunate thing to make yer acquaintance! If I can trouble you to gather his things, I'll be bringin' a wagon by momentarily to take him back." Lottie tearfully nodded and then returned to Joshua's side, collecting up his meager possessions in his bloody cap.

As she attended to the task, Joshua stirred, and mumbled, "O'Keefe! I saw O'Keefe in a dream!" Lottie wiped a tear from her eyes, and replied, "It was no dream, Joshua! He was here, he is coming to take you to a hospital." The sound of her voice caused him to open his one unswollen eye and exclaim, "Lottie! Are you Lottie Markley?" The recognition in his face caused her to cry anew. Through her tears, she responded, "Yes dear Joshua, I have found you! You must promise me you will live! I can bear no more death!" Joshua nodded, the talking had brought the pain back and he laid his head back, exhausted by the effort. He silently studied her, as he lay, enduring the fresh wave of pain.

Elliot Lacy returned to the loading dock and stood distant from Lottie and Joshua. Such a complex situation, beyond all luck and comprehension. A young lady betrothed to a dead man, whom she had known from his youth. Now the discovery of a childhood beau of the girl, not to mention appearing in the form of a Yankee soldier, only hours apart. While unseemly and unsettling, she understood. Striding over to Charlotte she announced, "Miss Markley, I have made arrangements for the interment of Captain Tinchant's mortal remains! I think it only fitting that you find some time to write his parents, by way of soothing them in their loss!" Lottie looked to her distressed but recovered her composure, "Yes Ma'am, I can do that, but I fear I have never had their acquaintance nor corresponded with them!" Elliot looked down at Joshua and asked, "This boy here, is he special to you?" Lottie nodded and explained the years of correspondence and their early life together. She bitterly explained, "In a fortnight, I have lost what I found and found what I have lost!"

Elliot Lacy softened her demeanor and replied, "Dear Charlotte, I do understand! I too, am stricken, as I have borne witness to a dozen deaths today of very fine, young men. Many who had wives and children! I dare say, I have witnessed more of death and suffering, on this one day, than I have in all of my 70 years of life. Do not feel shame, Charlotte, I of all people, understand what you feel!"

Lottie sullenly nodded. Lifting her soiled dress, she set out to find a litter. They would need one to move Joshua. After finding the canvas litter, she made her way back to the loading dock to wait. She looked up into the late afternoon sky. The December sun was fading fast, and she reckoned it was late afternoon now. The sounds of the battle continued as if it would never end and crowds of Union soldiers still filled the streets, trudging their way towards judgment. The orderlies were hearing rumors that the battle was turning into a slaughter for the soldiers in blue, some of the rumors speculated that General Lee would make a massive counterattack to retake the town. Lottie hoped the battle would not take that turn. She wanted Joshua to make it back to the safety of the north side of the river.

Corporal Alan O'Rourke prayed for the darkness to fall. He lay as flat as he could behind several dead men as the terrible and random sniping struck men all around him. Laying less than 80 yards from the inpenetrable stone wall, he could clearly hear the conversations of the Rebels. They were certainly charged up and swore frequently. From what he could gather, they were now making ready for another assault, coming up the slope. The sun had passed below the woods of the heights and it would soon be dark. Behind him, he heard the tremblor of the drummers as another brigade came up to make the attempt. O'Rourke remembered the words of the men they had passed at the swale. He bitterly realized that those men, whom he had regarded as cowards were terribly right in their assessment of this ground. The wounded called out for help that was not coming. Nothing could move on the muddy pasture. It was nothing more than a killing ground.

Hearing a harsh and low whisper off to his right, O'Rourke rolled his head slightly to get a glimpse of who was talking. "Corporal! Are ye still amongst the living?" croaked Private O'Malley in a hoarse voice. Alan uttered back, "Shush! They'll hear us!" The exchange drew several shots in their direction. One of the rounds struck the dead man next to him, the body twitched from the impact, making a meaty whack, as the heavy projectile struck bone in the corpse. A clear and distant voice rang out from the Rebel positions, "No worries Billy Yank, ya'll just keep playin' possum! Once it is dark, we are comin' to find ya with our bayonets!" Multiple men cackled and howled at the taunt. O'Rourke resolved, that once it was dark, he might run all the way back to New York, and no one would catch him. He tried to control his shivering as the sun set. An enormous eruption of musketry, off to his far left, tempted him to raise his head to look, but prudence prevailed, and he simply lay, and listened. The battle lasted only twenty minutes or so, and then the sounds of battle dwindled. It was clear to him from sound alone, that this latest assault, like thiers, was a failure.

Alan O'Rourke was grateful, as the darkness closed over the wet field. He finally risked rolling onto his back and stared at the stars above him. The Rebels continued to fire into the field, from time to time, each in response to noises when they heard them. The night was not as cold as he expected, and the moans of the wounded had subsided. He resolved to wait until the racket from the Rebels stopped. The activity along the stone wall remained high until late in the evening. The Rebels were jubilant at their victory and the noises suggested that whiskey was being handed out to them.

The strange lights above him caused him to forget about the horrors of the day and fleeing his predicament. The sky flashed with colored lights, like he had never seen. He could hear the Rebels remarking in wonder, as well. It was as if the spirits of the dead were marching to glory above them. Laying flat on his back, Alan O'Rourke forgot the damp misery of his wet clothes, and the dead friends who lay all about him. He found his rosary, and muttered the familiar words as he watched the heavens above put on her celestial show, filled with flashes of green and red. Losing sense of time and place, he closed his eyes and drifted off to sleep.

He jolted awake in the darkness when something wet touched his forehead. He pushed away a dim figure crouched over him, and heard a meek protest. "Sorry my son, I took you for a dead man!" Recognizing the French accent, O'Rourke realized it was Father Ouellet, "Father what the hell are you out, and about, here! Are you daft!" Ouellet shrugged, "Sorry my boy, there are so many here, so terribly maimed! I must give them the last rites!"

The hushed conversation attracted the attention of the Rebel pickets who shouted out wearily, "Who goes there?" The loud crack from a musket broke the still of the pre-dawn morning. Alan O'Rourke rose on his stiff legs, picked up his musket and grabbed Father Ouellet roughly by the coat sleeve, stating in a harsh whisper, "Lets leave this place! Stay right on my heels!" They ran with abandon, slipping on the dark mud and tripping over unseen bodies as they made their way back towards the dark structures of Fredericksburg. More tongues of flame spewed from the muskets of the pickets as they fired blindly after them.

The morning of the 14th of December 1862 shrouded the ruined town of

Fredericksburg with a dense and chilly fog. Sergeant Major O'Keefe and Quartermaster Sergeant Bollinger spent a hard night in the bed of an ammunition wagon, warming themselves with sips of whiskey from Bollinger's canteen. Movement by night was an impossibility as the streets were flooded with soldiers, descended from the murderous heights above the town. Near midnight, O'Keefe had located Sergeant Newby in a basement near the guns. The dawn found him sleeping in the other wagon with Corporal Cletus Woods, who drove the second ammunition wagon for Bollinger.

The thin rays of light filtering in between the cracks of the tarred canvas of the wagons, awoke O'Keefe. He turned, and shook Sergeant Bollinger, stopping his hideous snoring. Running his hand through his thinning hair, O'Keefe directed, "Lets get this outfit movin' we've work before us!"

As Corporal Woods fed the mule teams, O'Keefe, and Bollinger strategized. The retreat from the evening had filled the streets with disorganized infantrymen of the ruined regiments. Pointing up the sloping cross street, O'Keefe advised, "I think the street at the top of this ridge is Princess Anne Street, or a name of some such royalty! The provost guards said to avoid it, on account of the Rebel fire. On account of this fog, I think it is a fair gamble to get to the Warehouse." Quartermaster Sergeant Bollinger countered, "Bill, these here mules won't be doing no running in a fog, they can't see through. Furthermore, I ain't too anxious to yell at them, like I will want to. Them Rebs might hear us!" O'Keefe nodded, "Then it's a plan! Just be nice to your jackasses then! Once we pick up our boys at the hospital, we can dump down onto the river front and find a bridge. Just let me do the talkin' to them Provost Guards!"

They set off, steadily weaving the two ammunition wagons through the rubbled street. The fog cloaked them in a protective shroud and they soon reached Wolfe Street, which led down hill towards the Tobacco Warehouse. The fog stilled everything and they quickly navigated to the hospital. There, O'Keefe found Charlotte Markley, asleep beside Joshua. A folded Ralstead litter awaited use beside her. He turned to Sergeant Newby, and instructed, "Find me three others who have a chance and get them into the wagon! We'll load two per wagon." Lottie assisted O'Keefe in situating Joshua on the canvas litter. Corporal Woods and Quartermaster Sergeant Bollinger loaded him into the narrow bed of the ammunition wagon. The jostling of the litter in the loading process, caused First Sergeant Timmonds to moan in pain. Hearing the noise, Lottie clambered into the back of the wagon to soothe him. His eyes were squeezed shut from the pain and he blindly found her forearm and clutched her with a strong grip. Lottie asked, "Would you like some opium for the pain?" Eyes still closed, Joshua replied, through clenched teeth, "Stay, stay with me." Lottie tearfully nodded, "I will my dear. I am right here, beside you." Torn as she was, she resolved then and there to remain by him. Closing her eyes, she briefly uttered a prayer that he might live. Gradually the grip on her arm loosened as he lapsed into unconsciousness.

O'Keefe appeared by the tailgate and asked, "Miss, will you be needin' help to get out of the wagon?" Lottie shook her head, "I have decided to go where he goes!" O'Keefe's eyes twinkled, and he replied, "Good girl! I know some people who will be happy to help you!" Then all business, he turned and shouted out to his small detail, "Fasten the end curtains tight and let's get this show on the road! We need to get back across that river, now!"

Lottie listened intently, as the swaying wagon came to a halt by the river. The Provost Guards challenged the wagon at the abutment. Through the tarred canvas top, she could hear Sergeant Major O'Keefe arguing with the guard. It seemed the mention of General Hunt was all that was needed to permit the release to cross the bridge.

Soon the shouts and cracks of the leads increased as the tilt of the wagon indicated the ascension of a steep grade. Lottie held Joshua down on the litter to keep him from being jostled too much by the rough ride. Topping out at the top of the hill, the wagon came to a halt. Lottie could hear the tinkling of chains as the latches to the tailgate were opened. The dark canvas end curtain was thrown aside and she could see O'Keefe's face in the morning sunlight. She noticed that there was no fog on the top of the hill. He gruffly commanded, "Get on out, Miss! We'll handle the lad from here!"

Lottie stiffly exited the wagon, gratefully accepting Sergeant Newby's proffered hand to assist her. After she was down, he shyly remarked, "I seen your picture, Miss! Joshua didn't like us talkin' about you." Lottie smiled and nodded. Newby followed her, and blurted out, "I'm awful sorry, Ma'am, lettin' this happen to him, and all!" Lottie stopped for a moment, hesitant to do so, as Joshua was being carried into a great manor house that was obviously now a hospital.

Newby continued, anxious to clear his conscience, "I was right there with him as we were pullin' up the guns, then everybody was firing at us. It was horrible, everybody was hit, save me! I ran like a scalded cat and I ain't ashamed to admit it!" He was clearly becoming emotional and Lottie laid a hand on his arm. She assured him, "Sergeant, I understand, this cruel war has done terrible things to us all."

Newby continued, "I wanted to go check on Joshua, but the fellows in the infantry with us told me to stay put. The Rebs tried to get the guns and they shot them down. Then they started to capture our wounded and the boys shot them down as well!"

Lottie gasped, as she realized the import of Newby's account. He had described how Henri had been killed. She remembered his determination to obtain wounded Yankees in order to safeguard the hospital. She pondered the fates that brought the death of one good man, in order to save another. The thought brought another tear to her eye. Quickly rubbing it away, she excused herself, and hurried off to find where they had taken Joshua.

Rushing inside, she was taken aback by the number of wounded men inside the grand old manor. Beyond the crowded parlor, full of wounded soldiers, she noticed Sergeant Major O'Keefe engaged in conversation with a stern, dark headed woman. Lottie wove her way through the crowded hall, until she joined them. O'Keefe grinned, and introduced her, "Ma'am, this young lady is a close friend of First Sergeant Timmonds, she insisted on remaining with him! I trust you can tolerate her here? Her name is Charlotte Markley." The dark haired woman, appraised her coldly for a moment, before she asked, "My name is Clara Barton young lady, I am under the direct employ of General Letterman, and I am a physician! It is my understanding that you were assisting the Rebels. You are now amongst your enemies! Have you thoughts on this conundrum?" Lottie stammered, "Ma'am, I worked for the purveyor, accounting for medicines. I am not a soldier!" Barton nodded, her eyes piercing and bright, "You may remain here to see to your beau, that I understand, but I cannot afford idle hands, nor unproductive mouths! If you wish to shelter here beside him, you shall work under my direction! I fear we shall be shortly overwhelmed."

Barton then turned to O'Keefe, and dug into him, "Sergeant Major, you facilitated bringing this woman here, past our Provost Guard! Has she taken a loyalty oath?" O'Keefe, looked Lottie in the eye for a moment, before replying, "Absolutely Ma'am, administered personal like, last night, before I would let her into the wagon! She was real anxious to leave that place and to see to First Sergeant Timmonds! He's a good man and we shall need him back, as soon as he is able!"

Barton gave him a skeptical look, before replying, "Sergeant Major, the man is under medical parole with the Rebel army! He will not be able to return until he is properly exchanged, and judging from his wound, he will likely take several months before he can return!"

Clara Barton looked at Lottie and her demeanor softened, "Come child, I will take you to the kitchen house to wash up and get something to eat! Then I shall give you your tasks." With a tip of his forage cap, Sergeant Major O'Keefe took his leave, "Miss Markley, I will come back by to check on you and the First Sergeant. I apologize, but I got a war to attend to!" Strolling back outside, he hopped back into the wagon with L.G. and commanded, "Let's get the fook away from this place, Bollinger! It's pure hell, it is! Run by women!"

The mournful murmur of the wounded became audible again, with the burning off of the morning fog. Their plaintive cries drew General Joseph Kershaw to the window of his headquarters in the Bryce house. As he peered over the now still battleground, he could see the wounded moving as best they were able, in their attempts to solicit help. Some were painfully attempting to crawl back to Fredericksburg. Studying the ground, he found himself astounded by the cost; the Federals had been willing to pay for this impregnable position. The sheer number of the dead would certainly pose a problem for the good people of Fredericksburg.

Returning to the table he used for a desk, he took a clean sheet of paper and began to prepare a dispatch to General McLaws. He felt compelled to address the issue of the Yankee dead and wounded. If they attacked again, it might be a moot point, but since they had shown no inclination, perhaps it was appropriate to address.

A sharp rapping at his door interrupted his writing. Without turning, he shouted, "By all means, it is open!" As the door opened, Kershaw sighed. He instantly recognized his friend John's fifth son, Sergeant Richard Kirkland. One of the liabilities of command for him, was the care and keeping of so many precious lives. Particularly those of the children of his associates. Sergeant Kirkland blurted out, "Sir! It just ain't Christian, watchin' them suffer like that! I cannot stand listening to them anymore!" Kershaw, remaining seated, asked, "Who are you referring to, Son?" Kirkland motioned his arm towards Fredericksburg, replying, "Them Yankee wounded, Sir! I respectfully request to tend to them!" Kershaw nodded, "I see. I am sure you understand that their army is still there, possibly preparing a new round of attacks? What would you want me to say to your father, were you to be shot out there?"

Young Kirkland, insistently answered, "Sir, I'll take that risk. I could not abide in myself if I did not do anything, save wait on them to die." Kershaw, losing patience, said, "They are invaders! They make war on our people!" Sergeant Kirkland, nervous that he may be going too far, responded, "Sir, they are men like us! The have families like us! Should I use a white kerchief as a sign of truce?"

Placing his pen down, Kershaw solemnly replied, "No son, no truce is solicited, nor granted, at the moment. It would not be authorized, or proper. Since you are so insistent, you may go. I pray you remain safe!" With a hasty, "Thank you, Sir!," Sergeant Kirkland bounded down the stairs. General Kershaw slowly shook his head and then returned to his writing.

The warmth of the mid-day sun, woke Lieutenant Randolf Larkin of the 5th New Hampshire Volunteer Infantry. By now, he had fully expected to be dead. He lay helplessly, flat on his back, unable to move. In the attack, the evening before, something had burst in the air behind him. He could remember the sour smell of black powder smoke and of hot iron. Something had hit him in the middle of his back. At first there was a piercing heat and pain, but now, there was nothing but an unhealthy numbness, a deep chill and a terrible thirst. Unable to look about, he shouted out in a weak and hoarse voice for water. He was nearly mad with thirst, acutely aware of his nearly full canteen, now out of reach, by his side. The hours passed and he could no longer utter the cry for help. His tongue grew thick and sticky. Thinking of home and all he was about to lose, dimmed, and made foolish the ardor he had felt in joining the great cause of Union. He longed to see his mother again, instantly sorry for what his death would do to her. She had worried so when he had announced his commission, a year and a half ago. He could hear the voices of men nearby. He would then remember that they were those of his enemy. They had nearly reached the wall, in that hellish twilight. They had been so close. Closing his eyes for a moment, he lapsed into unconsciousness.

Clinking noises near him, brought him back to consciousness. He wondered if it was the Rebels coming to finish him off. Gritting his teeth, he tried to raise his head, only managing a few inches, until he gave out a dispairing grunt. A nearby voice softly sounded, "You is hurt bad! I can see that clear as day, mister!" Lieutenant Larken could only weakly respond, "Water. Dear God, give me water!" Opening his eyes, he saw a young man in a tattered hat and gray uniform. He held no weapons and had canteens strapped across both shoulders. The soldier observed, "You can't move, can you?" He studied Larkin for a moment, before he observed, "My apologies, Sir! I hadn't noticed you was an officer! Would you like to be propped up?" Lieutenant Larkin weakly nodded, he could feel the weakness rising in him and he felt very cold.

Sergeant Kirkland could see the man's eyes study the canteens. He could not say much, but the eyes watched the canteens. He was clearly mad from thirst and wounded in such a fashion that his limbs were useless. Seeing abandoned knapsacks nearby, he secured several and used them to prop him up. Gently pulling the cork from a full one, he held the precious liquid up to his parched lips. The man drank deeply and the glimmer of a smile of pleasure flashed across his face. Kirkland, soothingly observed, "Good, ain't it? Sorry it took so long." The Lieutenant looked him in the eye and weakly nodded. Kirkland gave him another long draft from the canteen, and apologetically said, "Sorry Sir, but I got to get to these other fellers! God bless, and if they come for you, thank the boys down there for not shooting me. I'm just doing my Christian duty."

Lieutenant Randolf Larkin savored the refresing drink, relieved, as the weakness crept on relentlessly. He closed his eyes, and thought of Christmas at home. The darkness steadily came until he drifted off into eternity.

9

EPILOGUE

As the sun set on the evening of the 14th of December, a cold weather front brought cold blustering winds across the wooded hills above Fredericksburg. Singly, then in pairs, followed by clusters, Confederate soldiers silently climbed over the stone wall to loot and strip the dead. Coveted overcoats, accouterments, weapons and shoes, became the objects of new owners, who treasured their quality and newness. Officers, elected by their own men, were reluctant to stop the barbarism of the action. In this cold, they could not begrudge their hard campaigning charges for wanting better. These were things the Confederate Congress promised much and delivered little.

By morning light on the 15th, the color of the slopes changed from blue to grayish pink as the naked bodies of the dead lay pitifully exposed to the frosty daybreak. The horrid spectacle did not escape General Lee's notice, and he resolved at once to send an envoy to Major General Burnside, via flag of truce. A folded message crossed the lines from the hand of a Confederate Staff Officer to a Union Regimental Commander, who duly had the message transferred to his Division Commander. An hour later, the neatly scripted communiqué arrived at General Burnside's headquarters. Brigadier General Parke broke open the wax seal and scanned the contents. Noting the signature, he quickly folded it and sought out General Burnside.

He found the General, carefully attending to the task of writing his initial report to General Halleck. Burnside still was greatly distressed by the returns from his Grand Divisions as his casualty numbers were exceeding 10,000 men, either dead or wounded. The bitter reluctance of his subordinates in continuing the attack, left him questioning his own capabilities and wisdom. Hearing Parke's trademark quiet knock, he looked up, dreading more bad news.

Parke, catching his eyes, solemnly remarked, "Sir, this dispatch has crossed the lines under a flag of truce. It is personal, from General Lee. I apologize if my opening it prior, violates your sensibilities."

Waving the apology away, Burnside accepted the message with a question, "Are you preparing the withdrawal orders?" Parke solemnly nodded. Burnside carefully unfolded the paper and read,

"Army of Northern Virginia
15th day of December, 1862

General
I respectfully request your solicitation of a general truce, to facilitate the interment of your fallen soldiers, and the recovery of those wounded, whom we have little capability to provide for. I implore you to consider sending sufficient forces forward to accomplish this task out of propriety, and respect for the families of the fallen. I shall provide officers with which to consult, in regards to appropriate burial grounds, and to safeguard your detailed soldiers, as they perform this task. I do not wish to burden the poor citizens of Fredericksburg with this onerous task.
Your Obedient Servant
Robert E. Lee, Genrl
Commanding
Army of Northern Virginia"

The tone of the message did little to improve Burnside's spirits, yet the general intent was admirably civilized. Nodding silently, he began to envision how he would accomplish this task amidst his planned withdrawal. The numbers revealed by the Divisional returns, implied a rather large task ahead.

General Parke intoned as he still held the message, "A Major Sorrell delivered the dispatch and has also provided us the name of the parole agent. They are anxious to negotiate an exchange, it would seem. I am prepared to begin planning for parties to return across the river, Sir. I only need your approval."

Burnside silently nodded, he returned his attention to his writing. The casualty returns were shocking. He was certain that the command, he had never requested nor wanted, would soon be taken from him.

The long awaited Regimental Colors had arrived, too late, on the afternoon of the 14th of December. General Meagher had paused from writing his depressing official report of the horrible battle to open the wooden boxes containing the emerald green banners. The Adjutant assisted him in unwrapping the gold trimmed muslin banners, and the General became maudlin and teary eyed as he beheld each Regimental flag. At last count, he had only 280 men present, after going into battle with nearly 1,200. Looking at the young Captain, he ordered, "Get the boys to display them on the dias, on stage, at the hall!" The young Captain nodded and quickly returned the banners to their packages.

In an earlier spate of optimism, Meagher had arranged for his rear detachment to hold a victory celebration for the Brigade's soldiers the evening after the great battle at the Colonial Citizen's Hall, on Princess Anne Street. The structure had endured only minor damage in the bombardment and the rear detachment had festooned the interior with evergreen boughs, and other decorations, for the occasion. The quartermasters had positioned the whiskey ration by the back of the hall, and barrels enough for the rolls of 1,200, stood ready for issue by the gill, for the soldiers as they proceeded through the banquet line. While the battle above them had raged, the cooks of the brigade had scrounged the abandoned homes for delicacies and preserves to spice up the repast. It was envisioned to be a "grand celebration."

Corporal O'Rourke and Private O'Malley, the only two remaining from their mess of six men, sullenly waited in line outside the theater with the others. There was little talking; First Sergeant Kirkpatrick, his wounded arm in a sling, had directed the scanty formation that the theater was where supper would be served. O'Rourke wanted his whiskey ration badly. In his mind, that was all his soul needed, at the moment.

The cold and hungry men pitched into the vast buffet that had been prepared for a thousand. There was much to be had among the 300 men assembled. What officers remained were limited to Lieutenants, Captains, and the few Majors that made for General Meagher's personal staff. All the others were dead or wounded. The hungry men marveled at the Christmassy adornments in the hall, but there was an ominous emptiness to the gathering. Most men looked around in vain for missing messmates, all heads turning when a new visitor came through the door, hoping to see a friend. The band had been pressed to play airs and jovial Irish tunes on the carefully husbanded Uillean pipes from each Regiment. The single unifying effect was the determined consumption of the whiskey ration.

As Corporal O'Rourke was growing sleepy in the smoky hall, the music stopped and General Meagher stepped up on the stage. His first act was to offer up an unsteady toast to the fallen. Sean O'Malley found him and plopped clumsily down beside him. He was well into an epic drunk, but remained determined to find more. Seizing O'Rourke's tin cup, he careened away, shortly returning with two cups full. Plopping down again, and spilling a fair portion from both cups, he observed, "Begorrah, the General is drunker than we! Jus' lissen to him!" Alan O'Rourke had to concentrate to make out the words over the noise of the raucous men. When he began to comprehend the General's speech, he caught the raw bitterness of the words. The effect was shocking to O'Rourke. General Meagher had always spoke of patriotism and service to the land of the free. Now he was hearing that the Army cared little for their lives, because they were Irish. He heard a General tell him that they were expendable, and few cared if they lived or died. The depressing turn of the General's words made him sad, and he turned to his cup. He would drink the sorrow away.

Officers from General Hancock's Division Staff were also invited and in attendance to the "Death Banquet," as the soldiers had taken to describing it. Some were acquaintances of the highest men in Washington and communicated their dismay in letters to those men. The word of his intemperate speech would ultimately reach the ear of Secretary of War Stanton. It would prove be a performance that General Meagher would not be able to live down. Further commissions for his service would be delayed, and the wounded hero, Colonel Nugent, would receive the orders to proceed to New York to raise replacements for the Irish Brigade, upon his recovery.

December in the Low Country, in and around Somerset Plantation, was a time of hunts, outdoor fires and gatherings free of the pernicious insects, which made life unbearable in warmer times. The blockade made the resupply of luxury items difficult, but with the season, oysters and other seafood items remained plentiful.

The pre-Christmas cookout and oyster roast at the Ravenel Home, marked the occasion of the shipment of the nearly completed *David* torpedo boat to Commodore Ingraham and Lieutenant Glassell in Charleston. E. J. Markley had been dismayed at the scanty payment the Confederate States' Navy had provided. The paltry sum of $1,800, had barely met the cost of materials, the steam engine in particular. David Ebaugh had reminded him that the Trenholm and Frazier reward still awaited them, once the sturdy little boat met success. Markley remained skeptical, but determined to hope for the best. The Torpedo Boat itself, was already on its way to Charleston, aboard a flatcar bound for Smith's Wharf. The navy would fit it out with iron plate armor and properly ballast her before the builders would be invited to her commissioning. He could not help but feel a sense of foreboding that the Federal forces harbored great plans to lay siege to Charleston. The Charleston Mercury daily provided dire warnings of the assembly of a great Ironclad fleet building up in vast numbers near Beaufort. Rumor also had it, frequently confirmed by Tom's letters, that major Yankee troop movements were underway with designs on the city of Charleston.

He watched, as Elizabeth exchanged pleasantries with the other ladies, carefully hiding her concern over Lottie's lack of correspondence. He had deduced she had been in the vicinity of the town of Fredericksburg. Now a place well known, by the great Confederate victory there as described in the newspapers. He had quietly prayed she remained well and safe from the dangers of the battle.

Doctor Ravenel interrupted his thoughts with a new glass of whiskey and pine. "Drink up, Sir! I shan't have my guests dry of thirst or unhealthy." E.J. smiled and nodded, accepting the potent concoction of aged bourbon, spiced with a splinter of sap-laden heart pine. Ravenel believed the rosin contained cleansing properties. E.J. reasoned, the health dodge gave the good Doctor an excuse to pull a cork. All things being said, however, he found he liked the drink. He enjoyed the off season immensely, and tried for a moment to forget about the war and the challenges of the spring.

The guests dined, danced and listened to the slaves playing fiddle music until late into the evening. Christmas would come soon to the low country and the good people of Old Berkeley County did their best to forget the war for a while.

⚓

Reid Markley waited for nightfall as he busied himself with his chores below decks of the *U.S.S. Pawnee*. After a thoroughly upsetting, bad weather voyage up the coast, the ship, and crew arrived at a magical place, Boston Harbor.

The Navy might be for some men, but Reid was quickly learning that he was not one of them. In the close confines of the voyage, particularly when the weather was rough, he learned the true disdain many of the crew held for Negro Landsmen. No one knew, or wanted to know, his name or his story. While accustomed to the useful invisibility that slavery had taught him all his life. On a ship, invisibility was impossible. Out of sight of the officers, he was taunted continually. Quickly he learned that the contrabands were a threat to the sailors, who held ratings. On the calm Sundays, after divine services, when the sailors were allowed to "Skylark" on deck, he perpetually was invited and coerced into Boxing matches. Often he held his own, but generally he received disturbingly hostile beatings.

Reid liked the life and the pay of a Freeman, but he could not shake the feeling that the ship and her crew were pushing him away. The realization made him feel strangely reckless. He determined that Boston would be his final port, once they arrived.

Their arrival to Boston Harbor late in the evening, on a December night, struck Reid spellbound. Unlike Charleston, Wilmington and the other hostile harbors he had served offshore near, Boston was gaily lit and thriving with shipping. There was no war here; it was a city of Freedom. His and the crew's excitement at arrival, was tempered by the Captain's stern orders the next morning, of limited liberties. Desertion was becoming a problem for the Navy. Suspension of the grog ration was one cause and recruiting enticements from Volunteer Regiments from the Army was becoming another.

Reid bided his time until it became dark the following evening and quietly slipped into the cold harbor waters, and swam his way to shore. In a small leather purse around his neck, he had secreted his pay, 13 dollars in all. He had no idea how much money this was or whether it would be enough, to make a life in Boston.

Finally arriving at the quay, he pulled himself up to the cobbled streets that were gloomy and empty at the late hour. Looking around the misty street, he decided to head uphill. Reid had not envisioned Boston to have hills within it. Gas lamps lit his way, but there was no one out for him to ask directions from, so he proceeded to walk uphill past fine shuttered homes lining both sides of the street. The richness of the place made him wary and he pushed himself, despite the cold, deeper into town. Soon he topped the hill and walked into a dark and heavily treed park. Spots of snow still remained on the grassy common and fine gravel walks wound throughout. Enormous buildings dominated one side of the park and he could tell that this was a very rich place. Tightening his woolen sack coat around his shivering frame, he pressed deeper until the city streets took on a more shabby and poor appearance. Finally he found a brightly lit tavern that still was full of patrons, despite the late hour.

Hesitantly he opened the door. Back home, entering a white man's club would have resulted in a beating, but as he entered, no one paid him any particular mind. The warmth of the tavern was a huge relief and he made his way to the bar lined with rough wooden stools. A middle aged woman with mussed up hair asked, "What would ye be having, Sailor?" Reid was shocked for a moment, until he realized he was wearing standard issue Seaman's clothes. Reid mumbled, "Somethin' to eat I suppose." After a pause he added, "And some grog if you have it." The older woman laughed and pointed Reid out to the proprietor, taunting, "Look Jonas, another sailor has swum in to get his grog ration!" Most of the tavern erupted in laughter. Reid confused, laughed along with them, not understanding the effect of the Navy suspension of grog rations, the very same year. Soon she placed a heavy bowl of stew before him, with a large chunk of bread, resting in the sauce. As she pushed a pewter tankard of grog towards him, she announced, "That'll be two bits, Sailor!" Reid, confused, pulled out a wet greenback from his neck pouch and handed it to her. The sight of the new paper money impressed her, "My, my! Union Navy must had pay day!" She quickly returned two silver quarter dollars to him. Reid returned the precious coin to his pouch and hungrily devoured the stew and bread. A weathered old Jack sidled alongside of him and asked, "What ship are you from, boy?"

Reid swallowed quickly and defensively responded, "Mister, I ain't no boy, no more! I'se a free man now! I ain't gonna say about that ship cause I ain't going back to it no more!" The older man laughed, "I seen your kind lots of times, son! No worries, I'll nae summon a constable on ye!" Leaning in closer, he confidentially whispered, "Stay well away from the docks! They'll press parties out to look for ye! It's best to stay uptown."

Reid nodded, as he took a swig of the strong grog. The old man presciently asked, "Lookin' for a place to lay yer head, as well, I suppose?" Reid quickly nodded, "Yassir! I is!"

Nodding, the old man shouted out to the old woman, "Mary! I found ye another lodger, if you have a room!" The tussle haired bar maid returned with a key attached to a wooden tag and tossed it on the bar in front of Reid, "That, sailor will cost you three bits!" As he finished the tankard of grog, he felt woozy. The last time he had drank strong liquor had been back on Somerset. Master Markley had encouraged them to drink rum on Sundays, in the belief that it hardened them against the miasma of the swamps.

As he unsteadily stood, he asked, "Ma'am where are the rooms?" The barmaid came over, and pointed out the back, "Go out the back door here and they are on the right." Picking up his key she continued, "This says you are in room number 3." She looked him in the eye for a moment, and adjusted her mussy hair, adding, "If you have desires for anything else, sailor, it will cost you four bits." Reid sturdily shook his head. It dawned on him, then and there that he had taken harbor in a bordello.

By February, Reid had exhausted his money and the proprietor of the bordello and boarding house, invited him to leave. He sent two large men to service this request. Reid reluctantly complied and trudged homeless and penniless into the bitter winter cold. For another week, he slept in alleys, and scavenged for scraps of food. Arising one frosty morning, he cast aside the scraps of newspaper he had placed over his head for warmth, when his eye caught a broadsheet advertisement on one of the inside pages.

His poor reading skills, only allowed him to make out "Colored Men," "$100 Dollar Bounty!," and "Pay $13 Dollars a month." Rising and dusting off his shabby clothes, he clutched the scrap of paper and rushed out into the street. Encountering a elderly Doorman outside a fine Inn, he asked, "Excuse me Sir! Can you read this?" The elderly Negro nodded and read aloud the contents. Reid asked, "What is today?" The older man responded, "The 17th of February, Son! This is yesterdays paper! You want to sign up to fight?" Reid nodded, knowing it was something he could do. The man directed him to the street corner only 3 blocks distant. As Reid rushed off to find the recruiter, the old man called out after him, "God bless you boy!"

Following the retreat back across the Rappahannock, The Army of the Potomac went into winter camp, in and around the hamlet of Stafford, Virginia. After one last disastrous and mud-laden attempt at marching to battle in January, General Burnside was relieved of Command and passed the burden of leadership to Joseph Hooker.

Concerted effort was dedicated to evacuate the surviving wounded from the makeshift field hospitals to a new facility, established in Annapolis, Maryland. The War Department had elected to use the recently evacuated Naval Academy facilities as a combination Parole camp and General Hospital. Once the facilities to transfer train cargo to steamships at Aquia Landing was complete; the general evacuation of wounded would commence.

The campaigning season over, and with troops in winter camp, General Henry Hunt and Sergeant Major O'Keefe dedicated an afternoon in late January to visit First Sergeant Timmonds at the Chatham House. Joshua was now ambulatory and able to eat, and talk again. He still felt very weak, mostly from his period of malnutrition, due to his wound. In between her chores, Lottie would dote on him and happily while away her free time with long conversation. Each fulfilled years of thirst for company and conversation. The time passed alarmingly fast when they were together.

Joshua stiffly rose when Hunt and the Sergeant Major entered that afternoon. Lottie instinctively followed suit. General Hunt warmly shook his hand, "First Sergeant, your wounding gave me quite a pause last month! I hope you will accept my apologies for our reckless use of your battery, last month!" Joshua solemnly responded, "Sir, do not trouble yourself! I would be happy to follow you to Hell!" Hunt and O'Keefe grinned broadly. Joshua turned, and introduced Lottie, "Sir, I am anxious for you to meet Miss Charlotte Markley! She came a long way, in difficult conditions, to arrive here! Miss Barton has her under her employ, and she has indicated that we are to travel to Annapolis, until I am paroled." General Hunt smiled, and took Lottie's proffered hand, "Young Lady, I am charmed to make your acquaintance! It may surprise you to know, that we have known about you for years! Sergeant Timmonds was terribly devoted to you!" The accolades from such a senior officer made Lottie blush. Hunt turned serious for a moment and asked, "Young Lady, are your parents aware of your current situation?" Lottie shook her head, replying, "No Sir! I have written a letter, but with no established postal facilities, I have nowhere to dispatch it." Hunt understandingly nodded and turned to Joshua, to ask, "Son, let me borrow Miss Markley for a moment, I need to give her some information." As Joshua nodded, the General took Lottie into the hall. O'Keefe used this opportunity to corner Joshua to talk future business.

General Hunt led Lottie to the cluttered office that Clara Barton had established in the trampled parlor. Dr. Barton rose from her desk when General Hunt entered, "Well good afternoon, Sir! It is indeed an honor to see you!" Hunt replied, "Doctor Barton, we as an Army are eternally in your debt, for your kind services!" Turning and motioning to Lottie, he added, "I understand this young lady is now under your employ?"

Barton cleared her throat, before responding, "Well, Sir, since you ask, no. At least not officially! She accompanied Sergeant Timmonds here, from the Rebel Hospital in Fredericksburg. I am afraid to say, she is an employee of the Confederate States Government and has no documentation, or proof of loyalty to our cause! I allowed her to stay here, for the sake of Sergeant Timmonds. Many of these men suffer here, with little such familial comfort!" General Hunt nodded, "Doctor Barton, we have been aware of her devotion to Sergeant Timmonds since 1856, when he first enlisted. She is nearly as much as family, as we Regulars could allow. I beg of you to allow her to proceed with First Sergeant Timmonds to Annapolis. I assure you that I can make provision for her, once I return to Washington. I will happily provide you with an endorsement under my signature."

Clara Barton's stern visage softened, "Sir, I sincerely appreciate this information. Forgive my sternness, but I have only this great task before me with limited vision to the backgrounds of these men. I should like that endorsement, not for me as I go freely through my own meanness. I should like the girl to have something, to assure her safe passage! Once she lands in Annapolis, I would be happy for her assistance, but she must be proofed with a loyalty oath, lest she be accused of being a spy!"

General Hunt turned to Lottie, and asked, "Do you understand this?" Lottie silently nodded. He continued, asking, "Is it your desire to go to Annapolis with Sergeant Timmonds? Or is your preference to go back across the Rappahannock and home?" Lottie sat silent for a moment, swallowed and welled up tearfully, "I want to follow him, to wherever he goes! I do not know what I shall do, but I cannot lose track of him again!"

Hunt nodded, "Young Lady, then that is what we shall do. Please provide me your letter. I will have it across the river today on our flag of truce exchange, this evening. I shall return tomorrow with an endorsement for you, along with a letter of recommendation for a family in Washington, with whom you can lodge. Leave it to us, young lady! The 2nd Regiment shall see to your needs, for Joshua's sake!"

Lottie tearfully thanked Doctor Barton and General Hunt and hurriedly excused herself to regain her composure. In her absence, Hunt asked Doctor Barton, "Now Clara, what is your honest opinion on this situation?"

Clara Barton replied, "General, it is a heartbreaking story, repeated over and over in multitudes by this horrible war! The girl is very good help and needs little urging. In some small way, she reminds me of myself. There is much character in her. I just cannot help my suspicion. She is from a rich, slave holding family! It is imponderable how she can lightly bring shame to that family, in this war!"

Hunt nodded, "Doctor Barton, I appreciate your concerns. I have much experience with the people of South Carolina, before the war. I think I understand her situation. She has been posting him regular mail, through the express services, since the beginning of the war. I am fairly certain that the family is aware of this relationship. I shall take responsibility for this matter and spare you the concern."

Barton rose and shook Hunt's hand. Hurriedly she excused herself to make the rounds as she perpetually had little time to supervise operations to General Letterman's exacting standards.

A week later, Lottie boarded a train with Joshua. She carried her endorsement from General Hunt, along with a letter of recommendation to be delivered to a certain Colonel Lawrence and Mrs. Mary Craig, in Washington City. General Hunt retained the loyalty oath, that he personally administered to her, for submission to the War Department. Daring Lottie had become one of the first "Galvanized Yankees."

10
ACKNOWLEDGEMENTS

To my readers, I cannot express in adequate terms, how exhausting this third book was to complete. I severely underestimated the level of research required to do this period of the war justice. My poor attempts to weave the civilian experience into the story took much research and effort to obtain.

Wandering through the streets of the still quaint city of Fredericksburg inspired some of this. To enthusiasts of Civil War history, I would implore you to visit this city. The well preserved old town, by the banks of the Rappahannock whisper the past to one, as they walk the tiny streets there. I recall my amazement at the narrowness of the river there. It became a wonderment for me to envision infantry forces contesting a crossing there. Much bravery was required for the Engineer Soldiers to establish a bridge there. Even greater courage was required to conduct an assault by bridging boats there for the supporting infantry that made that assault.

I would also recommend the student of Civil War history to make the drive along the quaint country roads from Leesburg, Virginia through Boonsboro, Middletown, and South Mountain to Sharpsburg, Maryland. In one sense, little has changed in this country. The flow of the land helps one to understand the "why" of General Lee's march. The area remains economically depressed and many of the original structures remain in place, as they stood 160 years ago. Such is our country. Not everything changes as fast as we think.

Moving into Sharpsburg, one can visit the Antietam National Battlefield Park and walk the hallowed grounds there. My last visit was covered in winter snow, but I was grateful for the lack of trees on the visit. Often, I have noted that the verdant and rich coverage from trees, we take for granted today, did not exist in the 19th century. We must consider that wood was the sole source of heat in the long winters of the age, and the people of that age chopped much of it down within easy reach for cooking and heat. The leafless backgrounds afforded me a vision of terrain, I never fully appreciated until I could see through the woods there. I found some of the positions selected by General Lee and General Longstreet to be extremely compelling. It became abundantly clear to me, in some instances, how well they could identify, "Good ground." This is particularly compelling at the sunken road, that leads to Porterstown on the far side of Antietam Creek. Approaching Union Regiments were denied the ability to see the position of the defenders, until they crested a slight ridge, well within rifle range of the Rebel positions. It took a considerable degree of genius to pick such an unlikely spot to defend from.

I noted that the grounds of the vast battlefield whisper to the visitor, if they listen closely. It proved to be a place of enormous suffering for both armies. The enormous cost of this fight to both armies, should never be underestimated, or unappreciated.

In my works, I attempt to avoid judgmentalism of the Generals that fought during this age. Many a historian has made judgments in regards to who was good, and who was bad. Having served 32 years in the army, I have enough humility to observe my own good times and bad times. No one can be at the top of their game all the time. Those who like to measure those events in the making of history should take care to appreciate the burdens of sickness, exhaustion, despair and weakness into consideration. Warriors are generally forgiving of these frailties, having felt them ourselves.

This is one reason why the revisiting of our most destructive past, compels me to continue. We are a great people who were once torn in two by our great passions. This war pitted our talents against one another, and ultimately we emerged united, albeit after a rather bitter 40 years of reconciliation. Each actor in this great drama, did his or her duty in the manner that they saw, as "The right way." Only hindsight has perfect focus. When you research the lives of these men, you begin to understand the motives, pressures, and challenges each faced. There are personal tragedies, debilitating wounds, and sickness that impaired their abilities. To lead, and to expose oneself to the heavy burden of responsibility often crippled able men, in the face of extreme adversity. It is easy for us on the sidelines of history to judge. It is a much harder task to research in order to understand. I ask every reader with an interest, to do just that. Study, analyze before you judge. In nearly every case, there is a human explanation for failure, and many a failure had exactly that for a cause.

I must take the time to acknowledge those who assisted me immaterially in this project. To Mary Alice Kotarski, who steadfastly refuses payment for her services. Yes, I am slowly learning what a comma does and why it was contrived. Perhaps someday, I will retain my lessons. In the interim, I remain forever in your debt for your generosity and assistance in these works.

To Sonny Hand, an exceptional author in his own right. I strongly recommend my readers purchase "One Good Regiment" as soon as possible. Sonny, your assistance in the accurate depiction of Civil War soldiers, terminology and commands, was of invaluable assistance. Perhaps someday I can make up for this assistance. In the interim, I appreciate your taking the time to assist me. Such help is rare and I sincerely appreciate your interest in my progress as a fledgling author.

To Jon Wood, one of my favorite New Hampshire Yankees. Jon spent invaluable time playing Devil's advocate of my prose. I found your edits stimulating and was driven back into further research frequently. Many an afternoon spent shooting Civil War muskets with Jon, gave me an appreciation for the craft of handling 19th Century military weapons.

To Marie Hoobery, perhaps the singularly most knowledgeable source of civilian life and dress in the 19th Century. Her expert advice helped me flesh out the character and mannerisms of Lottie, and hopefully have resulted in a more accurate depiction of a Civil War era lady. Marie not only understands the fashions they wore in the age. She is also a talented seamstress recreating the height of Victorian fashion.

To Ken Swanson, my infallible source of books and advice. I appreciate your commentary and ideas over the past year of writing this book. I implicitly rely on Ken for his insights into Civil War history in general, as well as the little documented aspects of Civil War naval history.

If this book creates interest in the Reader's mind, I strongly suggest reading "The Fredericksburg Campaign" written by Francis Augustin O'Reilly. This work reflects exhaustive research by the author and was invaluable to me in understanding this great and tragic battle. I also strongly recommend, "The Gleam of Bayonets" written by James V. Murfin. This work explains in great detail the events of the Battle of Antietam, and became another valuable resource.

ABOUT THE AUTHOR

Robert K. Lytle is a 30 year veteran of the United States Army. Born in Columbia, South Carolina he received his college education at The Military College of South Carolina and was commissioned as an Armor officer in 1982. He is a veteran of the Cold War in Europe, the First Gulf War and Operation Iraqi Freed